THE
SILENT
WAR

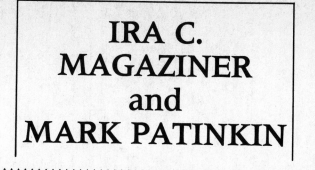

IRA C.
MAGAZINER
and
MARK PATINKIN

THE SILENT WAR

Inside
the Global
Business Battles
Shaping
America's Future

Vintage Books
A Division of Random House, Inc.
New York

First Vintage Books Edition, May 1990

Library of Congress Cataloging-in-Publication Data
Magaziner, Ira C.
The silent war : inside the global business battles shaping
America's future / Ira C. Magaziner and Mark Patinkin.—1st
Vintage Books ed.
p.   cm.
Reprint. Originally published: New York : Random House, © 1989.
Includes bibliographical references.
ISBN 0-679-72827-9
1. Competition, International—Case studies.   2. Corporations—
United States—Case studies.   I. Patinkin, Mark.   II. Title.
[HF 1414.M34   1990]
338.8'8—dc20   89-40489
CIP

Manufactured in the United States of America

10 9 8 7 6 5 4 3 2 1

For our children

Preface

On March 14, 1983, a Korean executive named Kyung Pal Park ordered a team of engineers to spend all night drafting a proposal for some visiting General Electric consultants who were due to fly back to the States in the morning. Mr. Park wanted to prove that his company, Samsung, could produce quality microwave ovens cheaper than GE's own factory in Columbia, Maryland. The visiting Americans were skeptical. This was a sophisticated product, up until then the exclusive preserve of the United States and Japan. But as the people of Columbia slept, eleven thousand miles away, the Koreans made their case. They showed they could beat GE's cost by 40 percent. Soon after, another piece of America's manufacturing base went overseas, leaving behind fifteen hundred unemployed workers and a few hundred million dollars a year added to the U.S. foreign debt.

In May 1969, the governments of West Germany and France agreed to commit $400 million each to develop a European version of a product many consider the most complex on earth—the commercial jetliner. Up until then, American producers made almost all of the Free World's civil jet aircraft. By far, the industry stood as our biggest exporter. Twenty years and $7 billion of government investment later, the new European Airbus had climbed to over 20 percent of the global jetliner market. By 1995, it will likely reach 30 percent. Airbus is now the second biggest jet producer in the world, having surpassed McDonnell Douglas and Lockheed. Its rise has cost America fifty thousand jobs, and over $4 billion a year in exports.

By EARLY 1981, a scientist named Paul Maycock had succeeded in making America the leader in the race to perfect a key energy technology of the future—photovoltaics. He'd done it by building a unique government program that funded private companies working on ways to produce electricity from the sun. The solar industry, Maycock felt, would be worth tens of billions in a few decades, and the United States seemed bound to harvest most of that wealth. Then, in October of that year, the new administration cut his budget by over half. Two months later, Paul Maycock's counterpart in Japan, a civil servant named Isao Kubokawa, got some very different news. He was granted all the money he'd requested for his own country's photovoltaic program. Up until then, America had 60 percent of the world's solar-cell market, and Japan only 23 percent. By 1986, America's market share had dropped to 27 percent, while Japan's had soared to half of all global sales. Today, Paul Maycock worries that we will lose the race.

EACH YEAR, companies and governments make thousands of decisions like these, decisions that determine whose standard of living will rise and whose will fall, which workers will get good jobs and which won't. More than ever, there are new rules behind those decisions, new rules for global business success. Nations that best understand them will prosper; those that don't are bound to decline.

FOR FIFTEEN YEARS, I've been an international business-strategy consultant. I've helped over one hundred companies in ten countries develop manufacturing and marketing strategies: U.S. companies like General Electric and Corning, foreign companies like Volvo and Mitsubishi. I've also helped government ministers in nations like Sweden, France, Ireland, and Canada frame economic-development plans. But I'm writing this book not just to talk about what I do. I'm writing because, after fifteen years of seeing how the world does business, I'm convinced other nations are moving faster than America, using new, more effective strategies to achieve prosperity. I've watched foreign companies become increasingly sophisticated, often at the expense of American ones. I've seen governments in countries such as Japan, West Germany, and France help their companies with factory investment, product research, worker training, and export. I've seen governments in Brazil, Singapore, and Ireland use incentives to lure U.S.

companies to build plants in their countries instead of at home. Meanwhile, as this silent economic war intensifies, I've seen our own government do little to fight back.

In 1973, when I started my consulting career, America had few foreign rivals. That year, we imported only 9 percent of our goods and exported the same. By 1988, we were importing well over 25 percent—almost a third of all cars, over half of all machine tools, over 65 percent of all radios, TVs, and stereos. Our exports hadn't risen nearly as much. The shift in foreign trade has caused a shift in wealth. In 1973, the average Japanese earned half the income of the average American. Today, he earns 20 percent more. Germans, who fifteen years ago were making two-thirds of our average income, are now a third ahead.

As I write these words in late 1988, our nation seems prosperous. American consumers have more money to spend than ever before. But much of the money isn't our own. It was borrowed, not earned. In 1982, the world owed us $140 billion. By early 1988, we owed the world $420 billion, a swing of more than half a trillion dollars in only six years, all because our rivals have been more successful at seizing global markets. As we continue to buy more from other nations than they buy from us, our debt continues to rise. Meanwhile, foreigners sitting on mountains of dollars have begun to use them to buy our assets—our land, our buildings, our businesses. Over 10 percent of our manufacturing assets, 20 percent of our banking assets, and over 35 percent of the commercial real estate in cities like Los Angeles were foreign-owned by mid-1988, and the buying spree continues.

For the time being, those purchases are pumping still more money into the United States, further buoying our sense of prosperity. But it can't last. If you sell your house and start paying rent, you'll feel flush with cash from the sale for a few years—but your children will be the losers. Long term, the banker always does better than the debtor, the owner better than the tenant. The solution is to become owner and banker again. But the only way to do that is to start earning more wealth, to start doing what Japan, West Germany, Sweden, and dozens of other nations are doing: to export more than we import.

In August 1971, when it became clear America was headed for its first significant trade imbalance since 1895, President Nixon considered it a time of crisis. He responded by imposing a 10-percent surcharge on all imports, and renouncing the twenty-five-year-old Bretton Woods monetary agreements so the dollar could float downward, making our exports cheaper. The trade imbalance that brought on this crisis, incidentally, was only $1 billion a year. By 1987, our annual imbalance had ballooned to $170 billion. Our response has again been to let the dollar fall, this time a full 40 percent. But it hasn't solved the problem. By the end of 1988, our trade deficit was still around $135 billion. Clearly, to outsell the world, we need a strategy far more complex than a lowered currency.

INDUSTRIAL NATIONS everywhere are developing such strategies. In most cases, government is integral—not government as meddler, but as partner of private business.

While America pours most of its research budget into defense, foreign nations pour theirs into commercial pursuits, supporting entire industries performing pooled R&D. While America focuses its training efforts around management, foreign governments have massive programs to help companies give ongoing training to hourly employees in the skills of the 1990's. While only 10 percent of American manufacturing companies export, three or four times that number do so in nations like Japan, Sweden, and West Germany—many with government assistance. Finally, while we talk about our service industries, governments in most other industrialized nations focus on manufacturing. They are convinced it is the wellspring of future wealth. After fifteen years of watching countries struggle for prosperity, I agree. If a nation is to prosper, it has to succeed at world trade. And ninety percent of world trade is goods, not services.

For the past fifteen years, America has been losing global sales in one industry after another: in textiles and steel, in cars and televisions, in appliances and telecommunications equipment. As our trade balance declined, we tended to explain it away. When Japanese products first began outselling U.S. brands in the mid-1970's, we said it was because of low wages and dumping—selling below cost. But by the late 1970's, we found that Japan's wages were as high as ours. We came to admit that they might be better manufacturers. Still, we insisted that they were copiers, not innovators. They would never catch us in advanced technologies like microelectronics and computers. By the mid-1980's, however, they had done so.

We have shown a similar short-sightedness about the rest of the world. "The Germans are too regimented and lack our entrepreneurial spirit." "The Swedes will sink because of high taxes." "Europe as a whole will fail because its nations can't cooperate with each other." "The Koreans are too backward to produce advanced products." But by the late 1980's, each of these countries was increasing its living standards faster than we were. And each had achieved a positive trade balance with the United States.

Today, many American businesses feel the trade crisis is ending. The lower dollar, in some eyes, is restoring our edge over the Japanese and Europeans. In truth, the low dollar has spurred our rivals to work harder than ever to make advanced products at low cost. The competitive arena that American companies will face in the 1990's will be tougher than ever before.

THE INDUSTRIAL MUSCLE of a nation does not atrophy overnight, nor even over a few decades. Despite fifteen years of competitive decline, America remains a major industrial power. In part, we've continued to prosper because our fathers and mothers sacrificed to build a highly productive economy. Through much of the 1980's, we've maintained the appearance of that prosperity largely by borrowing. That, however, is not the way to enhance wealth. We must once again earn our prosperity.

MY CO-AUTHOR AND I both had children born as this book was being written. As we traveled the world to write it, witnessing the economic progress in other countries, one question came up in our talks more than any other. What would it all mean for America's next generation? Would our children live in a declining society like Great Britain, whose people now earn wages only half to two-thirds those of their neighbors? Will they spend their lives working for foreign-owned companies, never able to rise to top management because of their nationality? Will they have to keep paying interest on the foreign debt we've run up while we enjoyed the 1980's?

It doesn't have to happen. We can still leave our children the same productive economy that our own parents left us. But we can't do it by borrowing. We can't do it with fiscal policies alone, or by lowering the dollar. We have to do it with strategies that enable us to outproduce and outsell our competition.

Some of our companies are already showing how that can be done.

IN THE MID-1960's, the Cross company of Rhode Island, maker of status pens and pencils, was doing almost no business overseas. Most of the foreign orders it did receive trickled in unsolicited. But management looked ahead and saw a time when sales could flatten if the firm restricted its horizon to America. With few immediate prospects, Cross gambled on opening an export division. Year after year, it gave its export people whatever money was needed to set up new marketing offices in new countries, even when the investment was ten times annual sales. Often, there was no payback for five years in a country, but Cross never pulled back. Today, Cross pens are among the most widespread American export, sold in 150 countries. Each year, they bring to the United States millions of dollars in wealth from nations like West Germany, Japan, and France. Today, Cross's biggest area of growth is from overseas.

ON SEPTEMBER 1, 1983, a team of General Electric executives flew to company headquarters in Connecticut to make a proposal. The key product in the firm's appliance group, the refrigerator, had come under sudden siege from foreign producers. New factories in low-wage countries like Brazil had begun to make refrigerator compressors—the heart of the machine—for half as much as it cost GE. Many in the company felt it was time to shut down its U.S. compressor plant and start buying from the competition. But the appliance team wanted to fight. With a $120 million investment, they felt GE's fifteen-dollar-an-hour workers would be able to make compressors both better and cheaper than foreigners paid a tenth as much. The company did make the investment. And soon, GE was beating its low-wage rivals.

IN 1977, a Corning Glass executive named Dave Duke was in Japan for a conference on a new technology his company was struggling to market around the world: optical waveguides. They were hair-thin glass fibers capable of carrying six thousand conversations at a time over a microscopic beam of light. Duke was convinced waveguides would eventually form the communications systems of the future, replacing copper phone wire. And Corning, he felt, was ahead. But now, he was finding out that Japan had launched a major challenge. The Japanese were planning to pour millions of dollars into a national research program. Although Duke knew Corning now faced the combined strength of the Japanese government and several huge companies, he did not give up. He got his people to redouble their own push. He had an advantage—Corning had begun research over a decade before, at a time when much of the science world doubted waveguides were possible. It paid off. Corning is beating the Japanese. Optical waveguides are now a $1 billion product, and Corning and its partners lead the world in sales.

IN THE following pages, I plan to tell those three American success stories, and six others from abroad. All are stories of how companies— and countries—have achieved world business leadership. In many, I was a participant, having worked with management as a consultant.

Lately, there have been scores of books on how America can become more competitive. My co-author, a journalist, and I felt it was important that our own book be not just another analysis, but a showcase of actual successes. So we set out to capture the human drama of people around the world who've fought for business leadership. The result, I hope, is a portrait of our rivals, of ourselves, and, most important, a testimony to America's economic promise.

IRA MAGAZINER
December 1988

Acknowledgments

EIGHTEEN MONTHS AGO, we sat down with Jason Epstein at a restaurant near Random House and laid out our vision for this book. It was an unformed vision, and we were fortunate that when the meal was over, Jason agreed to be our editor. We found him to have an immediate instinct for what worked and what didn't. During the course of this project, that instinct kept us on track. His encouragement and advice have enriched our effort immeasurably.

It fell to Kassie Evashevski, Jason's colleague, to usher our work along through many missed deadlines. We thank her for her patience, good sense, and commitment.

We owe thanks to three other editors, all of the *Providence Journal-Bulletin*, for the flexibility they gave—Carol Young, John Granatino, and especially, Chuck Hauser.

While each of us wrote and rewrote, Debra Morris kept us organized and made sure that this ever-changing manuscript stayed in one piece. We appreciate her skill, devotion, and hard work.

The book required detailed research in many parts of the world. For their assistance with this research, we thank Stephen Bloom, Hank Cauley, Sarah Cleveland, R. Barry Coates, Stephen Crolius, Marc Furtado, Joanne Riccitelli, Ted Rybeck, Michael Stone, and W. Edward Wood.

For reading our manuscript and offering advice, we thank Edward Caron, Willard Gallagher, Yasuhiro Kishimoto, Karen Kornbluh, the Patinkin family, Norene Rickson, Francis Scricco, David Stone, Nan Stone, and Rosalie Swedlin.

Finally, our deepest debt goes to our wives, Suzanne and Heidi, who, each day, gave us their wisdom and support.

Contents

THE
SILENT
WAR

Introduction

A Personal Awakening

IN 1973, at age twenty-five, I began working at the Boston Consulting Group (BCG), one of the country's major business-strategy consulting firms. While growing up, I'd always looked upon big American companies as unchallengeable. Even as late as the early 1970's, there were few imports on U.S. shelves, and most of those, such as Japanese radios, were low quality. If any economy held the secrets to business success, it was our own. Then I began to do international assignments. Slowly, I saw a different reality emerging.

My first consulting case was for LTV, a Texas conglomerate that had just bought America's sixth-biggest steel company, Jones & Laughlin (J&L) of Pittsburgh. J&L was losing money, and LTV wanted advice on how to turn it around. As junior member of the six-person BCG team, I was given what was considered a minor issue: overseas competition. Foreign steel, mostly from Japan, was coming into the United States at low prices. The industry believed the Japanese were dumping, and had lobbied successfully for quotas. My job was to analyze the real cost of Japanese steel, chiefly to confirm the dumping charges. On another issue, the U. S. industry's experts were all predicting a world steel shortage. In response, companies had begun asking Congress for billions of dollars in special investment tax credits for plant expansions. I was asked by my firm to confirm the shortage prediction by looking at global supply and demand.

I began by spending several weeks talking with company executives in Pittsburgh. Most told me it was a waste of time to analyze Japanese costs. The situation was already clear. Since American producers were more efficient, there was only one way Japan could land steel here at 20 percent below U.S. prices—dumping. To prove it, J&L managers gave me articles by steel analysts, many of them noted professors, all saying that Japan was behind in technology. Because the Japanese had to pay a premium to import coal and iron ore, they were behind in raw-materials costs, too. With low efficiency and high materials costs, there was no question that the Japanese were taking a loss in order to sell cheap in the U.S. "You'll see," they said.

I did see, though not what they expected. I flew overseas to visit some of Japan's mills. The first surprise was the technology. Back in the States, J&L was proud of having just replaced a fifth of its old open-hearth furnaces with doubly efficient basic oxygen ovens. The new technology, said management, made their plants among the world's most advanced. But in the first Japanese mill I toured, virtually all the furnaces were the new, efficient kind. And they were being run at 20 percent higher volume than J&L's, with 30 percent fewer people. Japanese rolling and finishing mills were also faster, and their blast furnaces bigger. Overall, the plants I visited were 30–40 percent more efficient than J&L's.[1] Meanwhile, it turned out Japan was paying no more for imported iron and coal.[2] The Japanese had put together long-term contracts with new, highly productive mines in Australia and Canada that were able to ship ore and coal cheaply by supertanker.

Japanese management attitudes were also different from American ones. In Pittsburgh, management did endless return-on-investment calculations, resisting any major modernizing. The payback, they explained, was too far away.[3] Instead, they preferred renovating selected parts of a plant, never redoing a whole mill. The Japanese had the opposite priority. Their main goal was to stay on technology's crest. They felt if they improved productivity first, profit would soon follow. They were convinced that pursuing a quick payback would eventually mean no payback at all. In America, most plants were built between 1900 and 1930 and were still of that era. In Japan, most plants had been built in the 1950's and 1960's and had already been completely revamped.[4]

Now, I focused on the other issue: the predicted steel shortage. I was supposed to find out how bad it would be. First, I wanted to make sure the prediction was right—that the experts hadn't overlooked anything, such as new plants. In Pittsburgh, they'd told me there were only a few major new mills being built in Europe and Japan, nowhere near enough to keep up with demand. When I asked about other nations, they said that developing countries didn't build modern steel mills. But I soon found that governments in Mexico, Brazil, South Korea, and Venezuela were all building big mills[5] after all, most with technical assistance from steel firms in Japan and Europe. All of them would be coming on line right about the time the U.S. industry was predicting a shortage. That would mean an enormous increase in world steel supply. Now I had to figure out whether demand would surpass it—as J&L managers had told me. Back in the States, I interviewed the country's big steel-using industries—automobiles and appliances. The people there told me they didn't see demand going up at all. In a range of products, they had plans to turn away from steel, toward plastic and aluminum.

Finally, it was time for our presentation. Our team gathered in J&L's boardroom. A dozen executives were there to hear us. I was one of the first to present. I began with Japanese steel, explaining their new technology, showing how their production was so efficient they were able to beat Pittsburgh's price, even after paying shipping and duties. Then I got to the predicted shortage. It wasn't going to be a shortage after all, I said; a boom in new plants and a decline in steel use would cause a glut.[6]

I presumed my findings would convince J&L to rethink its strategy, that the parent company, LTV, would move quickly to postpone plans for expansion and, instead, modernize the old plants. American business couldn't have become so powerful, I felt, if it weren't good at responding to sudden threats. The manufacturing vice-president of J&L was the first to speak.

"Look, son," I remember him saying, "I was over in Korea during the war. It's not easy to make good-quality steel. Those guys aren't going to be able to do it. I think you're overreacting."

Then the firm's president spoke.

"Every industry expert in the country is projecting something different than you are," he said. "I don't see how you can say what you're saying."

And that was that. They suggested I talk to the experts to understand what I'd missed. So I did, first asking about their prediction of a steel shortage. Each one pulled out his source material. Soon, I saw that it was all the same—all based on one original study done a few years earlier by some professors.[7] Some of the big changes—like plastic substitution and the boom in developing-country plants—had happened since then. When I mentioned those things, the experts dismissed them. If those trends were significant, they said, everyone in the industry would be talking about them, but no one was. I came away realizing American steel was a closed circle, where a few experts and executives talked only to each other, reinforcing a comfortable but outdated global view.[8] No one, it seemed, took world competition seriously enough to study it closely. I was convinced it was going to cost them.

I left the case bewildered. It wasn't that American steelmakers weren't smart, but they had a different way of seeing the world than did the Japanese. The Americans were convinced that domestic forces were all that mattered. The Japanese, on the other hand, based their plans on the world. For the Americans, investment in new technology took second priority to quick profit. For the Japanese, investment was everything. Their horizon was five to ten years out, rather than one or two.

A few years later, when the world steel industry indeed ended up in glut instead of shortage, the Americans were caught by surprise. They suddenly found themselves high-cost producers, and were hurt badly.[9] Still, I told myself, this was an exception. The steel industry had missed some trends, but the rest of corporate America was strong. Then I was assigned another international case.

THE CLIENT was Volkswagen. It was 1975, and the German mark had just strengthened against the dollar, forcing up the U.S. price of VWs by 25 percent. On top of that, VW had new rivals—the Japanese. Companies like Toyota had begun exporting small cars to the States, cutting into VW sales. Volkswagen was wondering if it should maneuver around both the currency and competition by building a plant in the United States.[10] Management was particularly interested in two questions. One, how boldly were the Japanese going to push into America? And two, were American automakers planning a push of their own into the small-car market?

I began my research by talking with U.S. carmakers. Whenever I brought up the Japanese, the Americans dismissed them, insisting they couldn't make a good car, and even if they learned, they'd never build ones to fit U.S. tastes. Perhaps Japan would get 4 or 5 percent of the car market, I was told, but no more. I asked what made them so sure. The executives all pointed to the late 1960's, when Toyota and Nissan tried a sales push into America. They failed. The cars were low quality, and so badly tailored that when many Americans sat down in them, their heads hit the ceiling. Forget the Japanese, the U.S. producers told me. They're not a threat. It struck me as curious that the Germans were more concerned about what Japan was going to do in America than the Americans were themselves.

Next, I went to Japan. In the U.S., car executives had told me that Japan's biggest problem was plant technology; they were way behind. But when I got to Japan, I saw the same thing I'd seen with steel. Japanese car factories were actually more modern than our own. They'd moved to unitized body construction, for example, which the U.S. firms had dismissed as not strong enough. The Japanese, however, had found a way to make it strong, and since the method used less steel and made assembly simpler, it lowered costs significantly. Eventually, the Americans would end up using unitized construction themselves. Meanwhile, the Americans were behind, and it wasn't the only area. The Japanese chassis and assembly lines were more mechanized than ones I'd seen in the United States, as well.

I could also see that the Japanese were gearing up for more capacity. They were building several new car plants, and expanding others. Soon, they'd be over 7 million automobiles a year, millions higher than what their own market could swallow.[11] Where would they be shipping the extras? Most European countries had a quota on Japanese cars. The obvious target was America.

I asked the Japanese why they were confident they could sell small cars in the United States. Well, they said, they knew Americans liked big cars, but they also knew gas prices were going up. In Europe and Japan, prices had been high for years, which was why small, efficient cars were so common there. They felt the same thing would happen in America. What impressed me most was how well their marketing people were tracking even subtler trends. For example, they spoke of the increase in working women in the United States, predicting it would lead to more two-car families. They showed me sophisticated U.S. buyer profiles. They also had plans to offer American car dealers bigger profit margins so they'd take on Japanese lines and push them harder.

All of them—Toyota, Nissan, Honda—had similar ideas. When I asked about their failed U.S. assault in the 1960's, they weren't shy about it. They talked about what they'd learned. Now, they explained, they were making far bigger passenger compartments, and increasing engine power. I had one more question for them. Why were they suddenly so export-obsessed? The answer was simple enough. The Japanese market was nearly saturated, more competitive than ever, and besides, they made more money on exports.[12] On top of that, they saw the economy becoming more global. Companies that wanted to grow, they said, would have to export. Economic health, they felt, lay beyond their borders.

Until then, I'd always thought of American car companies as invincible. But now the world industry seemed on the brink of major change, and no one in the United States saw it coming as clearly as the Japanese and Germans. It was the same problem I'd seen in steel—powerful U.S. corporations more inclined to dismiss foreign forces than confront them. But this was stranger still. Two foreign powers—Japan and Germany—were fighting over a piece of the U.S. car market being neglected by the Americans themselves. The U.S. companies even told me there was no point in gearing up major capacity for small-car production. It wasn't going to be a big enough market to make a difference; maybe 10 percent at most. By the early 1980's, it turned out to be 30 percent.[13] And our foreign competition took the majority of it.

I BEGAN TO SEE one other new foreign force during the car case. While interviewing overseas economic officials, mostly about exchange rates, I began to hear a novel phrase: "industrial policy." At first, I wasn't sure what it meant, but slowly, I began to see it was part of a new world vision. Governments were realizing the economy was going global, and felt they needed innovative policies to help their companies compete.

I remember one talk I had with an official at the German Ministry of Finance. The country's clothing firms, he told me, were having a hard time holding their own against new, low-wage competition. The industry had asked the government for help. One option, the German minister told me, was to let the deutschemark drop. That would make German exports—including clothing—cheaper. But a low mark also meant that German paychecks would be worth less, making imports and trips abroad more expensive. In the end, dropping the currency would cheat all citizens out of buying power, and that, he said, is not what a government wants to do to its people. A nation's goal, he said, should be to keep both its currency and its living standard high—a nation of $10- to $15-an-hour wages. To achieve that, he explained, you have to realize there are some products you can't compete in, like certain kinds of clothing. If something can be made well by unskilled dollar-an-hour workers, it's hard for a high-wage country to outdo them with ten-dollar-an-hour workers. Did that mean the German government should simply turn its back on the country's clothing firms and let them be killed by global forces? The Finance official didn't think so. Far better to help clothing companies move into new products—sophisticated textile products where advanced design, marketing, and manufacturing skills are important. Those, he said, are the kinds of areas where modern nations can compete profitably. In the same way, he said, if other industries with promising products find themselves challenged by foreign competition, you don't necessarily leave them to fight on their own. It's in the national interest for the government to help them stay ahead.

I asked how you do that.

That's where the new phrase, "industrial policy," came up. But the official was careful to avoid sounding interventionist. The answer, he said, was incentives. You don't impose government management, you offer government help.

What kind of help?

As an example, he began to talk about the German steel industry, which was facing the same kind of foreign threat as our own steel firms. The difference was that the German government was helping. The Ministry of Technology worked with local steel companies to find ways to become more productive—like researching techniques for burning cheap, low-grade coal more efficiently. To encourage a plan to keep Germany's steel industry competitive, the government sponsored coalitions of management, unions, and banks to chart a course together. Their recommendation was to close smaller plants, focusing production on bigger ones. That meant layoffs, which were sure to spark union resistance, something that could have derailed the whole effort. But government got around it by offering incentives to other German companies in growth industries to locate new plants near the closing steel mills. They even promised to retrain the laid-off steel workers for specific jobs in the new factories. It's not that government decided which industries should live or die—the world marketplace was doing that. Government's role was to understand the market, realizing it's better to help declining companies explore new paths than to prop them up with bailouts.

In Japan, I found government was thinking the same way. The Japanese had clear national priorities—high wages and high exports—and were far more organized than we in planning for them. The main mission of Japan's Ministry of International Trade and Industry (MITI) was to help the nation's companies compete abroad. As a foundation for that, MITI had an elaborate vision of how Japan's industrial structure should develop. For example, it had sent civil servants around the world to study how the country could build a strong national car industry. One ingredient, they found, was having sizable auto-parts companies. In Japan, however, parts firms were small and scattered. The government realized that individually, the firms would be unable to invest in the kind of new machinery they'd need to provide competitive parts to the booming car plants. So MITI offered incentives to spur the parts firms to merge. When several did combine, MITI offered more incentives, this time to modernize. MITI also imposed import barriers blocking foreign car parts from coming into Japan. Had government kept hands off, Japan's parts firms would have never become competitive, and probably would have folded. Not only would that have meant unemployment, it would have forced local automakers either to import parts or spend their own scarce resources on parts development, driving up car costs.[14] In the end, therefore, MITI wasn't just helping parts companies, it was looking after the broader economy. MITI's help wouldn't be needed forever—only until the Japanese firms could compete on their own with larger U.S. rivals.

Back home in America, by 1975 I'd had more than a dozen talks with U.S. Commerce Department officials. I'd found them to be skilled at special requests, like helping a company get foreign customs to clear goods, but there was no larger vision of how American firms could adapt to a global economy. I certainly heard no one in Commerce speaking about an overseas car threat. No one was warning about a steel threat, either. But both threats were unfolding: Foreign companies were coming at us with the support of their governments. Our companies, meanwhile, were being left to face this new competition on their own.

A FEW YEARS EARLIER, in 1969, while still in college, I went to El Paso for a national student-government convention. I remember walking across the border to the Mexican city of Juárez. It was depressing. Juárez was crowded, the poverty terrible, industry almost nonexistent. Except for some dirt farming and handcrafts, the main business seemed to be prostitution, aimed at the U.S. military base in nearby Texas. I hoped that would be the last time I saw Juárez.

But in 1975, I went back, this time for a client of BCG's—a Mexican company that sold paper to businesses which made it into cardboard boxes.[15] My job was to give the company a growth strategy. I decided to visit one of its fastest-growing customers, a box-making company that happened to be in Juárez. I couldn't imagine how a firm could be booming in a depressed place like that. When I arrived, I was surprised to see there were dozens of new factories. There was still poverty, but compared to six years before, Juárez felt like a new town. I sat down with the box maker and asked what had happened. He told me about the Maquila Program.[16]

It has been launched by the U.S. and Mexican governments to slow illegal immigration. The idea was to seed more jobs on the Mexican side by declaring it a duty-free zone, making it easy for American firms to put plants there and export back into the United States. The businessman told me it had grown slowly at first; American firms were wary of both a foreign environment and Mexican workers. But lately, things had blossomed. Dozens of plants were now in on the program, employing over fifty thousand people. That's why the businessman's box business was booming; many of the new companies were giving him orders. There were predictions that in another decade there would be enough plants along the border to employ over one hundred thousand workers—an underestimate, as it turned out.

At the time, most of the new plants were American, and few, I found, had been put there to expand production. Over 90 percent were replacement factories.[17] American companies had simply shut down U.S. plants and gone over the border for cheap labor. Most of the new plants involved low-skill labor—braiding wire harnesses, stuffing circuit boards, assembling motors. For years, those kinds of businesses had been naturals for low-wage countries, but U.S. firms had resisted going offshore. It was considered a tough leap to put your plant twelve thousand miles away, in Singapore or South Korea. The Maquila Program changed all that. Here was a low-wage country just a few miles from America's home market. Meanwhile, companies could keep their white-collar people in the United States, in El Paso or McAllen, just a twenty-minute drive from eighty-cent-an-hour labor.

At the time, 1975, unemployment in the States was high. Like many people, I'd been assuming the problem was rooted partly in the oil crisis and mostly in the kind of domestic forces I'd learned about in Economics 101—business cycles are supposed to dip every five years or so. But now I was seeing a new puzzle piece—international competition; first steel, then cars, now this situation in Mexico.

I wanted to understand it better, so I decided to do some reading. But all I could find on foreign competition were theoretical tracts. The latest writings by our most distinguished economists glossed over anything international. Usually, the subject was just an addendum. In one sense, there was reason for U.S. economists to ignore foreign competition. As recently as 1970, imports made up only 9 percent of all goods sold in America.[18] But from what I'd seen, a much bigger invasion was on the way, and at the time, no one was writing about it.

A few years after my Mexican visit, I was to see a specific casualty of the Maquila Program. In my home state of Rhode Island, I was having dinner with a colleague and a woman friend. They got onto the subject of business. She began to talk about how angry she was at American companies. I asked why.

Her mother, she explained, had spent twenty-five years working for a local GE wiring-device plant. Then, unexpectedly, the plant closed and moved to Mexico. After a lifetime of work, the woman's mother had been laid off without warning. GE tried to help employees find new jobs, but it was a bad local economy, and there wasn't much to choose from. The woman's mother ended up taking a counter job, at a big pay cut. The unemployment people, I'm sure, would have said everything had worked out fine; the woman, after all, had found new work. But the measure of an economy's success, I was realizing, wasn't just whether people had jobs—the question was what kind of jobs. This family was now struggling. The daughter told us she herself had to put her modeling ambitions on the shelf to take a second job; it was the only way the family could pay its bills. Her younger sister, a student, also had to begin working part time. Meanwhile, they were borrowing to make up the difference. For a long time afterward, I thought about that family as a kind of symbol. We were losing ten-dollar-an-hour factory jobs, and replacing them with four-dollar-an-hour behind-the-counter paychecks. It was the price of our not keeping up with the world.

I'm not saying we should have tried keeping the Maquila plants in America. In most cases, even millions of dollars in tax breaks would only have delayed the inevitable. Certain low-skill businesses are destined to migrate. Still, I realized, we should have been doing what I'd seen in Japan and Germany: giving incentives to get old companies investing in new technologies, and retraining their workers. The only way Americans could compete with eighty-cent-an-hour Mexican workers, it seemed to me, was to train our people to do more sophisticated work—ten-dollar-an-hour work. That's how a modern nation makes its living standard continue to go up, even with intensified global competition. If you can't undercut your rivals with low wages, you maneuver over them with more sophisticated products and factories. That's what Japan and Germany were doing: moving up the ladder of sophistication, and not just in advanced technologies. They were doing it in traditional industries like steel and cars. It was disturbing that *we* weren't.

IN 1976, I was sent to a new part of the world. A mining company—Conzinc Rio Tinto Australia—had just discovered a new coal deposit. It was middle grade—too pure for power companies, and not pure enough for steelmakers. Rio Tinto had asked BCG for a report on the best way to develop the find. I began by researching the world mineral industry. Until then, I'd thought of America as the most mineral-rich of all nations. Now, I found something unsettling. In most minerals, America's most accessible deposits had already been depleted. We were now having to mine for less pure minerals, in deeper, thinner deposits that were more expensive to get to. Meanwhile, big deposits had only recently been discovered in Australia, Canada, Africa, and Latin America. The new deposits were the type ours had been one hundred years ago—good, thick veins, up near the surface. All you had to do was put in a road, dig, and truck the ore or coal out. America's preeminence in raw materials had dwindled badly.

Rio Tinto planned to dig out its new coal with a technique called automated open-pit mining. I found it was using a similar technique with its biggest iron mine, so I asked if I could see it. That's what brought me to my true awakening on this trip. To get to the iron mine, we had to fly five hours by chartered plane over Australian desert. Finally, we came down on a private strip. The mine was enormous. It helped explain something I'd learned a few years before during my steel case. Australian ore, I'd discovered, sold cheaper in America than American ore itself. At the time, it cost about twenty dollars a ton to dig ore and get it from mines in Minnesota and Michigan to Pittsburgh. I'd been shocked to learn that Australia could land ore in Pittsburgh at an even cheaper price. Now, standing there in the Australian desert, I was seeing how it was possible. The mine was hundreds of times bigger than any I'd seen in the States. The ore was far purer and thicker— better, in fact, than anything we'd mined in fifty years.

Rio Tinto's technology was equally awesome. As I stood there, huge front-end loaders, triple the size of normal bulldozers, scooped the ore onto a conveyor that took it directly into rail cars. The cars then rolled to a deep ocean port less than a hundred miles distant. A mining company couldn't have dreamed of a more convenient find. My company guide drove me to the port, where we came upon the biggest ship I'd ever seen. It was like a skyscraper resting on its side, and had room for 450,000 tons of ore. That helped explain the cost. At that volume, shipping got pretty cheap. I watched as ore was sucked up by a machine so powerful it seemed to clean out each rail car in minutes. It was clear that this faraway operation was going to put a lot of American mining people out of work.

I spent the next few weeks in Rio Tinto's Melbourne headquarters, putting together statistics. When the Australians first began digging ore in the mid-sixties, they produced 2 million tons, a tiny amount. By 1970, they were up to 35 million tons. Now, in 1976, they were at 76 million, almost 15 percent of world demand.[19] Before I was done, I learned that the threat went beyond ore. Companies throughout Latin America, Africa, and the Pacific were finding rich new deposits in lead, zinc, uranium, copper, and bauxite, not to mention Middle East oil. For centuries, the United States had been one of the world's major suppliers of raw materials. That was now changing. America, I saw, was on the brink of becoming a net importer of most raw materials.

There was an important difference between this and the other big industries I'd seen. With the right investments, our steel and cars still had a chance to become competitive with the world. Our ore couldn't. I was beginning to see two categories of products—those that could be saved, and those destined to go over the border.

It made sense, of course, that our most vulnerable companies would be those in more traditional industries, such as steel, autos, and mining. But I was sure that in new technologies, we'd always be out front. Then I was given another case, involving one of the most advanced technologies of all, aerospace.

IN 1976, Textron's Bell Helicopter Division asked BCG for a study on how it could improve its international marketing system. The system was an uneven one, split between outside distributors and full-time company salesmen. Now that the company was expecting a boom in orders from timber companies, armed forces, and offshore oil firms, it wanted to make sure its global sales machine was organized right.

At the time, America dominated the world in aerospace. Aircraft had historically been our biggest export. Bell itself sold plenty of helicopters abroad—almost $500 million worth a year.[20] Most of its competitors were domestic, with Sikorsky the biggest and Hughes next. There was talk about France and Italy pushing into the market, but no one at Bell paid much attention. Despite what I'd learned about steel and cars, I didn't pay attention, either. France and Italy had never been technological leaders. Helicopters were especially sophisticated machines, and with our defense emphasis, I presumed this was one area where we couldn't be touched.

I began visiting distributors and customers alike. The questions I planned to ask were simple enough. What was good and bad about Bell's marketing? What was good and bad about its products? What needed fixing? In Singapore City, at a restaurant called Fatty's, I met with an Englishman who headed a regional Bell distributorship called Heli-Orient. He was there with a Sri Lankan colleague who had been in the British military. I asked about the competition—did Sikorsky and Hughes sell much in the area? The Sri Lankan answered in a clipped British accent.

"We're not worried so much about them," he said. "The people who are going to beat the pants off Bell are going to be the French."

He went on to describe a number of his customers who'd been approached by a company called Aerospatiale, which made helicopters. It seemed, he said, that they'd come up with some product improvements that outdid Bell. And their helicopters were cheaper, too. The French had set out to make a world-class effort, said the Sri Lankan, and were bringing it off.

My next visit was with the new head of purchasing for Indonesia's state-owned oil company. The Indonesians bought helicopters by the hundreds, which made them one of the biggest buyers in Southeast Asia. At the time, the oil company was recovering from an internal scandal. Its previous managers had just disappeared into Switzerland with tens of millions of dollars, leaving the company near bankruptcy.[21] The new purchasing manager, understandably, was a bit cost-conscious. I asked him whether Bell's distributors were meeting his needs. I didn't even think to ask him about France. If anyone was a reliable U.S. customer, this company was. Throughout its history, Indonesia had dealt almost exclusively with America for aerospace supplies.

"To be honest," he said, "we're not thinking about buying Bell helicopters anymore." He went on to explain that they were close to a deal with Aerospatiale.

I asked why.

Part of it, he said, was the machine's quality, but mostly it was the French financing—too attractive to turn down.

What kind of financing?

The French government was offering a 100 percent loan that came interest-free for five years. Best of all, Indonesia wouldn't have to pay a single installment for two years. Industrial policy, again: The French government was helping its companies compete globally. There was no such help, I noted, for Bell, which had to fight back on its own.

My next stop was Dubai, in the booming Middle East market. I met with the region's Bell distributor, and this time, one of my first questions was whether the French were becoming a problem in the Middle East.

"Yes," said the distributor, "they're our biggest problem."

"I understand they're offering good financing," I said.

"Yes, but the real problem is that their helicopter is better."

He described a range of new features. Aerospatiale had enclosed the helicopter's rear blade, for example, and turned it vertically, making it both safer and more efficient. The engine was more efficient, as well, and the helicopter flew faster.

A dozen other buyers in a half-dozen countries said the same thing. When I got back to the States, I told Bell management what I'd learned. They showed more concern than the steel and car people, but they just didn't believe Aerospatiale could be better. At that point, the French helicopter hadn't been officially unveiled. It was just finishing its standard testing, which had taken years. Still, the French machine wouldn't have been hard to check out. All you'd have to do was send in loyal customers to report back. Had the competition come from Sikorsky, Bell would certainly have done that. But the French were foreigners, with no reputation. It wasn't worth the trouble.

A month later, Aerospatiale showed its new model at an international air show in Los Angeles. I happened to be there, and saw that everything the distributors had told me was true. Soon afterward, Aerospatiale made a disturbing breakthrough—it got an order from the U.S. Coast Guard itself.

Throughout this time, I'd continued doing reading in economics. The few articles I'd found that spoke of foreign competition had always pointed to two American industries as unassailable world leaders. One was computers, the other aircraft. In products as technically complicated as these, our leadership was guaranteed. Now, I wondered. So far, I'd seen Japan and Germany as our sole high-technology competitors.

Since, neither had much of an aircraft business, that industry seemed safe. But suddenly, here were the French, known mostly as exporters of food and clothing, a nation never considered part of the high-tech club, and they, too, were closing fast.

BEFORE my business-consulting days, I'd thought that the market alone determined competitiveness. Government can't support industries, only the customer can. While that was true within a nation's borders, the global economy was different. How does a ten-dollar-an-hour country compete with those that pay one dollar an hour? How can a small American producer outdo European and Japanese conglomerates given millions of dollars in government support? What happens if we don't give similar support? We soon saw the answer. The ripples of foreign imports began to turn into waves. First textiles, steel, and cars flooded in, with American customers lining up for all three. Then televisions, semiconductors, microwave ovens, and machinery followed. The warning signs I'd seen were now unfolding into fact.[22]

I was becoming convinced that we no longer controlled our economic destiny. Decisions being made in Japan and Germany had begun to determine what jobs Americans would have next year, and what living standard our children would have next century. There had to be a way we as a country could respond.

That year, 1977, I asked my consulting firm, BCG, for a six-month leave to explore ways a country can stay competitive in an internationalizing economy. I spent my time traveling, reading, interviewing, and writing. After returning full-time to work, I gathered what I'd learned and made a proposal to my bosses. Perhaps it was time, I said, for the company to offer governments the same services we'd offered corporations—business strategy. Over the years, we'd developed unique ways of studying how industries could become more competitive. More than ever, governments were thinking about the same goals, but often using old economic theory geared more for domestic forces than global ones. My idea was to devise economic-development strategy based on business-strategy concepts. The company agreed to give it a try. I spent eighteen months doing this kind of work for BCG, and since 1979, have been continuing it through my own strategy-consulting group, Telesis. All along, I've continued spending most of my time consulting for businesses.

I've also tried to be part of the U.S. economic debate, writing two books, testifying in Washington, and giving advice to officeholders, candidates, and economic-development commissions. Throughout, I've pursued the same question I sought to answer when I began this career: How do societies achieve prosperity? That's what I hope to pass on in this book.

There is no single formula for building prosperity, but any solution must begin, I think, where I began in 1973—with understanding the world forces we face. The nine case studies I've chosen here show examples of these forces. Six of them show how foreign companies and governments are competing globally. But three show how the best of our own companies are proving that we Americans can still win this race.

Part I discusses America's challenge from developing countries, where low-cost production is the crucial threat. Part II illustrates competition with developed countries in mature products—cars and machine tools, for example—where our rivals are battling with superior quality, design, and service to win the world's higher-priced market niches. Part III focuses on competition in future technologies where the key to leadership lies with invention and rapid innovation.

Finally, the postscript explores what is perhaps our most compelling national challenge: what America must do to come into the twenty-first century as the world's economic leader.

I

Competing with Low-Wage Countries

THE NATIONS of South Korea, Taiwan, Hong Kong, and Singapore were responsible for over $30 billion of America's trade deficit in 1987.

Over 75 percent of our imports from these nations come from U.S.-owned or subcontracted plants, and are sold under American labels.

Despite the fact that wages and benefits average only $2 to $3 per hour in these countries, many of the products we source from them could be made competitively in the United States.

1

Korea: Winning with Microwaves

THE MICROWAVE OVEN, invented in America forty years ago,[1] just recently became one of the best-selling appliances in the world. It has created a multibillion-dollar industry that's spawned tens of thousands of jobs. Yet today, were you to buy a microwave oven in the United States, the odds are one in three that it was built ten thousand miles away, in South Korea.[2] The odds are one in five that it was designed by a forty-three-year-old engineer named Yun Soo Chu. His company, Samsung, is now the world's leading microwave oven producer.[3] But it wasn't until 1979, when millions of the new ovens were being manufactured each year in America, that Samsung set up its first crude assembly line. That year, the company made only a few dozen a week. Today, it makes over eighty thousand a week. The story of how Samsung succeeded speaks of the growing sophistication of our competition in the developing world.

WHEN CHU joined Samsung in 1973, it had just taken on a manufacturing challenge new to Korea: making home appliances. He started his company career designing washing machines, soon moving to electric skillets. Then, in 1976, he received an unexpected assignment. That year, on a visit to the United States, a Samsung vice-president named

J. U. Chung had been intrigued by a new kind of oven, heated not by electricity or gas, but by microwaves.

Chung knew there was no way he could market such an oven at home—few Koreans could afford it—but that wasn't a concern. In Korea, when companies consider a new product, the most common first question is whether they can export it. That same year, for example, Samsung had decided to make color televisions, even though there wasn't a single TV station in the country that could broadcast in color.[4]

Knowing that Americans like convenience, Chung felt the microwave oven was perfect for that market, the world's largest. When he got back to Korea, he asked Chu to form a team to design a Samsung microwave. Chu knew his company was starting well behind Japanese and American producers, but Samsung, he felt, had two advantages: low-wage workers, and a willingness to wait for a payback. The company's first priority, he knew, wasn't high profits; it was high production. Samsung was especially interested in modern products. For Korean industry, that was almost unprecedented.

Traditionally, low-wage countries have been content to let their factories lag a decade behind countries like America, making bicycles in the age of the automobile, black-and-white televisions in the age of color. Samsung was one of the first Third World companies to take a new approach, deciding to compete directly in modern products.

Chu began by ordering a new U.S. microwave model called the Jet 230, made by General Electric, America's leading appliance company. Soon, Chu was looking at his first microwave. He took it apart, but still had no idea how it worked. The plastic cavity seemed simple enough, as did the door assembly and some of the wiring; but there were several complex parts, especially the device that generated the microwaves— the magnetron tube. To build it, he could tell, required expertise Samsung lacked. He began to tinker anyway. His team was given fifteen square feet in the corner of an old lab that served the company's entire electronics division, which at the time consisted of three Quonset-hut factories. It seemed absurd that such a place could consider challenging major corporations in America and Japan, and Chu knew it. But he also knew Samsung's executives cared little about marketing at the moment. They'd told him they had only one objective right now—production. They'd worry about selling the oven later.

IT WAS around that time, 1977, that I got my first glimpse of South Korea, at the request of the British government. A few years before, Korean black-and-white televisions had begun arriving in England. At first, British TV producers hadn't been concerned. The Koreans gained only a small market share, and besides, this was exactly what developing countries were expected to do: compete in twenty-year-old products. But then something disturbing happened. Korean color televisions began arriving, also cheap. The British government wanted to know whether the assault would get more serious. I was asked to do a study.[5]

My first day in Seoul showed me that South Korea was more a Third World country than I imagined. My rental car, a tinny local brand, had a hole in the floor. The road from the airport was dusty, and much of the housing run-down. The city had only one first-class hotel, which lost power for a few hours shortly after I arrived. Only a decade before, the World Bank had listed South Korea as one of the world's poorest countries.[6] Could a nation like this be a threat?

At first, I didn't think so, except maybe in old technologies. But after a few days, I began to hear that the government was helping companies get into more modern industries. I purchased a copy of its latest official five-year plan,[7] then sat down with one of the country's leading economic officials. He explained that to invest in new factories, Korea needed foreign cash, so it had been encouraging export, mostly of textiles and black-and-white TVs. Korea's next goal was to export cars and ships. And recently, the country had finished a steel plant. I decided to visit it.

At the time, developing nations everywhere were breaking into steel. I'd seen several Third World plants, and had been especially impressed by those in Brazil and Mexico. I wondered if Korea's would be as good. It turned out to be better. The equipment was modern and the layout efficient. They'd done it by licensing foreign technology and hiring advisers from Japan.[8]

Next, I decided to visit one of Korea's auto plants. The hole in my rental car had left me skeptical, so I went to see the manufacturer, a company called Hyundai. A first glance left me even more skeptical. The workers were simply assembling old Japanese-designed models, then relabeling them, almost all for local sale. But just before I left, I met a British businessman who'd been brought in by Hyundai as an executive. He had good credentials—he'd worked as a senior manager at British Leyland, England's biggest carmaker. He, too, had at first been unsure about Hyundai, he said, but was now ecstatic. He was convinced that the ingredients were here for a real breakthrough—not just at Hyundai, but throughout the country. The nation, he said, had come to a consensus that manufacturing would be its road to prosperity. The workers were industrious, and South Korea's major corporations—with government help—were now poised to invest big dollars in new factories.

My next stop was Samsung, one of the companies exporting televisions to England. The company's electronics division, in Suweon, an hour's drive from Seoul, wasn't much. The factory floors were bare concrete, and people were hand-wheeling parts to and from the production line. I moved on to Samsung's research lab, which reminded me of a dilapidated high-school science classroom. But the work going on there intrigued me. They'd gathered color televisions from every major company in the world—RCA, GE, Hitachi—and were using them to design a model of their own. They were working on refrigerators and other appliances, as well. The chief engineer was young, well trained, a recent graduate of an American university. I asked him about Samsung's color-television strategy, telling him I presumed the company planned to buy parts from overseas, only doing assembly in Korea. Not at all, he said. They were going to make everything themselves—even the color picture tube. They'd already picked the best foreign models, he said, and signed agreements for technical assistance. Soon, he predicted, Samsung would be exporting around the globe. I wasn't convinced. Maybe in ten or fifteen years, I thought, but not sooner. To be a world player, you need world-class engineers, and that was something Korea was short on.

What I didn't realize was that the company's chairman, Lee Byung Chull, was investing not just in better technology, but better minds. He'd been sending waves of young Koreans to American universities, slowly building what was soon to become the biggest company engineering pool in any developing country.

HAD I LOOKED in all corners of the Samsung lab that day in 1977, I might have seen Chu, just beginning work on a microwave-oven prototype. By then, he too had gathered a number of the world's best models—GE, Toshiba, Litton—and was choosing the best parts of each. One thing that drove Chu was his failure at his last assignment at Samsung—designing an electric skillet. He just hadn't been able to make it work right. This time, he told himself, he had to succeed.

Samsung didn't have all the manufacturing machines he needed to make microwave ovens, so Chu began visiting press vendors, plastic vendors, toolmakers. When he couldn't find anyone in the country to do the kind of welding he wanted, he chose to seal his oven prototype with caulking instead. Slowly, it came together—brackets, outer panel, door. But when he got to the magnetron tube, source of the microwaves, he was lost. There was no way Samsung could make it, or even subcontract it locally. At the time, only three manufacturers in the world had that ability—two in Japan and one in Rhode Island. Chu decided to buy the magnetron tube outright, from Japan. As months passed, he drove himself ever harder, often staying in the lab all night. It took him a year of eighty-hour weeks to finish the prototype, but finally, he was ready to test it. He pushed the "on" button. In front of his eyes, the plastic in the cavity melted. So much for a year's work.

He spent more eighty-hour weeks to rebuild it, readjust it, redesign it. And again he turned it on. This time, the stir shaft melted. Even his wife began to question his obsessiveness. "You must be mad," she'd tell him. At times, he agreed with her. The Japanese and Americans, he knew, were now selling over 4 million microwave ovens a year, and he couldn't even get a single prototype to work.

MICROWAVE-OVEN technology was pioneered in the late 1940's by a U.S. defense contractor—Raytheon. While experimenting with radar microwaves, a researcher there noticed that a candy bar in his pocket melted. That led to the idea of an oven. Raytheon and another defense-oriented company, Litton, tried to sell the product in America, without much success.⁹ Few U.S. appliance makers saw promise in it. True, it was the first new major appliance in a generation, but in America it seemed unnecessary. Most households already had an oven. Who would want two? Besides, quick defrost for quick meals—a strong point of microwaves—wasn't yet the American way of eating.

The product seemed ideal for Japan, however, a nation with a taste for smallness—small houses, small kitchens, small appliances. And the Japanese cooking style did rely heavily on reheating. Though a few American companies were aware of the Japanese sales potential, they weren't interested. Exporting to distant markets wasn't worth the trouble.

That's how Japanese companies became the first major manufacturers of microwave ovens. They seized our technology, began perfecting it, and soon went beyond their backyard. They saw export as an opportunity, not a burden. They pushed the product overseas, harvesting a windfall when the world market took off, going from 600,000 units in 1970 to 2.2 million in 1975.¹⁰ Finally, in the late-1970's, American appliance makers like GE began serious investment in microwave ovens.¹¹ But they paid a price for being late. In 1979, the U.S. market became bigger than Japan's for the first time. But by then, Japanese companies already had over 25 percent of it.¹²

IN JUNE OF 1978, in the corner of his Suweon lab, Chu finally finished another prototype. He turned it on for a test, ready for the worst, but this time, nothing melted. His bosses were encouraged. They knew Chu's oven was still too crude to compete on the world market, but they told him to make more anyway. Chu himself had few global hopes. At best, he felt, Samsung would find a small, low-priced niche in the United States. But that didn't discourage him. The company's preeminent goal was production; marketing was second priority. Soon Samsung management did send out a few salesmen with the prototypes. They didn't have much success, but headquarters decided to put together a makeshift production line anyway. In case an order came in, they wanted to be ready. It was one of the company's rules: Never, ever, keep a customer waiting.

The production team began making one microwave oven a day, then two. Soon, they were up to five. By mid-1979, when over 4 million ovens were sold around the world, Samsung had finished only 1,460 of them. That's when the company decided to try its first real sales push. They chose to focus on the local market. Unfortunately, their low scale meant they had to charge an exorbitant six hundred dollars each—half the yearly income of an average Korean family. Almost no one bought. But management was upbeat. The machines worked. Having no sales was no reason to stop development.

Still, with the domestic push a washout, Samsung's sales people began to look abroad. They sent out brochures and hired distributors in dozens of countries. They offered to cut price and were ready to fill the smallest order. The first came in from Panama, for 240 ovens. By the time the ovens were all shipped, Samsung had lost money, but there was celebration in Suweon. The company had broken through. And besides, this would be a good way to learn what customers wanted. Samsung felt it best to refine the product in a few small markets before trying big ones.

The Panama sales gave them confidence to apply for underwriter's laboratory approval, necessary for exporting to the United States. Late in 1979, they got it. For Samsung, America wasn't a totally foreign market. Many of the company's managers had gone to school there; they had American knowledge, knew the American language. And Samsung was ready to do something few American manufacturers did at the time: tailor its product to foreign tastes. If that meant retooling production back in Suweon, Samsung would spend the money. Instead of planning on a single line of ovens for the world, its strategy was to make unique models for unique markets.

At the time, microwave ovens sold for $350–$400 each in America. One of the country's biggest retailers, J. C. Penney, had been searching for a $299 model. They hadn't had any luck with the two countries then producing microwaves—Japan and the United States. Then Penney heard about Samsung. The retailer saw an opportunity—a low-wage country capable of building a modern product. In 1980, Penney decided to ask Samsung if it could build a microwave oven to sell in America for $299.

By then, world sales were up to 4.7 million a year.[13] Samsung was being asked for a few thousand only. On top of that, Penney's order would mean designing a whole new oven and taking heavy losses, all in the name of gaining a fraction of one percent of the U.S. market. In Suweon, management was ecstatic anyway, promising Penney anything it wanted. To deliver, Samsung promised Chu any investment he needed. The firm put no pressure on him for profits; all it wanted was production.

Penney's technical people would be helping Chu with product quality, but Chu knew the greatest burden would be on Samsung. The challenge now was to turn a still-primitive assembly room into an efficient factory almost overnight. And Samsung would have to get it right the first time. This wasn't another Panama. These machines would be going to Americans, the most sophisticated consumers in the world.

CHU'S BOSS was a quiet mechanical engineer named Kyung Pal Park. Ask him why he chose manufacturing and he'll tell you of his memory of American soldiers during the Korean War. Everything about them suggested wealth: their clothes, their equipment, their vehicles. How, Park wondered, had America achieved that? In time, he came to see the answer as production. America was wealthy because it made things. Park wanted that for Korea, too: a nation not of rice paddies, but factories. In 1969, he joined Samsung. In 1980, at age thirty-nine, he was named head of home appliances. It was his responsibility to deliver the Penney order.

Soon he came up with his plan for organizing a team. In America, such a team typically would be headed by product designers; factory engineers would come second. At Samsung, production is king. So Park merged his product and factory people, stressing that design should be done with manufacturing in mind. He gave the team one unbreakable rule: No matter what, they would deliver on every deadline, not a day later. That responsibility would fall to Park's chief lieutenant, a production engineer just transferred from Samsung's motor division named I. J. Jang.

Before his transfer, Jang was managing the production of millions of motors a year on four separate lines. Now, he found himself in a division making five or six ovens a day. He didn't see it as a demotion. "There is one thing more valued at Samsung than high production," he explains, "the potential of high production." The best engineers aren't placed with boom products, but products that have yet to take off.

JANG IMMERSED HIMSELF in learning the product, spending hours talking with designers like Chu, then journeying overseas to Matsushita, Sanyo, and GE. Once he'd learned world standards, he began to make sure Samsung was living up to them. He studied the prototype test results, pausing on the microwave-leakage numbers, which seemed high. That was a problem. He asked if it could be fixed, and was told the seal design made it hard to weld any better. So Jang, one of Samsung's most senior production managers, personally went to the welding vendor to help upgrade his process. Of the one hundred outside vendors working on the project, he ended up visiting thirty of them himself.

Then he turned his attention to building the assembly line. He started with an empty factory room and a delivery date only months away. His senior people would begin at dawn, often working until 10:30 P.M., then take a few hours' nap before going back to work for the rest of the night. Even Jang's boss, Kyung Pal Park, one of the highest executives in Suweon, kept the same hours. Samsung's executives rarely ask a sacrifice they're not ready to make themselves. Actually, there was one area of privilege. There were a few cots littered around the factory. The executives got those, the others grabbed naps in chairs.

The line took shape, production began, but inevitably, there were dozens of bugs. The Samsung people decided they couldn't afford to lose production though, so they fell into a pattern of manufacturing by day, then running the line all night to fine-tune it. Production improved, up to ten a day, then fifteen. Soon, they got it to fifteen hundred a month, enough to meet Penney's order of several thousand.

Penney liked the ovens, and soon asked for more. Could Samsung deliver five thousand in another month? Samsung made that deadline, too, but there wasn't time for celebration. Now Penney wanted seven thousand. There was time only to work. "Like a cow," Jang would say later.

The team felt it would be wise to install more assembly lines and asked management for the money. "It was no problem," Jang said. As long as they got production, they would get the investment. By the end of 1981, Samsung had increased microwave production a hundredfold over the previous year, from just over a thousand to over one hundred thousand. Still, it was only a fraction of the world market. And almost none of the giants in America or Japan noticed. South Korea, they still felt, could never be a serious competitor in such sophisticated technology.

IN 1978, while working on a study for the Swedish government, I visited some Korean shipyards. I was surprised to find how modern they were—and more surprised when the managers said they planned to invest in even better technology. Then, in 1979, while in Athens to make a speech, I was given a Hyundai as a rental car. It was only two years after I'd all but written Hyundai off after touring their factory. But this car was much better. And I noticed a number of other Hyundai cars on the roads. A month later, on a trip to Dubai, I saw more Hyundai cars, as well as Samsung color TVs.

I decided to look into what was happening, and returned to Korea. After a number of days meeting with both corporate managers and government economic planners,[14] I learned that Korea's progress was driven by its government. The key player was the Economic Development Board. Its job was to think about where South Korea's economy should head and then give incentives to help business get there. EDB built industrial parks, subsidized utilities, provided tax rebates for export and low-cost loans for investing in selected new products. The incentives were of particular help to big companies like Samsung, whose managers met frequently with government officials, plotting strategy, trading ideas, and discussing projects. Both business and government understood the country couldn't depend on low-wage industries for long, not with even cheaper labor in countries next door. Just as America had lost thousands of clothing jobs to Korea, soon, the Koreans knew, they would be losing such jobs to Malaysia and China. To prepare, the government, in consultation with companies, developed incentives for investing in new industries. By 1980, the country had gone beyond textiles, into steel and ships. Now they were making automobiles. And they'd begun moving toward world-class electronics.[15] South Korea was developing faster than I'd expected.

IN 1982, Samsung's microwave production topped two hundred thousand, double the previous year. But Mr. Park and his team didn't think it was enough. They knew that Samsung was still a global afterthought. American manufacturers were making over 2 million ovens per year, and the Japanese even more—2.3 million at home, and another 820,000 in their U.S. plants. The giant Matsushita company had 17 percent of the world market. Sanyo had 15 percent, while Samsung had less than 3 percent.[16]

One problem was that the big producers were bringing their prices down, narrowing Samsung's key advantage. If Samsung was going to keep growing, it realized it had to lower its own prices even more. The executives looked over their cost structure. The highest item was the magnetron tube, which they were still buying from the Japanese. They began to wonder if they could make it themselves. It would mean millions of dollars of investment for a new, highly complex factory. They approached Japan's magnetron producers for technical assistance, but were turned down. That left only one other company to approach— Amperex, the Rhode Island firm that was America's only manufacturer. But that plant, Samsung found, had been unable to compete with Japan and was going out of business.[17]

ABOUT THAT TIME, in Louisville, Kentucky, the head marketing manager for GE's Major Appliance Business Group, Bruce Enders, was beginning to see warning signs in his microwave-oven division. Because GE had come into microwave ovens so late, it had yet to make money on them. In 1982, the losses began to get worse. The Japanese were chipping away at GE's U.S. share, pushing it down from over 16 percent in 1980 to 14 percent in 1982.[18] No one at GE thought of conceding ground, though. Japan's wage rates were no lower than America's and GE was just completing a multimillion-dollar modernization at its microwave oven factory in Columbia, Maryland. The company was convinced it would turn things around.

Enders knew that GE understood the American consumer better than any other appliance maker. It had just scored a tremendous success with the Spacemaker, for example, the industry's first under-shelf model. If the Maryland modernization could make GE cost-competitive, he was convinced the company could make the business profitable.

But then, in late 1982, the Japanese began to export a new mid-sized line of ovens at an alarmingly low price—it was even below GE's costs at its modernized plant. GE's manufacturing people insisted that the Japanese must be dumping. But Enders wanted to know for sure. He asked me to do a study.

THE STUDY was supposed to focus on Japan, so I spent three weeks there. But I knew Samsung had begun to make microwaves, so before coming home, I flew to Korea for a two-day visit. It was my first trip to Samsung since 1977. It was soon clear that there had been big changes.

In Suweon, the three Quonset huts had been replaced by a dozen new buildings. Some Samsung executives took me on a tour, beginning in the basement of the microwave building, where the machining was done. That part wasn't very impressive. Most of the equipment was old. Then they took me to the second floor, where the ovens were being assembled. It was a little better, but still backward. Samsung's wage rates, I thought, could perhaps outcompete GE, but not their technology.

Then they invited me to see their TV plant. The old one, I remembered, had long lines of women plugging in parts by hand. But this was different—as automated as any TV plant I'd seen in America. Next, they invited me to see their new television-tube factory. It was much larger, and more modern than I'd expected. The biggest surprise was a highly complex TV glass plant being put up in partnership with America's Corning Glass Works. Clearly, Samsung had been serious about producing every color television part by itself.

Finally, I went to the R&D lab. It had gone from an old high-school science room to a large, modern operation. Instead of a handful of engineers, there were five hundred. Everything Samsung had said it would do in 1977, it had done. I understood that the Koreans weren't showing me all this out of pride alone. They knew I was doing a study for GE and hoped I'd bring back a message: that they could do in microwaves what they'd done in TVs.

As I was leaving the Suweon campus, I saw a truck pull up, and men begin to unload equipment. I looked at it, then looked closer. Months before, I'd visited Amperex, America's last magnetron plant. Afterward, I'd learned it had shut down. Now, here in Korea, coming off this truck, I was looking at Amperex's equipment. Park and the others had decided to build their own magnetrons after all. In an almost disturbingly symbolic strategy, they were going to transplant an American factory that could no longer compete, and sell its goods—now Korean-made—back to America.

BEFORE FINISHING the final microwave report, I gave my initial impressions to GE in early 1983. The Japanese, I said, weren't dumping. Their plants and product designs were so efficient they could indeed land microwave ovens in the United States cheaper than those coming off GE's new assembly line.[19] They'd done it by first building volume and then investing the extra profits into brainpower. Matsushita, for example, had 280 engineers and technicians in microwave ovens.[20] That cost the company up front, but was now enabling it to get costs ever lower by continually redesigning both its ovens and plants. As for GE, it had only thirty engineers in its microwave operation.

Then there were the most disturbing numbers of all. GE's share was falling even as the world market grew. Global sales had gone from 4.7 million in 1980 to 7 million in 1983, but GE's U.S. market share had shrunk. It was down to 12 percent. Other U.S. producers had declined even more. The shift had almost all gone to the Japanese.[21]

I put forward two options. One was to invest as the Japanese had, in hundreds of engineers. It would be expensive, but in time, I was convinced, it would pay back well. The key word, however, was time. It might take GE a decade of heavy investment—and losses—to take the lead. It was a common strategy in Japan or Korea, but in America it's harder to tell stockholders to wait five or ten years for a return. Besides, GE was already pouring enormous investment into refrigerators and dishwashers, products where it led the market. Microwaves were a lower priority. They chose my other option—to get product from overseas, either through a joint venture or sourcing from a competitor.

While I was finishing my final report, GE management did decide to explore a joint-venture factory with the Japanese, though they wanted it built in the States. They chose to work with Matsushita, the biggest producer. Enders traveled to Japan to negotiate, and seemed to be getting close. He even got the Japanese to agree that a co-venture would be highly profitable for both. But in the end, the Japanese declined.

When they told him, Enders was surprised. He asked one of Matsushita's key executives why. If the co-venture would make them money, why wouldn't they agree to it? Because, the executive said, it would mean losing some of the American market to GE. In Japan, he explained, foreign market share is a key priority.

"Enders-san," he said, "you have to understand. In Japan, it's our destiny to export. If we don't export, we don't survive."

"That's what this guy said to me," Enders would say later. "Could you imagine a U.S. business manager thinking that way? I've never forgotten it."

Matsushita's decision left GE with one other option: sourcing—buying Japanese products and putting the GE label on them. No one in Louisville was ready to shut down the new Maryland plant, but maybe it made sense to source a few lines.

In April 1983, I finished my full report. In it, I raised a Korean option. If GE sourced only with Matsushita, I said, the Americans would be at the mercy of a direct competitor. Korean costs, however, were potentially low enough to undercut the Japanese. And because the Koreans were anxious for volume, it would be easier to negotiate a good deal with them.

Louisville was skeptical. The Koreans? Perhaps they were making a few ovens for Penney, but they were a Third World country. A high-quality firm like GE—selling a million ovens—couldn't risk depending on South Korea.

I showed them the costs differences. In 1983, it cost GE $218 to make a typical microwave oven. It cost Samsung only $155.[22] I went on to break it down.

Assembly labor cost GE eight dollars per oven; for Samsung, only sixty-three cents. The differences in overhead labor—supervision, maintenance, setup—were even more astounding. For GE, overhead labor was thirty dollars per oven; for Samsung, seventy-three cents. GE was spending four dollars on material handling for each oven, Samsung twelve cents. The biggest area of difference was in GE's line and central management—that came to ten dollars per oven. At Samsung, it was two cents. What did the companies get for their money? That was the most disturbing figure of all. Samsung workers were paid less, but delivered more. GE got four ovens per person each day, Samsung got nine. And once volume increased, Korean costs could go even lower.

The GE managers continued to waver. Japanese costs, though not at Korean levels, were better than those at GE. And Japan's products were clearly high quality. Many felt it was more prudent to source there. Still, to be sure, Enders decided to go to Korea himself. At the end of his first day, he asked Samsung's management for a proposal, including a cost breakdown, a delivery schedule, and a description of how they'd build the GE ovens. In America, it takes companies four to six weeks to develop that kind of plan. The next morning, Enders had a final breakfast meeting with Samsung executives.

"A group of engineers came in," Enders recalls, "and they gave us their proposal. Their hair was messed up—their eyes were bloodshot. Those guys had worked all night. And it met our target. I couldn't believe it."

A few weeks later, Roger Schipke, the head of the GE Major Appliance Business Group, decided to go to South Korea. He was walking down a Samsung corridor with his hosts when a crowd of white coats came bustling the other way. He had to stand against the wall to let them by. There were dozens of them, all very young. When they'd passed, he asked who they were. "Those are our new microwave-oven engineers," his host told him. There were more of them than Schipke had working in his whole microwave division, and these were just Samsung's newest hires. Louisville, he realized, was probably outengineered ten to one. He asked where the new hirees had been trained. The answer came back: Purdue, University of Southern California, University of Washington.

"I'm a simple guy," Schipke would say later. "I just looked around. And I said, 'Wow, I'm not getting into that game.'"

In June 1983, management in Louisville decided to begin sourcing microwave ovens from the Far East, but only small and mid-sized models. GE would continue to make full-sized ovens in America. The company's biggest order was with Japan. But GE did give Samsung a much smaller order, only about fifteen thousand. The Americans wanted to see if the Koreans could deliver.

IT WAS now up to Samsung's appliance director, K. P. Park, to produce high-quality goods at a cost America's biggest appliance maker could no longer match. GE sent technical people to Korea to outline its standards. In GE's thinking, this was simply quality control for a second-rate supplier. In Suweon, Park saw it differently. If he was a good student, he'd learn world-class skills. Once again, he told his people there was one unbreakable rule: Every deadline must be met. He knew he'd have to depend on his foot soldiers as much as his lieutenants. Managers like Park feel that Korea's most important resource is disciplined workers who give 70-hour weeks. Who, exactly, are they?

AT THE Suweon complex, more than half of those who do basic assembly are women. Most stay with Samsung four or five years, arriving with high-school educations and leaving with husbands to start life as housewives. Jo Yon Hwang and Jang Mee Hur, both in their early twenties, applied to Samsung because of its reputation for being good to its workers. They were among the third of all applicants accepted. Upon arrival, they were given blue uniforms, and after two weeks' training were put to work on the microwave line eleven hours a day, twenty-seven days a month. Everyone, even the senior people, works the same schedule. The two women say it's why they feel so committed to the company—their bosses make the same sacrifices they do. In 1988, their base wage was just over $350 a month—a little over $1.20 an hour. The male assembly workers are paid the same. Medical services are provided free by Samsung, and so is lunch. Dinner and breakfast, both offered in company dining areas, cost fifteen cents each. The workers are given gifts several times a year: clothes, shoes, hiking bags, tape recorders. The recorders are made by Samsung.

The two women get five days off in winter and five in summer, during which the majority go to a beach camp on the coast. It's run by Samsung. Like most of the women in the Suweon complex, Miss Hwang lives free in a company dormitory. There are 15 such dormitories, housing 420 women each, 6 to a room. Miss Hur chose to live outside the complex, in an apartment with a girlfriend. Rent is not a problem. Samsung lends her two thousand dollars, which she gives to the landlord, who invests it and gets to keep whatever interest it yields. Miss Hur, meanwhile, pays Samsung 10 percent interest on the loan. When she leaves, the two thousand dollars is given back to the company.

The two young women usually get up at six and have breakfast at seven. Miss Hwang walks to her factory, Miss Hur comes by company bus. At day's end, Miss Hwang has to be back in the dorm by 9:30 P.M., even on the three Sundays a month she gets off. On those days, she and Miss Hur like to watch television, read books, or go hiking. They also like music, particularly Michael Jackson. They know the Beatles are the most legendary of rock groups, but they don't care for them. "Too old," says Miss Hwang. Occasionally, they go on dates, though rarely to nightclubs; usually, they go for daytime walks in the park.

Though they'd welcome promotions, neither actively seeks them. When they think of their futures, they think of marriage. Most female Samsung employees wed between twenty-four and twenty-six. Thirty percent marry Samsung men. Most of the others wed men they've met through their families, though there's no obligation. Miss Hwang will tell you she's already rejected one parental choice. "I didn't like him," she explains.

The subject the two women are most enthusiastic about is product quality. Miss Hwang is convinced no workers in the world pay as close attention to products as those at Samsung. She herself checks her own work a final time even after an inspector double-checks it. Her specific function is to attach serial numbers and name-brand labels to microwave ovens. If you own a GE Spacemaker, chances are the label was attached by Miss Hwang, here in Suweon. She does twelve hundred GE labels a day. Miss Hur's job is to attach microwave doors—also about twelve hundred a day. They admit it's the same simple function, hour after hour, but neither thinks the days are dull. They see their jobs as a challenge to personal discipline, even integrity. Doing their work perfectly each time is a way of teaching themselves excellence. They feel their work should reflect their vision of themselves as people of quality. "I put my spirit, put my soul into this product," explains Miss Hwang.

As she does her work, she thinks of making each product as if she herself were going to buy it. She also thinks of the actual customer, some unseen American family. Such families are paying her livelihood; she feels she owes them a good product. Although neither has ever left Korea, both young women are keenly aware of global economic forces. They understand that a great company can no longer endure if it doesn't see the world as both market and competitor. They also understand that products sold abroad will improve the nation's standard of living more than products sold at home. They will tell you that exports bring in new wealth, while domestic sales only recycle it.

Like everyone, they would love higher salaries, but they're motivated by other considerations as well. They see themselves as planting seeds for both company and country. They feel that's a difference between Korean workers and Americans. Though they are in their early twenties, they still remember a Korea of dirt roads, few cars, and many slums. They've seen that change, and though they can't analyze all the reasons, they know manufacturing has been a big one. As factory workers, they feel they're part of that, part of something historic.

AT FIRST, Samsung's ovens were not up to GE standards. But with the help of GE's quality engineers, things soon got better.[23] Enders grew increasingly impressed, and eventually put in another order. Sales steadily improved. It was the GE label customers reached for, but Korean workmanship that satisfied them. On his next trip to Suweon, Enders was surprised at the changes. The assembly line had gone from roller conveyors to automatic-transfer mechanisms. Clearly, Samsung had the capacity to deliver far more than GE had been asking for. Enders put in a still-bigger order. Sales kept improving. It was around that time, mid-1983, that the factory in Suweon made a milestone. Samsung shipped its five-hundred-thousandth oven. For the first time since the company had begun four years before, Park said it was time to celebrate. The Koreans paused for a brief party. When the party was over, they went back to work.

IF SUWEON'S biggest regiment is the assembly-line foot soldiers, its second biggest is the engineers who work a notch above them. The company has thousands, all working the same sixty-eight hours a week. S. D. Lee is typical—a smart, energetic young man who's committed to staying with Samsung. He knows if he works hard, his managers will promote him when he's ready. Although he's a junior engineer, Samsung has already schooled him with extra knowledge. He'll tell you such training is the company's mainstay. Samsung has given him twenty days of full-time quality-control instruction, and once sent him to Japan for two weeks to learn technology from Toshiba. Before that trip, the firm gave him three months of Japanese-language training. "Three years after college," he explains, "you forget what you learned. Reeducation is needed."

What are Samsung's most lasting lessons? Two things, Lee says. First, management by target. You set a goal, then meet it no matter what, even if it means working through the night for a week. Second, you learn always to think several years ahead. It's not enough to be ahead of your competition today, he says. The question to ask is where things will be next decade. Lee's specific assignment illustrates that. Although Samsung's microwave ovens have the lowest cost in the world, Lee is working on factory automation to make the cost lower still.

Does he know Americans work only eight hours a day, five days a week?

He smiles. He is envious of that.

So why is it worth working so much harder, for less money?

Because you don't measure your success against Americans, he says, you measure it against the last generation of Koreans. And his lifestyle is going up faster than he ever expected. His father, he says, never could afford a car. Soon Lee plans to buy one. He sees even greater promise for his children. "If our generation doesn't work hard," he says, "the next generation will suffer."

BY THE END OF 1983, Samsung's annual microwave production topped 750,000, and by 1984, it passed 1 million. The Suweon factory expanded, as well. In four years, Samsung had gone from a few prototypes to ten mass-production lines. The product that began with melted plastic in an old lab was now becoming a major performer in America's market. But for Samsung, that wasn't good enough.

The company had grown concerned over some new projections.

From 1982 to 1986, U.S. microwave sales were expected to keep grow-ing at a healthy rate, but for the four years after that, the predictions said things would slow. It was time, Samsung decided, to seek out other markets. Europe, which was expected to grow by 20 percent a year, offered the most promise. The U.S. manufacturers were aware of the same trend, but Europe didn't seem a worthwhile market to them. The Americans didn't know those countries. It would take too much money to build a marketing network there, too long to get a profit. Samsung faced the same burdens, but its goal wasn't short-term return on invest-ment, it was long-term growth in volume. Among those assigned to Europe was a young marketing executive named J. K. Kim, soon to be named head of appliance-export sales before he was forty.

Like many Samsung executives, Kim is fluent in foreign languages and graduated from an American university. Although his parents had little money, they still found the means to send him to Berkeley. Edu-cation, he will tell you, is a Confucian priority. In South Korea, that and family come before all else. Even the poorer sections of the coun-tryside are over 95 percent literate—a far higher rate than in America. Kim still remembers arriving in California for school. The size of Amer-ica's cities, the number of cars, the wealth of the people—all of it astounded him. He returned to Korea with an urge to help build his own country. One secret of Korea's success, Kim will tell you, is the drive to escape poverty.

With his prestigious Berkeley degree, he had many career choices. Banking was one, lawyer another. Although it paid far less, he chose manufacturing. "I thought it could help more the totality of Korea," he would explain. "If I work for a lawyer's office, I can get my job, and my secretary's job. In Samsung, I can contribute ten thousand jobs." He knows Americans don't quite think that way. In the United States, young businessmen are more drawn to careers in finance. In South Korea, the prestige lies in factories. Services? "Britain," he says, "is a leader in services, but has one of the lowest living standards in Western Europe. Obviously, it's not the way to build a nation."

Kim found Samsung an ideal home. The hours were long, but he liked the idea of working for Korea's biggest company. Part of its appeal was the three weeks of training a year, another part the com-pany's willingness to invest. Samsung seemed to blend the risk-taking mentality of a start-up venture with the resources of a great corpora-tion. Most of all, he liked Samsung's drive to be a world player. Now, with the European strategy, the company was asking him to be part of that.

Curiously, it was America that taught Kim how to succeed abroad. It taught him what not to do. As most Koreans know, American firms rarely customize. "They just send us products made for Americans and say, 'Why don't you Koreans buy them?'" he explains. Sometimes, American exports are almost unusable. Although Korean households have 220-volt electricity, U.S. firms have been known to try selling refrigerators built for 110 volts, with only rudimentary converters. "Even the chocolate," says Kim. "My kids like chocolate very much, but they don't like American chocolate. Too sweet. You want to sell chocolate here, you have to know our taste."

Kim learned from that. Each market has its own tastes. If you're going to sell, you have to tailor. His company embraced the same philosophy. The Samsung people knew that would make things hard—each time they began in a new country, they'd have to design new products, retool lines, invest more dollars. They accepted it. The producer who doesn't tailor, Samsung felt, is the producer who will fail.

Kim began to focus on Europe, studying how it was different from America. Europeans, he found, like colder dishes. That meant the microwave defrost function should be different. Europeans like fish; Americans, meat and chicken. All that was fed back to Suweon's design division, which soon began tailoring new European models. In 1983, Samsung microwaves broke into Germany and Norway. In 1984, Samsung added France, Finland, Australia, and Belgium. And, all along, the Koreans kept pushing for a bigger piece of America.

IN MOST COMPANIES, it's the sales force alone that travels to learn buyer habits. Samsung doesn't think that's enough; it sends its engineers abroad, too. A successful production manager, the company feels, has to know more than just his assembly line, he has to know his customer. That's why I. J. Jang, head of production, was sent on regular marketing trips to America. Jang remembers flying in with a dozen other engineers from Suweon for an electronics show in Las Vegas. At one point, Jang took a side trip on his own to stores, visiting Sears, talking to salespeople. He asked what microwave models are most popular, what features attract customers. Once, he spotted a woman customer and went so far as to stop her and ask what she looked for in a microwave oven.

Why couldn't he rely on Samsung's marketing people? He will explain that there are some things an engineer has to see for himself. You can't describe color by phone or fax. Telling the designers to make a model red isn't enough. They want to know just what shade of red. They want to know exactly what size the knobs should be. They seek more than technical knowledge alone. They seek something subtler—a feel for America's tastes, its character, its people.

GE BEGAN SHIFTING more of its orders from the Japanese to Samsung. Soon GE's Korean models began to sell as well as those GE itself made in America, and at a much higher profit. Some of the executives in Louisville began to wonder whether it was time to shut down the new factory and source everything. The factory men resisted. How could GE stop production during the peak of the harvest? Microwave ovens, they pointed out, were blossoming into a $2 billion industry. Enders decided to give the plant defenders a final chance to make their case. He asked them for a proposal on streamlining. Soon they delivered it. It was an impressive job. They'd been able to get far lower cost than Enders had expected. But even if the company went through with the plan, its costs would remain far higher than those in Korea. It left management with little choice. In May 1985, GE publicly announced it would stop U.S. production of microwave ovens.

IN EARLY 1979, Samsung had produced exactly one crude prototype of a microwave oven. In 1987, it made 3.5 million microwaves[24] in 250 separate models for over 20 countries. Samsung had gambled correctly. Its appetite to produce had proven stronger than America's. From now on, GE would be doing the sales and service side of the product, Samsung the manufacturing. Soon, the people in Suweon would be the biggest makers of microwave ovens in the world.

SOME BUSINESSMEN IN America saw the Korean wage protests of 1987 as a hopeful sign. The higher their pay, the less competitive their products. But the fact is, South Korea is bound to remain a low-wage competitor into the next century. Even if Korean paychecks went up 20 percent a year and ours stayed flat—highly unlikely—it would still take a decade and a half for Korean wages to match our own.

And the political turmoil? It's possible that it could flare up from time to time, of course, but go to South Korea and you'll find a subsurface stability. Even at the height of the marches of 1987, many of the protestors were careful to put in their normal workday before going to the streets to demonstrate.

Koreans did not set out to chip away at our standard of living in order to build their own. But today, South Korea is dotted with factories that have replaced many in America. Its economy is growing at three times our rate. In 1987, the Koreans sold America $9 billion more in goods than we sold them. The trade balance has gotten so lopsided that Korea's version of *Business Week* recently ran a cover urging its readers to buy more American goods—to help America.

I RECENTLY VISITED with Suk Chae Lee, the Korean president's secretary for economic affairs. We spoke in a conference room near the Blue House, South Korea's equivalent of our own White House. Behind him, there was a portrait of traditional Korean warlords in full battle dress. They were on horseback, looking confident, poised on the edge of a river, ready to cross it. Lee began to speak of how the developing world has always been envious of America's industrial might. But today, there is surprise at America—a confusion over why we seem to be letting our industry decline. To him, it's a sign that we no longer care about world economic supremacy. He doesn't understand it. "America," he says, "isn't really tuned toward export." Later, he adds a thought: "In this age, you have to reach beyond yourselves. Nations are no longer islands. It's as important for American companies to sell in Japan as in Chicago."

He is quick to acknowledge that the world still sees America as a prosperous giant. But he wonders whether too much prosperity isn't part of the problem. When you've been the world champion for too long, Mr. Lee says, you have to remind yourself not to let your guard down. America, he continues, should know that nations like South Korea, which are striving for their first taste of prosperity, are now working harder than nations that take prosperity for granted. An aide sitting beside him at our meeting asks if he can quote a joke. Do we know how the two superpowers can destroy their enemies? There's an easier way than weaponry. "All Russia has to do," says the aide, "is send its enemies its economic planners. All America would have to do is send its lawyers."

Lee explains that a different kind of profession is preeminent in Korea. "Scientists and engineers," he says. "Our president treats them like heroes." True, he says, the nation's most revered businessmen are the chairmen of the great companies—but most of them are engineers themselves. It's hard even to start a company in South Korea, he says, unless you're an engineer.

The training of America's first industrialists, of course, was the same. Men like Henry Ford were inventors first, men of finance second. Perfecting the product was their priority. Speaking to Secretary Lee, you have the impression that South Korea is a glimpse of an earlier America, where people felt themselves part of a nation emerging through production. There's a sense of limitless opportunity here, but it's tempered. Even as Lee speaks of South Korea's achievements, he stresses that it has a long way to go. The reward will be there, he says, but only if they fear it won't be.

I RECENTLY HAD another discussion in Seoul, this time with a young Korean studying for an MBA and a career in strategy consulting. Though Koreans have historically been hostile to Japan, he doesn't hesitate when asked which country is his economic model. "Japan is the future," he says. He adds that he admires America more—its freedom, its spirit, its culture. But economically, there is more to learn from the Japanese. You need only look at one statistic to know that, he says. The Japanese have a trade surplus, America, a deficit.

IN 1970, Samsung, the largest Korean company, had only $100 million in sales. Its main businesses at the time were insurance, medical services, textiles and trading. That same year, General Electric had sales of $4.4 billion. Today, GE has grown dramatically into a diversified company with almost $40 billion in sales. Samsung has grown, as well. Today, it is one of the biggest industrial corporations on earth. Today, it too has almost $40 billion in sales.

At the gate of the Suweon complex, headquarters for Samsung's electronics and appliance division, a uniformed guard salutes all executive cars. Inside, the central offices are as modern as the most sophisticated in America. But the executives who staff them have not forgotten tradition. If you look under the fine wooden desks, you will often see a pair of slippers. In conversation, the managers sometimes speak of the values of Confucianism. "Less selfish," one explains of its essence. "More for the group."

Visitors to Suweon are first ushered into a screening room to see a video introduction of the company. It's broadcast on a Samsung TV with a Samsung VCR. The video begins with a statistic: Almost two-thirds of all the company manufactures is for export.

Speak with Samsung's managers, and a common theme recurs. What to manufacture next? What's on the world's horizon? Recently, employees at Suweon were wearing a button that said BREAKTHROUGH 87. Its point was to keep everyone thinking like entrepreneurs. "We are always looking for the next product," one manager explains. Samsung, he knows, will almost always be ready to invest in new ideas.

Today, the company designs and makes its own integrated circuits. In 1985, it began a data-systems division. In 1986, it started in aerospace. That year, net profits were only $182 million, among the lowest of the world's large corporations. It is by design. Samsung's priority for money is to plow it back into the company.

Samsung electronics now has over fifteen hundred engineers. In almost every building, showrooms display what they've done. There are VCRs, personal computers, video cameras, compact-disc players: products of the future, the kind that boost a nation's standard of living. There was a time when only high-wage countries had the vision to invest in such goods. No longer. Sometimes, even the opposite holds true. Although America invented most of these products, and buys more of them than any other country, we make almost none of them. In the case of VCRs and video cameras, we never manufactured them at all. Today, if an American company decided to start making VCRs, it would have to come to South Korea or Japan to get technical assistance. We remain the world's innovator, but others are challenging us as producers. Too often, the dollars we spend buying our own inventions are boosting the living standard of the Far East.

SAMSUNG is not alone in enjoying its microwave-oven success. General Electric is enjoying it, too. With Samsung's manufacturing help, GE's market share has shot up. Microwave ovens have become one of GE's most profitable appliances. In Louisville, management will say, rightly, that sourcing from the Koreans was good for the company. It allowed GE to leap over its Japanese and U.S. competitors to gain share and succeed.

But there is also the question of country. Over forty thousand Koreans make their living producing microwave ovens. In America, the number is a fraction of that. In 1980, almost 100 percent of every hundred dollars Americans spent on GE microwave ovens stayed in America. Today, well over half flows to South Korea.[25] While over eighty-four thousand microwave ovens are made in Suweon each week, GE's Maryland plant stands idle.

A lower dollar—America's key strategy to boost exports—won't change that. Even if South Korea's currency doubled in value, GE wouldn't be able to reopen that plant. The engineers are dispersed, the equipment sold. Nor will a low dollar dampen Samsung's resolve to produce microwave ovens. Currency levels alone won't correct our trade deficit. Only superior production will.

IN THE END, GE made a prudent choice in deciding to source from Korea. The company had discovered the potential for microwave ovens too late. By the time GE invested, the Japanese were way ahead. Going to the Koreans was a good way to leap past the Japanese and fight back. But the scenario could have been different. What if GE, or other American appliance companies, had acted earlier, not at the height of market demand, but ahead of it? If it had, it could have built enough scale to afford more product research and factory investment when competition got intense. Dollar-an-hour countries can be beaten. Our technology can often overwhelm low wages—but only if we're among the first in the arena. We can no longer afford to spend years analyzing new products. Too many other nations, like South Korea, are willing to seize them immediately.

Often, those nations do it with our help. Samsung would have had a hard time succeeding so quickly in microwave ovens without J. C. Penney and GE. The Americans helped bring Samsung world-class design, quality, scale, and legitimacy with other global customers—if GE sources from them, Samsung must be good. GE got a good deal in return—a low-cost source of ovens. But how long can an American company thrive by buying from the competition? Put another way, how long will Samsung be content to be a supplier? Its final vision, as with all great corporations, is to emerge as another General Electric, a household name. In some ways, this is already happening. Most luggage carts in West Germany's Frankfurt airport bear an advertisement for Samsung. Drivers in New York's Times Square, Chicago's Loop, London's M1, and even Tokyo's Keio Highway are beginning to see billboards with the same name—Samsung. Someday, Korea will no longer need to market its products through American labels, but will do it directly, as Hyundai is now doing in cars.

Gradually, the South Koreas of the world will move from supplier to competitor. If, by then, we've shut down our own factories, how will we ever fight back? GE made a good business decision for this decade. But what are the implications of this and hundreds of similar decisions for our children's generation?

EACH morning in Suweon, at 7:50 A.M., Miss Jang Mee Hur pauses before she begins work. Like all thirty thousand Suweon employees, even the division president, she stands silent as the company song is played throughout the complex. "We who gather under the flag of Samsung," goes the final stanza, "let's push ahead the wheel of new history." Then the song will end and all will begin yet another eleven-hour day.

Does Miss Hur really think Korean workers are better than American workers?

She is almost timid as she answers, but says she is sure they are.

Why?

Korean workers, she says, are driven not just by money, but by company, by country, by quality. American workers, she thinks, do it mostly for the money. Which product, she asks, would you want to buy?

Miss Jo Yon Hwang stands at a nearby line, continuing to attach company labels. "General Electric," the labels say. "Louisville, Ky. Made in Korea."

Does she feel bad that she has an American's job?

She says she wishes Americans only well, but is proud that by working harder, Koreans are now doing a job Americans had to give up. "Besides," she says, "in a sense, both countries are benefiting." Americans like to buy things, she says, and Koreans to make things—that is good for both sides, isn't it?

IT'S HARD for Mr. Yun Soo Chu, Samsung's microwave oven designer, to sit still for an interview. He'd rather be working. His office is no longer the corner of a primitive lab, it's a vast room filled with dozens of desks, and surrounded by another dozen rooms for research and test-ing. Behind his own desk are five clocks, each marking Samsung offices: L.A., Chicago/Mexico, London/Madrid, Frankfurt/Paris and New York/Miami. At the moment, Chu has a map of Sweden on his desk. Sam-sung began exporting there this year. The map is to help him organize trips for his staff; not marketing staff—engineers. He wants them to go to Sweden as often as possible. He wants them to know their customers.

Ask him what he works for, and he will tell you. His goal, he says, is to give his own children a higher standard of living than he knows himself. And so, each morning, he dons his company jacket, stands for the company song, and then goes back to designing the next line of microwave ovens that will fill the modern world's kitchens. On most nights, he is likely to be at the office very late.

2

Singapore: Silicon Island

THE OLD Singapore Airport at Paya Lebar was hot and chaotic, the customs lines over an hour, the taxi stand a war zone. When I finally did elbow my way into a cab, I noticed beetles crawling out of holes in the seat. There was no air-conditioning, and at seventy-seven miles from the equator, the ride was like a steam bath. Singapore, natives say, has only two kinds of weather—hot, and hotter. It took forty-five minutes across beat-up roads to get into town. My driver, who looked about three hundred pounds, spent most of the time cursing in Chinese and waving at pedestrians he'd narrowly missed.

The housing was mostly run-down, and the stores open-ended cubbyholes. I visited a few factories; all were in the familiar Third World mode: long lines of unskilled women, stuffing radio circuit boards and sewing garments. The country's biggest industry was trade, but of other peoples' goods. Singapore was a transit point for rubber, wood, and food from neighboring Thailand, Malaysia, and Indonesia. Within its own borders, Singapore had no natural resources at all, unless you counted low-wage workers.

The nightlife centered around seedy rows of food stalls. The best place, I was told, was a restaurant named Fattys. Fatty himself, the *maître d'*, wore a huge T-shirt that barely covered his belly. He was also the chief waiter, serving course after course as flies swarmed everywhere. The food was actually very good, as long as you didn't think about the kitchen.

My greatest challenge that week was trying to make a phone call to my office in America. My first night in Singapore, I tried to call a dozen times and didn't make it. I had the same problem the second night. By the third night, I was getting desperate. Finally, after a number of tries, I got a ring. A voice came on. I spent the first few seconds mentioning how relieved I was to have gotten through, then turned to business. Just as I did, the line went dead.

That was in 1974. Today, Singapore has changed. Drive around and you'll see very different kinds of factories—built by advanced-technology companies like AT&T, Hewlett Packard, General Electric, and Texas Instruments. There are now over two hundred U.S. manufacturing firms in Singapore, most making products to export back home. Altogether, they employ one hundred thousand Singaporeans, almost half in electronics, many with high-skill jobs.[1] The landscape has changed, too. The city is now filled with gleaming towers, the paved highways have late-model cars, the neighborhoods have modern apartment buildings.

In 1964, Singapore didn't even exist as a nation. By 1970, it was still illiterate and poor, its wealth per person only 18 percent of our own. Today, the country's wealth has risen to over 50 percent of our own, one of the fastest climbs of any nation.[2] Its living standard is now number two in Asia,[3] surpassed only by Japan. By 1995, the people of Singapore are expected to be richer than the people of Great Britain,[4] which first colonized the island in 1826.[5]

Its economic formula has been different from Korea's, where progress has been led by large local companies like Samsung. Singapore took another path, creating its wealth by drawing companies from outside, in part by building a good infrastructure. Once, that would have meant roads, telephones, and ports, but Singapore has added one more ingredient: an infrastructure of knowledge. Once, the world's best workers were those with strong backs; now it's those with strong minds. Singaporeans will tell you that brainpower is their only economic weapon. A speck of a nation, it covers only 225 square miles, has 2.6 million people, and no natural resources.[6] "Our brains," the people there say, "are all we have."

When they speak that way, they speak not of the corporate elite, but the whole work force. Today, the functional literacy rate in Singapore is 97 percent; our own is under 80.[7] Singapore's homes have a much higher ratio of personal computers than ours. Then there is the foundation of the new infrastructure: a score of advanced worker-training centers, most of which have better equipment than major American universities.

Singapore is two things. It is the competition we face. But it is also the promise before us. We're still far wealthier, but over the past decade, they've been building prosperity at a far quicker pace. Here is a Third World country that went overnight from slums to skyscrapers. It shows how quickly a nation can leap, even in a time of maximum world competition. True, it's easier for a poor country to double its wealth than a rich one, but America can move faster, and to do it, we need only understand the formula. Singapore teaches one piece of it: You don't build prosperity with low-paid people doing low-skill work, you do it by training high-paid people to work smarter. Invest in minds and you'll get your money back in productivity. One of the most sophisticated small factories in Singapore offers a glimpse of how that works; and how the country itself has blossomed economically.

I visited the factory in 1987. It was quite a change from the textile plants I'd seen thirteen years before. Instead of long lines of unskilled women, unmanned vehicles moved parts across the floor. Specially programmed vision robots did the assembly. The components were checked by automated testing systems, the finished goods boxed by one of the most advanced packaging machines in the world. Technicians with more training than many in America oversaw the operation. The product itself was an American symbol—the Apple II, one of the most successful computers ever built. But this was more than just a U.S.-designed assembly plant. Some of its most impressive automation improvements—the kind of developments that are the foundations of world manufacturing success—were developed in Singapore, by the Singaporeans themselves.

IN MARCH 1980, soon after being hired by Apple Computer, John Sanders was asked if he'd be willing to make a move—a long one. The company wanted to put a factory in Singapore, and needed a manufacturing man to oversee it. The factory would be small and simple, doing nothing more than assembling computer circuit boards, but it would be a doorway into Asian markets—as well as a cheaper way to make the boards. Not that the factory would lean on rows of low-wage workers. It would be a mechanized setup, with automatic component-insertion machines, but low skill nevertheless. No one at Apple was ready to farm out complex production to Southeast Asia. They didn't think the work force could handle it. You went there for new markets and low wages, not for high skills.

Sanders agreed to take the job for two years. It would be his first time working in the Far East. He'd later admit he had his share of stereotypes about what he'd find. He was convinced that setting up abroad—especially the Third World—would be a bureaucratic headache. He pictured endless hours in government offices waiting for permits. But at least, he knew, the company had already found a building. In fact, one of the reasons Apple had chosen Singapore was that the country's Economic Development Board, known by all as EDB, had a shell structure waiting. In early May 1981, Sanders went there to see it. It was a good building—solid, fine potential factory space, but still raw, with a dirt floor. He figured it would take a minimum of six months to put in services and start production. He lined up all the work he could, then headed back to America, telling himself not to be disappointed if it took far longer than he hoped.

HAD SANDERS looked around on that 1981 visit, he'd have seen plenty of other foreign companies setting up plants of their own. Like Apple, they were drawn to Singapore in part because of the vision of one man. If you had to pick a handful of nations most shaped by a single leader, Singapore would be among them. Lee Kuan Yew, its first head of government and head of government still, came to office in 1959, a one-time socialist student agitator who rose to power by speaking out against British rule. He was, however, hard-headed enough to think about prosperity as well as freedom, so complete independence wasn't his goal. He felt it would doom his people to poverty. Singapore, Lee knew, was not a blessed land—even most of its water had to be imported. Far better, he felt, to be part of its bigger neighbor, Malaysia. Such a marriage, he hoped, would offer Singapore a broad economic base, something it had always lacked.

Singapore's modern history began in 1826, when Britain claimed it as a port colony. It soon grew into a trading base populated by Malay labor, Indian bureaucrats, and Chinese coolies, talking at each other in scores of dialects. Its conquest by Japan in World War II laid the seeds for twenty years of disorder—first war, then poverty. Lee Kuan Yew's Malayan Federation was supposed to end that, but it didn't work. Malaysia was mostly native Malay, Singapore mostly Chinese. First came tension, then racial riots, and in 1965, Singapore was pushed reluctantly into independence, burdened with 30 percent unemployment.[8] Ironically, its one economic blessing was the British military, which had kept bases there, generating forty thousand jobs and 15 percent of the gross national product. Then, in the late 1960's, the British pulled out.[9] If ever a country was in danger of becoming an international welfare case, it was Singapore.

Most of the population was in trading or shopkeeping—a nation of middlemen. Lee didn't see any way to build wealth from that kind of base. To prosper, he felt, a people has to produce. But the country had almost no factories, just scattered, low-skill workshops. Nor were there any moneyed industrialists to build up manufacturing—no local version of Samsung. Lee was left with just one path. He looked outward. If Singapore's own companies couldn't build an industrial base, he'd lure world corporations that could. He knew he'd have competition. If governors throughout America were finding it hard to land good factories, how could he? Cheap wages would be one way, but Lee decided he needed more. For starters, he needed infrastructure. He moved quickly.

I took about a dozen business trips back to Singapore in the late 1970's, some only months apart, but each time, there were changes, sometimes remarkable ones—a new airport was built, the beat-up roads were paved, the phones got better. Other Third World nations began to build up, too, but not as fast. And there was another difference, as well. The other nations built through borrowing; in Singapore, Lee resolved to pay as he went. That way, he felt, there would be less danger of starts and stops. To raise capital, he set up an infrastructure tax akin to social security—the promised payback being roads, housing, industrial parks, and even roadside tree planting. Because people could see where their infrastructure taxes were going, they didn't view them as a burden. Besides, they were used to putting money away for the future. Singaporeans save 42 percent of their total national income; in America, we save less than 5 percent.

As I continued my trips to Singapore in the late 1970's, I began to see Lee's second step; you might call it social infrastructure. Understanding that global companies are wary of instability, he began to crack down hard on crime, even putting heavy fines on jaywalkers and litterers. The drug laws were fierce; possession alone could mean the death penalty. Slowly, I noticed, cabs got nicer, and elegant shops popped up. And Lee made sure the elite weren't the only ones to benefit. His biggest project was building modern housing for all Singaporeans.

In some cases, he did things most Americans wouldn't like. If you were male and wore your hair too long, the airport customs people gave you a choice—either they played barber or you took the next plane home. Elections were open, but dissent discouraged. Several international magazines, including *Time* and *The Asian Wall Street Journal*, have had their circulation limited for printing articles the government didn't like.

But Lee isn't a dictator. Elections remain open, and the administration is honest. In some ways, that's part of his economic vision, as well. Corrupt bureaucrats are too common in Third World countries. Getting rid of that, Lee felt, would do as much for economic growth as building industrial parks.

Then came Lee's final bait for luring factories—a package of incentives. It was more sophisticated than any I'd seen in America: tax breaks, low-interest loans, R&D help, and available shell factories. Soon companies began to come, first dozens, then hundreds. Apple was among them.

JOHN SANDERS returned to Singapore in late May, two weeks after his first visit. He'd braced himself for typical Third World problems: permit holdups, utility mix-ups, construction bottlenecks. The one scenario he hadn't counted on was the one he found: The plant was ahead of schedule. While Sanders was in America, the Economic Development Board had made sure everything went smoothly.

With the building coming together nicely, Sanders was free to focus on his other need—a work force. He admits he had concerns about that. He'd presumed the clichés were true, that Far East labor has a good work ethic but few skills. Would he be able to find workers with the talent to run a good computer shop? It would be a far simpler shop than the main Apple factory in California, but he knew all start-ups go through months of debugging. With Apple's other plants depending on the Singapore boards, he absolutely had to deliver, and that meant good people. Apple began to recruit and hire. It promised to be a long process, but the EDB said they'd help. Soon, Sanders had to head back to California.

When he returned again, only weeks later, he found that the employees had all been hired. Even more surprising, the building was finished. Sanders told California to start sending parts for assembly. He'd originally hoped that if everything went perfectly, he'd be able to start shipping finished boards back home six months after his first visit to Singapore. Instead, it happened in less than two months.

FACTORIES such as Apple's were like a tide, lifting the whole nation up from poverty. By 1981, foreign companies had created over two hundred thousand jobs.[10] Still, to a Westerner's eyes, Singapore remained the Third World. People were working and eating, but there wasn't much prosperity. Most of the factories were still low skill, which meant low wage.[11] Despite Lee's efforts, cheap labor remained the country's key lure. So jobs came, but wealth didn't. For Lee, that wasn't enough. His priority wasn't just low unemployment, it was a high standard of living. The only way to get there, he knew, was better paychecks.

Two years before, in 1979, he took the first step toward that goal. He declared a mandatory industrial wage hike of 10 percent a year. He was convinced no company would protest. Singapore was at full employment, so labor was scarce, a seller's market. The infrastructure was better than that of most developing nations. Singapore was still a good deal for companies, he felt, even at 10 percent more in wages a year. Nor did Lee think an across-the-board wage hike would cause inflation. Most employers were now foreigners. Instead of draining the local economy, a wage hike would simply draw in more money from the outside. A simple signature at the bottom of a decree, and Singapore would take a leap up the ladder of wealth.

IN 1981, I was asked by the Irish Republic to help it with a strategy for economic growth. I decided to go back to Singapore to look for ideas worth borrowing. Ireland, too, had grown by attracting foreign-owned factories. And now, like Singapore, it was hoping to nudge its new jobs to ever-higher pay scales.

One of my first stops in Singapore was the Economic Development Board. One of my first questions was about the wage-hike decree. How was it working out? The answer was obvious before anyone spoke. It had failed, and badly. The EDB people explained that they'd misunderstood why companies had come to Singapore. Good infrastructure was important, but it wasn't the main driver. Cheap wages were. Multinational companies, faced with the decree, didn't see the point in giving two-dollar-an-hour paychecks to unskilled Singaporeans when Malaysian, Thai, or even Mexican workers could do the same jobs for under one dollar. On top of that, all those countries had begun offering their own incentives to lure industry. So the Singapore shortcut was backfiring. Companies being courted went elsewhere. Some already there stopped investing. And a few got ready to pull out.

I asked the officials what they were going to do. They had a ready answer. They'd made a bad call and had decided to stop the mandatory wage hikes. "It was a mistake, to think that we could desire a higher living standard without first giving our people the skills to earn it," one of them said. Labor, they'd realized, was a product. You want to charge more for it, you have to improve it, giving companies more for their money. Then they laid out a grand scheme for doing just that. They planned to upgrade the skills of the whole nation. It would mean a tremendous investment in a training network vast enough to school hundreds of thousands.

It sounded almost too ambitious. I'd seen how Singapore had gone from slums to high rises, but in a sense, that was easy. It was just construction. Training was far more complex—especially the kind of training the EDB people were talking about. It wasn't just a question of putting up schools; they wanted a sophisticated system that would key itself to the specific needs of companies. The hope was to keep workers in the loop, going back and forth to customized training courses year after year. It wasn't enough, they explained, to just train young workers. To keep a whole country moving up the wage scale, a government has to help companies constantly improve the skills of their employees.

What intrigued me as much as the idea itself was the philosophy behind it—a philosophy of productivity. That's what the training would be about—giving workers the tools to help their companies improve productivity. Essentially, Singapore was saying, "Put your factory here, tell us what you want, and we'll train your employees to make your shop more efficient than you imagined." It was the lesson of the wage-hike failure. It made EDB realize you can't ask a company to pay out more money unless you first help it increase its profits.

"By the end of this decade," one of the economic officials told me, "we'll have the skills of a developed country." And then, he said, his people would have the wealth of one, too. In his mind, the two were one: skills and wealth. The vision was impressive, but the schedule, I thought, was overconfident. Maybe by the end of the century, but not much sooner.

JOHN SANDERS'S goal was to reach for more production. That meant eventually moving beyond boards—to building entire computers. California's strategy for Singapore was the same as EDB's. It's easier to sell computers in Asia, Apple felt, if you make them there. But that would mean a more complex assembly line, and better-trained workers to run it. At first, no one could be sure that was possible. Apple was new in Singapore. Making boards in a Third World country was one thing, making computers quite another. Success, they knew, would depend on whether they could upgrade their workers' skills. It was Cynthia Tan's job to make it happen.

Her title was human resources manager. Her mission, she says, was to get everyone, even the simplest of line workers, into a classroom. She knew she had the tools: the country's emerging training institutes. Still, she saw a problem. Many of the classes offered by those institutes ran two or three hours, several times a week. Apple would pay their tuition, but the workers would need to commit their personal time.

Cynthia Tan didn't think that posting notices would be enough to persuade people. So she went beyond that, organizing discussion groups, making sure to include each of the line people. They talked about the classes, about careers, and sometimes about larger subjects, like the global economy. How, she asked, could tiny Singapore keep good companies like Apple? By showing corporate owners that Singaporeans have better skills than those of neighbors like Malaysia or Taiwan. With that encouragement, the workers began to volunteer. A young woman named Jeanne Oh Chin Gek was among them. In a way, she is a symbol of how Singapore is changing.

IN APPEARANCE, Jeanne is a small, timid woman, but her story speaks of an inner resolve. She grew up in a four-room shanty, under a tin roof with thirteen people—seven children, two parents, grandparents, uncle, and aunt. The seven children all stayed in one room. There was no indoor plumbing, and two or three times a year, if the storms were bad enough, the house would fill waist high with water. Growing up, she watched the other women in the neighborhood take unskilled factory jobs, quitting when they got married. Men did physical labor. No one she knew had any specialized training. Most stayed locked on a low-wage track throughout their lives. That was Singapore. She finished school at sixteen, and eventually was hired by Apple as an unskilled assembler, doing the same simple function hundreds of times a day. Her first job was testing logic boards. She would take a board, put it in a machine, push a button, wait a few seconds, and then do it again—one logic board after the other. She did that job for nine months, then moved to visual inspection, another unskilled job. This time, her function was to look closely at each board when it was done, checking for surface flaws. She presumed she'd be doing that kind of job throughout her working life, and considered herself lucky.

Then, one day, Cynthia Tan's human-resource staff spoke with Jeanne about courses. It was one of the first times anyone had given her an opportunity to reach. She said she would. She enrolled at the Vocational Industrial Training Board, an entry-level technical school for full-time workers. Her subject, tailored to a skilled-job need at Apple, was electronic servicing. The course met twice a week, three hours a session, for two years. She worked days and went for training at night. It was a burdensome, difficult marathon, but when she was done, it left her wanting to reach for more. She signed up for another course, one with the same schedule. "I wanted to upgrade myself," she explains.

After finishing the second course, Jeanne was made an Apple process-control technician, a skilled job. Instead of just staring at boards for visual flaws, she was now able to trace and fix electronic problems in manufacturing machinery. The day of her promotion, she joined dozens of others who'd brought new skills back to Apple from Singapore's training network. With government's help, the company had been able to build a pool of low-wage Third World laborers into a team of skilled technicians. It brought California management to a major decision: Singapore was ready to move from producing simple boards to making the entire computer.

THE FACTORY was reconfigured, and soon, production began. Shortly afterward, something unexpected began to happen. Apple management had thought the company would get only one benefit out of training—people better able to keep the American-designed assembly line running. Slowly, though, the Singapore workers were going beyond that. They were actually improving the assembly line. They were innovating. In manufacturing, that's the heart of better productivity. An innovation can be as simple as inventing a machine that drives in one bolt or as complex as installing a bank of robots. Either way, the key to factory competitiveness is to constantly keep adding, streamlining, improving. That's harder than it sounds, chiefly because most assembly lines aren't upgraded with one sweeping step; more often, it comes down to a dozen complex ideas. A new device here, a shortcut there. Collectively, that's what keeps a plant world class. But the problem is that it's hard to notice possible shortcuts unless you're on the line every day. And those on the line usually lack the skills to envision possible innovations.

Unless you train them.

Now that Apple was doing that, its workers were beginning to have ideas. "Give to your people," Cynthia Tan explains, "and they'll give back."

Johnson Cho was among those who did.

CHO CAME TO Apple in 1981 as a repair technician, a moderately skilled job. His father was a carpenter; Cho himself finished school at eighteen. Then it was two years in the military, and a job at Apple. Each day, Cho took his place at the end of the line, repairing products with minor problems. He asked for no more. A mid-skill job like this would keep him happy indefinitely. But six months after Cho was hired, his boss asked if he was interested in taking a step toward engineer. That would mean serious training at Singapore's Polytechnic Institute. Apple, said Cho's boss, would pay his tuition. Like his colleague Jeanne Oh Chin Gek, Cho had never before had such a clear opportunity offered to him. Despite the time sacrifice, he didn't hesitate. It took two years, but he made it, moving from repair to maintenance technician. Now, instead of doing minor repairs on finished computers, he would be overseeing complex manufacturing equipment. He still was a few steps below the kind of creative thinking an engineer does, but that was all right. He never imagined he'd be smart enough to design machines. Fixing them was challenge enough. He could easily see making a career of this.

But again, his company urged him to take one more step. Again, he didn't hesitate, this time blocking out another two years of weekends to study electrical engineering. That meant more tuition costs for Apple management, but the firm didn't see it as social welfare. It was a hard business investment. In the end, Apple was convinced it would get more money out of a schooled brain than an unschooled one.

Soon, instead of simply maintaining the process, Johnson Cho started looking for ways to improve it, and now he had the knowledge to do so. For a long time, he'd had trouble with one of the automated testers—a chip kept blowing out. Every time it happened, Cho would replace the chip, but meanwhile, Apple was losing production. Still, both he and the company accepted it. In the past, replacing the chip was all he knew how to do. But now that he'd been trained as an associate engineer, he asked himself a new question: Why not find the root problem and fix it. He did, coming up with a more reliable chip. The problem was solved.

Soon, the company urged Cho to take yet another course, this one a customized class designed to teach Apple technicians programming. For Cho, it meant good-bye to weekends for another few months, but he signed up. So did twenty of his colleagues. In time, the investment began to pay off. Cho and a few others began to talk about factory problems among themselves, at one point focusing on a board-testing bottleneck. Workers had to lift the boards by hand, one at a time, put them in the appropriate tester, then manually put them back on the line. There didn't seem to be a way around it; different boards had to go to different testers, so someone had to pick and choose. But Cho and his colleagues began to experiment anyway, using their new software skills. Eventually, they wrote a program that acted like a traffic cop, channeling each board into the right tester. Then they designed the electronics to automate the system into the line. The unskilled manual-handling was no longer necessary. The boards now moved in and out of testers on their own. Productivity went up again.

These were small things, but they began to create a culture among Apple's employees—a culture of innovation. Soon, as the work force grew more skilled, the improvements became more significant.

Sanders was in his office when his chief of engineering, Patrick Lian, came in one day and said he'd been thinking about a problem Apple had been having. A number of their boards would suddenly fail in the midst of manufacturing, slowing things down. It happened to other computer makers, too. In the industry, it had long been seen as an accepted bottleneck. It was the nature of the technology—certain boards have weak links buried in places almost impossible to find. But Lian decided it didn't have to be that way. He felt if you could give the boards a quick, simulated three-month test—a fast burn-in—the bad ones would surface. He canvassed suppliers for a test system to adapt, but there was nothing for boards in a mass-production factory. That meant Apple would have to design an entirely new burn-in system. The research went from days to months. It involved working with two outside vendors to get proper equipment. But finally, they did it. A first-of-a-kind automated board-test system for the Apple II was developed by Singaporeans. And the computers coming off the assembly line became that much more reliable.

BY 1983, I noticed that *skills* was becoming a new international buzzword. Countries everywhere were talking about upgrading workers,[12] but Singapore was one of few to pour in significant investment. Each time I went back there, it seemed they were breaking ground for yet another new institute.

The heart of the plan was a network of training centers, built not around general courses, but specific high-technology job tasks. It was expensive. You can't teach advanced factory skills with lectures any more than you can teach flying from books alone, and the EDB people knew it. Instead of just talking about factory work, they had to simulate it, sitting students behind expensive terminals to try their hand at such things as computer-aided manufacturing—often with actual Singapore products in mind. That kind of equipment cost money; but they spent it. Because technology kept moving, it meant new equipment each season. They spent on that, as well. To get the money, Lee decided to tax businesses. In one sense, his disastrous pay-hike decree might have warned him away from that: The decree, after all, had showed that companies weren't going to let Singapore milk them. But this was different; it was an investment, a way for companies to get training they couldn't afford on their own. The levy began as a 4 percent surcharge on wages, and gradually was lowered to 1 percent.

Under EDB's supervision, the training network blossomed. The country built up seven general institutes[13] offering simulated factory environments. Then it added "craftsmen" centers for specific job categories. One area that intrigued me was precision machining and mechanics, essential skills for an industrial society. Back home, I'd spent a lot of time with U.S. machine-shop owners who were frustrated that few young Americans had those skills. The owners were even more frustrated that government gave them no help in training new hires. It was left all up to them, and they couldn't afford it. In Singapore, it was the opposite. EDB had built three "craftsmen" centers just to teach precision-machining skills. To make sure the courses were relevant, each center was built with the help of a leading company: Philips Electronics of the Netherlands, the Brown-Boveri Company of Switzerland, and Tata of India.

EDB had also gotten the governments of Japan, Germany, and France to set up major technical institutes, teaching subjects like control engineering, instrumentation, and software development. In addition, to keep on-the-job workers current, there was yet another program, called Continual Upgrading Training.[14] It's done in partnership with companies like IBM, Computervision, and Sanyo, each of which offers six-month courses to update technicians on everything from computer-aided engineering to industrial-robotics interfacing. Those kinds of skills may sound like technical mouthfuls, but they're what modern societies need to compete. Just as important, they give workers an opportunity to better their standard of living. I was surprised that those opportunities were being offered more aggressively in tiny, Third World Singapore than in the United States.

And there was one final program, as well. If those frustrated U.S. machine-shop owners moved to Singapore, they'd get all the help they needed to give their workers specifically tailored skills. They'd simply have to apply to the government's Skill Development Fund, which covers up to 70 percent of the costs of in-house training.[15]

Tens of thousands of students and workers, I found, were going through the training networks each year, an enormous number for a nation of 2.6 million. During the previous years, I'd been looking more closely at training programs in various countries, convinced it was a key to competitiveness. Singapore's program was clearly among the most sophisticated in the world. And the payback was obvious. The number of new factories on Singapore soil continued to grow. More significantly, so did the sophistication of the factories already there.

PATRICK LIAN'S burn-in system had brought Apple a leap in product quality. Now, he turned to his other priority: a leap in productivity. Lian would kick things back and forth with Richard Kwok, his production operating manager. Where were the bottlenecks? The possibilities? How could they make the factory more automated? They talked it out over lunch, after hours, even playing tennis. Soon they focused on one of the slowest, most worker-heavy parts of the Apple II line— bolting on the computer's bottom plate, a piece of flat metal locked into place with eight screws. As the computer came down the line, a whole team of people would have to take it off, spend several minutes tightening screws into the bottom plate, then lift it back onto the line. It was a cumbersome job; the screws were at different angles, and the plate needed to be held against the machine in an awkward way. It was one of those things that seemed impossible to automate. Apple's California plant hadn't been able to do it. Lian decided to try anyway.

He assigned Lye Wen Fong, thirty-two, as one of his point men. Lye remembers how his boss first got the idea to work on it. The two men were walking down the line one day and paused at the bottom-plate operation. "Gosh," he remembers Lian saying, "that's a hell of a lot of people on that." Lye knew his boss well enough to figure this wouldn't be the last he heard of it. He was right. Not long afterward, Lye was put on a team assigned to automate it.

Finding ways to mechanize the attachment of a flat plastic plate may sound pedestrian, but that kind of thing is the essence of automation. Spend time in even the most advanced factories and you'll see that most of the technology is geared around one goal: the automatic manipulation of simple parts. Staying competitive means finding newer and newer ways to do that.

The Apple bottom-plate team started simply enough, fixing nine automatic screwdrives onto a platform. They positioned the platform on the assembly line, then built in a mechanism to brace the base plate against each computer that came by, lined up with the screw holes. The idea was this: An Apple II would roll down, the bottom plate would automatically clamp into place, the screwdrivers would do their work, and that would be that. But with mass production, it's never that simple. Since the computers weren't rolling by at precise intervals, the team had to work out some complicated electronics to synchronize their new machine with the assembly line. It took long hours of trial and error. Finally, they got it, but then there was the matter of getting the screws to go in right. Every time they thought they had it, they'd give it a test, and screws would tumble into the works. They finally fixed that, but ended up with another problem—some of the screws were going only halfway in—or worse, nine-tenths of the way in. That produced a computer that seemed okay, but would eventually rattle on a customer's desk. They got around it by putting precision sensors at each point. They instructed the sensors to push the product off the line if one of the screws didn't go all the way in. That was an improvement, but still, they were just short of a solution. The final plate-clamping job was never quite right. They knew why, and had to admit it was something they couldn't get around. There was a central nut positioned just awkwardly enough on the bottom plate that it wouldn't mesh with their new mechanized line-up of screwdrivers. It threw the whole system off. They tried everything, but a solution was physically impossible.

Lian decided there was one chance—to get engineering in California to redesign the Apple II itself so the nut would line up better. That's not often done; usually, assembly lines are built around the product, not the other way around. But Lian knew more and more companies are realizing that the two should be designed around each other. So they sent the request to U.S. headquarters. There were anxious times while the Singapore team waited to hear the verdict. Finally, a decision was made. California liked the idea, and agreed to redesign one of the world's most successful computers around an automation idea developed by a few engineers in Singapore.

Sanders remembers heading down to see the new machine go through its maiden run. He watched as the first computer stopped briefly and nine screws were inserted in about ten seconds. Before, it had taken several people several minutes to do as much. With Eastern politeness, Lye Wen Fong looks a bit embarrassed when he explains the indelicate label given the new machine—Gang Screw. But productivity is now up. Sanders was exhilarated. It seemed they'd found the last key spot where things could be speeded up.

BEYOND THE Apple plant, Singapore's landscape continued to change. The Economic Development Board had moved to put a final overlay onto the economic infrastructure: a research network, one of the most ambitious in any small country. Research is one of the most expensive, risky investments a company can make. It's crucial, but even big firms find it hard to afford a world-class effort inside their own walls.

So Singapore decided government would help. As with the training network, EDB built in a number of loops. First, there is money for investment. Propose a research facility? Singapore will help fund it. Need land for labs? Singapore will subsidize it. Pour your capital into R&D? Singapore will match it.

Then came a second loop—brick and mortar. EDB built a modern campus called Science Park, teaming professors and companies around shared research in government labs. Then it added another loop: a national computer board. It was charged with computerizing the country's public offices, its schools, and, by 1990, a third of its homes.[16] In America, by that same year, the percentage will be less than 20 percent.[17] Next, Singapore tripled the size of the country's two engineering universities. Today, though still a Third World country, Singapore produces more engineers per capita than the United States.

And there was one more loop. The government built a $50 million venture-capital fund to encourage new technology start-ups.[18] One of the fund's approaches struck me as particularly visionary: It's not restricted to Singapore soil. If a Singapore businessman opens a venture in Silicon Valley, government figures it could lead to a future branch back home, so they'll fund it. The government even goes so far as to bankroll overseas start-ups by foreigners. For example, if the venture fund backs a California disc-drive maker, the thinking is it could coax him to expand one day in Singapore.

In one sense, their whole research program is a leap of faith. It's easier to measure the payback of investing in factory equipment than in knowledge. But Singapore sees this as it sees training: The country with the most knowledge will win.

AGAIN, the engineers returned to Sanders's office. They'd spotted still another bottleneck—the boxing operation, where the finished computer is packaged. This, too, had long been considered too quirky to automate. Assembly workers—usually sizable ones—would pull a flattened carton off a floor stack, set it up, and fold in the flaps. Then another worker would line it with polystyrene, and yet another would load in the computer. The team told Sanders they wanted to try automating it.

The brainstorming began again. But soon Lye Wen Fong, point man for this team as well, ran into technical problems beyond his expertise. Two years earlier, that would have derailed the project. The company simply wouldn't have been able to design new automation gadgetry beyond the expertise of its top engineers. But during those years, Singapore's training had given Apple dozens of people with specialized knowledge capable of unraveling a new range of technical knots. For example, to bring this off, Lye found, they'd have to tailor a pneumatic system. It turned out someone at Apple had recently studied pneumatics at an institute. Then there were software difficulties. Lye called on other technicians, who had just taken courses in programmable logic control. But what made the final machine a real success were a half-dozen ideas Lye had gotten from interviewing the boxing-machine line workers. Without training, they couldn't have offered much. But several had been to classes, and were able to talk technically about subtle day-to-day improvements Lye wouldn't even have thought about. It took the team four-and-a-half months, but they did it. Today, Apple Singapore has a machine that makes boxes from flat cardboard, puts in liners, packs a computer, adds accessories, and seals it all. Instead of five laborers performing the work manually, one technician oversees the whole operation. For this kind of job, it is one of the most advanced packaging devices anywhere, and Singaporeans designed it.

Sanders's people continued to eliminate other bottlenecks. Workers used to have to test each keyboard by hitting every key, one finger at a time. Now, a machine does it in seconds, with dozens of software-driven mechanical fingers—made in Singapore. They perfected a new software system for directing conveyor traffic, too. As Apple gave its people new skills, they continued to give back productivity.

IN JUNE 1985, Ralph Russo, Apple's vice-president of worldwide operations, traveled to Singapore to discuss a new proposal. He wanted to incorporate a "just in time" approach to Apple II manufacturing. It would mean no more big inventories, no more large warehouses. Invoicing and inspection would be easier, as well. It would also mean cutting back to fewer suppliers. That would simplify things, but the hard part would be to get those suppliers precisely coordinated: The parts would have to be better quality, the quantities guaranteed, and the deliveries frequent. Russo remembers the meeting in Singapore going about four hours. When they were done working out specifics, he realized that 40 percent of the suppliers would be nearby, but the rest scattered throughout Asia. That didn't bode well for precision scheduling, especially since this was the Third World. He left convinced it would be a few years before Singapore began to make good headway. One of the key ways to measure progress, he knew, would be how quickly the factory got inventory reduced.

Three months later, Russo was surprised to find they'd cut inventory in half. Another three months and it was cut in half again. Today, John Sanders boasts that inventories are down to below a month, with 60 percent of all parts going out in finished computers the same day they come in. Scrap rates are down, too, as are costs for warehousing, inspection, invoicing, and material handling. Russo's concern about Singapore being slow on this challenge didn't quite bear out. Today, the factory has the most efficient just-in-time system in the company.

THE PEOPLE AT Apple don't like to compare their plants with each other. Russo prefers to focus outside—on the competition. At the center of it, of course, is IBM, but he sees the Japanese coming. The Singapore plant, Russo explains, is key to Apple's strategy of fighting back, a beachhead in Japan's backyard.

"The company couldn't be globally successful if all manufacturing technology were centered solely in the United States," Russo says. Then he'll get specific and tell you how Singapore has benefited the whole company. He doesn't mention low wages, though that surely is an extra help. What Russo mentions is skills. Expertise. The breakthroughs Singapore has made in automation and testing techniques, he says, have strengthened manufacturing throughout Apple.

In early 1986, on a visit to Singapore, John Sculley, Apple's president, announced that the company would build a state-of-the-art plant to produce new sophisticated computer components there. It will cost over $25 million. It's a long way from where Singapore was only five years earlier: stuffing circuit boards. Today, Sanders succinctly sums up what his people have done. "We have one of the most automated lines anywhere," he says. "It's world-class manufacturing."

IN THE spring of 1987, an electronics company thinking of putting a research center in Singapore hired me to do a study for them. My first stop was in New York, where Singapore's EDB keeps a Park Avenue office. By now, I knew EDB was an organized shop, but its staffing was better than I expected. I was put together with Mr. Heng Yuen Chun, whose sole responsibility was Connecticut and Rhode Island, where my own company is based. Over the next month, he called a half dozen times, offering to visit me in Providence. Then another assignment forced me to move up my Singapore trip at the last minute. I called him with less than a week to go. He told me it was no problem, set up a full schedule for me, and rushed an itinerary my way in days.

The Singapore airport was a little different from the hot, chaotic terminal of twelve years before. Today, it's more modern than most in America. Usually, customs takes less than five minutes, and outside, a line of new, air-conditioned taxis is always waiting. The road to the city is now eight paved lanes, framed by modern apartments. I noticed signs on tall buildings as I cruised along. PROFESSIONAL ENGINEERING CORPORATION, one said. INTEGRATED CIRCUIT DESIGN CENTER, said another. The city slums were gone, as were the rows of open food stalls. They've been replaced by high-fashion boutiques and as many luxury hotels as in London or Paris. From my room, I was able to direct-dial anywhere in the world. These days, calls go through on the first try and are cheaper than in almost any other country. The street-side food vendors have also changed. For better or for worse, the government has moved most of them into a concrete structure with ventilators to suck up odors and inspectors to ensure health standards. Even Fatty has cleaned up his act. I dropped by to find him sporting a very large but fancy new shirt— made in Italy.

I was staying at the Shangri-La, generally ranked as one of the world's top ten hotels. I rode the Mitsubishi escalator to the arcade floor, where I found electronics from Japan and clothes from France, but nothing from the United States. Nearby was a modern discotheque with an array of large-screen Sony TV's. Then, finally, I noticed a sole American export. Madonna was playing on the video screens. That night, I stopped by another hotel bar, this one featuring an unlikely singing group—Matthew and the Mandarins. There were four of them, Malays and overseas Chinese. Their music was country-western. There in Singapore, a bar full of American businessmen listened to two Buddhists and two Moslems singing about cheatin' hearts, lyin' eyes, and don't let your children grow up to be cowboys.

AT MY REQUEST, the EDB had arranged a busy schedule—a dozen stops in two days. In some countries, schedules like that often unravel by the time you get there. In Singapore, that's rare. Mr. Ho Teck Hua, sent over to the Shangri-La by the board, met me in the lobby, promptly at 8:00 A.M. For the next few days, his job was to be my guide. He is a trained engineer, which meant technical questions would be no problem. The car, I soon found, was chauffeured, air-conditioned, and had a phone.

The first stop was an American disc-drive company called Micropolis. More disc drives are made in Singapore than anywhere else, most being exported back to the United States. I was met at the plant by a well-groomed young man named Wong Lin Hong, the firm's managing director. His background was typical: His father was a scrap dealer; Mr. Wong is an engineer. So are his three brothers. So is his sister. So is his sister-in-law. He explained that the plant was placed here by an L.A. firm only two years earlier. Already, nine hundred employees were working three shifts, and the firm was still hiring.

I presumed the plant was mostly for assembling American designs. Originally, said Wong, yes. But they've moved beyond that. "Right from the start," he said, "we saw the advantages of carrying out research and development here." It's only natural, he explained. Those who make the product can best see how to improve it. I asked where his people got the skills to innovate like that. The national training network, Wong said. But he's getting them even more schooling than that. Recently, he said, he sent eight engineers to the States for several months of education. "And that's just the first batch," he added.

Why did Micropolis pick Singapore?

"The computer industry here is booming," said Wong. It's the same phenomenon that's helped Silicon Valley: Once you establish a high-tech cluster, it's easier to attract newcomers.

I asked if low wages were a draw, as well.

"Wages are important, but not crucial," he said. Skilled workers were the bigger draw. "Disc drives," he said, "are hard to make." I asked Wong if American workers couldn't do this job as well. He admitted they could, but added that both yield and quality in Singapore have been going up. And not, he said, because of management alone; the workers push for it just as hard. They know, said Wong, that the more they produce and innovate, the more their living standard will go up.

"You are very strong individuals in America," Wong said, "very capable. Very brilliant. But individually, it's 'I do my own thing.' Here, we are willing to work as a group. It's a different culture. If you look at the United States and Japan, we are probably closer to Japan." America, he said, is more creative, but perhaps not as organized.

I asked what he meant.

He said a nation has to know what it can do best, then organize itself to do it. "We know as a country we have nothing except people," he explained. "How do we prosper? Only by maximizing our human resources. And offering those resources to the rest of the world."

Before I left, we toured the plant, typical of Singaporean industry. The employees looked like nuclear workers, wearing white suits, hoods, and masks. Some were testing the products with oscilloscopes;

the foot presses of modern Singapore. As he ushered me out, Wong talked about plans for a new company R&D center. Assembly, he said, isn't enough. His people want to pioneer technology, as well.

MY NEXT STOP was the Singapore Texas Instruments plant. Lee Ee Tee, company secretary, was my host. The words were beginning to sound the same everywhere. "The only thing we have is the brain," he said. "If the brain doesn't work well, the country will go down." I told him I was impressed with how quickly Singapore had begun moving from the Third World toward the First. I expected a confident reply, but he showed a healthy caution.

"If we're not careful," he said, "we'll go back to the Third."

I toured this plant, as well, finding another room of white-coated workers, peering through microscopes, overseeing the assembly of integrated circuits. This used to be unskilled work—one thousand people sitting in a line, manually connecting wires. Now, it's done by skilled technicians running automatic machines.

WE DROVE from there to the National Computer Board, which is housed in a large modern building with a grand lobby. It was initially set up to help computerize Singapore's government, but now also works to attract foreign software firms and boost industry's use of information technology. I was ushered into a meeting with a group of young engineers. One had just spent five weeks in Europe trying to woo software companies. Another said their goal was to get personal computers into every Singapore home. One of the engineers, Mr. Srang Boon, used a phrase I was beginning to hear often: brain-intensive industries. The board's mission, said Srang, is to bring such industries to Singapore. The country, he explained, no longer wants just any jobs.

I HEADED BACK outside. New construction seemed to be everywhere. We stopped at the country's Science Park, where more buildings were going up. One of the directors, Dr. M. Narendran, came out to meet me. He mentioned his background, a doctorate from MIT. Then he discussed his most important mission: linking professors and companies. As an example, he called a colleague into the room—Dr. Tjeng Tjung, professor of electrical engineering at the National University. Dr. Tjung explained how he's now helping develop a new disc drive that works by optics. The conversation soon focused on the Science Park itself. It was established only three years ago and already has twenty-five companies doing research, all for industrial application. "Our people are no better than people in the United States," Narendran said. "I'd say the United States has better people. But if you look at the whole concept of government playing a role, that's the difference."

I'D TOLD THE EDB I wanted to see a piece of the country's training network, so we headed for the French-Singapore Institute. Norman Chang is the director. I asked him about the curriculum, and as we walked, he ticked off a list: robotics, optoelectronics, design of microprocessor-controlled laser holographs—not exactly how most Americans picture the Third World. It's all direct application, Chang added, designed around the needs of local companies.

I asked if there's a basic set of courses for younger, school-age students.

"We begin by teaching advanced computer language," said Chang.

Not BASIC?

"No, most know it. They learn it at home."

"By age sixteen?" I asked. That's when many enter the institute.

"My kid is nine," said Chang. "She knows BASIC already."

Next, he took me to see student projects. They weren't what you'd expect from people the age of high-school juniors. One student had programmed a robot to weld seams automatically, guided around the contours by laser. It involved some expensive hardware, but cost wasn't a problem; most projects were sponsored by companies. In several cases, said Chang, firms have actually used techniques perfected by students in these classes.

The most intriguing emphasis here, I thought, was on design. In America, that's usually for engineers. In Singapore, they teach it to technicians. They want them not just to operate and fix machines, but to improve them.

I continued the tour, soon coming to a room with a half-dozen new robots. Altogether, the building had about thirty of them. That's more than in most American universities, and the students here were in their young teens. I asked Chang if the kids didn't find the curriculum grueling, or at least technically dull. "I have a problem to chase them out in the evening," he said.

As I left, I reminded myself there were a half-dozen other centers like this in Singapore, most less than five years old. They're only now getting up to speed. Their impact is just beginning.

MY FINAL INTERVIEW was at EDB's offices in a downtown high rise. I stood by the window with one of its directors, Foo Meng Tong, looking at a landscape that didn't exist ten years before. New skyscrapers were everywhere.

"We still have a lot to do," he said.

I asked about his background. Again, it was the story of a century in a decade. His father, a Chinese immigrant, started a small shop that sold coffee. Foo pointed out the window to one of the last rows of dilapidated houses in the central city. It's been left there as a reminder of the past. That, he said, was where he grew up; two parents and six children in two rooms. Today, like most Singapore government planners I met, Mr. Foo is an engineer.

PRIME MINISTER Lee Kuan Yew is not an American model. We don't want to borrow his system, or anyone's. But we can learn from what nations like Singapore have achieved. Most important, we can learn that to compete with them, our people's skills have to be superior. Our universities remain among the best anywhere, but there's a new kind of worker training evolving in the world, and we're no longer geared to keep up with it. Singapore has shown that a superior national skills system can be built in a decade. America, I'm convinced, can do it even quicker—if we find the will.

JEANNE OH CHIN GEK, who grew up in a wood-plank shanty that used to fill with water during the rainy season, is now a full-fledged technician. She's proud of having risen so high, but she no longer thinks it's high enough. "Technician," she says, "now is very common in Singapore." The next step would be associate engineer. It would mean her heaviest training burden yet—three hours a night, three times a week. She plans to do it. And she adds a thought. "I aim for higher than that, if I can." That would mean a full engineering degree at the national university—five more years of nights and weekends.

"Singapore is going more high tech," she says, "so we have to upgrade ourselves."

Was she ever worried, while on the assembly line, that automation would squeeze her out of a job?

The danger of layoffs, she says, isn't from automation, it's the opposite. Apple Singapore hasn't laid off anyone. Each time it automates something new, production goes up, allowing yet another assembly worker to be trained for a higher-skill job. The companies that resist automation, says Jeanne, will be the ones left behind. And the workers with them. Not long ago, she traveled to Thailand as a tourist. Singapore feels an affection for this neighbor, but the people were poorer than she expected. They seemed to have few job choices. It reminded her of how Singapore used to be. And something struck her: Here was the price that will be paid by nations that don't invest in skilled minds.

3

General Electric: The Heart of an American Product

FIFTY MILES south of Nashville, outside the city of Columbia, where the restaurants offer Bar-B-Q and catfish, there is an unlikely piece of smokestack America. There, nestled amid the pine and hardwood of rural Tennessee, is one of the world's most automated factories. Had it not been built, America's households might soon have had yet another product—the refrigerator—stamped MADE IN JAPAN. Instead, here in the heartland, General Electric found a way to build products both better and cheaper than those made by foreign workers paid a tenth our wages. The going has been rough, but GE's struggle shows the challenges we must meet if we are to compete against Korea and Singapore for world manufacturing leadership.

IN A SENSE, Tom Blunt is a figure from an earlier America. He loves factories. He's convinced they are the country's strength. He was disturbed, back in the late 1970's, to see so many shut down. It was around then that Blunt made a career change. He left Ford Motor Corporation, where he'd overseen plant automation, to work in major appliances. His new home was General Electric, Thomas Edison's company. He moved to Louisville, headquarters of GE's Major Appliance

Business Group (MABG). He found its manufacturing complex so huge that the parking lot needed dozens of traffic lights.

Blunt liked one thing in particular about this industry: Maybe foreign cars were succeeding in the U.S. market, and foreign steel, but not foreign appliances. The Japanese were strong in microwave ovens, but America still made better washing machines, better ranges, and, most important, better refrigerators. By the mid-1980's, refrigerators alone were to become a $4 billion industry in the United States. In 1979, they were already bringing in $1 billion of GE's $2.5 billion in annual appliance sales.[1]

But that year, shortly after Blunt arrived as chief manufacturing engineer for ranges, he found something disheartening. There didn't seem to be any clear direction at MABG. There were no great projects, just a lot of starts and stops. Most disheartening of all, he found that America's biggest appliance company made little money. No one could figure out why. There were almost no Japanese refrigerators landing at American ports, no German ranges in U.S. stores. Except for microwave ovens, there didn't seem to be any foreign threat. The group's executives told GE headquarters in Fairfield, Connecticut, not to worry. A few adjustments in marketing and they were sure profits would improve—probably by the next quarter.

But they'd been saying that now for a number of quarters. Finally, someone in Fairfield decided to act.

IN THE FALL OF 1979, Paul Van Orden had just been named GE's head of consumer businesses.[2] He had confidence in his Louisville people, but he feels it's occasionally helpful to get an outside perspective. He searched for a business consultant, and was given my name by his chief planner. Soon I flew to Louisville to begin looking at the profit problem. The group's executives were not happy to see me. Who was this outsider sent to tell them how to fix their own business? They already knew how to fix it: by finding a way to boost price. As a rule, that meant cosmetics—catchy features that could be added for a dollar cost while commanding ten dollars more in price. Bells and whistles, they called them. In appliances, group management felt, you can best compete by catching the consumer's eye. I didn't necessarily disagree, but my job was to look for profit problems everywhere, including the factories. They told me I'd be wasting my time. If GE knew how to do anything, it was manufacturing.

I began my detective work. Where to start? I didn't discount the bells-and-whistles theory. It's a classic marketing strategy that works with plenty of consumer goods: Develop unique features, add a good brand image, and people will be happy to pay a premium. But GE's features, I found, weren't unique. That year, the line's most promising innovation was size—a new model with seventeen cubic feet of space. Management was convinced it would be a breakthrough, but the competition had seventeen-cubic-foot refrigerators, too. I compared other innovations—ice makers, electronic controls, special trim. The competition had those, as well. Finally, I talked to store owners. Yes, they said, GE has a prestigious name and catchy features, but that's not enough anymore, not when everyone's selling something similar. Customers like cosmetics, they said, but in appliances, they like a competitive price and reliability even more.

If that was true, if high-priced features weren't sufficient, it left one other strategy for boosting profit: lowering costs. That meant making manufacturing more efficient. I discussed the idea with the managers in Louisville. Was it possible, I asked, that the problem—and solution—was on the inside, not the outside? They told me that if I knew appliances, I'd know the most important area is marketing. It was the accepted wisdom; if anyone was going to save MABG, it would be marketers, not engineers.

TOM BLUNT had been hired to upgrade MABG's range factories. His instinct was to do it from the ground up, but he soon found there wasn't as much capital for that as he'd hoped. The money was all on the marketing side, on product features. All Blunt was allowed was an adjustment here, an adjustment there, and he soon began to wonder whether leaving Ford had been the right move after all.

It was about that time that MABG brought in a new chief engineer. John Truscott was an Englishman by birth, but by passion an American—a believer in unbridled free enterprise. Throughout his working life, Truscott's real fulfillment had come from pushing technology forward. At each step of his career, he'd been able to do that, first on an aerospace team involved in breaking the sound barrier, then when he helped perfect medical CAT scanning. Now, GE had transferred him to Louisville, insisting it would be a step up for him; the money was better, and so was the title—head of technology for an entire group. But the atmosphere, Truscott found, was worse. The group was floundering. He felt you could actually see the malaise. "Everyone had a glazed look in their eyes," he would later say.

What made it especially hard for Truscott was the priority: adding gadgets rather than engineering all-new product designs. Worst of all, the gadgets didn't seem to be boosting group profit. First they changed the size of the refrigerator; it made no difference. They put chocolate gaskets on the door; it made no difference. They did similar things with the other products; no difference. Like Blunt, Truscott was beginning to think this was a bad turn in his career. From the sound barrier to CAT scanning to washing machines. Later, he would recall thinking a grim thought: I'd rather be dead than working in washing machines. It didn't look like Louisville would offer him much chance to push technology's edge after all.

AFTER PUTTING IN several weeks of work, I'd grown convinced that MABG's profit problem was on the inside—in the factories. But I wasn't sure where. As I walked through first one factory then another, I found plenty of inefficiencies. In some areas, the product flow was complicated, parts were strewn everywhere, and too many tasks were done by hand. The plants making refrigerators, the most important product, seemed the worst. A cost breakdown, I felt, might help me know what specifically to look for in the refrigerator operation, so I put one together. It turned out that the compressor—the pump that creates the cold air—was by far the product's most expensive part. It was also the machine's heart, as important as an engine in a car. If the compressor breaks, there's no refrigerator.

I decided to spend a few hours in the plant where compressors were built—Building 4. It was clearly the most antiquated at MABG. If you took a thousand old auto-repair garages and patched them together, it wouldn't look much different from Building 4. It seemed this was worth exploring more. I asked management if the compressor could be a problem. They told me it wasn't. The competition, they insisted, all had similar designs, similar factories, similar costs. No one in the business, they said, was producing a cheaper compressor.

Perhaps, then, there was competition management didn't know about. As I went from office to office, doing background interviews, I began to ask, Was it possible there was someone new in the business? Someone overseas, perhaps? Someone making compressors more efficiently? I was told it was out of the question. Appliances were an American bastion, and the world knew it. Whatever foreigners were doing, they were doing it worse. Besides, the executives told me, the Japanese and Europeans make different kinds of refrigerators—smaller ones. It made no sense for them to target the American market. A dozen times, I got the same answer. I asked about it one more time while interviewing an engineer who was about to leave the company. Foreign competition?

No, said the engineer. Nothing obvious.

How about a possible Japanese threat?

No, he said, nothing. Then, almost as an afterthought, the engineer added a brief sentence.

"But I did hear something about Canada."

He was speaking of GE's Canadian refrigerator plant, which did not report to Louisville. I asked what he'd heard.

"That the Japanese had tried to sell them compressors." He quickly added that it didn't seem significant. Compressors, he said, are all the same. You won't find any technological breakthroughs there, even from the Japanese. Perhaps he was right. But to be sure, I decided to go to Canada.

MANAGEMENT might have thought that marketing would save MABG, but Tom Blunt had his own theory. You build a great manufacturing company on one thing—great factories. During his first few months in Louisville, he made a point of walking through all of them. He still remembers the day he stepped into Building 4. It was a loud, dirty operation built around 1950's technology—old grinders, old furnaces and too many people. Finishing a single piston, he learned, took 220 steps. Even the simplest functions had to be done by hand. Workers loaded machines, unloaded machines, carried parts to the next machine. Then there was the scrap rate, which was ten times higher than it should have been. The plant was throwing out 30 percent of everything it made. There was only one thing Blunt liked about this plant. He liked the thought of beating it—changing it, rebuilding it. But it wasn't his place to suggest that. He was too new to start urging on major projects in someone else's department. Besides, he felt management would never pour huge dollars into redoing a whole factory. MABG's preference was cosmetics, not engineering.

I SAT DOWN with the head refrigerator executive of GE Canada. I asked if it was true that they'd been approached by the Japanese.

Yes, he said, it was. Matsushita wanted to sell them compressors.

I knew it cost MABG forty-five dollars to make each GE compressor. In Louisville, management insisted that the competition was building them for at least as much. If that were true, once Matsushita finished adding on profit and overseas shipping, I figured it had to be selling them for fifty or sixty dollars. I asked the Canadian executive what price the Japanese were quoting.

Matsushita, he said, was planning to build compressors in Singapore to cut labor costs. It was planning to land them in Canada for thirty-seven dollars each.

I asked about quality.

The executive had seen some samples of the Matsushitas. He said they appeared to be better than GE compressors.

Did Canada plan to buy them?

Well, said the executive, it would be hard to buy a product competing with one made by his own parent company, but he was about to start. He had to do what was best for his business.

I asked one final question. Had any other foreign companies approached them with compressors?

The answer was yes—an Italian firm called Necchi. It, too, had a lower price than GE.

AS MUCH AS Tom Blunt was bothered by the way MABG neglected its factories, something else bothered him even more: the way it neglected its engineers. He'd never worked with engineers who had such low self-esteem. It wasn't hard to see why. The money men had turned down their proposals so often that they no longer believed in themselves. It was routine, he said, to see engineers given $2 million for a $10 million automation plan and then scolded for doing half a job. Now, they were becoming timid, which Blunt felt could ruin an engineer. "To do technologically daring things," he says, "you have to get your people to say, 'All right, I'm willing to take a risk.' Instead, you had a climate down there for years that said, 'If you screw something up, you're going to get shot.'"

People, Blunt says, become what their bosses tell them they are. "And they'd been telling these guys," he explains, "that they were just a bunch of dumbheads." What Louisville needed, Blunt thought, wasn't better bells and whistles, it needed better technology. The only way to get it was with engineers willing to knock on management's door with new ideas. But most at MABG had become too timid to risk it. Pretty soon, Blunt feared, GE was going to be passed by, and he had a good idea who might try. During the 1950's, while in the air force, he had lived in both Japan and Korea. What struck him most about that part of the world was the attitude.

"They'd convinced themselves they can do things better than anyone else," he says.

Blunt is convinced that self-confidence is the key to innovation. "We're better than they are," he says, "but the difference is, they're allowed to try."

I RETURNED FROM Canada expecting Louisville management to be as stunned as I was by what I'd found, and also as relieved. I'd spotted a possible foreign threat while there was still time to respond. That hadn't happened with American steel, or cars—the Japanese had taken both by surprise. With refrigerators, the story could be different. I presented my findings at an executive meeting, then waited for the expressions of concern. There weren't any. The executives told me they didn't see why this was a problem. The Matsushita compressor wasn't a breakthrough; it was the same kind as theirs—a reciprocating model.

But your Canadian subsidiary, I told them, is convinced that it's a better machine.

They said I was being alarmist. Believe us, they told me, it will be a long time before an overseas newcomer outdoes the appliance technology of the General Electric company. They knew their competition, and it wasn't Matsushita; it was Whirlpool, or White. It was in America, not Japan.

But the Matsushita compressor, I told them, is also cheaper.

They told me there was a simple explanation for that. Dumping.

I mentioned the Italians, stressing that others were entering the field, and it was bound to get worse.

Again, they dismissed it. This wasn't an invasion, they said; it was a trickle. They'd seen such trickles before. None had ever amounted to much. This one wouldn't either.

TOM BLUNT was not in on that discussion, but if he had been, he'd have doubtless been more concerned. Later, he would say that while he had worked for Ford, he had learned the importance of looking overseas. What were foreigners making? What were they likely to make next year? How do we compete? At MABG, no senior managers asked those questions. Blunt knew of no engineer who'd even taken a business trip to the Far East. In Louisville, there was one measure of progress. It didn't matter what the rest of the world was up to, if you were doing 2 percent better than last year, you were making adequate headway.

PERHAPS management was right, I thought. Perhaps the Matsushita compressors were just a trickle, not an invasion. Still, it was worth exploring, so I booked a plane for Japan and Singapore. My first task was to break down Matsushita's cost. How much to build a compressor in Japan? How much in Singapore? Matsushita, of course, wasn't about to share that information with a competitor's consultant. So I decided to purchase sample compressors from repair shops, take them apart, and see what the Japanese were putting into them. I broke each down to raw parts—iron castings, powdered metals, silver solder—then called suppliers to get prices. I weighed the steel and copper wire being used, and got quotes on those, as well.

The next question was wage rates. Matsushita wasn't going to share those figures either, so I reviewed public reports the company had to file with the government which gave out that information. Next on my list was transport costs. Shipping companies were able to give me the standard rate. Finally, I wanted to know what Matsushita's version of Building 4 looked like. For that, I talked to Japanese machinery makers, the people who would have supplied Matsushita with motor wind-ers, grinders, and welders. After two weeks of gathering string, I was convinced. It seemed clear that compressor-manufacturing technology in Japan was far beyond Louisville. There was no dumping after all. Matsushita was simply making compressors more efficiently. By cutting labor costs with Singapore wage rates and using low-cost Japanese steel, Matsushita was able to tack on profit, pay shipment and duty, and still undersell GE by at least 15 percent.

Now, the other question: trickle or invasion? How many compressors were they making? This time, I approached Matsushita directly. They agreed to meet, partly as a courtesy to GE, and perhaps more important, because they hoped Louisville could be talked into buying compressors from them. They told me their Japan plant made a million compressors a year. All right, that didn't seem to be much of an export threat—Japan's domestic market took the whole million.[3] But what about the Singapore factory? Was that being geared for large-scale production? At first, my Matsushita hosts were hesitant to speak. Finally, during our last lunch together, one of them mentioned their plans. The plant, he said, was being designed eventually to produce 3 million compressors a year. As I sat there, it was hard to keep from reacting. Three million was more than GE made itself. And it was clear almost all of those would be for export. Where? Not to Europe; trade barriers there wouldn't allow it. Most would be going to North America.

THE MORE MABG's profit slide deepened, the more John Truscott, new head of technology, brooded. A confirmed smoker, he was smoking more and more. There were cigarette ashes everywhere in his office—on his desk, even on his pants. Like Blunt, he loved factories. Now, here in Louisville, GE's factories were struggling. Occasionally, he'd read articles proclaiming that declining factories were okay; the country was supposedly shedding its old, rust-belt skin, turning toward a more modern economy—a service economy. Truscott was of a different school. "How do you have a service economy without a foundation underneath?" he asked. He saw only one way to hold on to that foundation—by investing in factories. He found it disturbing that Japan and South Korea were doing more of that than America. He was convinced that if we didn't fight back, it would cost us. "Just because I have a U.S. passport," he says, "doesn't mean I have a right to a better standard of living."

He had a theory of how that standard came about. "Our fathers' productivity," he would say. "Our grandfathers'." When he looked for that same sense of mission now, he saw it in only one place, the Far East. They learned it from us, he felt; now was the time to relearn it from them. How? "There's no doing it with mirrors," he says. "You have to get right back to fundamentals." But at MABG, management wasn't letting him. Fundamentals—new factories—were considered too expensive, and too risky.

I RETURNED from Japan confident that even the most skeptical among Louisville's management team would be startled by what I found. First, I showed that Matsushita wasn't dumping. Second, I told them about the Singapore plant. But at least it wasn't too late, I said. If MABG responded now, it could fend off the threat. One of the executives spoke. He was sorry, but he just didn't believe those cost numbers. He still thought Matsushita was dumping. Someone else spoke. What about quality? He didn't think the Japanese could ever match GE.

"Your Canada man says they're better," I said.

"But they haven't really fully tested them yet," said the executive. Besides, he asked, what more could MABG do about compressors?

I asked them to think about Building 4. Everyone knew it was an antiquated factory. The executives said they already had plans to upgrade the rough spots, save a few cents on the final product here and there.

Wouldn't it be better to consider revamping the whole thing?

"Look," said one of the executives, "we can't even get one million dollars from headquarters to do little things, let alone one hundred million dollars for a whole factory."

"Maybe it's because your plans aren't big enough," I said.

Still they hesitated. To make a new factory pay off, they said, you have to have a new product—or at least a more sophisticated one. You don't get lower cost by building the same kind of machine. And the machine they had—a reciprocating compressor—was the only kind that made sense for a refrigerator.

Then look into redesigning the compressor, I said. Maybe you can make a technological leap. I'd seen how Japan had succeeded that way in cars and televisions. New technology's the only way high-wage American industry can fight back against low-wage countries: If you can't undercut them in labor costs, you leap past them in engineering—a better product, better automation, better productivity.

But reciprocating compressors were already mature, they told me. You can't make a technological leap with a product that's been taken as far as it can go.

I asked if there might be another possibility. While exploring Louisville, I had gone to Building 6, where air-conditioners were made. They ran on compressors, as well, but a different kind—rotary compressors. The air-conditioning engineering manager had told me rotaries were cheaper, quieter, and more efficient than the ones refrigerators used. He also felt they could be redesigned to fit a refrigerator. Even more significantly, GE had invented the rotary; that put the company in a good position to tailor it in a new way, which was the key to market leadership—being first in the world with a new, efficient redesign.

No, the executives said, out of the question. No point in even trying. Rotaries could never be durable enough to run refrigerators.

I looked around the room. Most of the executives there, I knew, were nearing retirement. Many of the voices, I noticed, were tired. Give us time, they said. We've got some great new features coming down the line. In a few months, everything will turn around.

IN JANUARY 1980, having failed to convince Louisville, I took my findings to Paul Van Orden, the sector executive who'd asked me to do the study. Together, we went over the numbers. Van Orden seemed disturbed and persuaded. He said he would discuss it with MABG. I hoped Louisville wouldn't be resentful. It's always best to galvanize an organization from the bottom up. But I believed strongly that I'd found a serious problem, and that it had to be addressed. I was sure it now would be.

A few weeks later, I got a phone call from Van Orden's assistant, whose message wasn't what I'd expected to hear. Van Orden had talked to Louisville's management, and they'd been adamant. They hadn't bought the compressor theory. They were convinced that they were competitive in compressors. They vowed that by July, their numbers would turn. Van Orden's assistant thanked me for all I'd done, and said his boss's decision was to go with his people.

JULY CAME, and MABG did not make its numbers. Instead, it had actually lost market share, and was now barely breaking even. That was the first sign that the problem hadn't been solved. Then came a second sign. In December 1980, the manager of GE's Canadian appliance plants told headquarters he wanted to increase his purchase of Matsushita compressors. In June 1981, there came a third sign. John Truscott had told his engineers it was time to take a closer look at the competition, especially the foreigners. The staff bought an assortment of refrigerators and tore them apart. Then they called Truscott to say they'd found something interesting inside a Mitsubishi. They'd found a rotary compressor—the type most in Louisville felt could not be used in a refrigerator. Finally, in July 1981, a fourth warning. It was the most unnerving of all. MABG learned that its chief competitor, Whirlpool, which had been making compressors in Ohio, had invested in a new compressor plant, to be located in Brazil, where wages were a tenth those in America. While Louisville had been focusing on bells and whistles, Whirlpool had looked abroad, glimpsed the future, and acted.

FINALLY, Van Orden acted, too. He called MABG. You said rotaries couldn't be done, he told them, and now they're being done. You said imports are no threat; Canada now wants more of them. You said your numbers would turn; they've gotten worse. You've got a compressor problem, he said, and it's time to fix it. Then he called me. Eighteen months had gone by since I had handed in my first report. Now, he asked if a second one could be done, this one of greater scope. It seemed clear that overseas forces were badly undercutting MABG's compressor manufacturing. It was time to explore whether anything could be done about it.

Don Awbrey, a Louisville general manager, was put in charge of the compressor project. His mission was to make GE competitive in compressors. He had nine months to develop a plan. My study was to be the first step. When we met, he made it clear that he wanted me to explore all options—to look at any potential technology, no matter how new, and to travel anywhere in the world, no matter how far, to find the right solution.

IT HAD BEEN a year and a half since I'd been to Louisville. When I was last there, in February 1980, the mood had been one of malaise. Now, in October 1981, it was more like confusion. The old fixation on bells and whistles was gone. There was a new obsession: What do we do about compressors? The confusion deepened when both Matsushita and Necchi approached MABG itself, in Louisville, offering lower-priced compressors that were indeed fine machines. Finally, management acknowledged it: Foreigners were building a better product. Had that happened ten years before, there would have been one response: Fight back. Even to whisper the word *sourcing* in Louisville would have been sacrilege. MABG manufactured at home—in America. Its factories were unequaled. It was unthinkable that a country like Japan should make anything for the GE label. Now, many in Louisville had begun to wonder if Japan could be MABG's deliverance. Instead of bells and whistles, people began talking of a new strategy—sourcing.

Lately, there'd been rumors that headquarters was so frustrated by Louisville's poor performance they were ready to sell the division, possibly to the Japanese themselves. No one wanted that to happen. Sourcing seemed a good way to stop it from happening. It would involve no investment and bring in fast profit. That was the goal—to turn the business around by next quarter, next year at the latest.

TOM BLUNT, who by now had been named head of advanced manufacturing for refrigerators, did not appreciate that kind of talk. Few things put him in a worse mood than a decision to close a plant.

"Sourcing makes sense in some circumstances, but you can't source everything," he says. "My instinct is always—always—to make things."

He did not think America was meant to become a service economy. "There are a lot of people who don't particularly want to work at Wendy's," he says. "I'm one of them." Colleagues tried to tell him it was time to face the truth: There are certain areas, certain products, that America can't compete in anymore. "Bull," he would say. "All we have to do is find a way to make it faster, cheaper, better."

John Truscott agreed, especially in this case. "The compressor is the heart of the refrigerator," he says. "The refrigerator is the heart of this group. I didn't want to give away our heart." No one was quite ready to go that far yet. Although sourcing was a compelling idea, it was still a new one. MABG needed more information. My new report was supposed to supply it.

I STARTED the research by looking again at the competition. That now meant more than Whirlpool and White, GE's U.S. rivals. My first destination was Japan. When I got there, I found that Matsushita wasn't the only company making refrigerator compressors. Four more Japanese firms had invested in new plants: Sanyo, Toshiba, Hitachi, and Mitsubishi. Two of them, Toshiba and Mitsubishi, were beginning to make rotaries. Sanyo was also planning to move into rotaries for refrigerators. None of this was a fluke. As obsessive exporters, the Japanese had spent the last few years traveling to America, probing the appliance market in search of a weakness—and had found it. They'd zeroed in on the compressor, the most important part of the most important appliance. This time, companies were anxious to show me their plants. They knew that GE was considering sourcing, and they all wanted to sell.

Next, I went to Italy, where I saw that Necchi was as great a threat as the Japanese. Necchi's new compressor plant was far more automated than Building 4. Finally, I visited the new Whirlpool plant in Brazil—Embraco. Nearby, GE itself had a subsidiary making refrigerators for the regional market, just as it had in Canada. It turned out that this plant, too, wanted to buy a rival's compressors—Embraco's.

An Embraco executive, anxious for GE's business, welcomed a meeting with me. I met him in a small, southeastern Brazilian town called Joinville, where the plant was based. I was surprised to find it a highly industrialized pocket, colonized mainly by Germans over the last few decades. The best hotel in town was called the Tannehof. The area's largest plant built Mercedes trucks. The three Embraco managers who met me, all Brazilians, were named Helmut Sommer, Gilberto

Krause, and Johann Richter. The cultural touch went beyond the surface. The plant itself had been shaped by a German work ethic. It was efficient, mechanized, and had good quality control. While parts in Louisville's Building 4 were manually machined, most of the operations here were automated.

It seemed that in every corner of the world, GE was being outmanufactured.[4] In February of 1982 I returned to Louisville to give my interim report.

MABG'S executives gathered to hear what I'd found. I began with the numbers. It now cost MABG over forty-eight dollars to make each compressor. Necchi and Mitsubishi were doing it for between thirty-two dollars and thirty-eight dollars. Sanyo, Hitachi, and Toshiba were designing plants that would be making them for under thirty dollars. And Embraco and Matsushita's Singapore plant were planning to be at twenty-five dollars—almost half of GE's cost. One reason was labor. GE was paying over seventeen dollars an hour, including benefits. That compared to Matsushita's $1.70 in Singapore and Embraco's $1.40 in Brazil. Even more astounding was the difference in productivity. It took GE sixty-five minutes of labor to make a compressor, compared to forty-eight minutes in Singapore, thirty-five minutes in Brazil, and under twenty-five minutes in Japan and Italy.[5] A company that's paying higher wages for lower efficiency doesn't have much of a chance.

Then there were the competitors' export plans. Embraco, already shipping ten thousand compressors a month to America, was aiming for ten times that amount within four years. Meanwhile, Necchi had just boosted exports to 1 million a year, and Matsushita would soon be in the multimillions. Overnight, foreign companies had gone from a few percent of the U.S. market to a full 20 percent. And the biggest invasion had yet to begin.

MABG's biggest product—the refrigerator—was in jeopardy. If management didn't act soon, I said, it could be disastrous for the whole group. The options? One possibility was to source. A second option: build a factory overseas, in a low-wage country, perhaps in a joint venture. Third, invest in a new, more efficient factory here at home.

I waited for the response. It turned out to be the opposite of what I had heard before. "If they're that far ahead of us," someone said, "how can we possibly catch up?"

"We ought to just go for the source," someone else added.

The report made even John Truscott waver. What most shocked him was the difference in labor costs. For each compressor MABG made, it was paying out $19.73 in factory labor. The others were paying between $1.12 and $3.32 per compressor.[6] How, he asked, can a company—one with average wages and benefits of $17 an hour—compete with dollar-an-hour workers? GE was clearly being outcompeted, which was a shame, and it was a bigger shame to think about closing a factory, but a company's first mission is to survive.

Everyone knew that this was only an initial overview—my final report was still two months away. But for many, this had been enough. The sourcing bandwagon began to roll. It was a measure of how far MABG had come that most executives were now asking why anyone would even think of manufacturing compressors in America. Awbrey, the new project leader, who'd been discussing sourcing for months, sensed it was now the likeliest option. He decided to speed up plans to be ready. I agreed it was a good idea. Even if GE were to build a new plant, which was doubtful at this point, it would still take years. Meanwhile, they'd need a bridge, and sourcing could be it. Soon Awbrey went beyond planning. He had to get away from those forty-eight-dollar models. He began to arrange to source smaller compressors for the low end of the refrigerator line from Necchi, GE's Italian competitor.

ALTHOUGH Tom Blunt had not yet met me, he'd decided he didn't like me. He was convinced I'd been sent down by GE headquarters in Fairfield with a preordained mission: to recommend that the compressor factory be closed. Blunt dislikes people who close factories. He dislikes the idea of sourcing just as much. "All everyone wants to do these days," he says, "is find someone overseas who makes something, someone over here who wants it, and then pat it on the fanny for thirty percent as it goes by." He will tell you that's not how a great nation maintains a high standard of living.

I made an appointment to meet him. As the day approached, Blunt recalled later, his resentment grew. If consultants had their way, he felt, there wouldn't be a plant left in America. They'd turn MABG into one big shipping and receiving station. Its factories would become warehouses, and its engineers retired as obsolete. Why should he meet with someone who thought he and his staff weren't as good as the Japanese? I remember the meeting clearly.

"You're a hard man to get hold of," I said as I was shown into Blunt's office.

"I don't want to see you," said Blunt.

I asked why.

"Your study's just a setup."

The truth, I said, was that I was here to learn what he'd recommend.

That was easy, replied Blunt—a new plant. Give us enough money to build one, and we'll make more in the long run.

I said I'd take that into account; I was there to explore all options.

"No, you're not," said Blunt. "You're here to say what they want you to say. Which is to close down a plant."

"That's not why I'm here."

"Bull," said Blunt. "You guys are all alike."

I told him I intended to do a fair report, and for that, I hoped to interview a number of his engineers.

"They're busy," said Blunt. "I'll tell them to cooperate because I have to, but don't take too much of their time."

AS COMPELLING as sourcing seemed, I knew there were still good arguments against it. Once you shut your plants, you're in danger of being hostage to your suppliers.[7] Buying Matsushita's compressors would turn around next year's numbers, but what about next decade's? And what if Matsushita decided to market its own refrigerators in America? They'd no longer be simple suppliers then, they'd be rivals. And a rival wouldn't sell to you cheap. Eventually, they'd hike their compressor price to give themselves the edge on the showroom floor. With its plant closed, how would MABG fight back then? Of course, it could turn to a different supplier, but that would mean retooling its refrigerator for a new machine. And who was to say that new supplier wouldn't become competition, as well? Could MABG afford to stop being a producer of the most important part of its most important appliance? To source a product when you're a second-level producer to begin with—as GE was with microwave ovens—is one thing. But to source the heart of your biggest product when you are the market leader is a much larger risk. I knew the tide in Louisville was moving toward sourcing. It might be the right tide, but I wanted to explore alternatives.

THE IDEAL alternative would be to build a new American plant that could make compressors cheaply enough to undercut those built by the dollar-an-hour people in Brazil. Could a high-wage country do that? Theoretically, yes—through automation. But not with the standard model, reciprocating compressors. The Germans at Brazil's Embraco had automated those about as far as they could go, and with low-wage workers, GE's only choice was to explore a new kind of compressor. The rotary was the main hope. Because it had fewer parts, there seemed a good chance of making it quicker, boosting productivity. Toshiba had plans for making rotaries much faster than Embraco was making the recips, as they were called. Could MABG do even better than Toshiba with rotaries of its own? I was doubtful. Not by themselves, anyway. It's hard to become the leader in a new technology that a competitor has already started to run with. But there was no need to do it alone. If GE could get the leader—Toshiba—to help them with either a joint venture or a technology license, it would have a better chance, and at less of a gamble. At least, I decided, it would be an alternative. But even to propose it, I'd need to come up with a plan.

I WENT BACK to Tom Blunt's office.

"I hear you've given away the store," said Blunt. He was talking about my interim presentation. It had accelerated the sourcing bandwagon, and he wanted to let me know he wasn't pleased.

In fact, I told him, I was here to explore an alternative to sourcing. I went over the idea of a rotary plant, adding that proposing it would take more than rhetoric; it would take a plan. That's where Blunt came in. Could he put one together?

He nodded. That's what he did for a living. If we wanted a plan for a factory, it wouldn't be a problem, he said.

I told him he needn't design it from the ground up. GE could possibly work with either Toshiba or another Japanese producer.

Blunt had a standard way of reacting to that kind of suggestion. "You tell a manufacturing engineer someone's better than he is," he'd say, "and he'll want to prove they aren't." If we gave his guys a chance, he added, they could outperform the Japanese. But he doubted management would allow him to try.

"We can do it alone," he said, "but they won't let us. The decision's already made."

"As far as I know," I told him, "it's not already made."

"They'd never give us the money," he said. "A factory wouldn't be cheap."

I knew that. And I knew that in the last few years it was almost unheard of for a U.S. smokestack company, surprised by foreign competition, to fight back with an expensive new plant. But I told Blunt not to think about money for the moment. Just come up with a plan. If he didn't want to work with the Japanese, I suggested involving some engineers from the air-conditioning business who knew rotaries. I had a feeling that wouldn't be easy; the two divisions had a rivalry going and barely talked. But an outside enemy, I thought, could bring them together.

"All right," said Blunt, "we'll do it. But I don't think anything will come of it."

BEFORE going forward with the factory option, I wanted the support of one other man. I met with John Truscott. He was intrigued. His career, in his words, had always been a search for the technological Holy Grail. Having left the sound barrier and CAT scanning behind, he'd begun to think he'd never find the Grail again. But now, for the first time since coming to Louisville, he saw a possibility. If aeronautics was the frontier of the fifties and medicine of the sixties, this could be the challenge for this decade—automating smokestack America. Everywhere, it seemed, the sun was setting on American manufacturing. Now was the time to show the trend could be reversed. High-wage America, Truscott felt, could still be the industrial leader of a low-wage world. But it would take investment. It would take leadership in both product design and factory automation. He wanted to be part of showing it could be done.

He spent some time studying the rotary with an engineer's eye. He found it could indeed be made simpler than the old-fashioned reciprocating compressor. He also found that even the Toshibas were far from perfect. There was room to take this technology to new heights, beyond the competition. He assembled a team to come up with a new design.

TRUSCOTT'S engineers spent several months designing a GE rotary compressor. The challenge was to make it as simple as possible, with low noise and high efficiency. Then there was the hardest challenge of all—durability. Refrigerator compressors had to work far harder than those in air-conditioners. The design would have to be for a tough machine. At the same time, GE couldn't load it up with too much metal, or it would cost too much.

After a few months of work, the engineers came up with a model that could be made in America even cheaper than the Japanese models being made in Singapore. The design, however, had a problem. It called for the key parts to work together at a friction point of fifty millionths of an inch—about one hundredth the width of a human hair. No product on earth had ever been mass-produced at such an extreme tolerance. No one had even tried it; most engineers thought technology hadn't advanced that far. Tom Blunt knew there were some machines—like jet engines—that operated at those tolerances, but those things weren't mass-produced. Their parts had to be tooled one at a time, over long hours. Was it possible to get such precision in a plant that made three thousand pumps a day? Everyone they talked to doubted it could be done. Blunt took the design to Truscott anyway. Truscott looked it over. "It looks possible," he said. He told Blunt to gather the manpower necessary to plan a factory. Blunt knew he'd just bargained himself into an obsessive few months. Designing a new factory, he will tell you, is an enormously complex job, with a hundred new headaches a day. But that is why he likes doing it. "Because it's hard," he says.

BLUNT knew this would be a first of a kind—one of the world's most automated factories. To design it, he figured he'd need forty people. Where could he find ones with the right skills? Many GE colleagues advised him to go outside. To pioneer new technology, they said, you have to find designers already on technology's edge. Blunt decided against that. He would stay with his own people. But where in MABG would he find them? He gathered up many from an unlikely place: Building 4. "We didn't go out and get a bunch of Star Wars guys," he would say later. "Most of these people came from one of the most non-automated places you've ever seen in your life."

Why did he risk that? Blunt is convinced that American industry doesn't have to recruit experts for breakthrough projects. Most seasoned engineers, he thinks, can do it. All they need is the backing—and confidence. At MABG, he knew his people had neither. "Some of the engineers here were the brightest people I had ever seen," he recalls. "They had degrees coming out of their ears. But they'd never been allowed to do anything." For years, they'd been free to innovate on gadgetry, but not basic manufacturing. That cost too much. It left most engineers in a malaise. What made it worse, said Blunt, was that they were treated as the group's second-class citizens. It was the opposite of how things were in the Far East. There, he knew, manufacturing engineers were heroes. Here? "A lot of people thought we couldn't walk and chew gum at the same time."

If they were to come up with a worldwide breakthrough, Blunt felt they first had to believe they could do it. That is where he started—on morale. "I had to spend a long time convincing them that they really were worth a shit," he says. As they began their work, Blunt pep-talked them. The reason he'd plucked them from Building 4, he said, was because he needed people who knew factories—and still believed in them. He knew they could design a better one than anyone in Japan or Korea. As they progressed, he kept up the pep-talking. It was true, he said, that no one had ever built a factory that could mass produce parts of this precision. It was true that no one had ever achieved interchangeability at fifty millionths of an inch. None of that mattered. Here in America, in Louisville, they'd be the first. One of his favorite approaches was to remind his team that few outsiders would understand why they'd chosen to build factories for a living. You get no credit for it, he'd say, even though it's about the most difficult thing there is to do. But that's why they'd picked it; because of the challenge. And then he'd give his most heartfelt line: "Anyone can source," he'd say. Gradually, his people began to feel more confident than they had in years.

THE PROBLEM with most manufacturing, Blunt felt, was that factories are designed around products. This time, with the compressor plant, he and Truscott decided to design the two together, adjusting each as they went. They began by moving the product and manufacturing engineers across the hall from each other. With each day, there was more and more movement across the linoleum. Gradually, they fine-tuned the pump down to the most automatable of models—a stationary vane rotary. It was also the simplest; it had fewer than twenty parts. The computer simulation said it would work, but only if the machining went far beyond anything the Japanese were doing. To help find a way to do that, Blunt brought in specialists from GE's jet-engine division. He brought in computer-modeling engineers he'd met at Ford. He brought in the head of the Swiss Institute of Technology and consultants from the Structural Research Dynamics Corporation. But they were just for occasional advice—and even many of them doubted Blunt's team could bring this off. He still relied mostly on his own people, the people from Building 4.

His main rule was never to allow them to say it couldn't be done.

"We figured it was the way to drive our people beyond state of the art," says Blunt. "If you say it can't be done, you won't do it. But if you say, 'We don't care that it's never been done, we're going to be the first'—then you have a shot."

Slowly, week by week, the plan came together. "There weren't great Eureka breakthroughs," Blunt recalls. "It doesn't work that way. The whole thing was block-and-tackle grunt work." As he expected, there were one hundred headaches a day. There was constant frustration. There were late nights. Blunt hadn't enjoyed work this much since he'd come to Louisville.

The factory began to take shape on paper. Each time the engineering team finished roughing out a new piece of it, they taped it into a matrix unfolding along a corridor wall. The matrix soon took up a quarter-block of space. To keep it going, they had to find empty offices and extend the paper in there. They spent a lot of time just sitting, drinking coffee, and looking at it. How to integrate the grinding and the gauging? The loading and the material handling? They moved around pages, deciding what to automate and what to do with manpower.

And then it was done. "But that still didn't mean anything," says Blunt. "It was just a bunch of sheets of paper. Anybody can do that." Now came the second stage. Could they design machines that would make the parts the paper called for?

BLUNT had one other rule. He wanted every piece of equipment in this plant to be made in America. His stated reason was that it's too hard to deal with vendors twelve thousand miles distant. But there was another reason. He wanted to show that America could outdo the world with only its own resources.

One of Blunt's chief engineers was Dave Heimedinger. Under his direction, a team of engineers began to negotiate with suppliers of grinding and gauging machines. The vendors would look over the plan to mass-produce parts at jet-engine precision and then shake their heads. Heimedinger and Blunt remember a typical conversation.

"You can't do that," one vendor said.

"We think we can," said Heimedinger.

"Well," said the vendor, "it's our equipment, and we don't think it'll do that."

"We think we can find a way to make it do it."

"Well," said the vendor, "all right. We'll sell it to you. But it won't do that."

One maker of grinders insisted on putting a clause into the sales agreement saying the purchasers had been warned they would not be able to get the tolerances they hoped for. He also added a no-return clause. Heimedinger bought it anyway.

Blunt's theory of how to make machines do something they weren't built to do was simple enough. "We played around with them," he recalled. "We knew that five things determine how good a grinder is. First, there's the way the machine spins the grinding wheel. Then there's the wheel itself. There are the fluids that lubricate the process, the computer that fine-tunes it, and, finally, there's the material that's being cut." Heimedinger and his team began experimenting with combinations that had never been tried before. Blunt describes how they brainstormed: "If I take this machine, and combine it with that wheel and use this fluid on that material, and then tell the computer to have the whole thing act this way, let's see how far we can go."

Often, people would come by and ask Blunt why he was bothering. MABG is in trouble, they told him. Why gamble on a factory? Let's just source and get on with it. You can lose with a factory. With sourcing, it's a guarantee. Blunt smiles at the memory of it. "I just put my head down and said, 'Well, we're working on the son of a bitch.'"

THE FIRST prototype machines started to work. They began to deliver parts the manufacturers had warned they could not. Blunt knew it still wasn't final proof. Test machining is a good guide, but when you're building an unprecedented manufacturing process, the only real test, he says, is the plant itself. "A first-of-its-kind factory," says Blunt, "is its own prototype."

In one sense, he considered that a welcome risk, a sign of limitless potential. "If we could have proved this would work," he recalls, "it would have meant we were breaking no new ground." In another sense, it made for sleepless nights. Until it was done, and the switch was thrown on, there was no way of knowing whether the plant would succeed. Blunt did, however, have one test he used to gauge whether each of the new ideas would work. He calls it the eye test, "If you look into an engineer's eyes," he explains, "you can see whether he feels good about something, or whether he's afraid of it." Then there's the "I'll try" test. If an engineer thinks an assignment is impossible, says Blunt, he'll say, "I'll try."

"If you hear someone say, 'I'll try,'" Blunt says, "you better look real close, because he's afraid." When they'd finally finished their plan, no one was saying, "I'll try."

ONE THING made Blunt more nervous than the technical question—the financial question. Would this plant, if built in America, make cheaper compressors than anyone else in the world? It was up to me to make those first projections. Both Blunt and I knew that if they didn't add up, it wouldn't matter how brilliant the design was. Headquarters couldn't possibly go ahead with it.

First, there was the estimate of the cost of the plant itself—$120 million. Then it would cost tens of millions more to redesign the refrigerator so the new compressor would fit it. It would add up to one of the biggest single investments GE had ever made in a factory. It was a lot to gamble on the hope that it would still produce cheaper goods at seventeen dollars-an-hour labor than rival factories paying less than two dollars. It was beginning to loom as an almost unacceptable risk. Then GE's engineers came up with a way to make it more attractive. GE had a Columbia, Tennessee, plant that made air-conditioning compressors—rotary models. Instead of going from nothing to the new prototype factory in a single leap, we could begin by adapting the machinery already there. It would allow a quicker move into rotaries and a chance to work out the bugs in advance while the new factory was being completed. The numbers on that proposal looked better. Even at ten times the wages, it would still be lower cost than any other compressor plant on earth. At least on paper.

Blunt knew that was no guarantee that GE's Connecticut headquarters would back the proposal. Fairfield was wary of huge capital investments, especially since GE had recently lost money on a failed washing-machine plan. How could MABG convince management to invest an even bigger amount on an even higher-risk venture? Especially when they could source for almost nothing?

I finished my calculations and called Blunt. He asked me what I thought. I said I'd weighed the two options carefully—sourcing or building—and had decided to recommend that GE invest the $120 million. I took Blunt's reaction as a compliment. "You really are a crazy son of a bitch," he said.

I WENT to Don Awbrey, who was overseeing the compressor project. When I finished my presentation, he hesitated. Awbrey had made it no secret he'd been leaning toward sourcing, and now told me it still struck him as the safest route to better profits. Over the next hour, I carefully showed him the numbers proving the factory could do it better. I pointed out the risks of sourcing your core product—long term—from potential competitors. Afterward, Awbrey called together people from marketing, production, quality control, and finance. He told them that he was prepared to go with the factory. But he wanted an airtight proposal.

JIM LEHMANN had been a finance man with GE for thirty years. His job was to be skeptical of any big spending plan. Like all good finance men, he treated money requests as if they would be coming from his own pocket. At first, when asked to review the $120 million, he was doubtful. He'd never seen so high a figure before. He forced us to recompute the numbers with every possible risk factored in. But finally, everything seemed to add up. And in truth, after so many years of bells and whistles, he was drawn to the challenge of a major manufacturing project. His support eventually proved crucial. Later, when Don Awbrey suddenly left General Electric, Lehmann was named to replace him as head of the compressor project.

Like Blunt and Truscott, Lehmann had sensed for years that Louisville had been in malaise. Now, from his new helm, he was able to feel the atmosphere from a different angle. He was surprised at how changed things were. Even those who'd been most inclined to source were now excited. "There was electricity in the air," recalls Lehmann. "It was like the early days, when we were proud of being technology pioneers."

THE COMPLETED plan was finally sent to the head of MABG. A new man now held that post: Roger Schipke. Many in Louisville were surprised when Fairfield took him from head of dishwashers, the smallest of MABG's products, to head of the entire group, one of the premier positions in General Electric. Schipke doesn't fit the profile of a corporate titan. In many ways, he is the opposite of the man who gave him the job—Jack Welch, the chairman. Welch is demanding and constantly energized. Schipke seems more like the kindly owner of a small-town general store. "I'm just a simple guy," he often says, and he isn't being disingenuous. He is low key, and readily jokes that the only thing he knows about engineering is that you don't glue two shiny surfaces together.

The main reason he'd been selected as group head was his success a few years earlier in managing the redesign of a new dishwasher, both product and factory. It was one of the few MABG projects in a decade that went beyond bells and whistles. Its success was still a matter of pride in Louisville; the project did all the things the Japanese were then known for doing—a long-term investment that cut costs, improved quality, and doubled market share.

But this didn't mean that Schipke favored big investments. By nature, he was conservative, another reason Welch had selected him. Though proud of the dishwasher project, Schipke had come up through selling, knew the importance of profit, and like most in Louisville, had gone beyond the early seventies mind-set about having to manufacture everything in America. A manager can't make decisions on patriotism, he'd say. The priority is to keep the company's numbers strong. Schipke's other priority, upon taking over the group, was to get rid of the Louisville malaise. When a division becomes lackluster, he saw, people tend to turn on each other. He worked hard to change that, getting rival managers to work together and stressing cooperation with unions. It worked. Slowly, MABG was settling into more cohesion. It was around then that we brought him the compressor proposal.

Still new at his post, Schipke didn't know much about refrigerators, and knew less about compressors. We began by trying to explain to him the differences between rotary and reciprocating. That kind of discussion tended to bore him. "That wasn't my thing," he would say. "It was a big yawn to me. That was Truscott's job." He did understand that compressors were losing money because foreign competition had a seemingly unbeatable edge—a tenth the labor costs. But the compressor team had numbers proving the new factory would overcome that. It would be more than ten times as productive as any other factory, they said. A high-wage country can fight back, they argued—with technology. The plan was to apply it on two fronts: Both the plant and the product would be the world's best.

Schipke looked it over. The proposal seemed to make sense to him. Because of the high automation, labor costs weren't nearly as big a factor as he'd expected. He said it was time to take the proposal to Jack Welch, the chairman in Fairfield.

SCHIPKE, Truscott, and Blunt flew to Connecticut to sell the proposal to Welch. I was not part of that final meeting, but did all I could to brief Welch's top staff people in advance by phone. I knew their briefings of Welch before the meeting could make a difference.

Later, Blunt would recall the plane ride from Louisville to Fairfield. The betting was that they would not get approval. They knew there was a new world outlook in GE headquarters. A few years before, management had been almost haughty about the Japanese; they could never touch GE's quality, or technology. That had changed. The Japanese had become manufacturing geniuses. Why try to beat them when you can borrow from them? Or buy? Words no one dared speak before—words like "sourcing"—were now accepted wisdom.

It was Blunt's first time in the Fairfield boardroom. It was nearly empty as he filed in along with the Louisville team. Then a half-dozen executives from headquarters, including Jack Welch, entered the room. The Louisville people made their pitch.

"Then Jack poked at us three or four times," recalled Blunt.

The chairman asked some of his colleagues their opinion. A few said they doubted it could be done. It had never been done before, and seemed too great a risk. Welch looked at Blunt. "Why should I believe you people can do this?" he asked. "Why should I? You've never done anything like this before."

"No one ever asked us to," said Blunt. "And I believe we can do it."

Welch nodded.

"Essentially," Blunt would say later, "it boiled down to, 'You bums have never done anything worthwhile down there—why should we let you try this now?'"

Welch turned to Ed Hood, a vice-chairman of GE and one of his most trusted technical advisers. Blunt watched as he drew out Hood's comfort level. Blunt was counting on three things. Welch, he thought, had faith in Schipke's new management team. He'd seen the numbers showing the plant could do it—if the technology worked. Finally, the chairman wanted to keep major appliances as a core business for GE, and was concerned enough about Louisville's slide to know that only major investments could turn things around.

Welch turned back to Schipke, Truscott, and Blunt.

"Okay," he said. "Go ahead."

IT WAS up to Keith Moore, recently transferred from GE's lighting business in Cleveland, to start up the new factory. First, that meant retrofitting the old Columbia, Tennessee, air-conditioner-compressor factory with the new processes developed by Blunt's engineers.

Moore's people soon found that it's easier to design a new process than to make it work. The warnings of the machinery suppliers proved true. At first, GE couldn't make the equipment do what Blunt's engineers wanted. It took endless hours of debugging, and hundreds of changes to each machine. The required tolerances—one-hundredth of a human hair—were so extraordinary that even the tiniest slippage could throw a whole process off. Ultimately, to keep the equipment at absolute precision, GE had to develop new gauging and sensing systems to get the machines to instantaneously readjust as they worked.

Deliveries of machinery were two months late at the start, and up to fourteen months late at the end. Management found it hard to shepherd the process from Louisville, two hundred miles from Columbia, so they rented twenty-two apartments in Columbia to house engineers. The company even started a daily air shuttle between the two cities. That way, they could instantly fly lab results in from Louisville and test experiences back from Columbia. Finally, by October 1985, they'd begun Phase One. The old factory started producing the new compressor—first five per day, then ten, then one hundred. By month five, they were up to volume production, with the quality holding just fine.

But if they were to succeed at Phase Two—making the new fully automated plant work—GE faced another challenge just as important as improving its hardware: improving its people.

A HIGH-WAGE country can't compete with better technology alone; its other weapon has to be a better-trained work force. Could MABG create that in a place like Columbia, Tennessee, where the biggest annual celebration is Mule Day? Could blue-collar American workers in the rural heartland run one of the world's most automated plants? GE knew it would have to try. It would be too expensive to hire high-salary technicians from around the country. At seventeen dollars an hour—benefits included—the new plant could still beat the competition, but not at twenty-five dollars or thirty dollars an hour. So GE planned to staff the new factory with the same assembly people already employed next door at its Columbia air-conditioner complex. Most were unskilled, and few had more than a high-school education.

Historically, U.S. companies have put little investment into shop-floor training. With this kind of technology, GE management knew they had to make it a priority. They ended up deciding on yet another major investment: one of the most sophisticated blue-collar training centers ever built in an American factory. The cost would be over $2 million, which would have been difficult had GE not gotten help from a welcome partner: government. The state of Tennessee gave the company a training grant to help build the center.[8] But MABG was still left with a problem. It wouldn't be able to afford the additional expense of paying workers for the hundreds of hours it would take to train them. That left one choice: asking unskilled men and women to sacrifice between 120 and 400 hours in classrooms, labs, and computer stations at no pay and with no guarantee of promotion, either; that would depend on how they performed. All GE would offer was the promise of a skill. Would the workers volunteer? Would they show the same kind of commitment to company most associate not with Americans, but Asians?

PAUL VARNER, who'd been named by GE to help run the new training center, thought it a bad mistake. Having been an assembly worker in Columbia himself, he knew most on the line were conservative souls, wary of anything new. They already had secure jobs; what would be the point of sacrificing up to a year of nights and weekends for no pay? His guess was that almost no one would volunteer. "It took me two weeks to realize I was totally wrong," Varner says today. "I ate crow."

Workers lined up for the training. Partly, it was because of the prestige GE gave it. Those who got through it were offered diplomas and graduation dinners. But there was another draw, as well, the same one that had prompted Varner to apply for a training-center job himself. He was aware of the world. He knew how vulnerable his job was. He saw why plants throughout America were closing: foreign competition. He was convinced it was a question of time before distant forces put him out of work as well. "We knew what the Japanese could do," he said. "A lot of people were aware we were fighting for our lives." As an assembly worker, Varner knew he didn't have the weapons to fight back. Columbia's old machines were antiquated. How, he wondered, could they hope to beat 1980's rivals with a 1960's factory?

Then came the announcement of a new plant. Finally, here was the means to fight back. Varner wanted to be part of it. He didn't mind unpaid nights and weekends in the training center. For him, joining the future was incentive enough. Still, he was at first convinced most others would need more than that. He was wrong. Hundreds of workers flooded into the training center. Clayton Russell was one of the first.

RUSSELL had been hired by GE Columbia in 1974 for an unskilled assembly job. "That's all we had then," he explains. His job was to put four screws into the rear case of an air-conditioner. He did it 712 times each day. Gloria Anthony began the same year, also on the line. "A monotonous job," she says. "Over and over and over." Then construction began on the new plant. To have a chance at being part of it, they were told they'd have to put in hundreds of hours of training, all on their own time. It didn't matter. They began to do so—mornings, nights, weekends. "Whenever we had a chance," says Russell. His reason was similar to Varner's. He'd heard this would be the world's most automated plant; he wanted a piece of the future. He trained almost three hundred hours.

Dan Edlin, another line worker, put in four hundred hours. Like the others, his motivation was more than the chance of a bigger paycheck. "For me, money wasn't the major factor," he says. "I wanted the opportunity to be in on something totally brand new. This is where business is going—automation."

Was there any resentment that automation would cost jobs?

"Machines aren't taking people's jobs," he says. "Machines are making new jobs. Anyone who wants to get off his duff and train can have them."

Gloria Anthony saw it the same way. "You have to start thinking skilled labor," she says. "If you don't get on that bandwagon, you're lost."

"It's the wave of the future," says Clayton Russell. "And it's already here."

In the first year of the training center, the workers of GE Columbia spent over fifty thousand hours, all on their own time, learning new skills. Paul Varner was taught a lesson: Give an American worker an opportunity and he'll sacrifice for it. "From Welch on down, they were saying, 'You can do it,'" says Varner. "We wanted to prove their faith in us."

SOON, Keith Moore, head of compressor production, was facing his next challenge: moving manufacturing from the converted air-conditioner plant into the new factory. Making the just-completed factory perfect, he knew, would mean thousands of adjustments. He also knew that his floor workers would be best able to spot many of those adjustments. So, right from the start, he involved them in developing the final setup. He began holding meetings with workers and engineers sitting shoulder to shoulder to discuss how to get better quality and efficiency. Moore was just as likely to reorganize a part of the plant at the suggestion of an assembly worker as an engineer. When they came across tough trouble spots, Moore would put the two groups together on joint teams to figure out solutions. He soon got an unexpected payback from spreading responsibility down through the ranks. In the past, even if a small thing went wrong, line workers would call a supervisor to deal with it. Now, they fixed it themselves. Part of it, says Moore, is that the training gave them the knowledge to know what to do. But it was more than that. By being involved in the planning, they'd started to feel as though they owned their part of the factory; that making it run right was on them, not their bosses.

"To this day," Moore says, "the facility runs without a manager or supervisor calling the shots on what has to be done." That, he says, can save an enormous amount of time. "If a supervisor has to become involved, you're an hour or two behind before it gets fixed. If you don't need the supervisor, you only lose minutes."

Moore also got workers involved in writing training manuals for the equipment. He figured that if they were compelled to teach the techniques, they'd learn them better themselves.

Finally, he laid down a rule against finger pointing. When things went wrong, Moore noted, the instinct was for workers to blame each other. That didn't solve anything. So he announced that any failed project would be considered the fault of the whole team. That way, Moore hoped, if one worker was having trouble, everyone would rally to back him up. That's exactly what happened.

Looking back, Moore realizes how important it was to keep up camaraderie. Frustrations could have easily gotten out of hand. The late equipment deliveries backed up the timetable. Dozens of times, processes that worked in the lab ended up failing on the factory floor. It meant late nights and occasional 7:00 A.M. Sunday morning meetings. But they made it; the plant opened on schedule, in March 1986. Both production and quality went smoothly, though inevitably there were bugs. It turned out to be a blessing that they had the older plant to occasionally fall back on while they worked the bugs through. GE will also admit it had to pour in more investment than expected. The managers there will tell you that happens when you're pushing technology's edge. But the factory is working. Ask Moore to point to one thing that did it and he won't mention hardware; he mentions the freedom he gave his workers. "We provided people with the tools to run their own businesses on the factory floor."

AS THE new plant was being built, John Truscott heard rumors that GE was thinking of putting him back in aerospace. A few years earlier, he'd have done anything to leave low-tech appliances for a high-tech division like that. But now he told his wife he wouldn't be interested. He wanted to stay where he was, in appliances. Aerospace, he felt, wasn't the cutting edge anymore. America's most urgent technological challenge, he felt, now lay in something as hard to master as space itself: factories. He explains the challenge: "Revitalizing American industry. Chrome-plating the rust belt. Turning around smokestack America. That's the best way to reestablish ourselves as a world power."

Ask him how a high-wage country can do that, and he'll give you a ready answer.

"Productivity," he says, "is the only tie-breaker."

When Truscott first arrived in Louisville, colleagues from GE medical and aerospace kidded him about getting factory dirt under his fingernails. The kidding bothered him a little. But now, with the compressor plant nearing completion, he'd grown proud of being a factory man. "You know what's the cutting edge for graduating engineers today?" he says. "This. Doing compressor factories. Automation. Robots. It's another sound barrier. Building missiles was exciting, but that's old hat now. I'd rather do things that've never been done before."

Four years after deciding he'd rather be dead than working in washing machines, the man who worked on the sound barrier and CAT scanning had found his life's greatest challenge in an appliance factory.

BLUNT, too, saw how important the plant was. It was especially plain to him when he went to Columbia to visit the site. Other factories outside the city were struggling, mostly because of faraway competition. Foreign companies were modernizing, America wasn't, and this was the price. It bothered him to see those plants in decline—Blunt never likes to see a factory go under—but what bothered him as much was the way newspapers seemed to focus only on that: plant failures, never successes. "A lot of us get really riled up when the popular press beats the hell out of us for not being competitive," Blunt says. "The truth is, we can be. It's just that most companies don't have the balls to spend money on productive capacity. Manufacturing may not seem like a lot of fun to people who don't do it—but it's necessary. And if you're going to do it, you can't short-sheet it."

As he drove past Columbia's older, struggling plants, he was proud that in this case, MABG was doing it right.

But eventually, he was to find the struggle wasn't over yet. Being at the cutting edge of new technology often involves risk.

IN JANUARY 1988, twenty-two months after the first compressor rolled out of the new factory, a problem arose. Some of the larger compressors—those in GE's bigger refrigerators—began to fail.[9] It was only a small percentage of the plant's total production, but GE clearly had a problem. For a consumer product like this, reliability is essential. So is customer satisfaction. Immediately, a team of design engineers was formed to find what was going wrong. They worked for weeks, often through the night. What made the job especially difficult was that only a small portion of the compressors had actually failed. But based on those few, they'd gone into a massive program of testing and found that others could fail in the future. Soon, the team solved the riddle. There was a lubrication problem with one of the compressor's smaller parts, causing it to wear quicker than they'd expected. It was mostly affecting the compressors that had to work hardest—those in the biggest refrigerators in the hottest climates, but some others were affected, too. Eventually, Truscott found that GE wasn't alone. The Japanese companies using rotaries were having similar problems.

Now that the cause was isolated, finding a fix became Louisville's obsession. A new team worked on it for months. Finally, they came up with a better design and showed it to Roger Schipke. Fearing the disaster of a second mistake, he told them to keep improving it—and to keep testing. Meanwhile, he approved a plan to immediately replace any compressor that broke down by dispatching servicemen to customers' homes at GE expense.

But Schipke still faced a serious dilemma. True, the projections showed that only a few percent of the compressors would fail. But the redesign of the lubrication device would take months to implement, and Schipke didn't want to risk GE's reputation by shipping refrigerators that might develop problems. To be as safe as possible, he made a painful choice. In the spring of 1988, he decided that MABG would start to source medium and large reciprocating compressors from abroad while the engineering team perfected a fix. It would mean a temporary layoff at the old plant in the Columbia complex. It would also mean a high-cost burden. GE had to pay top dollar for the sourced recips, and take longer contracts than it needed.

In November 1988, GE decided to go into the field and replace all rotaries that might someday break down. The one-time financial penalty was very large—well over $150 million. The losses will offset several years of savings from the program. But GE will continue to make rotaries with the corrected design for most of its refrigerators at its automated Columbia facility. The failure problem has drawn hard criticism from both the competition and the press. Some at GE are embarrassed at having been forced to source foreign compressors. Others are irritated at how much money the problem has cost. Still others are angry that it was potentially avoidable. Early lab tests showed the compressors would last twenty years, but obviously the truest test is performance in the field. Looking back, many GE executives see a lesson. When using a brand-new technology, it may be wiser to introduce it gradually, working out the bugs over a year or two, rather than converting your entire production immediately.

The irony is that over 80 percent of GE's compressor investment—and risk—was tied up in the factory, by far the most complex technical challenge. And the factory worked well. It was a relatively simple part of the product design that caused the problem.

Still, GE management preferred facing the problem to giving up. Occasional product recalls are part of the price of being willing to gamble on new technologies. It happened with fuel-injected car engines, electric shavers, and microwave ovens when they were first introduced, and now it was happening with rotary refrigerator compressors. The cost to GE is high. Profits are seriously off in 1988 and morale is low. But the achievement still stands: Here in America, GE is fighting to make compressors that are 20 percent cheaper than any made by dollar-an-hour competition.

CLAYTON RUSSELL, who used to put four screws into the rear case of an air-conditioner 712 times each day, now runs a seven-hundred-thousand-dollar synchronous machine with twelve different stations. Gloria Anthony is now a skilled controlperson who can operate machines by computer, adjusting them whenever the terminal tells her there's a slight quality problem. "I never thought I'd go this high," she says. "When I began, I was just sweeping." Both are proud to be part of a plant that makes twice as many compressors as the old one, with less than a quarter the people. Productivity, they say, is the only way America can compete. "There's a good feeling to it," says Russell. "We got production. That's a feeling of pride."

Edward Fite, director of the training center, dressed in gray pin-stripes gives a tour of the automated Columbia plant with the pride of someone showing off a new home. Overhead, compressor pieces roll down long, winding chutes, into machines that stamp, cut, and refine; computers direct them to the next machine, warning that they're on the way. The machines work and work, never stopping. Grinders, welders, testers, and robots do their drilling, milling, tapping, and gauging. There may be no other mass-production factory in the world that makes goods this precisely. Most of the line people stand before computer terminals: They're symbols of the new American blue-collar worker, equipped with the tools to outcompete the world.

"They knew that if the work had stayed the way it was," Fite says, "it would have been a matter of time before it went overseas." They knew about dollar-an-hour Brazilian workers. They knew they had to outproduce them. They knew if they failed, they'd be lucky to be back in unskilled jobs, stuffing wires into panels, for half the pay. "To be trusted with a plant like this," says Fite, "that made them prideful. They know they've met an extreme challenge that's never been done before. And they know they're bringing the whole community up. They're making it a skilled community."

It sometimes surprises Fite to know that today, at thirty-six, he's come from stuffing wires to teaching workers how to run a high-technology plant. He sees people like himself as the final mission of a factory like this: They give common workers a standard of living beyond what they ever hoped for.

JOHN TRUSCOTT, recently retired from GE, will tell you that now, more than ever, he knows the risks of trying to pioneer new technologies. But he'll tell you that if GE—and America—are to compete, we have no choice but to take those risks.

"Our future is not dependent on the bells and whistles," he says, "or even distribution. Those aren't the things that will make or break you in a world-class environment. What's really important is having world-class cost leadership, and world-class quality leadership." He makes one other point. America still has a productivity problem, but it's not because our workers aren't as good as foreigners. It's that they're not used as well. Give them the best of factories, he says, and the best of training, and they can still outproduce the world.

"It's the major need for the nation," he says. "Call it the Third Wave in industrial products—call it what you will. It's our biggest challenge." Three years ago, he recalls, few people felt smokestack America could meet that challenge as well as the world's Japans and West Germanys. "Well," Truscott says today, "at Columbia Tennessee, we are doing it."

IN A SENSE, Tom Blunt will always be a figure from an earlier America. The noblest kind of business, he will always believe, is manufacturing; the highest form of architecture is a factory. "I like the gritty stuff," he says. His father was a toolmaker, and he proudly traces his ancestry back through eleven generations of factory mechanics. But he knows America can lead the world in factories only by building a new kind. At his desk in Louisville, he leans over a computer terminal and punches a few keys. A moving diagram appears on the screen. He explains that he is now monitoring the Columbia factory. Sitting here in Louisville, two hundred miles away, he can peer by computer into the guts of any machine he wants to—judging how it's working, how many parts are made correctly, how many had to be set aside for rework.

"Let me show you something interesting," Blunt says. He punches a few more keys, then leans back, clasping his hands behind his head. "Since seven A.M.," he says, "we've made 3,413 pumps." He pushes an update button. "I'm sorry," he says, "3,415." He pushes the update button again. "3,417." He's a big man, well over six feet. He finds it hard to get through most sentences without at least a mild oath, and few things make him smile. But when he works this computer, if you look close, you can almost see the trace of one.

"So far," he says, "we've only had five defective parts today." He pushes another button and nods; the computer is showing him a diagram of the day's tolerances for one of the machined parts. "The problem was with one of the grinders that went down," he says. "It's fixed now." Is there any other plant in the world that has this automated an information system?

"There isn't," says Blunt.

BUILDING 4 still stands a few hundred yards from Tom Blunt's Louisville office. Only now, it's half-empty. Even if Columbia hadn't been built, he points out, Building 4 still would have been dead by now. Its time was up. The choice was simple: Either it was replaced with a foreign plant or an American plant; a foreign payroll or an American one. He's glad GE chose to go with this side of the ocean. Sourcing, he says, is not America's future. He's come out of this with one main lesson.

"I'll tell you something you just think about for a while," says Blunt. "In late seventy-nine, early eighty, this place was the garbage dump of the universe. Could do no good. Bunch of dumbheads. Low tech. Well, I didn't go out and hire a bunch of world-class experts to fix it. I didn't bring anybody in. The people that fixed it were mostly here. You stop and think about that. The only thing that really changed was that we told them they could do it. And we let them. We've starved the manufacturing community for challenge—and that's what we thrive on. Challenge."

As much as mastering technology—that, he feels, should be industry's goal: confidence. If a floundering corporation can start believing in itself, he says, it can beat the world. "I don't think the battle in American industry is mainly a technical battle," he says, "it's an attitude battle. People become what you tell them they are. If you tell them they can't do it, they won't."

THERE ARE other lessons, often overlooked. Most wouldn't have thought that compressors—which have been around for decades—could have been turned into a technological breakthrough. It's how most old, smokestack products are seen. Once low-wage countries begin making them, it's supposedly over; the only choice is to source—or put a factory overseas yourself. In truth, we need only lose a minority of products. Most can still be kept ahead of world competition with new technology. But only if we invest in time. Had Louisville slept another few years, it could have been too late. By then, foreign refrigerator compressors would have flooded America, forcing a decision to source forever. That's what happened with microwave ovens. The only defense is to track the competition and know when to act. But you can't win with technology alone. Eventually, the world will match it. To stay ahead, you also need the most skilled workers. That's far harder for the competition to match.

Finally, there must be a willingness to take risks. That means being ready for failures. Some might argue that if GE had sourced compressors to begin with, it never would have had the product-failure problem in 1988. But there are ways to minimize risk. GE probably moved into the marketplace too fast with its new compressors. A year or two of limited field testing would have exposed the minor design flaw, allowing a fix with limited financial losses.

GE's basic decision to manufacture was the right one. Sourcing so essential a product would have left GE's appliance group vulnerable, and America without a vital piece of its production base. Because GE risked, and persevered, in the long run it will be ahead of the world in both technology and cost. As long as the company maintains that lead, it's guaranteed to win. Had it sourced instead of invested, it would have no guarantee at all.

At the moment, Louisville is still fighting to recover from the compressor's design flaw. A special team of senior engineers has come up with a final idea for a fix, but MABG is moving cautiously, making sure to do the most thorough possible testing before rushing into production.

Meanwhile, the cost of the flaw has been high. Some at GE have called it a financial disaster. Much of the reason has to do with GE's obsession with reliability. Altogether, several million new rotaries were made and sold. Because of the flaw, it was predicted that a small percentage of them would fail in the field. But instead of waiting for that to happen, fixing them one at a time, GE has decided to go out and replace in advance almost every one of the new rotaries—a decision that will run into hundreds of millions of dollars.

There's no reason most companies battling foreign rivals must pay the kind of price GE is now shouldering. Its problems point out two key lessons. First, when sailing into uncharted technological waters with a traditional product, it's often wise to introduce a breakthrough design gradually. Second, thorough accelerated life-testing is crucial, and with a new technology it may be necessary to rethink the way that testing is done. Today, GE engineers say it's an important area for university researchers to now refine.

Despite it being a painful time in Louisville, MABG stands behind its rotary strategy: In the long run, GE is convinced it will win with rotaries. Taking a technological leap in both product and manufacturing remains America's only hope for fending off foreign challenges. GE's commitment shows the tremendous will America's smokestack industries are capable of mustering to win global business battles. And the biggest, riskiest part of this investment—the Tennessee factory—is working fine.

Tom Blunt, Dave Heimedinger, Don Awbrey, Jim Lehmann, and the hundreds of others who made the compressor factory happen have never made the cover of *Business Week*. We're more prone to celebrate CEO's or even brokers and speculators. Many Wall Streeters, of course, do contribute to a vibrant economy, but there's something more important. Drive fifty miles south of Nashville, outside the city of Columbia, into the rolling hills of tobacco country, where the restaurants offer Bar-B-Q and catfish, and you'll find a symbol. It's a symbol of how, with the right vision, and investments, and risks, we can still keep our trade balance, our jobs, and our quality of life, from going overseas.

II

Competing with Developed Countries

OVER $30 BILLION of America's trade deficit in 1987 resulted from imports of traditional products—steel, cars, machinery, televisions, and clothing from European countries like West Germany, France, Sweden, and the Netherlands.

Most workers in these countries are paid higher wages, have more social benefits, take longer vacations, and work fewer hours than American workers.

With the proper investment strategies, we could have positive trade balances in these products with these countries.

4

West Germany:
The Sophisticated
Machine

THE manufacturing manager was waiting for me at his U.S. company's headquarters. It was the summer of 1987, and the firm's textile business was under foreign siege. To help them fight back, they'd asked me to suggest ways to make their plants more efficient. As we drove to the firm's biggest factory, my host told me how proud he was that so far, they were holding ground against the foreign threat. He gave me a passionate speech against those who wrote off the U.S. textile industry. America, he kept saying, can't afford to lose its traditional industries. We have to keep producing, stay competitive. I noticed an American flag on his lapel. He was a real economic patriot.

Then, halfway through our plant tour, some brand-new equipment caught my attention; spinning machines, texturizing machines, cutting machines. Clearly, they were the most modern machines in the factory. I stopped to look at the labels. They were all German. Most of the company's older equipment was American-made, but not these. I asked the manager why he hadn't kept buying American. Were the German machines cheaper?

No, he said. They were much more expensive.

"So why buy them?" I asked.

"Better quality," he said. "More reliable."

I asked him what he meant. It started him on a five-minute monologue even more fervent than his earlier patriotic talk.

The German machines needed less power, less space, and less maintenance, he said. The software was simpler to use and more versatile. The cutting heads were steadier, the safety guards less cumbersome. Service was better, too. If there was a breakdown, the manufacturer would have a locally based technician by within two hours, even at night. The American companies, he said, usually took two days. The Germans, said the manager, even trained his workers to run the machines. Finally—and he said this was key—you could adjust the German machines for new jobs three times faster than American machines. In the textile business, he explained, one of the worst drains on productivity is downtime for machine setup. By using equipment that could do it quicker, he was saving thousands of dollars a week.

It occurred to me that with the cheap dollar, it would cost him 40 percent more to buy German machines now than a year or two before.[1] Would that convince him to buy American in the future?

"No way," he said.

I asked why.

Price isn't everything, he said. For a lot of products, like machines, performance is more important. It's like this, he said. Maybe he has to spend more up front, but if the machine delivers better productivity, the payback will be bigger in the long run. So, yes, he'd be happy to pay the premium. He wasn't happy to pay it to foreigners, he added, but it was his only choice. No American producers offered the same performance. Too bad they didn't, he said, because he'd prefer to keep his dollars at home.

I didn't feel good about what he'd told me, but I wasn't surprised. For years, many of my company's clients—in all industries—had been turning to imported factory equipment. It was hurting the majority of U.S. machinery makers. Most people don't realize how enormous an industry machinery is: over $600 billion a year worldwide, from steel rollers to plastic injection molders.[2] Machine tools, one of the biggest pieces of that industry, with $30 billion in annual sales, is one of the most troubled U.S. industries.[3]

MACHINE TOOLS, which form and cut metal, are the guts of industry. Some are as big as houses, some as small as bench tools. They're used to shape everything from coin-sized watch housings to huge bulldozer shovels, from car-engine blocks to massive power-plant pumps. They are industry's cookie cutters, stamping, drilling, and milling. Without them, there would be no mass production of cars or appliances, of airplanes or cameras. For decades, America was a world leader in machine tools, with over 15 percent of global production in 1977.[4] That has changed. By 1986, our share had dropped below 10 percent.[5] Imports to the United States meanwhile, have soared from 16 percent of our market in 1977 to almost 52 percent in 1987.[6]

By late 1986, our machine tool makers had lost so much ground that Washington felt compelled to step in and protect them, pressuring foreign producers to accept import restraints.[7] It wasn't just for the sake of jobs, it was for national security. A sophisticated machine-tool industry is necessary for making everything from fighter aircraft to high-tech tanks, and the government felt ours was in dangerous decline. I agreed, but was just as concerned about the commercial threat. To keep competitive, I felt, America had to keep automating, keep making more compressor plants. For that, we'd need state-of-the-art machine tools. Of course, you can always buy them from abroad, but it's much tougher to work with suppliers who are ten thousand miles away. Besides, machine tools aren't like tape recorders or microwave ovens; they're more integral than that. Factories in almost every field depend on them. A modern economy that loses its machine-tool industry risks losing its economic independence.

Despite that, many analysts point to our new machine-tool rivals—Japan and Taiwan—and say there's no point in trying to compete. We could never match Taiwan's low wages, and as for the Japanese, well, they seem to have already won the battle, more than tripling their world share, to 24 percent, during the same decade ours tumbled to under 10 percent.[8] Better for America, the analysts say, to move into future technologies, like computers, leaving traditional products like machine tools to the Far East. It's supposedly not the kind of industry a high-wage Western nation can compete in.

But that's just not true. The proof lies across the Atlantic, in West Germany. In the late 1970's, Germany's smokestack industries were hit just as hard by Far East competition as our own were. The German landscape was dotted with near-bankrupt factories. Its wages and workers' benefits are even higher[9] than ours. But in Germany there was no serious talk about moving to a postindustrial age. Instead, the country resolved to resurrect traditional industries, and succeeded. In 1987, they sold us $10 billion more in cars than we sold them, $4 billion more in machinery, $2 billion more in steel, and over $5 billion more in chemicals.[10] That same year, when America had a trade deficit of $170 billion, Germany had a surplus of $60 billion, most of it from its revived traditional industries.[11] One of the most impressive parts of that revival was machine tools.

In 1977, Germany was just ahead of America in machine-tool sales, with slightly under 20 percent of world production.[12] By 1987, when our own machine-tool sales plummeted from a 1981 high of $5.1 billion to just over $2 billion, Germany had its best year. Its sales were $7.6 billion, and its world market share still 20 percent, despite the rise of the Japanese. That share was now more than double our own,[13] impressive for a nation with only a quarter our population.[14]

Lee Iacocca once asked why the country of Eli Whitney has to import so many machine tools. The answer is, we don't. High-wage Western countries can win in traditional industries. Two companies from West Germany show how they've succeeded, and how we can, as well.

FOR THREE DECADES, it had been one of the old standbys of German machine tools—the Traub automatic lathe. The company created it in 1938, and had kept it a strong seller ever since, the mainstay of its product line. Like the Volkswagen Beetle, Traub's lathe endured for decades; no need for many changes. The market endured as well—lathes were among the most commonly used of machine tools. Just about any metal rod, from a drive shaft to a lamp arm, had to be finished on them. Most of that work was done by small machine shops, Traub's main customers. Hundreds of those customers were nearby, in Stuttgart's industrial valley, serving the region's car and appliance plants. But Traub sold all over Germany, as well, and even to the world. It wasn't a big company—about $20 million in sales in the late 1960's—but it was solid, profitable, comfortable. It seemed to have found a guaranteed niche.

It was around then that American toolmakers made a major breakthrough. Up to that point, machine tools were controlled by a cumbersome array of cams and gears. One headache was adjusting them for each job. It could take hours or even days to get a line of machines ready to shape a new part. Toolheads had to be replaced, angles adjusted, clamps shifted. The American breakthrough cut that adjustment time way down. It was an invention that allowed the machines to be programmed. That way, instead of having to change settings by hand, you could do it automatically, and with far more precision. The technical name for the process was numerical control (NC). It worked like a player piano, although with magnetic tape. The breakthrough put the United States way ahead technically, but the Germans weren't surprised. They expected that from the Americans. U.S. machine toolmakers had always been world leaders, and with this particular technology they'd had help—government support. The Department of Defense needed better machines to cut new high-precision aircraft parts, so it gave U.S. companies money to develop the NC idea.[15]

Some considered NC the start of a new age in machine tools, but across the ocean, Ernst Ehmann, one of Traub's directors, wasn't concerned. NC was interesting technically, but not relevant for Traub. First of all, Ehmann knew it would double the price of an ordinary machine. Second, what did it offer? More precision and flexibility, but who needed that? Maybe U.S. jet-engine makers did, but not small German machine shops. For them, the old Traub automatic lathe was fine. First of all, most machine shops didn't need to deliver aeronautics precision. Even more important, they didn't need flexibility—quick adjustment time. This was the 1960's, the age of manufacturing standardization. Whether you were making cars, cameras, or refrigerators, companies avoided variety. To make mass production easier, most firms had only a few product models. For machinists, that meant huge orders for a handful of basic parts. Auto companies routinely ordered batches of fifty thousand at a time—one shape. For that, machine shops found the old cam-controlled automatics all they needed. They'd receive orders, take a day to adjust their Traubs, then spend the next few weeks cranking out the batch. Often, they kept machines at one setting for months. Why spend for flexibility when you didn't need it? Traub decided not to bother with the NC concept.

THEN, in the early 1970's, there was another surprise. Japanese companies, never big players in the industry, suddenly unveiled their own NC machines. For the first time, Ehmann and his colleagues began to worry. Obviously, the Japanese weren't developing NC for defense or aerospace applications, which didn't exist in Japan. Their goal had to be commercial products. If that was true, it could mean direct competition. Perhaps, thought Traub's directors, it was time to think about getting into NC themselves. But there was a problem. It would take an enormous investment to make that leap, and Traub had neither the electronics expertise nor the money.

Then a Japanese firm made Traub an offer. It was looking for a distributor to help push its NC machines into Europe. Would Traub help? In one sense, such a setup would be perfect. If the product failed, it would be Japan's problem. If it succeeded, Traub would harvest part of the profits. Some of Traub's managers said the company couldn't lose. But Ehmann hesitated. The short-term reward could be lucrative, but helping the competition into your own backyard, he decided, wasn't a good long-term investment. Still, maybe there was an opportunity here. If Traub could license the Japanese NC components and build them into its own machines, it could avoid big R&D costs. That way, the company could afford to gamble on this new technology while keeping the competition at bay. Traub made the proposal. The Japanese, seeing it was their best option, agreed. Soon, using Japanese NC technology, Traub had created its own NC prototype machine. Management showed it to their customers. Ehmann still remembers the response.

"It's crazy," the customers said. "It's foolish." They were happy with their old, mechanical Traubs; they wanted no part of the new ones. "Too expensive," they said. "And who needs the flexibility?"

In a sense, it would have been logical for Traub to have been relieved at that. Why throw more money into a new product line if your customers are happy with the old one? Still, Ehmann was concerned. Germans—even those born in the forties and fifties—often speak of the poverty of the 1920's, when hyperinflation drove the price of a pound of sugar to 250 billion marks. Then there was the postwar devastation, less talked about but still a source of insecurity. Few Germans take a good economy for granted. Most recognize how important it is to stay ahead of the competition if prosperity is to be preserved. It would be perilous, Ehmann now felt, to ignore the new NC products.

But that left Traub in a bind. NC, the company felt, might well be the future, but move into future products too fast and you'll go bankrupt waiting for the market to catch up. On the other hand, if you wait until your old product has begun to decline, you could be too weak to invest in a new one, especially if the competition has already done so. The smart move would be for Traub to do both—mechanical and NC alike. But the firm wasn't rich enough. The solution Ehmann and the others came up with was a bridge strategy. Instead of charging outright into NC, Traub would first upgrade its mechanical line. Ehmann and his colleagues would do it knowing that in a few years, if the NC market came around, they'd shift their main focus that way. But they'd need that bridge step—a better mechanical line—to build strength for the greater investment ahead. The strategy began to work. The upgraded mechanical machines boosted sales better than ever—building reserves for investment. By 1975, Traub began to talk about finally moving into its own NC line.

Then came yet another surprise.

THE Americans unveiled an entirely new generation of machine tool—computerized NC machines. Instead of programmed tape, these had microprocessors aboard. It was a powerful technology. You could adjust a machine to a new part in minutes, and boost precision enormously. The Traub people were caught off balance. It was as if they'd been poised to move from biplanes to single-wing props when, suddenly, the competition announced the jet engine. If their strategy was to keep up technologically, they couldn't ignore it. But some at Traub argued that they should. It was the same hesitancy they'd had when NC came out:

The NC computerized machine was for high-precision aeronautics jobs, not mass-industry use. And it was far too expensive. A machine like this, Traub figured, would have to cost two hundred thousand dollars. That would put it beyond the reach of small machine shops, Traub's standard customers. They decided not to invest in it.

But once again, the Japanese did so, unveiling computerized machines of their own. They didn't make much headway, but they were aggressive, and their prices were much lower than those of the U.S. versions. Ehmann remembers giving a speech five years earlier, in 1972, to a group of German machine-tool executives. Afterward, during the questions, there was only one subject on everyone's mind: the Japanese. People spoke of how they'd come from nowhere to develop NC machines, and were now building share in world markets—threatening everyone else.[16] That year, Ehmann says, the Germans realized Japan had to be taken seriously. Now, in 1977, with Japan having leaped to computerized models—CNC machines—the Germans took it as accepted wisdom that they had to fight back.

Still, in Traub's boardroom, it was the same dilemma. Could they afford to invest in a new technology that their market wasn't ready for? Traub decided to ask the question a different way: Could they afford not to? Admittedly, there was little demand for computerized machines, but in a global economy, Traub felt, companies that wait for customers to come knocking will wake up to find them already captured by the competition. The Germans already saw that happening in America with subcompact cars. They didn't want it to happen in their own backyard with machine tools. They decided they had no choice but to invest in a computerized line.

And if the market resisted? They told themselves they'd just have to find ways to pull the market along with them.

IT WAS at about that time, 1977, that I had a chance to look at the world machine-tool industry. The British government had asked the Boston Consulting Group for a report on whether Japan was likely to hurt England's machine-tool producers. After taking a trip to Japan, I flew to West Germany for the annual European machine-tool show, an efficient way to do research. It would have taken two weeks and a dozen plane trips to interview the people I'd be able to get in one hall in two days.

I knew the Germans and Americans were the industry's leaders, but I also knew Japan was planning to challenge them. I began by sitting down with an executive from one of Germany's bigger machine-tool companies. I explained what I was doing, and started off by asking about the Japanese.

"Yes," he said, "we are worried." He told me of a recent trip he'd taken to Tokyo to see if the threat was real. It was. The Japanese were smart, aggressive, and in a hurry. Other German machine toolmakers had flown there, too, he said, coming back equally alarmed. The German industry was now organizing a combined study to come up with a strategy for fighting back. Most German companies were planning to develop sophisticated products, he said, but they wanted to study Japanese plans in more detail to be sure their new designs could win. A half-dozen other German producers told me the same thing.

I also spent an hour with a representative from Germany's Ministry of Technology. He was at the show, too, and just as concerned about Japan.

"We can see they're improving," he said. "We've also had a few of our companies lose sales because of Japanese tools."

Instead of simply gathering data from the sidelines, the ministry was trying to help. One way was to research future toolmaking technology, like laser cutting. Another was to help companies invest in new products.

My next round of interviews was with the Americans. Their outlook was a bit different. The talk I had with a marketing executive for one of our bigger companies was typical. "I've just returned from Japan," I told him. "The Japanese are coming on strong. What kind of response are you planning?"

He said his company hadn't given it much thought. He'd never been to Japan, he said; he really didn't know those firms. "We're not worried about them," he added. "The Japanese aren't really a threat." He assured me they'd never be able to penetrate the American market. They weren't skilled enough, either as producers or marketers.

Altogether, I sat down with executives from eight American companies. Only one knew the names of the new Japanese competition. And even he wasn't worried. He admitted Japan was making good products, but he told me America's large machine-tool users would never buy from them. The automobile companies were anti-Japanese because they were fighting them in their own business, he confidently explained, and the aerospace industry wouldn't buy foreign for national-security reasons. It turned out that a decade later, both industries were heavily invested in Japanese and German machine tools, and his own company, once an American leader, no longer made them.

Before I left the show, I looked around for U.S. government people to see what they had to say. None were there. And it wasn't just because this was overseas. Later, I would go to an American machine-tool show. There were no Washington officials there, either. The German ministry people, however, were just as plentiful on our side of the ocean as their own.

TO BEAT the Japanese, Traub began its plan of developing a computerized lathe. But should it design one from scratch? Its first problem was expertise. Traub's technical people were machine designers, not electronics specialists. How do you computerize your product if you don't know computers? The obvious solution was to do what they'd done with their NC prototype: license designs from the experts—the Americans or Japanese. It would be far cheaper and less risky than doing it on their own. But Wolfgang von Zeppelin, head of Traub's design department, didn't want to license.

The way Zeppelin saw it, you can't stay out front in a competitive industry if you just keep licensing technology from your rivals. If machine tools were truly moving toward computerization, then software would soon end up the product's centerpiece. How, asked Zeppelin, could Traub remain a leader with hand-me-down software? It was similar thinking to what I would later see in Louisville. Whether it's compressors or software, you don't want to source the heart of your machine. Traub might have thought differently about licensing had it been based in Taiwan or South Korea, where low price is often a central strategy. But a high-wage country like Germany couldn't hope to compete on low price. Its strategy had to be high sophistication. To bring that off, Zeppelin argued, Traub needed to be a technical leader.

Others at the company finally agreed; Traub would develop its own computerized machine. Later, Ehmann would recall that decision with a fatigued smile. "If we'd known at the time what kind of adventure we'd started on," he said, "we might never have begun."

The challenge of computerizing Traub lathes fell chiefly to Zeppelin—a descendant of Count Ferdinand von Zeppelin, the blimp pioneer. He knew of no one in West Germany who had the expertise he needed—no specialist in machine-tool software writing. The idea was too new. His obvious move would have been to hire a team of general computer experts and teach them about machine tools. Many advised him to do that. If software was the new priority, you start with people who know it—computer eggheads, as they were called in Germany. Zeppelin decided against it.

"Eggheads may know how to program," he would say later, "but they know nothing about turning." That was the essence of the Traub lathe—turning. But there were a thousand subtleties to it. To know those subtleties, you had to have worked with machine tools for years. Zeppelin worried that free-lance software designers couldn't master those subtleties, no matter how many briefings he gave them on turning. He didn't want Traub's new lathe to be grounded in computers, he wanted it grounded in shop-floor practice. He felt he could best get that not by teaching machines to software experts, but by teaching software to his own machine experts. Of course, he'd have to hire eggheads for backup, but his own machine designers would be the center of the effort. It was an echo of Louisville. When Tom Blunt sat down to design GE's new compressor plant, the core of his team was his own staff, people who knew the product.

IT TOOK Traub one year to finish its first machine. In 1979, management proudly took it to the European machine-tool show in Milan. But they found themselves criticized from both sides.

First, an American executive stopped to look Traub's machine over, judging it by the aerospace standard he knew back home. "Forget about it," he told the Traub people, "you're not sophisticated enough." Then came the German machine operators, Traub's customers. "Foolish," they said again, insisting it was even more impractical than the NC prototype of a few years back. They pointed to the price—over $150,000. Why should they pay that much for a machine tool?

Traub tried to make its case. It's more flexible than ever, they said, easier to adjust to new parts. But the customers didn't need flexibility. Their standard order was still big batches. What they needed was a low price.

Traub's managers left the exhibition shaken. "Whenever you try to introduce a new technology," Ehmann would say later, "you run into some resistance." But they didn't expect this much. Creating this market was going to be harder than they thought. Still, they were committed. No one was ready to pull back yet.

In Stuttgart, they talked out what to do next. Price, they decided, was a bigger priority than they'd realized. All right, that's how they'd beat the Japanese. Zeppelin and his team went back to the design lab to cut costs. It turned out to be good timing. The price of computer hardware was falling. They worked for another eighteen months, and by mid-1981 had finished a new product. Management was convinced that this time, Traub had done it—a good machine at a good price. The company took it to the European trade fair in Hannover, Germany, convinced they'd stun the industry. Instead, they were the ones who were surprised.

The Japanese were everywhere. There must have been a dozen companies, almost all with cheaper machines than Traub's. Most disturbing, the Japanese quality was as good. Manfred Hekeler, Traub's marketing director, remembers it as a bad time for all German toolmakers. "A lot of companies in Germany nearly panicked," he recalled. What worried them most was the size of the threat. The Japanese had once again doubled production in only four years. And with their new, low-priced machines, they were poised to boom even more. Already, they were grabbing share from dozens of U.S. companies. Germany, Traub knew, was equally vulnerable.

I remember being at that same Hannover show for my compressor study. I was there to find out whether machines indeed existed that could give Louisville the tolerances it wanted. I noticed a difference from the show I'd attended four years before. Back then, German companies had the biggest presence, Americans second, and the Japanese an afterthought. Now, the Japanese dominated, and it was the Americans who were hard to find. The Germans were somber. They weren't quite sure what had hit them. Still, they all spoke of fighting back. "It's a matter of survival," one executive told me. "If we stop investing now, we die." An official in the Ministry of Technology was just as resolute. "We cannot let the machine-tool industry in Germany die," he said. "Without your own machine tools, you cannot be an industrial power."

After Hannover, Traub's management sat down to decide what to do next. Was there any chance to compete on price? It didn't seem promising. Ehmann and the others spoke of what the Japanese had done with watches and calculators—getting costs down by 20, 50, even 90 percent. They were already working on the same strategy with machine tools. With lower wages and high worker discipline, they'd probably keep succeeding. So low price was a bad strategy. The Germans decided to go back to where they'd started. If they couldn't do it cheaper, they'd do it better. More sophisticated. Leave the Toyota niche to Japan; Traub would design a Mercedes. But would their customers pay for a Mercedes? One trend convinced Traub that they would.

INDUSTRY, the Germans felt, was going through a fundamental change—a change beyond standardization. A new age of individualism seemed to be dawning. Customers were demanding more variety. Gradually, companies were responding with a greater selection of product models, from cars to cameras. If that trend kept going, Traub felt, it would change the nature of machine tooling. Factories would begin to need a bigger variety of parts—in smaller batches. That meant toolmakers would have to be flexible enough to adjust quickly from one to the next, delivering fast turnarounds. Traub's mechanized lathes couldn't do that. A computerized model could.

The change in manufacturing, Ehmann noticed, had already begun to happen. Ten years before, the average batch size Daimler-Benz wanted from machine shops was about fifty thousand. By now, 1981, Daimler had tripled its model selection, adding dozens of options. That meant batches of 10,000–25,000 were more common. It was the same in other industries—appliances, cameras, fixtures. Ehmann was convinced that machine shops, industry's cookie cutters, would soon find themselves having to deliver ten times as many shapes.

Then something else began to drive batch size down even more.

Factories began to rethink the habit of stockpiling big inventories. Here and there, companies moved toward the idea of just-in-time manufacturing. Instead of bringing in a backlog of twenty thousand parts to carry them for months, they began rolling in deliveries a fraction that size every few weeks, or even days. Just-in-time producers were also reducing the number of suppliers they used. To survive, machine shops would have to become larger, more flexible, able to make fast deliveries. Ehmann eventually saw average batch sizes going as low as a few hundred in the next decade, a mere fraction of what they used to be. The only way to juggle a steady flow of such small batches would be with sophisticated computerized machines.

So Traub decided there would indeed be a market for a Mercedes line of machine tools after all. They began to pour money into developing one. In Traub's design lab, Zeppelin hired more engineers. The company's R&D space grew from a small room to an entire floor. The new machine grew with it, capable of performing more functions at faster speeds with faster changeovers. One new machine could do the work of several older ones, and in less time. Soon, the next trade fair came. And there was Traub, unveiling its new Mercedes amid an array of Toyotas.

BUT AGAIN, the customers were hesitant. The Japanese models are cheaper, they said.

True, said Traub, but ours is more flexible.

Why, the customers asked, would we need that?

You're getting smaller orders these days, true?

Yes, that's true.

You're spending more and more of your time retooling for new parts?

True.

Well, this will speed that up ten times. The Japanese model won't perform as well. You want to make ten thousand loaves of bread, it's worth spending six hours setting up. But is it worth it for one loaf?

Batch sizes aren't quite that small, the customers said.

But that's where the world's going, said Traub. More variety. More tailoring. More speed. Factories aren't going to want parts six weeks from now; they're going to want them tomorrow.

Then the Traub people began to demonstrate. They took a complex component that would normally require ten settings on five machines and showed how it could be done on one Traub. What impressed the customers most was the changeover speed—only minutes to readjust, as opposed to hours or days. Cycle time[17] was so fast that even at $150,000, the machines proved cost-effective after all. In time, a few firms put in orders, then a few more. The strategy was beginning to work.

Then, late in 1982, the bottom fell out. The world slipped into recession. It was about the most damaging thing that could have happened to Traub. Heavy industry cut way back on equipment buying. It was worse in Europe than in America. Sales of the new Traubs, the ones management had gambled the company on, plummeted. For the first time in its forty-six-year history, Traub lost money.

SOME AT Traub felt the problem wasn't just the recession—it was the product. The world machine-tool industry was contracting. In the United States, dozens of firms were going under. The only people getting bigger were the Japanese. There was one explanation—the Toyota strategy had proved the right one. The pessimists at Traub weren't alone in thinking that way. When the company's 1982 loss figures came out, the specialized German press began to write Traub's obituary. Even Ehmann himself wondered. Soon he began to think the unthinkable—maybe Traub should simply stop production and start sourcing product from the Japanese. "We had a nicely developed distribution in Germany," he would say later. "Why not just take on the Japanese machines? Was it worth really continuing?"

In America, dozens of machine toolmakers were asking the same question. Between 1981 and 1983, one quarter of all producers decided to get out of the business.[18] Many who stayed asked for protection against Japanese importers, claiming unfair competition.[19]

But in the end, Traub decided to keep fighting. Forget about sourcing, Ehmann decided. He saw only one route to a secure future: production. Traub's pessimists eventually agreed, but at least, they argued, the company should cut costs to get through the bad times. Their first choice was R&D, which had grown faster than any other cost. That's fine in flush times, but during a squeeze, they said, R&D had to be held way down.

On paper, in the finance offices, there didn't seem to be much choice. In the design lab, however, Wolfgang von Zeppelin resisted. He argued that there was no such thing as temporarily stopping R&D. "What does it mean to cut R&D costs?" he would say later. "You have to fire people. Once you start doing that, if you try in a year or so to recuperate, you can't."

The board ultimately agreed. Zeppelin felt it was exactly why American machine-tool companies were going bankrupt. "They tried to cut costs by starving their R&D departments," he said. "You do that, you will have a hell of a time reversing it."

So Traub made a decision. It did cut the research budget some, but nowhere near as much as other functions. Even in this time of potentially disastrous losses, Traub kept research a priority. Management still looks back on that period as its most difficult time. "Whenever we were debating whether we should spend this deutsche mark or not," recalled Ehmann, "we were more inclined to say, 'Let's spend it.' It was painful. But if we did not, the end was coming nearer."

There was one other area they didn't want to cut—training. Their machine tools were becoming ever more sophisticated. They knew they'd need sophisticated workers to build them. But they also knew they no longer had enough money to keep their training programs going. So they made a hard choice; they sold off two subsidiaries—a local material-handling company and a production shop in Singapore. It may sound strange to give away concrete assets in favor of such immeasurables as research and training, but Traub considered them as investments. Today, Ehmann says it might have been difficult to hold to that strategy had Traub been an American company. In the United States, he says, there's too much pressure to pay dividends every few months. In Germany, where companies don't even issue quarterly reports, things are different.

"The temptation for management to take the shortsighted decision is not here as in the United States," Ehmann observes. "And in the machine-tool business, short-term acting is the surest way to death." Manfred Hekeler, marketing director, explains that further. "It takes at least four years until you get a penny for your first new machine," he says. "America's management doesn't like that. They need the quick dollar."

Traub's bank helped. "They were convinced they should help us to sustain—even when we were taking a loss," says Ehmann. He didn't even have to explain away his big research and training budgets. The bank understood. It's often that way in Germany, partly because banks tend to be major shareholders in companies. But even when they're not, they usually take the long view.[20]

None of that gave Traub a guarantee. Sales continued to lag. But throughout, Traub continued to invest, making machines ever more sophisticated. Management had faith that in the long run, industrial trends would favor them. Some of the old machine shops were indeed getting bigger, as factories gave the bulk of their business to the most sophisticated few. And factories themselves were buying machine tools. Frustrated by vendors who couldn't deliver small batches fast, they'd begun moving more functions in-house, buying their own machines. A big company, Traub knew, would be more willing, and able, to pay for the best products available.

THE 1983 European machine-tool show was in Paris. The evidence of recession was on the floor. The Americans were hardly there at all.

Lean times had meant little investment by most Europeans into new models. Traub and a number of other German companies were the exceptions. Customers began to come around. By now, operators were clearly seeing batch size plummet. They were seeing other sources of pressure as well. Casting technology was becoming more precise, which meant fewer machining steps on new parts. On top of that, strong new plastics were replacing metal parts altogether. The business was shrinking. The survivors would be those with the most sophisticated machines. It was clear to Ehmann that Traub's gamble was about to pay off. "Yes," he remembers being told by several Austrian machinists. "We can imagine this machine for our range. We cannot afford to buy it now—but that's what we will need." Some didn't even mention price. They encouraged Traub to just keep pushing for better flexibility.

And soon, the customers did begin to buy. Gradually, Traub edged back into profitability.

STILL, management wasn't complacent. The Germans knew the Japanese would soon challenge their high-end niche. That had always been Japan's strategy—start with simple, high volume products, then work up the ladder of sophistication. They'd done it in TVs and motorcycles, were doing it in cars, and seemed to have the same plan in machine tools. Traub's solution was to keep climbing higher still. The firm had understood that it needed to invest to get past bad times. Now it saw that to sustain good times, it had to invest even more.

Every time Wolfgang von Zeppelin asked for more research money, he got most of it. The same company that had relied on one kind of lathe through three decades now designed four new generations of machines in six years. Today, Zeppelin admits he couldn't have done that had there been a drop in R&D a few years before, during the recession. Many of the new breakthroughs he was now making were begun during the lean times. In 1980, for example, he had been at the Technical University in Berlin when he saw an impressive computer-graphic-simulation system. It was for office use, but it got him thinking. If Traub could couple that with a machine tool, allowing an operator to watch a simulated run of each job on a video screen, it would guarantee better quality. The problem was expense. The university people told Zeppelin that the system cost about thirty thousand dollars. He began working on it anyway, continuing through the recession. Eventually, he was able to build a simulation system for under five thousand dollars. When it was introduced, it put Traub years in front of the Japanese.[21]

That and other innovations pushed Traub sales up 50 percent from 1983 to 1986. And 84 percent of those sales were in the machines the company had almost avoided: computerized ones. But Zeppelin's team still didn't stop. The R&D department, with over a hundred people by 1984, decided to move into new machines that could be linked up with computerized factory scheduling systems. By late 1985, they had introduced a machine group that could automatically reset itself for a new order, changing tools and settings when directed by a central factory computer. The R&D people even added new functions to their machines: drilling, milling, and sawing.

By then, 1985, some were saying there was no longer a clear leap for Traub to make. Its machines were as advanced as the market could take. But when you're asking for Mercedes prices, Ehmann felt you have to deliver more than a superior product; you need superior service, as well.

Instead of having to take a malfunctioning machine apart, Traub developed a system to let technicians peer inside and track down the problem by computer. Then they took it one step further: diagnosis by satellite. It was an idea first conceived by an American company, but Traub perfected it. Sitting in Stuttgart headquarters, Traub technicians could dial a phone, then look into the circuitry of machines ten thousand miles away. They knew the system would push up their prices, but it was all part of the Mercedes strategy; people will pay more if they get more. After the technology was in place, Traub found itself up against a Japanese rival in a final bid for a big British aerospace contract. Traub got it. One of the deciding factors was diagnosis by satellite.

BY 1986, Traub was facing a problem it wouldn't have expected in 1982: how to keep up with booming demand. The company had so much work, it often took a year to deliver—far too long when Japanese firms were delivering in three months. The only answer was to invest in a major plant expansion—hiring hundreds more workers. There was no way Traub could afford that as a family-owned business. On the other hand, there were lots of arguments for staying family-owned. A private company allows management more flexibility. Besides, Traub's family tradition was a long, proud one. But its priority was competitiveness. So the decision was clear: The company went public, and used the new funds to begin an expansion, hiring hundreds of workers. From 1986 to 1988, Traub sales continued to soar.

AT A TIME when the world machine-tool industry continues to shrink, there is new construction everywhere at Traub's Stuttgart headquarters. In the last three years, says marketing director, Manfred Hekeler, Traub has put $12 million into manufacturing investment alone. It has also invested another $3.5 million in a new training center, used for Traub's customers as well as its workers. To compete, says Hekeler, it's no longer enough to sell sophisticated products; you also have to sell the knowledge to run them. It's costly, but he insists it's worthwhile. "Sophisticated users make more frequent buyers," he says. "So we see training as a profit center." The number of trainees has ballooned six times in four years. In 1984, Traub put five hundred people through the center, most for a two-week course. In 1987, the number had risen to three thousand.

It's common in Germany to have this kind of center. Traub's has fifteen machines, all the latest technology, just for teaching. The center is only one part of the company's training expense. There's also the apprentice program, a key part of the German working culture. Almost all firms have apprentices—young high-school graduates who come aboard for three years of in-house classes, shop-floor instruction, and local schooling before moving on either to college or official employment. Although Traub pays apprentices only a small stipend, the program's cost is $1.5 million a year. The company spends still more to upgrade skills of more seasoned employees.

Does Hekeler ever worry that after all that investment, his newly trained people will leave for other companies? He shakes his head. Traub's turnover, he says, is a mere one percent—partly because training keeps workers challenged.

Not far from the training center is Traub's design department, a vast floor filled with over a hundred computer terminals, forty draftsman's boards, and technicians in white coats. Ten years ago, Traub had only a handful of software engineers. Today, 10 percent of the company's twenty-two hundred workers are in R&D. Traub spends 8 percent of sales on it, more than triple the average U.S. rate for machine-tool companies. The department looks as if it would fit better in a computer company than a machine-tool business, but Hekeler says that's appropriate—Traub is now part computer company. Not only does it design its own software, it even designs two-thirds of each machine's integrated circuits.

On the factory floor, Hekeler discusses some of the work-force issues that management must grapple with. In early 1988, West Germany's average work week was 38.5 hours. It is soon due to come down to thirty-seven, and the unions are pushing for thirty-five.[22] They'll probably get it. Meanwhile, German wages continue to go up faster than American wages. Hekeler concedes this is a big problem. Then he explains how Traub plans to respond.

"We'll have to automate to a higher level," he says. Ten years ago, he points out, each Traub worker produced the annual equivalent of thirty thousand dollars in value. Today individual production is triple that. Hekeler says part of that was achieved through training.

"I give lectures all over Germany," Hekeler says. "Never stop training yourselves. Your knowledge today is worth only fifty percent after five years. Technology is progressing."

Hekeler points to his bicep. "Today," he says, "you are not paid here." He pauses, then points to his temple. "You are paid here." He says it's one reason American machine toolmakers have slipped behind; they've neglected their work force.

"The most sophisticated machines we make we couldn't produce in the United States," he says. "It would be difficult to find the skills at a reasonable cost. This is something we've been complaining about to Americans. You must install proper means of education and training. You will have to invest far more money—in technical institutes, in vocational schools, but also in the companies. We have 120 apprentices here. We base our work-force planning primarily on these people."

Don't any U.S. manufacturers produce state-of-the-art computerized machines?

"A few," he says, "but more than fifty percent of the sophisticated machine tools in the United States are made by Japanese companies."

Does Hekeler worry about the Japanese?

"They produce very good computerized machines at a much lower price than we produce here," he says.

So why do people buy Traubs?

"Because Traubs do more."

IN 1968, Traub was a $20 million company. It spent the next ten years on a cautious strategy of upgrading its old mechanical line, which helped it grow to $40 million. That's when it took a less cautious leap into advanced technology, building computers into its machines. It turned out to be a powerful blend. Today, Traub is a $200 million company.

That isn't huge, but it's sizable enough to make it easier for Traub to invest, to export, to compete. Smaller companies have had a harder time keeping up, but some have managed. In the northwest corner of West Germany, near Düsseldorf, in the city of Mönchengladbach, a company called Scharmann is one.

THE PEOPLE at Caterpillar Corporation's world headquarters in Illinois had a problem. Their machining—the foundation of their manufacturing process—was painfully slow. It was that way for most industrial firms forced to deal with large, multi-ton metal parts. You couldn't stamp those out like watch housings. Caterpillar's worst problem was with its biggest part, the eight-ton bulldozer chassis. It was the vehicle's skeleton; the engine went in it, the cab over it, the tracks on the sides of it. It could take weeks to finish each chassis. One of the plants where the bottlenecks were the worst was in Gosselies, Belgium. In 1976, the manager there, Pierre Guerindon, decided to do something about it. His hope was to automate the machining, something long considered impossible for hugh parts. Still, Guerindon wanted to try. After researching machine toolmakers, he called Scharmann, a small company in Germany. He'd heard they'd been experimenting with the industry's latest technology—NC machines. He asked if they'd come across the border to Caterpillar to take a look. Heribert Vogt, now the company's chairman, made the trip.

THE DRIVE to Gosselies took ninety minutes. Guerindon walked his guest, Vogt, over to the machining plant. It was about half the length of a football field. Vogt watched as the process churned on. Each chassis came into the factory as a ten-by-six-foot raw metal frame, mostly solid. By the time it was milled and bored, it would look like Swiss cheese. That, however, would take four machines, dozens of steps, and weeks to finish. Vogt watched as a chassis was lifted by crane onto an enormous machine tool, at least thirty feet high. "A monster," Vogt said. Then it was clamped like a piece of wood in a carpenter's vise, but to picture it, you have to picture a station wagon being strapped to the side of a house. The clamps were the size of large tables, weighing six or eight tons themselves. Despite the size of each chassis, the machining had to be done to a thousandth-of-an-inch precision. That's why it took long hours to set up each step; there was no room for error. Then there was the ordeal of setting up the toolheads, the actual instruments that did the metal-on-metal surgery. Most weighed over a hundred pounds, and had to be aimed just right. Only then, hours later—when the chassis was clamped and the tools adjusted—could the machine begin the simple process of boring a bolt hole. And that was only the first operation. There were still dozens more to come. That meant carefully unclamping the frame, swinging back the crane, lifting it to the next machine—and the next, and the next. Vogt saw that it was anything but a smooth handoff. There were bottlenecks everywhere. Tools often wore out, stopping everything. Work breaks stopped everything, as well. So did shift changes. Increasingly, Caterpillar was adding new features to its bulldozer line, which meant almost every chassis had to be machined differently. That slowed things even more. A chassis could sit against a wall for days, waiting for a turn on the next machine. Not exactly high productivity.

As he stood there, Vogt saw no easy way to automate the operation. You certainly couldn't put eight-ton parts on a conveyor belt. That's fine for cars, where most models are identical and work cycles only a few minutes per station, but not with different-shaped eight-ton pieces, where one machining step could take up to six hours.

Guerindon wanted Vogt to try anyway. The current method, he said, was so inefficient that Caterpillar's machine tools spent only 8 percent of factory time doing actual work. The other 92 percent of the time, the machines were either being set up or simply idle. The capital cost alone for a machine to just sit there was $150 an hour, and lost production time cost more still. Caterpillar desperately needed a more flexible machining system. Vogt drove back to Mönchengladbach to see what his staff could come up with.

AT THE CENTER of the discussions was Helmut Maschke, the company's sales director. He was hired in 1970, after working four years in Seattle, modifying machine tools for Boeing. When he decided to come home to West Germany, he knew his U.S. years had spoiled him. "The American machine-tool industry was far superior," he would recall. Most German manufacturers, he soon found, didn't realize that. He remembers being in the Scharmann boardroom right after he came on staff. The chief engineer gave a briefing on a machine under development—a numerically controlled model that could be programmed to follow a rough contour, going from point to point around a geometrical shape. Scharmann was proud of its sophistication.

"I raised my hand," Maschke recalls. "I said 'This doesn't impress me at all.'" At Boeing, he told them, they had just commissioned a Sunstrand Machining Center that could be programmed to mill a replica of George Washington's face. He conceded it was for high-precision aeronautics, not standard industrial use, but the technology was there—far ahead of anything Germany had. For the others in the boardroom, Maschke's speech was an education, but not a concern. Scharmann didn't have to worry about fighting for sales. It was a seller's market around the world, the tail end of the sixties industrial boom. All Scharmann had to do was wait for orders. It got half its business simply by showing up at each year's trade fair. As Maschke would point out later, when you have two years of deliveries lined up, you don't worry about competition.

Then things changed. First the oil crisis, then recession, and then, in the mid-1970's, another shock—the first wave of low-priced Japanese machines. Not only had the market suddenly shrunk, but new players were vying for pieces of it. Maschke remembers it as a time of endless talks at Scharmann.

Could the Germans match the Japanese with cost cutting? Not likely, not with Japan's low wages. One other thought was simply to outwork them, but the Germans knew that wouldn't be possible, either. Despite Germany's renown for discipline, workers there put in fewer hours than Americans, and far fewer than Asians.

"We work for seventeen hundred forty hours a year," Maschke

would say. "In the Asian world they are working twenty-two hundred—that means four hundred or five hundred more hours a year."

There were other differences, as well. "People in Germany are talking about their vacations, about social benefits," says Maschke. "That is the way of thinking. You know the old saying, 'Germans live for their work'? That was changing. So we were worried."

Inevitably, Scharmann was left with one strategy, the same one as Traub: If you can't beat your rivals in price, you beat them in sophistication. "To bring a technical solution that our competition cannot easily copy," explained Maschke.

The first idea was to move into the industry's newest technology—NC. But by the mid-1970's, lots of people were doing that. Adding a Scharmann version to the heap wouldn't be enough. They needed to innovate, not duplicate. So they decided to focus on an area that had yet to be mastered—automating the machining of big parts. That included anything from ten pounds to ten tons. Whether you deal with pump housings or bulldozer sections, once you move beyond the small sizes, machining becomes a different world—a cumbersome one-at-a-time process. It was time to speed that up. But how?

Scharmann focused on medium-sized parts—those that weighed between a few dozen and a few hundred pounds. Like pump housings. A key bottleneck, Scharmann knew, was the need to constantly clamp and unclamp. First you'd clamp the pump housing to the machine, adjust it, mill it, remove it, and only then could you start clamping the next one. No one had found a way to do the clamping in advance. You had to just kill time until the machine cleared, leaving the next piece sitting idly in a bin, or against a wall. Scharmann's idea was to design a new kind of machine, shaped like a hut, or cell, and roll preclamped parts inside it. That way, you could get them ready beforehand, on a pallet—a small table with wheels. It opened up all kinds of possibilities. You could put six preclamped pump housings on a lazy Susan, for example, spin them one at a time, and roll them on their pallets into the cell, cutting way back on downtime.

Scharmann's first model sold well, but the firm knew its lead would be brief. Bigger companies were experimenting with the same idea. Soon it would be hard for Scharmann—with only eight hundred employees—to keep up. To prosper, Scharmann would have to specialize in an even more sophisticated niche, one that couldn't easily be copied. But management wasn't yet sure what niche to choose. That's when they received Caterpillar's call.

WHEN Heribert Vogt came back from Gossilies, everyone at Scharmann agreed the challenge was certainly unique. But rolling twenty-pound pump housings into a single machine cell was one thing; routing an eight-ton tractor chassis around dozens of steps on four massive machines was something else. In a sense, it wasn't even Scharmann's business. Instead of designing machines, Caterpillar was asking it to design a factory. It would be an expensive challenge, probably taking years. Scharmann saw it as a double risk. First, the company could simply fail, which would be ruinous. Or it could succeed for Caterpillar, and then find that no one else wanted this kind of system. The alternative, however, was to sit around Mönchengladbach watching big toolmakers pass them by. In a declining market, Maschke argued, the only small-company survivors would be those gambling on a unique niche. Scharmann decided to gamble.

The first problem, a big one, was that the company didn't have the technical expertise. The nerve center of a system like this would have to be a computer, one designed to act like an orchestra conductor, directing all the plant's machines to act in concert. It would involve a lot of complex software, something the company knew nothing about. Even so, the Scharmann people had the same instinct as Traub—they didn't want to rely on computer eggheads who didn't know toolmaking. Traub had gotten around that by giving its mechanical engineers software training. Not so easy for Scharmann. This would be far more intricate than any Traub machine. Scharmann would have to design an entire silicon nervous system for a factory. You'd need more than a crash course in computing to do that. Scharmann would need a dual expert, someone who understood machine-spindle speeds as well as microchips. In 1976, the Scharmann people started to look around, but found no one in Germany who combined the two talents. For the time being, it seemed that they were stalled.

Then, one day, Vogt flew to Austria on another job, visiting a company that did crankshaft milling. He was talking about NC machines when the Austrian company president mentioned that he'd been working with a professor from the technical university in Vienna—Dr. Helmar Weseslintdner. Vogt asked about him. He was a mechanical engineer, the president said, his academic specialty being machine tools, a common discipline in Central European technical schools. But what made him interesting, the president added, was a dual discipline he'd pursued; he was also a computer engineer.

Vogt asked if there was any chance of meeting him. Soon he was sitting down with the professor. "Listen," said Vogt, "I have a problem." He told him about the Caterpillar project—the challenge of linking four machines under one computerized orchestra conductor.

"Interesting," said the professor. "I was also thinking about this type of problem." The professor began to throw out some ideas, and soon, there was no question Vogt had found the perfect person. But he knew he couldn't do this job if his main expert was five hundred miles away. An occasional visit wouldn't be enough. That's when the professor mentioned something else. He was due for a sabbatical. Vogt made him an offer. A month later, he moved to Mönchengladbach to begin a new partnership.

DETLEV VAN ZEELAND had spent the last few years computerizing some of Scharmann's business functions—mostly personnel and production scheduling. Then, in 1977, he got a call from the company's manager of development. Scharmann had just taken on a major new project, Zeeland was told—automating a plant in Belgium. Zeeland was one of few on staff who knew computers. Would he join a professor newly brought from Vienna to form a team?

Soon Zeeland was at the Belgian factory studying the problem. The plant was clearly inefficient. The machining of the scraper—the blade used for plowing—typified it. Because of bottlenecks, so many scrapers were piling up they had to be carted back to Caterpillar's warehouse to wait their turn on the next machine—again and again. Over forty people were needed to truck the scrapers back and forth. If you could automate this, thought Zeeland, you wouldn't need all that material handling. You could finish each piece in a day or two, with no warehousing. As things stood, it took weeks, and by the time a scraper was done, its parts had been moved several miles. There had to be a better way to do this.

THE FIRST challenge was to get each piece—each scraper or chassis—into a smooth flow between machines. But because of their size, the pieces had to be moved by crane, something you couldn't automate. It was as impossible as getting a computer to build a skyscraper. You couldn't program a crane to swing an eight-ton chassis onto a machine tool any more than you could program one to swing a girder into just the right fix-point on a building. Obviously, the Scharmann team would have to replace the crane, but they weren't sure how. Their first idea was to clamp each chassis onto an immovable platform, anchored in the middle of the shop like a big altar, then have the machines move up to it one at a time to do their boring and milling. But they decided this would leave the parts too exposed. This was industrial surgery; if you left parts open to grime, they could be ruined.

They finally came back to the idea Scharmann had developed on a smaller scale, the enclosed hut and movable pallet. But what kind of pallet can move something that weighs eight tons? Not a table with wheels. They decided to try a small train car. That way, they could move it by rail. In turn, that meant designing enormous, custom-made machining cells, ones you could wheel a chassis inside and close up like a house to keep out debris. If you built rails right up to them, you could roll in your pallet, do the job, then roll in the next one. It seemed doable.

Now came the computer part—guiding all those scrapers and chassises through the whole routine. Zeeland and the Austrian professor started with a central computer. Its first job would be to tell each machine to get ready for the next chassis, automatically adjusting its angles and toolheads. Then, precisely when the job was done, the computer would order the pallet to roll out, following the rail to the second machine, and the third, and the fourth. To make the process efficient, it would have to be a precisely timed ballet. That was the hard part. You'd have a score of other pallets rolling around the plant with different parts on them. Some might only need an hour in a machine, but others might need three hours. That would leave clamped scrapers waiting for tied-up machines—a bottleneck again; perhaps a worse bottleneck, since you'd have pallets getting into a traffic jam. The Scharmann team came up with a solution. They would design machine tools so flexible they could do any job. That way, if machine number three was tied up on a six-ton chassis, the computer could reroute a waiting eight-ton chassis to whatever machine was available. In normal mass production, it's the parts you make interchangeable. Since most of Caterpillar's parts were different, they solved the problem by making the machines interchangeable.

After a few weeks, they'd diagrammed a pattern they thought would work. But Detlev van Zeeland and the Austrian professor knew that paper models often become a mess in practice. How could they test it? They came up with what may be one of the most peculiar trials ever used to gauge an advanced new technology. They began moving coins around on a desk. Each coin, they decided, would represent a pallet. They spent long hours just sitting there, moving the coins up and down. The coin test soon showed them they indeed had problems. If a machine broke down, the coins piled up. They made a note to design a holding area. There were also collisions. To solve it, they built crash avoidance into the software. There were a dozen other problems like that, and it soon got too complicated for coins, so they decided to go to computer simulation instead. They tried a few programs, but soon found none were advanced enough. Their simulated video pallets ended up racing around the screen too haphazardly to track.

Soon, what was to be a one-year sabbatical for the Austrian professor turned into two. Then Zeeland came up with an idea—forget computer simulation; why not build a model? A working model run by the actual software? They hunted down a firm that did models for architects, and after three months and forty thousand dollars, they had it set up like a child's train set in the Scharmann boardroom, complete with computer. It was worth the price. It showed, for example, that their design would be too big for Caterpillar's plant. They scaled it down. But then their pallets started colliding. Finally, they saw they had to throw out their plan of using twenty pallets, and brought it down to about a dozen, which worked. It took months to debug the programs, but it was far better to do it on a model than in the plant. Eventually, they were even able to do the training of Caterpillar workers using the model. At one point, they added up the time put into the project and found Scharmann had spent one hundred man-years. But finally, they were ready.

Had this been a routine industrial project, all they'd have to do now was build the hardware; the machines, pallets, and computers. But they knew this would take more than that. It would take training. It was the same issue GE faced with its compressor plant—you can't get unskilled workers to run a sophisticated factory. Scharmann had learned that lesson a few years before.

IN THE EARLY 1970's, over half of Scharmann's machine tools were mechanical. Then the company began to move quickly up the ladder, first NC, and then the big leap: closed machining cells with lazy Susans. Management decided, of course, to use Scharmann equipment in its own factory, machining its own parts. The company confidently installed a bank of the new machines, but immediately ran into problems. The jobs kept coming out wrong. First the executives thought it was bad design, then bad parts. Finally, they realized it was something else; it was their workers. They hadn't trained them sufficiently.

They would admit later that they'd tried to hire unskilled people— ex-bakers in several cases—to save on payroll. They were convinced they could get away with it. The theory was that their machines were so state of the art, they'd run themselves. All the operators would have to do was push a few buttons. On the contrary, they quickly realized, state-of-the-art technology needed state-of-the-art workers. It was an awakening. It wasn't enough to compete with machines alone. You had to compete with minds, as well. But that was all right. Scharmann came to understand it was the best way to stay ahead of its rivals. It's somewhat easy for competitors to duplicate your technology, far harder for them to duplicate the skills of your work force.

Scharmann knew it would take years to give its people the needed training, but it had an advantage. West Germany's apprentice program is one of the world's strongest worker-education systems.[23] The experience of Gunther Zebbities, a Scharmann line worker, shows how the program works.

Zebbities finished high school at sixteen, and, like 80 percent of his classmates, went into an apprenticeship. In West Germany, choices aren't restricted to blue-collar jobs. Some apprentices go into banks, others newspapers. In the mid-1970's, Zebbities joined Scharmann. His stipend was too small to survive on, but like most young German apprentices, he lived with his parents. The training wasn't like a summer internship, where you learn while working; it was structured education. Zebbities would spend a day and a half in company classrooms, two days on machines in Scharmann's training center, and another day at a nearby technical school studying machine-tool theory. It was relevant theory. The teachers at the school took week-long courses at Scharmann once a year to keep updated. When Zebbities's third year was up, he had a choice; either to begin full-time work or continue schooling. Like many, he chose school, spending two years at a technical college in industrial electronics. Afterward, just when Scharmann began its Caterpillar project, Zebbities returned. His first assignment was to get more training; he spent two weeks learning about computers, and then he was ready. So were dozens of other ex-apprentices— most coming to their first day of work with five years of specific preparation. Scharmann wouldn't have needed that had it been asking workers to stand on an assembly line like automatons to build identical machines. But the firm had moved beyond that. Now it was making different machines for almost every order, tailored machines. You couldn't do that with hands, only with trained minds. Scharmann had them.

THE COMPANY completed Caterpillar's new Belgian system in December 1980, four years after Heribert Vogt first journeyed to Gosselies. A team from Scharmann was there to watch the trial run. This time, it was a different picture from the one Vogt had seen on his earlier visit. There were no more groups of workers clamping a crane-lowered chassis; no more need to manually readjust tools for each job; no more trucks hauling backlogged scrapers to the warehouse. Everything was automated. Frames moved fluidly on pallets, guided by a computer-directed nervous system. The computer electronically adjusted the machines for new parts, then monitored the jobs, silently directing each chassis to the next available machine. During worker breaks, the machines did not stop. The pallets kept moving, the tools milling. Machine use went from 8 percent to about 70 percent. Jobs were done in days instead of weeks, sometimes quicker.

There was celebration back at Mönchengladbach. They'd done it. Experts and industrialists came from everywhere to study the Belgian breakthrough. For Scharmann, it seemed the firm was on the brink of a boom. It had some of the most advanced technology in the business. Scharmann presumed customers would start to line up. Then came a surprise. Nothing happened.

Months went by without another sale. Then a year. The few times the Scharmann people were asked to make proposals, they gave it all they had, spending months coming up with tailored engineering plans, but in all cases, the companies backed away. Too risky, they said. Too expensive. Scharmann's system, the customers pointed out, cost 50 percent more than stand-alone machines, a tough capital investment, especially in a recession. True, Scharmann promised better efficiency, but it wasn't enough. Companies wanted not promises, but a track record. And this system was too new to have one.

Soon two years had gone by, and still not a single purchase. Sales of Scharmann's traditional machines were down, as well. It was that way throughout the machine-tool industry. At Scharmann, a faction began to push for phasing out the development of the new factory systems. It was time to face reality. It wasn't working. The Caterpillar job was a one-shot fluke. Why waste R&D money on new designs? They insisted that R&D—the biggest drain—should simply be cut.

Helmut Maschke, sales director, disagreed. R&D cutbacks, he said, would mean firing, and the cost of that would be high. These were skilled people. Let them go and you've let go five years of expertise. He even argued to increase investment. "It's not the main point to make profit all the time," Maschke would say. "The main purpose is to produce. You can't survive if you have no products for the future."

He and those like him prevailed. Despite this being the low point of company performance, they got Scharmann to actually increase investment, boosting its software R&D staff from a half-dozen to twenty people. And the firm put most of its money into the product that wasn't selling—the Caterpillar-style flexible machining system.

"If there is no business, do you just give up?" Vogt would say later. "No."

Nor, he said, do you give up improvements. The Germans knew they already had the world's most advanced system, but they felt that wasn't enough. They had to upgrade it. You don't get a product moving with marketing alone, Maschke will tell you—only with technical advances.

"You go window shopping on Christmas Eve," he would say. "They are planning for Easter already—they should have all the windows with the Easter bunnies. You have to plan for the future."

Scharmann began to look for new ways to streamline its Caterpillar-style system. What were the lingering bottlenecks? The most obvious was the replacement of tools. In the Belgian plant, it had to be done manually. That meant the machine had to be stopped, a new tool selected from inventory, then installed by hand. Before you got things going again, it could be an hour or more. Why not replace the tool automatically, with robots? To do it, Scharmann came up with the idea of using computer-guided vehicles to carry the tools to the factory floor—to the exact point where the machine's robot could grab them. It would cut down tool replacement from hours to minutes. Gradually, Scharmann perfected the process. Meanwhile, the company poured money into other ideas. But still, no sales. Scharmann leaned entirely on its traditional product lines to keep afloat. And even that wouldn't have been enough had it not been for one other corporate priority: export.

MUCH LATER, in 1987, when the low dollar reduced the price of U.S. goods around the world, a number of American machine toolmakers were pleased to get unexpected inquiries from overseas.[24] For U.S. firms, foreign business often happens like that—customers come calling on their own. Scharmann, like most German companies, took a different approach. "If we would be just sitting here waiting for requests from someone who needs our equipment," says Maschke, "it wouldn't work." Scharmann, though a small company, invested in a worldwide sales network.

One of the company's first targets was America. As far back as the 1950's, Scharmann began making arrangements with U.S. dealers. Although it's often best to start that way—with local distributors— Scharmann found it could do better by investing in its own subsidiaries. Soon the firm had built its American branch to twenty-five employees. "We couldn't sell to the States without a Scharmann-owned company there," says Vogt. "How can you sell in a foreign country unless you are willing to meet that market?"

That meant adapting Scharmann's machines to local needs. American toolmakers, Maschke says, rarely do that. He remembers running into the frustrated representative of a U.S. toolmaker at a European show. The representative had lost several deals with countries that liked his machines, but needed them tailored. He had to tell them his company didn't do that. For Scharmann, it went without saying that it would customize, no matter what the headaches. Tailoring was the only way to create exports. And exports, he says, are essential, not just for expanding business in good times, but more important, for weathering recessions. The German industry's Russian sales are an example. In 1981, a year when German machine-tool exports to the U.S. fell by $17.7 million, the country increased sales to Russia by $8.8 million. That kind of counterbalancing, Maschke says, happens all the time. A few years ago, China bought 10 percent of West Germany's machine-tool exports—a welcome market at a time when orders from European countries had fallen. A few years later, China was down to only 3 percent.[25] But by then, Sweden, Italy, and Switzerland were back on the rise.

Spread your business he says, and you can ride out the bumps—the world cycles; American companies don't do that enough. And they rarely sustain it when they try. Historically, Maschke says, U.S. machine toolmakers had a hold on the Swedish market. Then, when American machine sales picked up in the mid-1970's, U.S. companies neglected the Swedes, feeling they didn't need them. That's when Scharmann and other German firms moved in. Not long after, when business softened in the United States, American firms tried to go back to Sweden, but found the Germans had displaced them.[26] "The Americans must learn something," says Maschke. "There are always peaks and valleys. If you give up on a nation as soon as you hit a valley, you'll never succeed."

Scharmann now keeps 50–60 percent of its business abroad. Recently, it began negotiations with Romania and Poland. It tried turning to South Korea as well, but soon ran into a problem. The government told the Germans they could only sell there if they licensed their technology to local firms. That meant handing their inventions to a competitor. Scharmann did it. "We are not afraid of giving away our current technology," says Maschke. "The moment they are up to our standards, we have to be ahead of them again."

WHILE exports of its basic products sustained Scharmann in the early 1980's, its continued investment in Caterpillar-style systems remained a drain. Even after two years, Scharmann still couldn't get a single buyer. Vogt, however, kept telling himself that one figure was more important than profits: investment. In the mid-1970's, he recalled, Scharmann's profits were much lower than those of American toolmakers—only 5 percent compared to 15 for the star U.S. performers. Scharmann began to wonder what it was doing wrong. Then the numbers from America began to turn. Some of the companies that had been profiting the most went bankrupt. "We realized where their profits had been coming from," says Rolf Horchler, Scharmann's finance director. The Americans had been putting almost nothing into R&D. While Germans were investing in new technology, the Americans had cut that back to keep profits and dividends high. Later, that would hurt them. Far better, Scharmann decided, to harvest 5 percent profit for fifteen years than 15 percent for five years, and then bankruptcy. The company redoubled its commitment to Detlev van Zeeland's research. That was one part of Scharmann's recession strategy—stepping up R&D. Scharmann poured over 6 percent of company sales into it, compared to an average 2.3 percent for U.S. machine toolmakers. Of eight hundred Scharmann employees, ninety were assigned to development.

Another part of the strategy was to step up training. That, management knew, came with a risk. Is it worth pouring money into workers who could move on at any time? Scharmann's bet was that the training itself, as well as the challenge of ever more sophisticated work, would keep that from happening; both would leave workers more fulfilled than ever. The gamble paid off. In 1969, when Scharmann's work was less skilled and the company did little employee education, turnover was 20 percent. Today, it's down to 4 percent.[27] Ask workers at Scharmann if they're bored, and it doesn't occur to them that it should be an issue. Every year, sometimes every few months, they find themselves building new, more complex machines.

The workers also speak of feeling trusted. German law gives workers a say in how their jobs are organized, but Scharmann gives them even more freedom.[28] Hans Dieter Gabler, head of manufacturing, says it's a question of productivity. "If you give workers more freedom," he says, "you get more efficiency. They are partners. They are not subordinate." He gives an example. In 1987, Scharmann's production goal was 100 million dollars. In the first six months, they only made 30 million.

"So we appealed to the workers," says Gabler. "Help us. We are in a hole." They responded well, he recalls, even coming in on weekends. They were paid overtime, but that wouldn't have been enough. To get performance, Gabler says, you have to give workers authority as well as money.

"Flatten the organization," says Maschke. "Not too many cases where one reports to the other, and then to another. In Germany, we have broad skills, not pyramid skills."

In his visits to American plants, Gabler has seen the opposite—too much hierarchy. Far better to delegate jobs to trained workers, he says, than reserve training for an elite few supervisors. "That is very important," he says, "that they improve work methods by their own activities." To do that, you have to give them knowledge. In 1966, Scharmann had 228 unskilled workers. Today, they have only thirty-eight.

Gabler now sees American firms working hard to come up with new technology. He says that alone won't help them compete. They are neglecting the other ingredient. "The people," he says, "aren't trained enough."

IN 1982, Scharmann began talking with the Swiss company BBC, maker of turbochargers for big diesel engines. They were interested in speeding up their machining. Scharmann engineers drew up a tailored version of a Caterpillar system. One key feature seemed of particular interest to BBC: replacing tools by robot. It was the feature Scharmann had developed during the recession, when many other firms were cutting out R&D.

BBC agreed to buy. The dry spell was over. Soon Scharmann made another sale—an even more sophisticated system—to a big British forklift truck maker called JCB. Next, some General Motors executives flew to Mönchengladbach to talk with Scharmann. Maschke took them to see the BBC factory, and got the order on the train coming home. Then came a real coup. Caterpillar chose Scharmann to install six more systems in its plants around the world, including four in America. Though Caterpillar had at one point commissioned a U.S. firm to try automating one of its American plants, the company felt Scharmann had come up with better product. Curiously, Scharmann decided to buy fully half the individual machines for these latest systems from other companies—even some from overseas. Maschke explains why. Many of the machines, he says, are simple models that dozens of firms build. Scharmann prefers to keep its resources focused on the most sophisticated machines only.

"With our high labor cost," Maschke says, "we don't want to simply do grinding machinery work. We'll only do things we can be world class at. We won't build the heavy, stupid machines. We should build the intelligent ones."

Today, the Scharmann people see themselves on the brink of a boom. Ten years after they completed the Caterpillar job, the market is finally coming wide open, and Scharmann is out front. "We are sure that beginning with the nineties," says Maschke, "Flexible factory systems go like this." He draws a finger up a steep, imaginary graph.

Is he worried that by then, low-wage nations like South Korea will be making the same systems? He explains that the same question was asked of him by the chairman of a big Korean corporation. "Tell me," Maschke remembers him saying, "what are you going to live on in the future? You in Germany work only a little bit more than seventeen hundred hours per year, four hundred less than we do. Soon you go down from thirty-seven hours a week to thirty-five. Your apprenticeship means your young people only enter the work force at twenty, and you retire them at fifty. And your apprentices get paid more than a manager in South Korea. Your absentee rate is eight percent, ours is two or three percent. Tell me," he asked Maschke, "how will you compete?"

"I gave him a very nice example." Maschke recalls. "I am living twenty miles outside of town. One morning, I drove to the company and there was one lane—the outgoing lane was blocked off for about three miles. There were three people with some heavy equipment, that's all. In the evening, when I came back, this obstacle was gone. Three miles of country road were done. There was a new coating on the road. It took only three people—with equipment—one day. Then, three years ago, I was in Nanking, China. They drove me to a machine-tool plant. On the way, we passed maybe one thousand Chinese, digging. I came back at night, and I still saw one thousand workers—there was no progress. The message is one thousand people without expensive equipment achieve less than three men with the proper equipment." That, he told the chairman, would be Germany's strategy—to make machines more sophisticated than the Koreans', with better-trained workers.

EVEN in its success, Scharmann, like Traub, guards against complacency. Recently, the company helped contract for a study of Germany's toolmaking future. Its prediction was stark. Competition will get worse, and technology ever more advanced. To stay ahead, Scharmann will need to hold on to a unique niche. That will be more expensive than ever. In 1970, Scharmann's average machine sold for one hundred thousand dollars; the average now is a $4 million factory system. Since all systems need tailor-made software, each job will take a big research investment—without guarantees. It's now routine for Scharmann to spend over a year making blueprints at its own expense before completing a deal. And three-quarters of those jobs never go ahead. Just as disturbing, enormous competitors are now developing their own flexible factory systems. It's a battle that will favor companies with the deepest pockets. Like Traub, Scharmann realized it couldn't keep up without a cash infusion. So it came to a hard decision: to find an angel, a big parent company willing to take Scharmann over.

Some in the firm considered it a disappointing move. Why sell out at the height of success? Maschke thought that was the wrong way to look at it. It's irrelevant, he says, to ask how you're doing at the moment. The question is, how will you be doing ten years from now? Maschke argued that if Scharmann wasn't big by then, it wouldn't be able to compete. If you're the first company to market a personal computer, you can survive fine while still small. But once the world's IBMs begin to challenge you, the only way to meet them is to grow. Scharmann's management resolved to grow.

The Scharmann people searched carefully, spending years looking for just the right conglomerate. It wasn't enough to find someone with cash alone. Scharmann wanted a firm that understood high-tech machining, whose management would be patient with heavy investment. The one it chose, the J. M. Voith group, had both qualities— Voith was twenty times Scharmann's size and had a commitment to push its own machinery business upscale. On January 1, 1988, the deal was closed.

IN 1970, Scharmann made 150 machine tool sales. By 1987, that number had been cut in half—only 72 sales. But they were Mercedes sales, and the dollar comparison speaks of the strategy. In 1970, the firm's total receipts were $18 million. In 1987, on half as many sales, they were up to $100 million. Such is the harvest of making smart machines. Lately, more orders than ever have been coming in. "It cannot be the price," says Vogt. "We are very expensive. It is the sophistication."

THE NEXT WAVE of machine-tool competition has now arrived. At the 1987 European fair in Milan, the Koreans were everywhere, with prices almost 30 percent below most others. There is no way, says Helmut Maschke, that a high-wage country can beat them head to head. Western manufacturers that don't develop smarter machines, he says, will be forced into the role of traders, marketing relabeled goods from low-wage South Korea and Taiwan—even India and Czechoslovakia. In Germany itself, he says, there are some toolmakers who have yet to realize this. "Their death," says Maschke, "is predictable." But many others took the same risks that Traub and Scharmann took. The country has benefited. Germany's machine-tool industry is robust.

In Stuttgart, a few hundred miles southeast of Mönchengladbach, Traub's Ernst Ehmann feels no victory in seeing U.S. machine toolmakers falling behind. He'd prefer to see America remain the world's industrial leader, not Japan. He fears that won't happen if the United States can't compete in machine tools. "In order to make a good piece of modern military equipment," he says, "you need absolutely perfectly machined components."

But his bigger concern is for America's overall economic health. Few realize, he says, how deeply a nation's machine-tool sophistication affects its industrial capability. That's truer now than ever, he says, and he'll tell you why. The age of standardization, Ehmann explains, is truly passing. The age of product variety is replacing it. People have begun buying everything from cars to industrial pumps depending on how quickly they can get specialized models. If a factory hasn't brought in flexible, computerized machining, it won't be able to stay competitive. America, he says, now lags behind. That's one reason the United States is awash in imports—foreign manufacturers have more flexible machines; they're better geared to speedily deliver new products into the marketplace. Nations that succeed at that, he says, will have the highest standard of living.

The government of West Germany understands that. It works hard to funnel both loans and grants into commercial-toolmaking R&D. Like most German businessmen, the executives at Traub and Scharmann don't like to talk about that. It's a matter of pride. Government assistance, they say, has been minor. But in the past five years, Traub has received almost a million dollars in government research-and-development aid, and Scharmann several million.

In the last decade, the American machine-tool industry has shrunk by almost two thirds. It didn't have to happen. Nor does it have to continue. Even as U.S. plants have closed, Japanese and European machine-tool makers have built new plants on U.S. soil. A handful of American toolmakers have gained ground, as well, upgrading products and attacking world markets, but their numbers are too few. And it's the same across the range of machine making—from manufacturers of textile equipment to steel-rolling mills.

Ernst Ehmann does not think it's too late for America's machine industry to come back.

"Nothing is permanent," he says, "American companies can regroup. But it can't be done in a year. It will take a long-term strategy. If the U.S. companies have to continue to show a profit every three months, then it's going to be very difficult."

WEST GERMANY isn't ignoring high-technology industries typical of those in Boston and Silicon Valley. But drive around its industrial enclaves and you'll see an even more widespread use of advanced technology. It's blended into factories, built into machines made by companies like Traub and Scharmann. Many Americans are still convinced we should move from the smokestack era to the information age. The Germans think differently. Modern nations that lose traditional industry, they feel, will lose a mainstay of their wealth. They don't believe it has to happen; not if old and new are married together.

5

Sweden:
Producing
the Future

O N A September day in 1977, my boss at the Boston Consulting Group told me some executives from Volvo were coming to visit. Their first priority was to discuss corporate strategy, but they also wanted to talk about a broader issue—Sweden. In their view, the Swedish economy was in crisis. For the first time in forty years, its trade balance had gone consistently negative, and some of its biggest firms were almost bankrupt. As Sweden's largest company, Volvo wanted to understand why. The Volvo people thought I might be able to help.

I'd just taken a six-month leave to pursue an idea I'd been thinking about for more than a year—developing ways to apply corporate strategy to nations. I was especially interested in why certain countries succeed at world trade better than others. A Volvo planning team had apparently heard about speeches I'd given on the subject in Japan, and wondered if I'd do a presentation for them. I had two weeks to prepare. I knew little about Sweden, so I began research right away, wiring money to Stockholm for the country's annual statistical reports. I looked at where Sweden's employment was growing and where it was falling. I made lists of what companies were exporting and what companies investing. I tried to understand why some of its industries were expanding and others failing. I then compared Sweden's progress with other countries I'd been studying, such as Japan and West Germany.

The Boston meeting date came. There were three Swedes in the delegation. I waited while a BCG colleague finished our standard corporate-strategy presentation, and then it was my turn. I began by pointing out what they already knew—that Sweden's economy had grown in the 1960's, but stagnated in the seventies. The question, of course, was why. I told them it would take more than a few weeks' work to say what the problem was, but meanwhile, I could say what it wasn't. It wasn't lack of investment. Swedish industry had spent more on new projects in the seventies than the sixties, and more relative to its size than most other countries. But for some reason, it wasn't getting a payback anymore, either in productivity or export.[1]

As I spoke, one of the Swedes got up and began to pace. I kept going, pointing out that Sweden's biggest trading falloff had been with Central Europe, particularly West Germany. That, I said, would have made sense had their currency gone up against that of other European nations, hiking the price of their goods, but it hadn't. Something more structural was going on. I showed them some tools I'd developed for applying corporate strategy to countries.[2] With more time, I said, I thought we'd have a chance to understand Sweden's problems.

The Swede who'd been pacing was named Bo Ekman, Volvo's top planner. He asked if I'd be willing to make this same presentation to the company's chairman. Volvo, he said, might want to push for us to try something unique—a business-strategy study on how a whole nation could become competitive again.

I PREPARED for the meeting with Volvo's chairman, starting with some general reading on Sweden. The world business press, I found, had a uniform view on why the country was in economic trouble. First of all, most Swedes didn't work enough—1,640 hours per year compared to 1,930 hours for Americans and over 2,100 hours for Koreans. The country's unions were among the world's most powerful—90 percent of the work force were members as opposed to 21 percent in America. Workers' wages were high, and benefits were the most elaborate anywhere. Have a baby and you and your spouse could split a year off with pay. If either you or your children got sick, you could stay home at 90 percent salary, with government covering all medical bills. Retire after age sixty and you'd still get 90 percent of your salary. Interested in more education? You could go back to school full time whenever you wanted, with your job guaranteed and government covering tuition. If your company no longer needed you, government would retrain you with pay and find you another job.

To support all that, Swedes paid some of the highest taxes in the world. Nevertheless, at the time, 1977, the government was in deep debt. Its budget deficit was about to pass 10 percent of the country's gross national product, a dangerously high point.

Workers who don't work enough, cradle-to-grave welfare, high taxes, high wages and benefits, strong unions, big government debt— it was a recipe, the business press said, for economic failure.

Then there was Volvo. It was in trouble, as well. At the time, auto experts were saying a car company needed scale to succeed globally— at least 1 million cars per year—but Volvo was making only two hundred thousand. The experts also said a competitive car company needed flexible worker rules. Volvo didn't have them. Management couldn't lay off workers, close plants, change factory processes, or make any major investment without a nod from the union. Then there was the Swedish work week. At a time when the Japanese were getting ever more aggressive and disciplined, Volvo's employees worked fewer hours than those of any other automaker. The company also had the smallest home market—8 million people compared to 60 million in West Germany and 216 million in the United States. Making things worse, it had to share that market with Saab. Volvo, the articles were saying, was like Sweden itself—strong unions, short work week, small home market, uncompetitive scale—a sure recipe for business failure.

Today, twelve years later, things are a bit different. Sweden's living standard is among the world's highest, its trade balance in solid surplus, its federal treasury in balance.[3] As for Volvo, it's now one of the most profitable automobile companies in the world, exporting more cars to the United States than BMW, Mercedes, Renault, or Peugeot—all of which are bigger.[4] I did do the study of Sweden's economy Bo Ekman suggested. I also worked several years on Volvo's corporate strategy. I had the advantage of seeing, from the inside, how both company and country turned themselves around.

A FEW WEEKS after the meeting in Boston, I flew to Göteborg, Sweden's second biggest city, home of Volvo. I gave my presentation to its chairman, Pehr Gyllenhammar, not yet forty at the time. When I was done, he said it echoed what he'd feared, that Sweden's problems were more than a phase in the business cycle, they were signs of decline. Since his own company produced 90 percent of its cars and trucks at home and sold a full 85 percent abroad, he worried that an uncompetitive Sweden would pull Volvo down with it. He wasn't sure how to fix the problem, but thought a good place to start was the kind of study I'd proposed. He told me it would need the backing of government, and asked if I'd be willing to give the presentation once again, this time to the minister of industry.

A week later, I did. When I was done, we spent an hour talking.

The minister told me how the downturn was affecting his own office. He was being buried by bailout requests from struggling companies— big requests. At first, it was easy enough to handle. If you're in charge of national industrial development, and a major employer—a Swedish Chrysler—is about to go under, you do whatever is necessary to save jobs. If that means bailouts, so be it. But what happens when four Chryslers come to you with their hands out, and then six, and a dozen? That was now happening. Shipbuilders, paper companies, and steel-makers had all come to the government for money, some returning a second and third time.[5] The minister no longer knew what to do. Were bailouts saving the economy? Or were they pouring hundreds of mil-lions down a rathole? That, he said, was one of the things Sweden's government had to figure out. Until it did, Sweden's economic policy would be no policy at all, just crisis management. It reminded me of America's approach, where government gives plenty of handouts—bil-lions of dollars each year in quotas, tax breaks, and loan guarantees— but not by coherent design; it's all determined by who lobbies the hard-est. Sweden, said the minister, wanted a better strategy. And he, too, felt a study of the whole economy would be the way to start. Could we do it? I told him we'd never done anything on that scale before, but if they were ready to experiment, we were, too. He asked how soon we could start.

Afterward, things happened quickly. To fund the study, the minister worked with Volvo's chairman to form a coalition of government, cor-porations, and banks. I organized a Boston Consulting Group team of eight people, setting up in Stockholm in January 1978. Our goal, in essence, was to answer one question: How do you turn around a high-wage, Western, trade-imbalanced nation?

I HAD more than a few midnight sessions with Bo Ekman. He helped me to understand Sweden: the outlook of business, unions, the public. Our study, he said, could be crucial. As a planner, he saw Sweden not for where it was but where it was going, and it worried him. He was especially alarmed at the foreign deficit. How could a nation be sover-eign, he wondered, if it's beholden to foreign bankers? One reason Sweden had gotten that way, he felt, was the country's attitude toward industry. Manufacturing was seen as part of the past. Few among the young wanted to go into it. They were drawn, instead, toward services. Most of the public thought that was good for the economy. Services were the future. Sweden was shedding its industrial skin, moving toward a new, more promising era—the information age. But Ekman saw it differently, not a nation shedding its skin, but one losing its mus-cle. Industry, he felt, was fundamental. It was what created wealth. It created service jobs, too. Maybe only 20 percent of the jobs in the economy were in manufacturing, he said, but another 40 percent grew directly out of manufacturing. Legal jobs did, accounting jobs did, computer jobs did. Close down factories and jobs like that will eventually disappear, as well. In short, thought Ekman, lose industry and your standard of living will decline. It's not that he resisted change; he agreed industry had to evolve. You don't keep making horseshoes—you switch to tires—but you need production. Too many Swedes, he felt, didn't understand that anymore.

THE country's problems, our study team found, began during its greatest prosperity—the early 1970's. Sweden's trade balance was positive, its industrial production at an all-time high, and company profits booming. Then, in 1974 and 1975, the boom helped unions win a 40 percent national wage hike.[6] It took effect at the worst of times—just after the energy crisis pushed the world into recession. Global auto demand went from 30 million cars in 1973 to 25 million in 1975.[7] That, of course, hurt Volvo and Saab specifically, but most of Sweden's industries were hit just as hard. Government came up with a clever but risky response. It urged companies not to cut back on production. Better to keep manufacturing, keep Swedes working, build big inventories so Sweden would be ready to meet demand when recovery eventually came.[8] Most companies did just that, but the policy failed. The recession stretched on, leaving Swedish industry buried in backlogs, unable to sell. Then the Swedish crown strengthened against the dollar, pushing export prices up and sales down even more.[9] Men like Ekman saw the country in crisis.

But the public didn't. Ekman later told me how audiences dismissed him when he'd give speeches warning of bad trends. What crisis? Unemployment was low, consumer spending high. No one cared that it was because overproduction and foreign borrowing had falsely pumped up the economy. As long as things seemed good on the surface, it didn't matter what was going on underneath. Yes, there was a foreign-trade deficit, but to most, that was just a phrase. All these warnings about manufacturing decline—they didn't square. Weren't there always economic doomsayers? Perhaps a few industries were struggling—shipbuilding, steel, forestry—but they'd come out of it. This would pass.

Then, in 1976, the struggling industries began to go over the edge. A shipbuilding firm went bankrupt, and another followed. One of the nation's big iron-ore mines went bankrupt. Forest-product firms went bankrupt and steel mills followed. The equivalent for the United States would be to have Ford, IBM, International Paper, and U.S. Steel go under, all in one year. The government was forced to go beyond bailouts; to maintain jobs, it had to take over companies. That kept unemployment under control, but people were finally alarmed. The crisis moved from the business section of the newspapers to the front page. The country, however, was divided over what to do.

Corporate Sweden charged that the crisis was labor's fault. Labor was bleeding industry white, driving wages and benefits out of control. Government monetary policy was the other villain; Sweden's currency was too high, making it tough to sell goods abroad. The corporate world's solution was clear-cut: lower wages, lower benefits, lower currency.

Labor, on the other hand, saw an equally clear-cut solution: better management. Swedish executives, the unions felt, were making the wrong investments. And exports were going down not because of high currency, but bad marketing decisions.

Government was in the middle, shoveling bailout money. The newspapers, meanwhile, were full of other theories—the breakdown of the school system; the bad work ethic of the young; the decline of Western civilization. As for solutions, many felt it was best to simply let industry decline. Sweden's salvation would be a service economy. In the midst of that debate, we began our work. It was clear we faced a political problem as well as an economic one. Our proposals would mean nothing if we couldn't get a national consensus behind them. And at the moment, the country was badly split.

JUST AS the nation's problems began during the prosperity of the early 1970's, Volvo's did, too. The company made more profit during those years than ever before. Still, when Pehr Gyllenhammar became company president in 1971, he saw dangerous signs. Sweden's young—the most educated generation the country had known—wanted little to do with industry. Those who did go into manufacturing were alienated, and Volvo was paying a price. Absenteeism was high, over 15 percent a day. Annual turnover was higher, over 55 percent, and 300 percent in the worst departments. It got so bad that Volvo had to import the majority of its labor. More than 85 percent of new hires at its biggest plant—Torslanda—were foreigners; mostly Norwegians, Finns, and Yugoslavs. For years, Volvo's manufacturing strategy had been to buy the best technology. But the Torslanda plant was bristling with it, and both productivity and quality were still down. Space-age hardware, Gyllenhammar realized, wasn't the only answer. Something had to be done about the work force, as well. He turned to Berth Jonsson, his young director of human resources.

Were you to picture a typical champion of factories, it wouldn't be Jonsson. He comes across more like a social worker—soft-spoken, caring, a good listener. Industry's greatest goal, he'll tell you, is worker dignity. But he doesn't say that because he's a do-gooder, he also believes it's the best route to profits. It's a modern age, he'll insist, an educated age—the age of the mind. Start tapping that resource on the factory floor, Jonsson feels, and you'll find a new source of productivity. But back in the early 1970's he saw few corporations doing it. The mass-production world, Jonsson knew, still tended to worship Henry Ford's assembly line. Jonsson felt it was time to rethink that. Assembly lines had been fine for the last fifty years—and were still fine for unskilled Third World countries, but not educated nations. You can't hire people who've spent fifteen years training their minds and expect them to be happy tightening seven bolts a minute, no matter what the pay.

Jonsson still remembers arriving in Göteborg after being hired in 1971. Things were worse than he expected. The company's major plant, Torslanda, was a classic assembly-line behemoth. The main building was two thirds of a mile long and filled with thousands of workers at thousands of stations, each with a simple function—turning bolts, attaching a door lock, putting on a plastic strip. The cars cranked relentlessly down the line, allowing each employee only ninety seconds to do his or her job. It was mind-deadening labor, though Torslanda workers would tell you there were few minds to deaden. As the saying went, you left your head outside the factory fence.

Decades before, assembly lines had been welcomed—a better paycheck, an exciting opportunity to help build a new Sweden. But things were different now. People wanted to be craftsmen, not cogs. They wanted the right to use their brains—their judgment. The frustration of not being able to, Jonsson felt, was costing Volvo tens of millions of dollars. He could even measure it. First, there were the quality problems. Seventy percent of all cars had to be fixed after they came rattling off the line. The payroll was bloated by quality supervisors, absentee replacements, and people fixing flaws. The key measure of efficiency—man-hours per car—seemed frozen. Volvo tried to improve productivity with technology—more robots, more electronics, more automation. But that only alienated workers more. The lesson for Jonsson was clear: An uninspired work force means uninspired profits.

Pehr Gyllenhammar agreed. He decided it was time to think about an entirely new kind of plant. He assigned a committee, including Jonsson, to come up with some ideas. Its goal was to devise a plant design that would break assembly-line boredom without breaking mass-production efficiency. After months of research, the committee still had no solution. No one in mass manufacturing, it seemed, was doing anything different. Then the committee talked with Torgny Karlsson, quality manager in Torslanda itself. Karlsson, Jonsson found, had been experimenting in parts of the plant with alternatives to the line. Torslanda was such a sprawling operation, it was possible to try new things unnoticed. Now, Jonsson's group began to notice.

Yes, Karlsson said, he had some ideas—but no one was listening to him.

What ideas?

Well, he said, instead of an assembly line, Volvo should use teams. That would allow workers to assemble entire sections of the car. Not only would that offer more challenge, Karlsson said, it would garner more loyalty. Workers would feel like craftsmen instead of automatons. They'd feel they were building Volvos instead of just tightening bolts. To heighten loyalty and improve productivity even more, Karlsson urged that the teams be allowed to supervise themselves; no foreman looking over their shoulders. Each group would decide for themselves who should do each task—assembly, material handling, machine maintenance, quality control. Let them use their heads, not just their hands, said Karlsson. He conceded it would be a leap of faith. You'd have to trust workers to run themselves. But he was convinced that employee alienation had become industry's greatest problem. You want productivity, he said, you need to win back loyalty, and teams were the way to do it.

The project team thanked him.

Karlsson told them he doubted his ideas would make a difference. He'd been trying to talk about these things for years, and no one listened.

This time, it was different. Karlsson's experiment became the basis of the new plant proposal. Instead of putting cars on a conveyor with ninety-second work cycles, the committee proposed a movable dock. Each team would do one section of the car. When they'd finish, they'd pass the dock along to a second team; and on and on, until the car was done. It wasn't a complete break from the assembly line. There would still be repetition. The car would still physically move from stage to stage toward completion as the dock was handed along. But instead of spending only a minute or two on the same job over and over, workers would spend around half an hour on a whole range of tasks. It would be a step away from the human robot, a step toward craftsmanship. That is, if it worked. The gamble was that shop floor employees would be able to oversee themselves—not just with competence, but heightened efficiency. That was especially important. The new plant design would cost 10 percent more than a traditional assembly line. If it was going to pay for itself, it would have to deliver better productivity.

Most of Volvo's manufacturing people were against the idea. Industry had spent fifty years refining the assembly line, they said. This would be a clear step backward. The final decision was up to Pehr Gyllenhammar, the CEO. He'd shown before that he was ready to go against the status quo. When he came to Volvo, he decentralized management, cutting the headquarters staff from 1,500 people to 100. Now he decided to do the unorthodox again; he backed the new plant design. In 1972, in a city in southeast Sweden called Kalmar, Volvo began construction. It wouldn't be a big plant; it would assemble only about thirty thousand cars a year, less than 15 percent of company production. But it would be framed around a team concept, perhaps the first time in decades a modern mass-assembly plant had broken with the legacy of Henry Ford.

JONSSON expected the idea would be ridiculed throughout the car world. He was right. Other mass manufacturers considered it idealistic, or just plain dumb. Inside Volvo, Jonsson and the project team were called radicals, out to gamble a great company on a social experiment. It would never work. It was clearly inefficient.

The project team argued that the old assembly line was even more inefficient. First, they said, it ignored personal pace, forcing slow workers to do half a job and fast ones to waste time waiting for the next car. Second, if someone made a mistake, there was no way to stop the line; instead, you had to break the car open at the end to fix parts that weren't tightened, headlights that didn't work, engines that didn't run smoothly. Third, the line bristled with unnecessary bodies—foremen to watch over workers' shoulders, material handlers to feed the line, trainers because of turnover, quality-control people to eyeball everything. And you still needed dozens more to fix bad cars. Teams, Jonsson felt, could do most of those jobs themselves. It would also get around one of the biggest inefficiencies of all—balance problems. That's a technical term that becomes very untechnical if you ever see it. Take the assembly person assigned to put on cruise control. It's only needed on every fourth or fifth car, so between them, he has less to do. His time's wasted. That's a balance problem. Add dozens of other special-feature installers and you have a lot of waste—enough to cut a line's efficiency by 20–30 percent. With consumers demanding more options than ever in their cars, the problem was only getting worse.

Teams, Jonsson felt, would solve all that. They'd also allow for craftsmanship, camaraderie, and the kind of caring that would encourage workers to want to build it right the first time. Loyalty, Jonsson felt, meant productivity.

The skeptics didn't buy it. They told Jonsson he was living in a fantasy world. Talk to the workers sometime, they said. Half don't even speak Swedish, and the other half don't care. They barely follow orders as it is, how can you trust them to run things?

The hope, said Jonsson, was to attract the new generation of

Swedes back in—the educated young who felt industry had grown too depersonalized, too hierarchical. There was only one way to woo them, he said: by offering a challenge as well as a paycheck. Teams would allow that—a chance to use their judgment; a chance to do work they could control.

Soon, Kalmar was completed. The plant started badly—full of bugs. Jonsson expected that. This was untried territory. He knew it would take a year or two to get to speed. But things went even slower than that. The mid-1970's drop in world sales happened right after the plant opened, forcing it to produce fewer cars than planned, only 18,000. That hurt efficiency.

The skeptics weren't patient. Day to day, they would approach Jonsson.

"Academic stuff," some said.

"Experimentation," said others.

Each had his own point. There was the materials-flow man. At Torslanda, Volvo had an army in charge of that, forklifting loads of parts back and forth on a structured schedule. Workers were like baby birds, they swallowed what they were fed. At Kalmar, however, it was up to the teams to order what they needed by computer. The parts would then be brought their way on unmanned vehicles. At first, that went badly, and the Torslanda man told Jonsson he could have predicted as much.

"You can't let people decide what they want," he said. "You have to give them what they need."

But slowly, Kalmar began to prove itself. First, there was absenteeism. At Torslanda, it was usually over 15 percent. At Kalmar, it went down to 9 percent—high for America, but well below the Swedish average. Then there was turnover. It had been one of Jonsson's biggest worries about Kalmar. To work there, you needed training—computer literacy, management talent, a craftsman's skills. It took months to teach that. If someone at the new plant quit, the company couldn't just plug in an untrained hire as replacement. There was no way Kalmar could afford Torslanda's turnover, which was over 55 percent. It turned out Kalmar didn't have to. Turnover was less than 10 percent.

Then there was quality. It started a little rough, but in time, defects plummeted a full 40 percent below Torslanda.

That left one crucial measure: productivity. If it lagged too far behind the assembly line, Kalmar would be a failure. Jonsson tried to tell the skeptics to be patient. But after two years, Kalmar still lagged. Jonsson was told to face it: The team idea was a slower way to build cars. It was lousy business.

Then productivity began to climb. The Torslanda people still weren't sold. It's no surprise that productivity would speed up a little, they said, but it would top out. Then, after three years, Kalmar made it. Its man-hours per car had equaled Torslanda. There were grudging admissions. All right; it was as good as the assembly line, but not better. And if you figure that the plant cost 10 percent more, it was still a step below in profit. A few months later, in the summer of 1977, Jonsson was in the office of Karl-Eric Nilsson, Kalmar's plant manager. They'd just gotten the latest productivity sheets. They put them side by side—one from Torslanda, the other from Kalmar. On direct labor alone, Kalmar was slower—three man-hours per car more than Torslanda. But because of better quality, there were two man-hours less of fixing time at the end. Then there was the biggest boost: Because the Kalmar teams managed themselves, the plant needed fewer foremen, production planners, material handlers, and machine-maintenance people. When they added in those savings, the lines crossed. Kalmar's productivity was ahead.

Subordinating machine to man was proving more efficient than man to machine. The difference, Jonsson knew, would be tens of millions a year in profit. Even Henry Ford, Jonsson was convinced, would listen to that kind of argument. But Kalmar was still only a small plant, a small experiment. The big challenge, Jonsson knew, would be converting Volvo's main assembly plant in Torslanda.

But that would have to wait, if it came at all. Before Volvo could afford another major plant investment, it would need a major leap in sales. Sales, however, were falling. That left Volvo with another challenge as difficult as its assembly-line crisis. It needed a new product.

IT HAD BEEN almost ten years since the company had designed a new car. The last model was called the 100 series. It had since been upgraded to the 200 class, though that had mostly been cosmetic. The basic machine had now become old technology. The corporation's car division told Gyllenhammar he had to invest in something new. The chairman said it would be difficult. Designing a new line would cost the company a half-billion dollars, a huge risk. Volvo wasn't like General Motors, which could easily weather a few failures. If Volvo gambled on a new model that didn't sell, it could go bankrupt. Gyllenhammar didn't want to chance that without a cushion. It left him with one alternative. All over Europe, small car companies were merging with big ones to get the scale to survive. Audi joined VW, Lancia joined Fiat, Citröen went with Renault. Car gurus said Volvo would have to do the same: either merge or decline. During the early 1970's, Volvo resisted, but then came recession. By January 1977, with sales having dropped from a 1974 high of 224,000 to under 180,000, Pehr Gyllenhammar gave in. He called Marcus Wallenberg, the legendary Swedish banker who controlled Saab, and found a sympathetic ear. Saab, even smaller than Volvo, was locked in the identical tailspin. On May 5, 1977, a deal was announced. Sweden's two car companies would merge. Publicly, it was put forth as a great, visionary marriage. Privately, a lot of people knew the companies had no choice. It was hard for such proud corporations to give up their independence, but once the principals got past that, there was excitement. A merger would mean pooling resources, and for Volvo, a chance at finally designing a new model.

But at the last minute, factions within Saab began to rethink the deal. The white-collar union, convinced they'd be overshadowed by the more powerful Volvo elite, pulled back. So did the head of Saab's truck division. The deal unraveled.

It was around then, 1977, that I first met Pehr Gyllenhammar. I remember him as a man weighed down by problems. Gambling on a new product, he knew, could be ruinous, but with sales falling, not gambling could be equally ruinous. Meanwhile, except for Kalmar, productivity and quality were suffering. The solution was to build the team concept into Torslanda, but with the Saab deal aborted, he couldn't afford that investment any more than a new-model investment. All he could do was begin a search for another angel to give Volvo the funds it needed. At the moment, there were no prospects. And then there was his other concern—Sweden itself. The economy was in decline, and Gyllenhammar worried it would drag Volvo down with it. That's why he'd pushed so hard to get our Sweden study launched.

THE RESEARCH took us eight months. We began with statistical reports, then visited hundreds of companies, analyzing their costs, their market prospects, their foreign competition. Most of our team members were in our late twenties, all of us charged up by being in on something groundbreaking. We interviewed during the day, then stayed up past midnight trying to piece our material into a pattern. At first, we did our best to live like Swedes, eating herring and fish paste, but soon gravitated back to burgers and pizza. Industry by industry, we peeled back the layers. It was clear many were in trouble, but not for the reasons each side said. It wasn't high wages or bad management after all; the true problems lay far beyond Sweden's borders.

Ore mining was typical. We journeyed north to see one of the country's best-known mines. It was obvious the company hadn't held back on investment. Going into that mine was like descending into the twenty-first century. Here we were, north of the arctic circle, and the company had still managed to burrow a mile underground, drilling ore most firms would have dismissed as inaccessible. The technology was state of the art, the conditions humane. But it wasn't enough. Even another billion dollars' worth of equipment wouldn't have been enough. The ore mine I'd seen two years before in Australia had veins fifty feet thick, right at the surface and of top-grade purity. Brazil had discovered some extraordinary reserves of its own. This mine, on the other hand, was like most in Sweden: It had veins a half-foot thick, full of impurities, and thousands of yards deep. For the last few years, the Swedish industry's one advantage had been location. Since it was right there in Europe, it was able to ship ore cheaply to its neighbors, many of whom were major world customers. But the birth of the supertanker changed that. The Australians—and Brazilians—were now able to land ore in nearby Rotterdam 30 percent cheaper than Sweden could.[10] The Swedish mine managers had known about the foreign threat, but hadn't seen how fast it was growing. Clearly, for this industry, the days of growth were over.

Our study team's next focus was Sweden's shipbuilding industry, the biggest in Europe and second biggest on earth. I went to see one of the country's largest yards, in a southwestern port city named Udde-valla. Again, the shipbuilding companies hadn't held back on invest-ment. There were dozens of huge cranes lifting massive steel plates, which were speedily attached to the skeleton of a ship with automatic welding machines. It was as automated a yard as you could build. A manager there insisted its technology guaranteed it would turn around. He conceded the yard was losing money at the moment, but was con-fident it would bounce back.

We began to explore whether he was right. The yard's losses, we found, certainly hadn't been due to bad management. The shipbuilders had seen the foreign threat early, first Japan, then Spain, then Brazil, and finally South Korea, and they'd acted. They knew they couldn't beat dollar-an-hour competitors on wages, so they tried to leap past them with automation. They shifted their product line to supertankers, the easiest kind to automate, then bought the latest equipment. Yards all over Sweden did the same. It was the one way, they felt, for a high-wage country to win: increasing productivity. It was an admirable strat-egy. But despite the yard manager's confidence, it seemed to be failing.

To find out why, I went to see the competition. I chose a new yard on the southern coast of South Korea. The moment I arrived, I saw that the battle was over. The Koreans had just finished installing new Euro-pean equipment, almost as sophisticated as what I'd seen in Uddevalla. It was an unbeatable combination—low wages and advanced technol-ogy. The Korean manager told me he'd recently received his first super-tanker order. They'd be delivering it for millions below anything Sweden could match.

Much later, GE would use part of Uddevalla's same strategy with compressors—leaping past low-wage rivals with automation. And they'd win. But there were several differences. One, GE made a leap in product design, too. The Uddevalla yard hadn't; all it had done was to take a straightforward product, the supertanker, and improve manufacture alone. Second, GE had designed its own unique factory technology, making it hard for rivals to duplicate. The Swedish shipbuilders, on the other hand, had bought standard equipment easily accessible to the Koreans. And unlike GE's new compressor factory, Uddevalla's equipment was simple to operate. Low-skilled Koreans had no problem running similar machines. If a high-wage country's going to leap past Third World rivals, it can't do it with just any technology, it has to be with technology that requires high skills. Swedish shipbuilding hadn't been able to do that. Uddevalla's yards were still better, twice as efficient, but with Korean wages an eighth of Sweden's, that wasn't enough.[11] Certain industries are destined for the Third World, and this, our study team realized, was one. Finally, we found Sweden had made one other global miscalculation. Just after the Swedes had geared up to build supertankers, high oil prices drove down world demand. It left Swedish shipbuilders in the worst of positions—competing for fewer customers with a costlier product.

So far, we'd looked at two industries, and in both cases had found the same problem. The Swedes were being undercut not by forces at home, but from afar. And no bailouts, no reasonable wage restraints, no better marketing, no investments, no new technology, would make a difference.

HAKAN FRISINGER had spent most of his career building pieces of Volvos—he ran the company's engine and transmission plants. In 1975, he was given a major promotion—Pehr Gyllenhammar made him head of all Volvo car factories. If Frisinger was honored by his new job, he was disillusioned by what he found. "Worse than anyone could expect," he would later say. He discovered cars being shipped out with terrible paint jobs, doors that wouldn't open, engines that leaked. In America, he found that Volvo had an absurd oversupply—thirty-two thousand cars in storage at the harbor, many of them rusting. At one point, he noticed a backlogged car that was unintentionally two-toned—light green on top and dark green on the bottom. He felt forced to spend $40 million to recall and repaint tens of thousands of cars, money he could ill afford. With sales dropping and Kalmar still unproven, it was more urgent than ever that Frisinger improve company performance. That meant making better cars and more efficient factories, but he had to do it the hard way. Since he didn't have the money for sweeping restructuring or major technology investment, he had to do what Tom Blunt would call block and tackle grunt work: hundreds of subtle adjustments. Frisinger feels that should always be part of a manager's strategy. A successful company, he will tell you, must be open to building new Kalmars, but it's equally essential to keep fine-tuning old operations.

He went to work, chopping costs, thinning executive ranks, then taking on quality. He met with plant managers, then supervisors, and even went to each factory floor to rally workers with speeches. He formed thirty quality teams, and personally trained each one. He set hard goals for performance, but allowed each plant to come up with its own strategy for delivering. At one point, he ordered two Oldsmobiles, which cost half as much as Volvos, and had them parked at the gate of each factory. It was Frisinger's way of reminding everyone that Volvos had to be worth twice as much. Another time, in March 1976, he learned that Volvo's Belgian factory was lagging badly. Frisinger's response was to order production stopped. Then, the next day, he flew down. The machines were silent, the workers sitting idle. Frisinger began to move from department to department, talking out why the plant couldn't meet its goals. Each time someone gave him a specific, he promised it would be fixed. When some workers complained that their tools weren't good enough, for example, he made sure they got new ones. By the time Frisinger left two days later, dozens of changes had been made. Within weeks, the factory began to improve. By 1977, Frisinger felt his streamlining was beginning to pay off. But sales still lagged. Like many others at Volvo, he knew there was only one answer to that—a new model.

The chairman, however, still didn't have the cash to invest in one. So far, Pehr Gyllenhammar hadn't been able to find an angel to replace Saab as a partner. Finally, he decided there was only one other place to turn—government. Lately, it had been bailing out bankrupt steel and shipbuilding firms. It seemed logical there would be help for the country's biggest company, as well. But government said no. It conceded Volvo was going through rough times, but it wasn't the same as going bankrupt. It was ironic, perhaps, that government was so drained by keeping sinking companies afloat that it couldn't help promising companies invest in new products, but in essence, that's what its policy had become. It was a policy of crisis control rather than growth. And the people at Volvo felt they were being forced to pay part of the price.

That's when the company tried its boldest move—some would say its most desperate. The search for an angel took Volvo to the door of an unlikely partner. Just before Christmas of 1977, a memo was hand-carried from Gyllenhammar to Norway's prime minister. The proposal was to sell 40 percent of Volvo to the Norwegian government. In return, Gyllenhammar wanted two things. One, enough cash for that sorely needed investment. Two, a piece of the oil and gas reserves Norway had just discovered beneath the North Sea. Energy was a boom business, something Gyllenhammar felt Volvo needed to strengthen its future. The response was good. Norway was happy to have a piece of the region's biggest company. After months of negotiation, the two sides agreed.

It became an emotional issue for Sweden, spread across the front pages every day. Selling part of Volvo to outsiders, some felt, was like selling a piece of the flag. Bo Ekman, Gyllenhammar's chief planner, was at the forefront of the debate, arguing that the deal with Norway would make Sweden's biggest company stronger than ever. It was even a matter of survival, he said. He pointed out that the competition—the German and French automakers—were getting further and further ahead with new models of their own. Volvo had to respond. And even if the company started designing now, it would be five years before its first new car was in a showroom. Waiting much longer could make things truly desperate. Volvo management gave all it had to make the Norway deal happen.

OUR study team soon found that another big Swedish industry—steel—was being overwhelmed by the same kinds of forces that were crippling Swedish ore and shipbuilding. It was foreign competition again; the Koreans, the Brazilians, and, most of all, the Japanese. All had poured hundreds of millions into new mills, and were now invading Europe with cheap steel. In this case, Sweden had a chance at becoming competitive again with big investments, but there was a problem. Now that the world's carmakers and appliance makers were using more plastic and aluminum, the steel market was falling. Even in special high-strength and tool steels, long a Swedish preserve, competition was intensifying. It seemed to us that Swedish steel's only hope was to drastically downsize.[12] It would cost the country thousands of jobs. And there was yet another Swedish industry that seemed to be in trouble—forest products.

Forests are one of the country's proudest resources. Many Swedes we met had relatives who owned forests. The minister of industry himself had come from a forest company. Only a few years before, forestry had been a thriving field. But now, it, too, was threatened. Forest firms in western Canada, the southern United States, and Brazil had begun to push hard into the world market. Sweden fought back well, investing in modern pulp and paper mills, but as with ore, the competition had an advantage that was hard to match—nature. In Sweden, trees took eighty-five years to grow; in the southern United States, twenty-five years. In Canada, the trees grew almost twice as thick. Further, many of Sweden's forests were in hilly, rocky terrain, which made it terribly expensive to transport logs. Put all that together, and it was difficult for the Swedish forest industry to stay competitive. That didn't mean the companies were doomed. If they merged, rationalized, and invested in niche areas like coated writing paper, where production techniques were more important than raw-wood costs, many could succeed.[13] But like steel, this industry, we felt, had little chance of growth.

It seemed we had our answer to why Sweden's world trade was declining even as business investment increased. In the early 1970's, ore, steel, ships, and forest products made up 40 percent of Swedish exports. Now, despite massive investments, all four were in trouble. And it was clear government bailouts weren't going to turn the situation around. If the country was going to compete globally, government needed new kinds of policies.

In the summer of 1978, we finally sat down to write our report. By now, our team had become a national story. The press watched us closely. Soon, we knew, we'd be causing a lot of controversy. We were about to come out against bailouts for four major industries that had given jobs to generations of Swedes.

But we weren't going to leave it at that. Letting ore, steel, ships, and forestry decline might have been unavoidable, but it was no solution. Our basic mission was to help Sweden create wealth. That was the second part of our study.

At the same time we'd been researching Sweden's problems, we'd also been looking for companies with growth potential. Volvo was one, and we found others.[14] L. M. Ericsson, for example, had promise in phone-switching equipment, and Alfa Laval in plate heat exchangers and automated dairy farms. ASEA had a leading position in robots and power generation, Sandvik in cutting tools. There were other strong companies in transport, engineering, chemicals, and pharmaceuticals, all big exporters. They seemed to have three things in common: They'd studied the world market for niches they could win in, poured money into technical leadership, and developed good global-distribution networks. Atlas Copco was succeeding in rock-drilling machinery, Tetra Pack in packaging equipment and SKF in large ball bearings. Volvo's truck division succeeded by focusing on large vehicles. Clearly, the country had enough promising companies to rebuild Sweden's strength. But most needed help. Like Volvo, they were small in global terms, and burdened with Sweden's high wages and benefits. To stay world competitive, they needed to make large, risky investments in new factories and products.

Our idea was to have government start offering incentives for firms that could grow, not bailouts for firms in decline. The government wouldn't decide who could grow, but if a company was ready to invest in new plants, new products, or more export, government would help. Far better for Sweden to do that than waste money propping up bankrupt companies. But that left a problem. What about the workers of those bankrupt companies? Our solution was to put new industry where the old was declining. Yes, some of the ore mines had to be left behind, but not the miners—not if government could use incentives to steer new factories into ore-mining regions. Perhaps shipbuilding had to shrink, but the yard workers could be retrained to work in more competitive plants. It would be a two-pronged strategy: investment in tomorrow's products, retraining for yesterday's workers.

IN 1978, Hakan Frisinger got another promotion; this time, he was put in charge of the whole car corporation. By then, the Norway negotiations were moving well. In Frisinger's eyes, the deal would be essential, the key to bankrolling a new car generation. He was confident enough to begin hiring the design staff to do it. In mid-1978, he had 650 engineers. He gave orders to build that to two thousand by 1980. To help pay for it while he waited for the Norway deal to go through, Frisinger began looking for ways to save money inside Volvo. It was the same kind of proccess he'd gone through before—instead of searching for big windfalls, he sought to streamline through a hundred subtle adjustments. He studied balance sheets, walked through factories, and one by one, came up with ideas. Inventory, for example, was a problem. There seemed to be a lot of money tied up in it. Engines, transmissions, and pistons sat idle in warehouses for weeks. Cars themselves sat in warehouses too, waiting to be shipped. Once they arrived to the world's import yards, they sat in other warehouses waiting to go to dealers. To solve the problem, Frisinger formed a twenty-five-person team. They started by trying one of the first just-in-time systems in Europe. Gradually, they got engine inventories down from over a week to thirty-six hours, and soon even less.

Then they turned toward the overseas-warehousing problem. In some cases—green cars, for example—there were backlogs. In other cases—perhaps cars with leather seats—there were shortages. They solved it with a system that told shipping schedulers in the company's Göteborg headquarters precisely what models were sold around the world every week. That way, instead of simply filling import yards randomly, Volvo would know exactly what dealers themselves needed. The company then shaped production plans around the dealers' needs. That precision helped cut the total cars in the factory-to-dealer pipeline from two hundred thousand to sixty-five thousand, a huge savings. By 1979, Frisinger's fine-tuning had freed up an extra $200 million in cash, a healthy start on paying for his expanded pool of design engineers. Once the Norway deal went through, Volvo would be able to start on the new model immediately.

Soon the deal was voted on by the Norwegian government. It said yes. So did the Swedish government. The Volvo union, whose go-ahead was necessary, said yes, as well. Volvo was almost there. All the company needed now was the approval of two-thirds of its stockholders. They were set to consider it in February 1979.

They did not give their approval.

Frisinger and Volvo were stalled.

USUALLY, business-consulting reports are kept confidential, restricted to boardrooms. Our Swedish study was different. Soon it would be released to every newspaper and TV station in the country. We were hoping it would spark a fervent public debate. If these ideas were to pass, Sweden first had to understand its competitive problems—and hopefully be alarmed enough to act boldly. We knew that wouldn't be easy to make happen. Global economics isn't the kind of issue the public gets passionate about. And even if we did get it on the front pages, there was still the problem of convincing people our solutions were right. We weren't sure what would be harder to sell—specifics like ending shipyard bailouts, or our philosophy: that Sweden's future lay not in services alone, but in manufacturing. The philosophy part wasn't just words. As Berth Jonsson was finding out at Volvo, unless the young turned back to industry, the country's factories would languish, unable to compete with the Germans and Japanese, both of whom were seeing some of their best and brightest drawn to manufacturing.

We unveiled the study at a press conference in September 1978. We soon saw we wouldn't have to worry about engaging the public. The debate got hot quickly. Stop bailing out shipyards? Ore mines? That would be national suicide, people said. Of course those industries could be rescued. What's wrong with helping companies get through bad times?

Some called us Caesars, deciding what businesses should live or die. We argued that it was the world marketplace that was doing that, not us. Our job was to find a way to boost potential survivors. Besides, we weren't planning to pick winners and losers. We weren't saying cars should be supported first, machinery second, steel last. Our point was simply to replace handouts with incentives—such as loans for companies willing to invest in new products. If a steel company was ready to take on such loans, fine. But far better to offer incentives for growth than bailouts to bankruptcy cases.

But the criticism continued, from all sides. Conservatives felt we were being interventionist, giving government too big a role. The real problem, they said, was high wages and benefits, and we'd all but ignored that. Social Democrats, meanwhile, couldn't believe we'd neglected to criticize bad management. And they felt government should be given an even greater role than what we proposed.

Some of the criticism was useful. After speaking at the Swedish

Academy of Engineering Sciences, I was approached by Bertil Ohlin, one of the fathers of global-trade theory. He said he backed us, but would mix in one more ingredient: devaluing the currency. If industry was going to restructure—let go of old products and invest in more competitive ones—it would need all the help it could get to sell around the world. A lowered currency would give that help, making Swedish products cheaper. It was something we hadn't thought about. We'd grown convinced—rightly, I think—that fiscal policy alone wouldn't save Sweden; you can't tinker your way out of a declining economy. But restructuring alone would probably fail, as well. Ohlin made us see that Sweden needed both.

Altogether, we made seventy public presentations. The controversy continued throughout. Our sponsors had wanted a national debate on Sweden's competitive problems, and they got one. Magazines did cover stories. Sweden's version of *Business Week* started a regular column on what was dubbed "the Boston Report." Over morning coffee, Swedes were now talking about the importance of reviving manufacturing. Global competition had become one of Sweden's top issues. The daily financial news heightened the sense of urgency. The country's bad economic performance continued: By 1980, the national trade balance had fallen to its lowest point in history.[15] Clearly, that was because of industrial decline. Sweden simply wasn't selling enough goods to the world. Business saw it, unions saw it, and most important, the public saw it.

WITH THE Norway deal canceled, Volvo had only one place left to look for salvation—within. Gyllenhammar, the chairman, realized he had to leap into a new product line, despite having found no safety net, no angel. He knew he could fail for a dozen reasons—even bad timing. What if the new car was unveiled during a recession? Or fuel crisis? What if it got hit by competing lines from Germany or Detroit? What if it was simply a dud? All you had to do was remember the Edsel to realize new designs can be treacherous. The difference, Gyllenhammar knew, was that Ford had enough models to survive a bad gamble; Volvo didn't. A new car would cost the company a half-billion dollars. If they guessed the public's taste wrong, good-bye car company. What made it especially risky was the lead time—five years, minimum. What if they'd begun this in 1969, shooting for a big, powerful car—perfect for the times—and then, half a billion dollars later, found themselves starting production the day OPEC doubled the price of oil? Then there was the hardest challenge of all. Because Volvo exported 85 percent of all it made, the car would have to be right not just for Sweden, but a dozen countries.

Throughout 1979, Gyllenhammar struggled with ways to minimize the risks. Finally, the company came up with a strategy—a bridge strategy. It was the same approach used by Traub when it decided to first upgrade its old mechanical machines before leaping into computerized models. Volvo would take some of the features it was planning for its new car and first put them into an upgraded version of their standard car, the 200 series. They could have that done by 1981. Hopefully, it would reinvigorate sales, helping Volvo sustain investment in the new model, due in 1983, to be christened the 700 series.

NOW CAME the challenge of designing the product itself. With Volvo losing money,[16] management had to succeed. A young engineer named Dan Werbin was one of the key designers.

Werbin became interested in the auto business early, as a teenager, when he and a friend scraped together enough money to build a working sports car in a neighbor's barn. Their goal was to be as big as Ford one day. Then, having spent all their money, they took their one new car to be government-certified. A clerk told them that all they'd have to do was prove its safety by crash-testing three of them. That ended their car company.

But as he got older, safety became a fixation for Werbin. At college, he did his thesis on safety for trucks. Then he joined Volvo and found just the right culture. Safety had always been a priority at Volvo. Seatbelts had been installed in all Volvos as early as the 1950's. Pehr Gyllenhammar reaffirmed that commitment when he became Volvo's chief executive, organizing a team to come up with an experimental safety car that would be ahead of government regulations. Werbin was put on the team. He helped Volvo become the first company to make shoulder seatbelts standard, first to develop an antiskid braking system, and first with a steering wheel that folded away from the driver's chest on impact. Then there was the idea of making the car's front end crumple. American safety theory had been to make cars like tanks. But Volvo found that too sturdy a frame could cause bad whiplash, the most frequent crash injury. So Volvo's front ends were made to crumple—more damage to the car, but less to the passengers.

Gyllenhammar had also made Volvo a pioneer in pollution control. A few years later, when other carmakers were saying new pollution laws would be too costly to meet, Volvo had already met them. Werbin knew there was a reason Gyllenhammar had emphasized safety and pollution control. The chairman saw them as Swedish values, and was convinced that the most successful products are those that reflect a nation's best values. Werbin agreed. But when the time came to design a new model, he'd come to understand that something more was needed. Swedes, for example, tended to be practical, nonflashy people. So, through the mid-1970's, Volvos had reflected that value—they were practical, nonflashy cars. "A hairy Viking," is how Werbin once described them. That worked fine for a while, but Werbin had grown convinced the world market was getting ready for something more styled. He'd come to think that way in America, where he was sent as Volvo's resident engineer from 1973 to 1977.

Volvos, Werbin soon found, were seen by Americans as one step above the VW Beetle. They were transportation capsules; durable and reliable, but dull. "It will last for eighty years," people would say, "you can jump on it and it will survive." That had been fine for the non-materialistic sixties, but now Werbin saw the culture changing. Consumers were moving toward designer clothes and even designer appliances, like Cuisinarts. Soon, Werbin felt, the young professionals buying upscale jogging shorts would be affluent enough to afford upscale cars.

It helped him see where Volvo should go—toward prestige. In a way, it was the perfect niche for a high-wage manufacturer like Volvo to compete in. The big Japanese automakers were coming on strong with good, cheap cars, with the Koreans planning a similar assault. There was no way a small, high-wage company like Volvo could compete with them on price. When you have to pay your workers $15 an hour, it's hard to make a profit selling five-thousand-dollar cars. But you can do it with ten- or fifteen-thousand-dollar cars. And if you build those cars with quality, customers will pay the premium. Werbin's time in America was teaching him there would soon be more customers for that niche than ever before.

In 1978, Werbin returned to Sweden, now one of Volvo's chief designers. Soon he was named head of the product-development team assigned to upgrade the 200s and create a new 700 line. The goal was to meet a niche priced about 30 percent higher than the company's old transportation capsule. Higher price, Werbin knew, meant higher standards, so the first thing he did was to introduce a more rigorous testing system. He didn't want the same kinds of problems Volvo had in the early 1970's, when both its fuel-injection system and pollution controls malfunctioned after being introduced too quickly. If that happened at premium prices, it could sabotage the whole effort. When people pay more for a product, they want reliability.

Then it was time to move on to the actual design work. Werbin knew there would be limits. True, Volvo planned to go upscale, but it couldn't triple its prices to Mercedes levels. His goal was value for dollar, his target somewhere between Volvo and Mercedes. Knowing what to leave out would be as important as what to put in.

My consulting firm was able to help Werbin with that. Like most car companies, Volvo didn't have a good fix on exactly how much new features cost.[17] Instead, it made a rough guess by factoring in direct costs alone. For example, when the company computed the cost of a sunroof, it only added in two things: the parts and the pay for the people who installed it. We showed that more subtle factors—like the cost of design—were just as essential. Up until then, design costs were considered general overhead, like insurance and the light bill. We changed that by adding up engineers' time sheets to see exactly how many hours were spent on each new feature. We were able to key other general overheads to specific features, as well, like the cost of repairing assembly-line breakdowns. We were able to prove that many of those breakdowns were caused by one specific add-on—say, cruise control. The extra factory-repair expense, therefore, should be part of cruise control's costs. Similarly, we found that each retractable antenna needed another five dollars of labor at the receiving docks. That had never been factored in, either. This wasn't just nitpicking. With Werbin having to decide what new ideas to leave out or leave in, it was an enormous help to know precisely how much each would add to the overall budget. Color-coordinated interiors were one example. At first, Werbin had thought of offering more color options on the upgraded 200; material costs, it seemed, would add only another thirty dollars per car. We showed, however, that all the extra inventory, parts handling, and purchasing would make it over one hundred dollars. Werbin decided against it.

He did, however, want to make the car more luxurious and a bit sportier. So he upgraded the engine, even adding a turbocharge option, but he didn't go to the power levels of U.S. cars. It was more important, he felt, to spend that money on passenger comfort. So he did so, adding power mirrors, seat heaters, and an adjustable back support for the driver. But he stressed the hidden engineering most of all. Reliability, Werbin felt, was worth any ten cosmetic options. He added a new suspension system with redesigned dampers and springs for better handling. Werbin was especially concerned that the car perform well in all climates. Because of Swedish winters, Volvos had been fine-tuned for cold weather, but not hot. So Werbin himself began spending two weeks each summer in California's Death Valley to test the car. The first year, his Volvo shut down as soon as he got there—vapor lock. The engineers soon solved it, then turned to the air-conditioning, which tended to fail if the car idled too long. They fixed that, too. Each year, Werbin kept coming back, always renting the same house— Dante's Inferno section, Furnace Creek neighborhood. Finally, there came a moment when he knew he'd made it. On a particularly hot day, Werbin headed for a long uphill. He could see cars on either side of the road, all overheated, but Werbin kept going, even with a three-thousand-pound supply trailer on his bumper. Still, he wasn't satisfied. One more test. He flipped on the air-conditioner and accelerated. The car sped up the hill at fifty, and out of Death Valley.

The upgraded 200 series was introduced in 1981. Over the next three years, sales soared from 173,000 to 236,000.

In 1983, the 700 line was ready for production. Werbin felt the car was just the right blend of such old values as durability and such new ones as performance. He would later point to one model as a symbol of the blend: a family station wagon with a turbocharged engine. But would they sell? Could a company now known for ten-thousand-dollar cars succeed at peddling models costing sixteen thousand dollars and more?

VOLVO management knew that a good car alone wasn't enough. If they didn't market it right—upgrading sales and service—their half-billion-dollar investment could fail. In the United States, the job of selling was up to Bjorn Ahlstrom.

He was assigned to America in the heart of the company's boom period, 1972. That year, Americans bought sixty thousand Volvos. Then came a string of setbacks. Sweden's wages and currency went up, Volvo's quality and productivity went down. By 1975, U.S. sales had plummeted to forty-three thousand. Ahlstrom began to fight back. First, he brought over Dan Werbin to suggest ways to adjust Volvo cars for U.S. buyers. Normally, that would be done by taking marketing surveys of customer preferences, but Ahlstrom thought an engineer could do it better.

Next, Ahlstrom turned to dealers. He dispatched teams of Volvo salespeople to talk with each U.S. dealer about upgrading operations—larger showrooms, more service bays, modern office equipment, better locations. He preferred coaxing the dealers through negotiation, but he was firm. Those who resisted were dumped. By the time he was done, total Volvo dealerships actually went down, from five hundred to four hundred. But because the survivors upgraded, coverage was broadened.

Ahlstrom used surveys to study his customers. Upscale buyers, he found, were more educated and demanding. He wanted to make sure his sales and repair people had the professionalism to serve them, so he increased the company's American dealer-training centers from four to twelve. The surveys showed that most customers' biggest fear was having a car tied up in the shop for weeks while parts had to be sent over from Sweden. He decided to solve that by getting parts inventories up to the same levels as American carmakers—about 96 percent. The carrying costs, he knew, would cut deeply into profits, but he was convinced it would win him more sales, and a payoff in the long run.

He also knew Volvo needed an upgraded image to match its

upgraded cars. That meant new advertising. He had to convince America's new upscale buyers that Volvos were no longer transportation capsules. But he didn't think putting the word *sporty* or *prestigious* in an ad or two was enough. Far better, he felt, to get the name associated with the right kind of life-style. To do that, he got Volvo to sponsor boating regattas and tennis tournaments.

He did, of course, do direct advertising, but targeted it. No network TV, for example. No reason to spend your budget hitting 20 million people, most of whom would never be customers. Instead, he chose publications like *Gourmet* and *Fortune*, to reach the few million most likely to buy. In the ads, he kept pushing the upscale image, but kept an equal focus on the car's soul—its safety and durability. Like Gyllenhammar and Werbin, he felt values win as many customers as luxury features.

Ahlstrom's program began to work. His marketing helped sell the design department's engineering. U.S. sales went up. By 1981, they'd climbed back to the sixty-thousand high of 1973. By 1986, they were almost double that—111,000 in America alone. And half of all cars bought were the expensive 700s.

The dollar's decline forced up Volvo's price, but it still managed to maintain its U.S. market share. The more it improved its cars, the more it improved service. Volvo was among the first to introduce a three-year comprehensive warranty. It was the first car to offer a twenty-four-hour-a-day 800 number to ask for quick breakdown service. More recently, Volvo started a ten-year financing program, both to help younger drivers move upscale and to underscore the durability of the car.

Volvo's other "Ahlstroms" achieved similar success in other nations. The company now produces three hundred thousand cars each year, up over 40 percent from the late 1970's, despite the average price being 25 percent higher. By the mid-1980's, the gamble on the new model was paying off.

But Volvo might not have succeeded had it not taken one other gamble. Most industrial companies rest on three broad pillars. Design is one, marketing is another. The third is manufacturing. In 1979, at Volvo, manufacturing was still in crisis.

THE PROBLEM was symbolized by Torslanda, the company's biggest plant. Despite Frisinger's efforts, its turnover remained high, its productivity low. Later, Gunnar Johansson would speak of the reasons. From 1974 to 1979, he worked on the line. Like most of his colleagues, he says, he left his head outside the factory gate. His job was to lift body sides onto a moving conveyor so they could be welded. He did one every minute, eight hours a day. He reported to work at 5:54 A.M. and left at 2:36 P.M. He remembers the times precisely—on the line, he says, you often watch the clock more than your work.

Did he ever stay on an extra minute or two to finish up—until 2:37, perhaps?

"No," he says. "Two-thirty-six."

What did he think about while doing the job?

"Nothing."

On occasion, he'd see problems with efficiency or design—problems that slowed production. He never mentioned them to his bosses. He didn't feel his ideas would be welcomed.

Did he at least check for quality?

"It was impossible," says Johansson. "As soon as each one was done, it got carried away."

In almost all of Torslanda's departments, other workers felt the same. Most will tell you they were either unwilling or unable to do a good job. The cost to Volvo was easily tens of millions of dollars in lost profits.

Frisinger knew that. He also knew that the team approach in Volvo's Kalmar plant was showing a very different result. Absenteeism there was down, productivity up. Beginning in 1979, Frisinger introduced the team concept to the engine plant in Sköde and the transmission plant in Köping with good results. Then, in 1982, Frisinger decided to try putting the team concept into Torslanda itself.

He did it one section at a time. Gunnar Johansson's department, the press shop, was one of the first. The difference, Johansson would say later, was night and day. Instead of a foreman giving orders, he and his colleagues were formed into teams, each allowed to manage itself. To keep everyone challenged, the job of team leader was rotated every two weeks.

The teams would begin each day with an informal meeting. Soon Johansson found himself arriving early to talk with the last shift about problems—machines that needed fixing, supplies that needed ordering. Then he and his teammates would divide up the day's jobs; material supply, machine maintenance, quality inspection. Every so often they would switch, to keep things interesting.

The people savings, Johansson says, were significant. The old way, they had fourteen foremen; the new way, six. Quality control? Johansson remembers men in green uniforms swarming everywhere to check each detail. Now, the teams were doing most of it themselves, a cut of twenty-five jobs. They also were able to order their own supplies by computer, which allowed the company to reduce the material-handling staff by ten people.

Turnover, Johansson found, fell drastically. With teams, it went from 40 percent to 12 percent. Quality problems fell too. Before, there were so many defective bodies waiting to be fixed, they had to be stacked in an outside yard. Soon flaws dropped by 90 percent, and the yard no longer had to be used.

Does Johansson today think Volvo team employees work harder?

No, he says, they don't.

"Smarter," he explains.

They work more conscientiously, as well, and he gives an example. In the old setup, if your machine broke, you yelled for maintenance, then sat down and hoped it would take as long as possible to fix it. In the new system, you have to fix it yourself. It's another job, but a welcome one.

"It means I'm important," says Johansson.

As other parts of Torslanda were converted, other workers found a new enthusiasm as well. Patrick Askfors's background was typical—a year of high school, a year of military, then the factory. Volvo put him on the engine assembly line. He hoped it would be the start of a career, but within months he hated the job. He felt like a cog. A foreman stood on one side of him, a conveyor belt on the other, both telling him what to do.

"If you can't influence your work," he would say, "you stop thinking."

Then he was put on a team. In place of an engine conveyor belt, the company installed a dozen workstations. Instead of having two minutes to do one task, Askfors was given up to an hour to do a whole section of the engine.

"Earlier," he says, "you just put one thing on, then you had to jump to another. Now, you get some feeling of building the whole engine. Much better, much better."

He used to touch 240 engines a day, now it's just 15 or 20.

Quality?

On the conveyor, when engines were done, workers would have to repair an average of eight or nine faults in each. Now, it's down to one or two.

"On the line," says Askfors, "I'd have thought twice, maybe three times, before I'd buy a Volvo."

And now?

No longer any question. He smiles. "Especially the engine."

With the new 700s selling well and Torslanda turning around, Volvo's corporate strategy was moving well. But Pehr Gyllenhammar was still worried about something he had less control over—Sweden's economy. If it continued to suffer, he knew Volvo would suffer with it.

He was glad to see that a consensus had begun to form around restructuring Sweden's economy.

THE worsening economy in 1979 and 1980 certainly helped people face the need for change, but looking back, I think something else helped even more: the worldliness of most Swedes.[18] They understood that their country was being threatened by new competitors playing by new rules. They were ready to admit they could no longer prosper by sewing patches on yesterday's industries. They needed new strategies, new niches suited to Sweden's strengths. Even those with the most to lose—unions representing declining industries—saw it.

I remember journeying north to visit a steel company. I'd arranged to meet with the mill's union leaders. Three of them were waiting for me in a small, cluttered office. I figured this was going to be rough. Here we were, foreign consultants in suits and ties, about to tell them that their mill couldn't compete; that the work force would have to face it. I said as much, then waited for some arguing. It didn't come. One finally spoke.

"Yes," he said, "we understand."

He went on to tell me he'd been part of a union tour of world steel mills. Japan, he said, was particularly disillusioning. Mills there were all using modern, efficient blast furnaces. They were even able to use cheaper coal in their coke ovens because of new blending techniques. His own company, he conceded, was too small to afford the same technology.

I asked what made the union decide to go on that trip.

Two reasons, the union men explained. One, to help them bargain with management. And two, to be better board members; the law in Sweden said that union representatives sit on company boards.

Other union members we spoke with were similar. They cared about wage hikes, of course, but saw it was no victory if their companies didn't stay competitive. That's why they'd been willing in the past to accept flexible work rules and new automation. It's why most were now ready to admit Sweden should perhaps let go of declining industries and start nurturing new ones.

Swedish management realized the same thing. After a year of front-page debate on global competition, they conceded that in certain industries, freezing wages wasn't enough to beat dollar-an-hour rivals around the world. The only way to export more was to find more promising product niches.

To get there would take cooperation, and it began to happen. Managers and union leaders began to discuss ways to develop growth strategies for their companies. On occasion, I was asked to help. For example, I worked with the metalworkers' union and machinery-industry executives on a study to develop export strategies. In a way, that was a symbol. After a long national debate, Sweden's two sides were working together. At a press conference releasing this particular study,[19] in the fall of 1980, the changed attitudes were ever more apparent. There was no union-management name-calling. Both sides were there at the podium stressing cooperation for a common mission: spurring more competitive manufacturing in Sweden.

By 1982, the government had begun to shape policies to help industry become more competitive. First, bail-outs were ended. Sweden had been spending between $500 million and $1 billion a year on that.[20] Now, that money would instead go into incentives for investment. Next, research support was increased. Soon Sweden would be spending a higher ratio of public money on commercial R&D than any other country—over 4 percent of GNP.[21] Sweden went on to improve its export insurance and financing packages, then started a loan fund to help companies develop products with a long lead time.[22] To get the loans, companies would have to invest, too. If they succeeded, the loan would be paid back at high interest. If they failed, it would be forgiven. In time, that program was actually making a profit for taxpayers.

Finally, there was the centerpiece of Sweden's restructuring efforts: a program to steer new factories toward hard-hit regions, near the declining ore mines, shipyards, and steel mills. Americans might think it unpalatable for government to order industry where to build, but this involved no pressure, just incentives. In Sweden, corporations are allowed to pay their taxes into a reserve fund.[23] It's set aside for future investment, but companies can only dip into the fund if the government agrees a project is in the national interest. Since it gives companies a chance at recapturing their taxes, none object. Now, the fund was opened wide to companies willing to locate in distressed areas. As a second incentive, government beefed up its already strong training network. Locate a plant near a closed ore mine, and the network would train the laid-off miners for you at state expense.[24]

As an umbrella over all those policies, the Swedish government added a final touch: the devaluation of the Swedish crown. Five years before, that might only have made lazy companies relax as their export prices fell. Now, it was different. Sweden's firms understood the danger of resting on old products. Companies everywhere had begun investing in new ones. The lower currency helped good products get attention in global markets.

Volvo was a symbol. In 1981, the corporation's car division lost money. In 1982, it made a profit of $125 million, chiefly because of the revamped 200 line. Management then projected a $300 million profit for 1983. Instead, the devaluation sent profits soaring to $800 million.

By 1984, Volvo sales were at an all-time high. Soon Torslanda and Kalmar couldn't keep up with demand. Pehr Gyllenhammar had a problem he would have never envisioned during the bad times of the late 1970's—he couldn't make enough cars. That meant he needed a new plant. But it left him with two dilemmas. One, where to put it? Two, could he afford it?

Volvo was still small for a world car company. It had just spent a massive amount of money on the 700 line. Despite two boom years, a major plant investment was well beyond its reach.

But it was just about then that Sweden's new industrial policies were taking hold. The bailouts had all but stopped. Older industries were downsizing or closing. The government was working hard to steer new plants toward regions where old ones were shutting down. Swedish officials were particularly concerned about the shipyard town I'd visited back in 1978—Uddevalla. Here was a city of forty-four thousand people with its main industry on its way out. Thousands faced losing work. Government saw the problem as its responsibility. It saw Volvo as an answer.

THE Uddevalla shipyard, begun in 1946, soon became one of the world's biggest. At its peak, in the mid-1970's, it's payroll was forty-five hundred—a quarter of the city's work force. Another forty-five hundred jobs rippled out of the yard. Then came foreign competition . . . and losses . . . and bailouts. Finally, the bailouts ended. In December 1984, it was announced that the yard would be closed. Some foresaw a local disaster. That's when government knocked on Volvo's door.

It wasn't by fluke. The Swedish Ministry of Industry stays in touch with Sweden's major companies. It knew Volvo needed a new plant. It knew the company was worried about financing it. The minister offered to help. Volvo, he said, would be allowed to tap into its tax reserve fund, on one condition: if it built the new factory in Uddevalla. By then, Volvo's fund was over $1 billion, more than enough. The offer was tempting, but Volvo had two concerns. If it was going to expand outside of Göteborg, it would need to transport parts. The sixty-mile road between the two cities, however, wasn't wide enough. Would the government build a better one?

The minister agreed.

Now Volvo had another concern. Management had decided to make the new Uddevalla plant a unique experiment. They wanted it to carry Kalmar's team concept to its ultimate form. At the new plant, each assembly team would probably be allowed to build the entire car, an ideal employee challenge but one that would demand the most skilled autoworkers in the world. Volvo wasn't sure it could afford retraining shipbuilders for that kind of job.

But again, no problem. Government agreed to set up a special school in Uddevalla and pay for the training itself.[25] Since the government had already allocated 2.5 percent of Sweden's gross national product for training—more than any modern nation—it could afford it. The two sides shook hands.

It wasn't government's only effort to help Uddevalla. Volvo planned to employ one thousand people there. When you added on everything from parts vendors to restaurants, another two thousand jobs would spin off. It was a blessing, but still short of what was needed to replace the yard. So government began trying to seed other business start-ups in Uddevalla with a fund geared for areas hit by economic shock. If you were willing to start a new venture in such areas, you could get cheap loans, or even outright grants—usually enough to meet half of your total investment.

Altogether, on top of releasing Volvo's tax funds, Sweden ended up spending $100 million to keep Uddevalla working. In one sense, that was high. But in America, we'd have paid $40 million for unemployment benefits alone, and after the money ran out, the workers would be on their own—their jobs gone, their skills useless. Something close to that happened when U.S. ore mines shut down. In Sweden, government steered enough new companies into declining ore-mining towns to employ most who'd lost their jobs. In America, ore mines in Michigan and Minnesota were also hurt by foreign competition. There, unemployment soared, and has stayed high for years.

IN THE SHADOW of Uddevalla's shipyard cranes, the new Volvo plant is now nearing completion. Instead of a single, sprawling factory, like Torslanda, it will be broken down into six gymnasium-sized workshops. The workers will be their own bosses, allowed to decide how to organize production. Each team will be given control of its own budget—allowed to buy tools and recruit new members. Instead of automatons, they'll be craftspeople, but backed by some of the world's most advanced technology—computers to order parts, robots to bring them, microprocessor-controlled hydraulic platforms to angle the car into more accessible positions.

Volvo chose to keep one of the Uddevalla shipyard structures a part of its new factory. It cost more to convert the structure than to build from scratch, but the company felt the symbolism was important. In that converted structure, through 1986 and 1987, Volvo began experimenting with its first workshop. One of those on the trial team was Kristina Hallberg.

She'd begun work at the Uddevalla shipyard in 1973, in her mid-twenties. She presumed the yard would always be there. It had seen fathers, sons, and even grandsons follow each other through its gates.

Then Kristina Hallberg began to hear about falling profits, and government bailouts. In 1984, when an offshore oil company canceled two tanker contracts halfway through construction, she understood it was only a question of time. Soon afterward, she heard the news. The yard was done, and so was her welder's job. But she soon found she had options. Sweden's National Training Board quickly set up a new center near the yard. She enrolled in a machinist's course. Worried about Uddevalla's future, she grabbed the first job she could, at a paper company. But it was dull work, so she took one more try, applying to Volvo. The difference, she will tell you, is remarkable. She quickly found there was no reason to worry about getting along with her boss; she didn't have one. There was an overall supervisor, but the decisions on how to do each day's work were left to her assembly team.

Was it that different at the shipyard?

"Do that—do that," she recalls. "It's all they said." At Volvo, she feels something she never felt at the yard: loyalty. It's because the company lets her use her judgment. In return, she wants to give back productivity. She feels that she and the company share a mission: finding ways to build cars faster and better. She'll tell you it's the only way for a country like Sweden to beat low-wage competition. She'll also tell you she wants to prove to management that workshops can be efficient. All her colleagues feel the same, she says. It's why they constantly suggest ways to streamline production. She never made suggestions at the yard, but this job is different; she wants it to succeed. She wants to show the company it's worthwhile to let her use her head as well as her hands.

Martin Rybeck, Torslanda's plant assembly manager, speaks of how important it is to get worker suggestions.

"All cars have some bad design," he says. "It costs money to assemble bad design, and it'll cost in the field. But if you have knowledgeable workers, they'll point it out, so you can change it."

Kristina can't imagine finding a better job.

"People who work on a line," she says, "they're not satisfied."

Is she?

She smiles. "I don't look at my watch."

VOLVO's management understands Uddevalla will take years to perfect. But they're convinced it will become the company's most productive plant. As of late 1987, Torslanda was taking thirty-six man-hours to build each car. At Kalmar, because of better-quality and leaner staff, they did it in thirty-one man-hours. Berth Jonsson predicts that Uddevalla will get well below that. He concedes that a traditional assembly line will be able to pump out cars faster than Uddevalla's teams, but Uddevalla will have fewer supervisors, fewer material movers, fewer machine breakdowns. Teams won't have balance problems. They'll do their own quality control. At Uddevalla, there will be far fewer flaws to fix. Management there won't have to replace nearly as many absentees. It won't have to constantly retrain new workers to keep up with turnover. Add that all in, says Jonsson, and you'll beat the cost of an assembly line. He estimates that Uddevalla won't reach its potential until 1996. Too long to wait? Martin Rybeck, the Torslanda assembly plant manager, says you have to look at the long view. You don't create new eras overnight, but he thinks the manufacturing world is due to start.

"We're assembling the car the same way Henry Ford did in 1929," he says. "I think it's time to make a change."

He also sees it as the only way for Sweden to compete. Any nation, Rybeck says, can now put up a robotized assembly line. So Volvo can't beat Japan that way. Or Korea. But it can win with minds—with uniquely skilled workers equipped to build a sophisticated product.

IN THE MID-1970's, Volvo was said to have little chance of survival. It was weighed down by high wages, high benefits, and a short work week. It was burdened by powerful unions and a small home market. Today, those things haven't changed. But Volvo is now one of the most profitable car companies in the world.[26] Each year, its exports to America alone bring over $2 billion into Sweden. It now produces three hundred thousand cars annually, up over 40 percent from the late 1970's.

Volvo's strategy was fourfold. It redesigned its product, moving upscale. It sharpened its service and marketing. It organized its factories to get the most it could out of its educated, high-paid workers. Finally, it pushed export.

The Sweden of the mid-1970's was also said to be destined to decline economically. Its workers didn't work long hours, its wages were high, its benefits indulgent, its unions all-powerful. That's still the Sweden of today. But the country now has one of the healthiest economies in the world, despite the decline of some of its major industries. In 1970, steel, shipbuilding, forestry, and ore made up over 40 percent of Sweden's exports. Now, they contribute under 20 percent. In 1977, Sweden employed twenty-eight thousand people in shipbuilding. Now, it employs none. Nevertheless, the country's exports are up and its unemployment down—below 2 percent.[27] Look for the source of the resurgence and you won't find it in services or high tech. Most of Sweden's growth has come through modernizing traditional industry.

There are a lot of differences between Sweden and America. Sweden is a more homogeneous country, making it easier to shape consensus. It's a small country, making it easier to move from declining industries to new ones.

But there are similarities, too. We're both high-wage Western nations. We both face aggressive new competition. We both can win with high-value products.

But first, to win abroad, our companies need a supportive government at home. We need to embrace industry and export. We need to redouble our commitment to training, to plant investment, to new product development.

Most important, we need not work harder, just smarter.

6

A. T. Cross: The Mighty Pen

I N L A T E 1987, I was in France talking with executives for Airbus, the new European jetliner challenging Boeing. The French, I knew, tend to be chauvinistic about their products; they buy local. Airbus itself is a symbol of the country's resolve to manufacture at home. That's why I was surprised to see the corporate gift they gave out. It was an American product.

You can find the same product in Tokyo, Hong Kong, and in stores throughout Munich. In total, it's exported to over 150 countries—not by a Fortune 500 company, but one with sales of under $200 million. Nor is it an advanced product. It's simple, low tech. Look at the breast pockets of businessmen in most of the world's cities and you'll see them—Cross pens and pencils. Each year, they bring millions of dollars of Japanese money into America and millions more from Germany. They're exported to both Israel and Arab countries, throughout Africa and South America. They're exported to Fiji in the Pacific, and even Andorra, a tiny nation of forty-nine thousand people nestled on a sliver of land in the Pyrenees.

"Anywhere you can do business today," says Cross's international vice-president, John Lawler, "we do business."

He reminds himself of that with a poster he keeps on the corridor outside his office in Cross's Rhode Island headquarters. It's a photograph of a store—it looks more like a weather-beaten trading post—in the sands of Dubai. It's one of Cross's dealers. The company considers it as important as any of the high-class shops that stock its goods along New York's Fifth Avenue.

There are a lot of reasons why Cross should be finding it hard to compete globally. Its product is a traditional one. Over the years, its design has changed little. It faces a half-dozen aggressive rivals, all pursuing the same markets. But for decades, Cross sales—and profits—have been growing at over 15 percent a year. It's a premier American manufacturing success story, and it would never have happened had the company stayed within America's borders.

NOT long ago, I did a study for a $150 million company that sold goods to hospitals. The company wanted to grow, but knew it had gone as far as it could go in its traditional products. It had a full 80 percent of the U.S. market, and with few hospitals being built, there were almost no new customers. That left two choices; either develop different products or attack a different market, perhaps nursing homes. Management asked me for some ideas on both those options.

I came back a few months later with a report on some possible new products the firm could develop. Then I raised an option the managers hadn't brought up. Why not export? The company was the world's largest producer of its particular goods, and probably the highest-quality one. The potential, I said, could be enormous.

But management hesitated. Export seemed like too much of a headache. It would mean setting up warehouses, hiring new sales forces, redesigning the product to meet local regulations. It might even involve building foreign plants. It just wasn't worth it, too risky.

I told them it wasn't any more risky than gambling on new products or markets in the United States.

Well, they said, at least they knew America. With foreign markets, there were too many unknowns. It wasn't for them.

I've had dozens of talks like that with American businessmen. Many had the same promise—they were world-leading producers and wanted to grow. But they just weren't ready to cross borders.

The obvious price is lost potential. To avoid export in a world economy is as limiting as deciding to sell only east of the Mississippi because west of it is too far. But there can be an even greater price. Let your rivals have the world to themselves, and if they build enough strength, it's likely they'll one day invade your own backyard. That's what the Japanese did with motorcycles, the Koreans with microwave ovens, the Germans with machine tools. The best way for American companies to keep that from happening—is to go overseas first, facing down the competition in their markets first. The competitive test is no longer within countries; it's between them. Manufacturers are finding it ever harder to keep their lead in isolation. Most foreigners understand that. We seldom do.

Few U.S. firms even try to export. Of America's 360,000 manufacturing companies, fewer than 10 percent do any foreign business.[1] Only a handful of those do it seriously: Almost 80 percent of our export comes from only 250 companies.[2] And even those often don't match their overseas competition. The fifty largest corporations in Germany sell 40 percent of what they produce abroad. In France, it's 28 percent. In America, it's about 6 percent.[3]

A. T. Cross is an exception. It sells over a quarter of its products to the world. It succeeds despite fierce competition. Its formula is the same as that of Volvo, Traub, and Scharmann: It sells a high-quality product at a premium price, as aggressively beyond its borders as within. The Cross story shows that even in a mature, low-technology industry, moderate-sized U.S. companies can succeed around the world.

JOHN LAWLER was just out of college, about to join the FBI, when a friend's father, George Fisk, spoke to him about another kind of career—export. That's what Fisk did for Cross writing instruments. He was its first international marketing manager, though at the time, 1965, there wasn't much to his department, just himself and a secretary. Still, for an American executive, he had a rare challenge: selling to the world. He told Lawler he felt that was the future. Without export, Fisk thought, many U.S. producers would one day be unable to keep growing.

Lawler came aboard, joining a company founded fourteen years before the Civil War by a Yankee inventor named Cross, who, lacking heirs, sold out to one of his toolmakers, a man with just the right name to own a company—Walter Boss. After the firm went near-bankrupt during World War II, Boss's two sons gambled on a novel idea in the mid-1950's: a high-status American ballpoint at a time when foreign-made fountain pens were the world's premium writing instruments. Ten years after that, it was Walter's two grandsons, Brad and Ron, the current management team, who decided on another novel idea: selling abroad. That was now up to George Fisk and John Lawler.

By the mid-1960's, the writing-instrument business could be divided into three categories: cheap 19-cent Bics, three-dollar Papermates, and then the luxury lines—ten dollars and up. The competition in that niche was intense. Parker and Sheaffer were Cross's biggest rivals. Next to them, all over the world there were strong local brands—Mont Blanc in Germany, Waterman in France, Ballograf in Sweden.

When Lawler came aboard, the export division wasn't doing much business; about one hundred thousand dollars total, well under one percent of Cross's sales. International revenues would sometimes arrive rather unimpressively, in envelopes containing a few travelers' checks.

Lawler began the way all exporters must begin, learning the paper work; how to make out a bill of lading, an export declaration, a letter of credit. Then came the key step of actually finding foreign customers. George Fisk taught Lawler to start with local independent distributors. They know dealers, Fisk told Lawler, you don't. He taught Lawler one other rule—you begin by seizing any opportunity, no matter how small.

ONE DAY, a letter was routed from the company mail room to Fisk and Lawler's office. It wasn't much, just a customer's request. It came their way only because the postmark was foreign. A Costa Rican business-man who'd bought a Cross pen in the United States was looking for a refill. But the letterhead interested Fisk. The businessman worked for a distributor of religious periodicals. That meant he was probably tied in with stationers and bookstores—good possibilities for selling pens. Fisk wrote back, enclosed a catalog, and asked if he'd be interested in taking on Cross's line. The Costa Rican put in a tiny order. It was too small for Cross to make much money, but they shipped it anyway. All that mattered was that it was an order. "Any business was some business," Lawler explains. Cross was in Costa Rica.

Another letter arrived from an Israeli Air Force colonel, also look-ing for refills. Parenthetically, he mentioned that he was looking for business too. He got side income selling imports, he wrote, and won-dered if Cross was represented in Israel. The answer was no. Lawler sent the colonel a few pens, and now Cross was in another country.

Still another letter came from a Belgian who distributed to duty-free shops. He thought he could get Cross pens on the national airline, Sabena. This one involved more of a risk. To do it, the Belgian said, he'd need financing. Fisk decided to take a chance.

Lawler would later say that thousands of prospects like that slip by U.S. companies simply because no one's assigned to do export. There's no one to pursue leads, no one with the knowledge to do the paper work, so the world is ignored, considered too hard to penetrate. Lawler was now finding it was almost easy.

But spend all your time waiting for reps to come knocking and you'll end up with fifty pens in Costa Rica and twenty to Sabena. So Lawler began to travel, quickly becoming a half-million-mile-a-year man. Fisk sent him everywhere. No country, he felt, was too small, too far, too unstable. Lawler will always remember one of his early trips.

Hong Kong was his first stop. It was Cross's best foreign market, chiefly because its local distributor pushed products around the whole Pacific rim—Taiwan, Singapore, South Korea, the Philippines. Lawler was looking forward to the trip. He'd never seen this side of the world. It turned out to be more exotic than he wanted. His plane touched down at Hong Kong's Kai Tak Airport in May 1967, and proceeded to stay put on the runway for over an hour. Finally, the pilot came on and explained why; there'd been rioting in the city. Soon some police came aboard to check passports. After that, everyone was allowed to disembark, but warned not to leave the terminal. Because of the violence, all roads were closed. Lawler got ready to spend the night in the lounge when he heard his name paged. It was the Cross rep's brother, who worked with Pan Am. The brother told him he had a Jeep. Would Lawler like to go into town? They headed in together, down a road lined with burning cars. It was that way for the next few days. Because of martial law, Lawler had to be back in the hotel every night at six. But he got business done.

His next stop was Iran. It was the time of the shah. It was also a quick lesson in how foreign businessmen can be a bit different from those Lawler knew back home. His Tehran distributor had three wives. After that, Lawler went to Beirut, still a beautiful city at the time. His business was tricky; he had to disengage from one distributor who wasn't performing and link up with a new one. The new man welcomed him to Beirut, then told him to get out as soon as he could. There were rumors the airport could close because of some trouble no one wanted to talk about. Lawler left that day. A few days later, the Six-Day War broke out next door in Israel.

By then, Lawler was safe in Athens; or thought he was safe. He arrived just in time for a coup. At least it was bloodless, but the streets were filled with tanks. Atop the Hilton Hotel, where he was staying, there were machine guns. That's when he got a telex from George Fisk.

"Maybe you better think twice about coming back," he remembers it saying. "Things are going well here."

Still, Lawler made headway. In most countries, the sales were modest, but the total began to add up. Lawler, however, was still having problems breaking into large markets. Most big nations had strong local competition. Customers were loyal. Distributors were hesitant about new brands. West Germany was typical.

Mont Blanc was made there, one of the big names in premium pens. Lamy and Pelikan were sold there, too, as was Waterman of France. When Lawler first arrived in the late 1960's, almost no one had heard of Cross. He made the rounds, then came home with names of possible reps and began to write them. It was a bit different from Costa Rica and Israel. Some in West Germany didn't even write back, and all politely refused. Sorry, they said, your product is unknown here. The other lines are strong. One said Cross was a guaranteed local loser—the product was too thin. Germans like big, thick pens. They also like to buy German.

Fisk sent Lawler back to West Germany anyway, this time to a stationery trade fair. On a hunch, Lawler chose to stop at one of the biggest exhibits, sponsored by a line of greeting cards named Suzy. He asked if Suzy represented any writing-instrument lines. The booth attendant said no. Lawler asked if he could talk to someone about it. He was introduced to a Mrs. Borofsky—president and owner. She gave him a glass of champagne and said she'd never heard of Cross. Lawler showed her some pens.

"They're very slim, and feminine," she said, adding that Germans are used to large black models. "You'll probably have difficulty selling here. You're unknown. A different kind of product."

He did his best to talk her into it. She said she'd think about it. He later found he'd at least gambled on a prominent company. Suzy was the Hallmark of West Germany, tied in with the best stationers. A week later, back in company headquarters in Rhode Island, Lawler sent Mrs. Borofsky a small supply of Cross pens, suggesting she try a sample order. If it didn't work, Cross would take it back. No risk. It did work; she agreed to take a thousand dollars' worth of merchandise. It was almost nothing, but Cross spent money to follow up with a display case. Lawler didn't care about profiting at that point, just investing.

A month later, Mrs. Borofsky sent in a second order for 50 percent more pens. Many would have felt it was an ideal contact; Cross had stumbled on a major national stationer. But George Fisk wasn't convinced. A big distributor, he felt, isn't always best, and he told Lawler why. Even if Suzy increased its pen orders ten and twenty times, Cross would remain one of its minor items. Suzy had dozens of other products that would always be bigger. The best distributor, Fisk explained, is one who's hungry, one who will seize your product as a priority. Still, that was long-range thinking. At the moment, there was no need for a change. All that mattered was that Cross was in West Germany.

BY 1970, the division had gained good ground in dozens of countries, building close to $3 million in sales, almost 15 percent of Cross's total. It involved lots of paper work, lots of plane tickets, but the headaches, Lawler felt, were no worse than doing business at home. Once you learn the rules, and keep pushing, you've a shot at making as much progress in Hong Kong as Pittsburgh.

More customers brought in more money, but instead of taking profits out, Cross plowed them back in, expanding its home staff to keep up with international correspondence. Lawler brushed up on his French, and went to nearby Brown University to study Spanish. That year, the company's foreign sales were even noticed by government. Cross was given the President's Award for advancing U.S. trade. It came with a flag the company promptly began flying outside headquarters—"E" for excellence in export.[4]

Still, Cross wasn't the only company to get that flag. Had Fisk and Lawler stopped there, this would be an unremarkable story. But they kept going, gradually building themselves into one of America's top small-company export performers. Lawler readily admits he couldn't have done it on marketing alone. He could have had ten times the staff and still failed—if the product itself had been anything but superior. That was the other ingredient to Cross's export success: product quality.

In a world of nineteen-cent Bics, the average Cross model was priced at fifteen dollars. Whether you're selling cars, machine tools, or pens, you can't get that kind of premium unless customers believe you're high value. And you can't get customers to believe that through advertising and cosmetics alone. If that's all you do, you'll have a fad on your hands at best. To succeed around the world with a premium product, and maintain it, a company needs superior service and engineering. In a high-wage country, those are two of the most essential competitive weapons.

RON AND BRAD BOSS, Cross's owners, will tell you how they've built their product's value. First, they point to something almost unique in the world of manufacturing—a forever guarantee. If your Cross pen breaks fifty years after you buy it, Cross will fix it, even if it's been run over by a truck. Cross ends up fixing or replacing about 2 percent of all the pens it makes, at a cost of a bit over $1 million a year. They think they get a better return on that investment than from their most advanced factory equipment.

"I can't tell you the number of letters we get on this," says Ron Boss, president. "People saying, 'Thank goodness today someone still cares.'"

It's curious who takes advantage of it. The Bosses have had pens mailed into their Rhode Island headquarters from the middle of China, the tip of Chile, and the heart of the Yukon. They've received broken pens from Teddy Kennedy, Bob Hope, Richard Nixon, and Henry Kissinger, all sent in by their personal secretaries.

Then there's the engineering side of the formula: the product itself. At Cross, they talk of it as Dan Werbin talks of his Volvo, as Ernst Ehmann at Traub talks of his machines—a matter of the best engineering. Spend a day at Cross's factory and you'll hear them speak of quality almost as if it were a religion. For twenty years, Larry Farmer has been at the center of developing it.

He joined Cross around the time Lawler did, the mid-1960's. He remembers his first visit to the Rhode Island factory. "I saw lots of machinery and not many engineers," he said. "It sounded like fun." At Chrysler, where he'd previously worked as a mechanical engineer, they had jokes about talented people ending up as upper-right front-ball-joint engineers. This promised him more range.

In one of his first assignments, he quickly saw where Cross's manufacturing priority lay. The assignment had to do with Cross refills—the ink cartridge and ballpoint itself, the heart of the pen. The refills, he learned, had a plastic cap plugged into the end to keep ink from backing up. He also learned that the cap was plugged in by hand. Now, he was asked to design a machine that would do it automatically. He worked on it for almost a year, finally going to Frank Wilwol, the plant manager, when he was done. Farmer was proud of what he'd created, boasting that he'd tooled the machine to run at an especially high speed. He stressed how it would be great for productivity. He presumed Wilwol would think that was terrific. Instead, Wilwol asked a different kind of question.

"That's all very well," he said, "but is the product any good?"

"I had to think a minute," Farmer would say later. "I hadn't really concentrated on that."

Productivity was important, Wilwol explained, but quality was essential.

Farmer found that, always, there was money for quality. Whenever he'd show the Boss brothers a way to make their pens better, they'd all but push investment at him. Early on, Farmer remembers the company having problems with the quality of its refills. It had been buying them through an outside vendor for years, and though the pens wrote well, they weren't much better than other pens. Occasionally, for example, they'd leave tiny freckles of ink on a page. Or the ink would come up light and thin instead of bold. Farmer spent a lot of time pushing for improvement. The vendors resisted.

"This is the way we make it," they told him.

"We understand that," Farmer would say, "but can't you make it a little better for us? We'll work with you." He went on to talk specifically about the blot problem. He conceded it might not seem serious, but Cross didn't think a fifteen-dollar pen should do that. It wasn't enough for the product to *look* superior, it had to *write* superior. To drive the point home, Farmer, Wilwol, and Ron Boss headed down to New Jersey one day to talk to the vendor about it in person. But the vendor resisted again. Cross's standards were too high, he said. Plenty of status pens used this kind of refill.

On the way back to Rhode Island, the three of them began to talk about what it would take to do it themselves. The initial investment would be a quarter-million dollars, and much more by the time they reached full production. That was a lot of money at the time; the company was under $20 million a year in sales. Farmer presumed it would take months of discussion before they made a decision. Instead, there in the car, while still en route, Ron Boss said he'd made up his mind; they'd do it.

Soon Cross had bought five expensive machines to make the refills. They were similar to those used by big-volume low-end pen companies. Usually, to save on manpower, companies like that assigned only one person to oversee about twenty such machines. But Cross decided to start out by assigning one person to each. Most producers would have considered that overstaffed.

"We felt it was the only way to maintain quality," explains Farmer. Gradually, as the process was mastered, the number of machines run by each worker was increased. It is a classic principle of good manufacturing; it's easier to pick up speed once you have quality than to pick up quality while already running at high speed.

Now that refill manufacturing was going well, Cross faced the question of making sure there was no slippage. The obvious approach would have been to do spot testing, perhaps one of every thousand, or hundred, or fifty. But what if an occasional bad one slipped by? Cross saw only one solution: to hand-test every refill. That was something you couldn't possibly automate. It would mean another dozen workers or so, not exactly the way to save labor costs, but it was a typical Cross call. Whenever there was an argument between quality and lower manpower, quality won.

Cross gave its new hand-testing people the power to reject any refill they deemed substandard. For years, the firm had given the same power to virtually every employee in the factory. Anyone could reject any part at any time. The most unskilled of assembly people had as much right to discard a pen as the company's top quality-control supervisors.

"You have to keep people involved," Farmer explains. "If they don't care about it, they won't produce good work."

Much later, Japan's manufacturers would start using a similar policy, but Cross had been one of the pioneers. The policy had one other result—worker loyalty.

"It's our way of saying, 'You're important,'" says Farmer, "'We need you. If you don't do it right, it's not going to be done right.'"

The lifetime guarantee and the investment in quality are expensive, but in the long run, the price premium Cross earns more than compensates.

FISK AND LAWLER continued to find the most lucrative markets the hardest to crack. Germany was going slowly, as were France and

England. The competition was strong, and worse, the markets were partly protected. Cross had to pay tariffs on anything it shipped into the Common Market. Usually, that forced the firm to push its European prices 15 percent higher. For Lawler, it was frustrating. Here were big, prosperous nations, filled with potential customers. A good market share in any of them would offer ten times the business Cross could ever get from a Costa Rica or an Israel. But with those tariffs, it would be tough to stay competitive. Fisk and Lawler began talking out possible strategies with the Boss brothers. Then, just as they were wrestling with the problem, a sudden opportunity opened up. Cross's U.S. plant hit full capacity. It was time to expand. Ron Boss made a proposal: Since we need a new plant, why not put it in Europe? If you manufactured anywhere in the Common Market, you could ship throughout Europe without paying duties.

At the time, other big American firms were thinking of building their own overseas factories, but there was a difference. For most, it was to take advantage of cheap labor, no other reason. If you could get work done for a dollar an hour in Singapore, why not shut your home plant and build there instead? The Boss brothers didn't approach it that way. They were committed to their workers; they even had a no-layoff policy to win loyalty. Nor were they feeling squeezed by competition. Their company was still earning high profits; there was no urgent reason to save money on labor. And there was certainly no intention to close their U.S. plant. In a sense, the idea of expanding abroad was to do the opposite—fortify Cross's American manufacturing base. The Bosses believed that to be strong, the company had to keep growing at a 15-percent-a-year pace. They knew that would be hard to sustain— unless they began to become a top world performer. The European community was the world's second-largest market, next to the United States. But to compete there, Cross had to produce there. That, the Bosses decided, would be their strategy. It would also allow Cross to take on the European pen makers on their own turf. The best way to keep your competition from surprising you in your own market Lawler will say, is to invade theirs first.

But there was a problem: money. Cross was still small in 1971, its sales around $20 million, not necessarily enough to invest in major foreign construction. Lawler began a search to see what kind of assistance Cross could get from foreign governments. He and Ron Boss looked at the Netherlands, Belgium, England. Then Lawler noticed some ads placed in U.S. magazines by Ireland, offering tempting investment incentives. Meanwhile, a business associate of Cross's chairman, Brad Boss, was touting Ireland, as well. The associate's company had an Irish subsidiary and it was working out well. So Lawler set up a talk with the country's Industrial Development Authority (IDA). Almost immediately, he saw that money would be no problem.

Ireland, Lawler found, was ready to give grants covering a full third of Cross's investment in buildings and machines. In addition, the Irish offered to suspend taxes for fifteen years on export profits.[5] Since Cross was planning to ship out almost everything it made in Ireland, that made a big difference. The IDA even offered to pay the costs of flying Irish employees to Rhode Island for training.

Cross chose the town of Ballinasloe, on a patch of ground as far as possible from the local livestock-rendering plant. Irish wages were a bit lower than those in the United States, but material was higher, so costs were a wash. Clearly, the strategy wasn't to replace U.S. jobs, just to compete in Europe. It was an offensive strategy, not a defensive one. By 1972, Cross had begun production inside the walls of the Common Market.

THE Irish incentives showed Lawler just how aggressive foreign nations had become at seeding economic development. The United States certainly didn't do anything like that.

"I could get into trouble for saying this," he says, "but I think the U.S. government does less for the exporting manufacturer than countries like Ireland, Japan, West Germany, and France."

In the early 1970's, the United States did make one effort. It was a program called DISC—Domestic International Sales Corporation.[6] The idea was to encourage companies to export by giving a 50 percent tax break on overseas profit. Cross signed on. Lawler expected DISC would draw other firms to start exporting, but it didn't happen. Most who signed up were the few already selling abroad. Others, it seemed, were still afraid of taking on the unknown. "The export field is a mystery to a lot of manufacturers," Lawler explains. "They feel there's a lot of red tape and restrictions they don't understand. They're happy to concentrate their resources on the domestic market, which, of course, is the largest in the world."

It wasn't enough just to establish the DISC idea, he thought—to make it work, government had to promote it, send people into the field to sell it. They never got that going. In time, DISC was repealed.

THE Irish plant gave Fisk and Lawler a powerful new weapon, but something was still holding them back. In too many countries, they were dependent on local agents, many of whom saw Cross as a low priority, one of a dozen imports they sold. The only way to become a major exporter in large markets, Lawler will tell you, is to have your own people pushing your product. He and Fisk decided it was time to start doing that. It would mean major investing at a time when overseas profits were just beginning to come in, but profits weren't their priority. They wanted growth. Hiring their own foreign salespeople seemed to be the best way.

They started with one experiment, in Ireland itself. It struck them as the least risky. It's always easier to sell when you can claim you're a local producer, and besides, there was no Ireland-based rival. Still, at the time, Cross was well back in sales—fourth after Parker, Sheaffer, and Papermate. In 1973, Fisk and Lawler began. They hired two salesmen and spent seventy thousand dollars for advertising, more than double their previous year's total Irish sales. But it bought them first-class exposure, crucial for a status product. Within a year, the investment began to pay off; sales doubled. They plowed the profits into still more advertising, giving their salesmen cars to help reach dealers all over the country. Soon they were putting 25 percent of receipts into ads. They even spent fifty thousand dollars on a lit sign at Shannon Airport. By the early 1980's, their Irish sales had passed $1 million, making them first in the market.

But it was far from Europe's biggest market. And as they began to look beyond Ireland, toward mainland Europe, they were finding once again that bigger means tougher.

THE partnership with Suzy in West Germany was suffering. Suzy was simply too big, Cross too much of an afterthought. Lawler saw it as a kind of Catch-22. Suzy felt that until Cross pens began to sell big, they wouldn't be worth pushing. But of course, without pushing, the pens weren't selling. Finally, Suzy told Cross it should face up to reality and give up on Germany. The two parted amicably, but Lawler didn't stop trying. He moved on to a new independent, a smaller one that he hoped would be hungrier than Suzy. But now there was another problem. The new agent, though hungry, couldn't afford a hard push. Lawler would talk to him about advertising, but he was hesitant. Deep down, Lawler understood. Small reps usually can't afford to gamble. Again, it left him in a Catch-22. As long as there was no promotion, stores would keep Cross on the back shelf. But as long as Cross was on the back shelf, the German rep felt it too risky to gamble on promotion.

Then Lawler got a call. It was from his old Belgian distributor—the one who'd gotten them on Sabena. He'd been itching to move beyond his duty-free market, into retail. He wasn't a German local, but he seemed especially aggressive, willing to risk. Cross began to talk about a three-way partnership: the Belgian, their German rep, and themselves. Lawler realized it would start his department on the road to his biggest foreign involvement. Yes, Cross had gone hard into Ireland, but that was a country of only 3.5 million people. West Germany had over

60 million. To make it there would eventually involve enormous spending. When you go through local distributors, promotion's on them. When you buy into your own sales operation, it's on you. Management in Rhode Island talked about it and decided the company was ready. In 1975, they began.

The first year they started modestly, putting in twenty-five thousand dollars. The second year, they did the same. Sales crawled up, but slowly. Lawler saw that if they were to succeed, it would take a lot more. You don't buy brand image in a huge country for twenty-five thousand dollars a year; and they needed brand image. You can't ask someone to spend twenty dollars on a pen no one has ever heard of. In 1978, Lawler decided it was time to invest much more.

But there was a problem. The German partner still wasn't ready to do that. He wanted a strategy that kept profit flowing. To Lawler, it was understandable. The partner was getting older. He didn't want to wait five years for a payoff. So, for the time being, Cross agreed to continue slowly. The distributor had been loyal, and Lawler felt Cross should always be loyal in return. Then, in 1979, the partner offered to sell out. Cross purchased his share, and finally, they were ready for a major push in a major market. They knew that the difference with Ireland wasn't just size. In West Germany, there was aggressive competition, and a public who'd long been loyal to other brands.

"I knew it would be a long, hard road," said Lawler.

Cross hired salesmen and printed literature in German. The company stepped up visits to dealers, and contracted for larger spaces at trade fairs, at one point spending twenty-five thousand dollars on a floor display. To make sure Cross was promoting itself right, Lawler worked with local ad firms. They helped him see that the campaigns Cross used at home probably wouldn't work in West Germany. In the United States, promotional posters often come with a theme—a pen photographed against a mortarboard, for example. In Germany, Lawler was told, posters would work better if they simply showed a stark picture of the product itself—a direct approach for a direct culture.

Cross pushed advertising from twenty-five thousand dollars a year to one hundred thousand dollars, a quarter of its German sales. Lawler focused it on a few high-end publications, feeling it's better to target selected readership than go scattershot in national magazines. Even with all that, Lawler told himself to be patient. He knew you don't buy market leadership overnight. Nor can you do it if you're itching to grab profit early. So he blocked out a five-year plan, keeping with his same targeted publications. He also decided to keep investing 25 percent of sales into advertising. The more money he made, the more he'd plow back in.

"Our real interest was in growing the business," said Lawler.

It went quicker than he expected. By year two, business had doubled. Was he tempted to cut back at that point to bolster profit?

"That would be good for today," says Lawler, "but what about tomorrow? You have to determine whether you're in this for the short term or the long term."

Was there pressure from management?

"We had a five-year plan," he explains. That way, there was no expectation to deliver short term. But Lawler points out that one part of the company did get profit. Cross had a rule that even its own distributorships would pay its Irish plant the standard factory prices for pens. That was key at a time when the goal was to get the factory up to full capacity. It also forced the sales operations, like the one in Germany, to make it without a crutch. In time, Lawler's patience paid off. In one of the world's most competitive writing-instrument battlegrounds, the newcomer from America surged from a few back-shelf sales to a full 15 percent of the market. Lawler doesn't remember much celebration over it, though. By the time West Germany's momentum was picking up, his attention had turned to France.

The competition there was even more intense. The French brand—Waterman—dominated, of course. But others were there fighting hard. Parker, Sheaffer, and Mont Blanc all had factories in France. Each was doing millions of dollars in business. One of the biggest local sellers was a product Cross didn't even make—the fountain pen. Cross decided to go in anyway, opening its own French sales office. That meant paying high Parisian rents and high French salaries—a commitment of several hundred thousand dollars in a country where Cross profit at the time was a tenth that. But as Lawler would explain later, he felt no pressure from management to prove himself short term. The company had a five-year plan.

THROUGHOUT its history, one of Cross's distinctions had been a small product line. By the late 1970's, after 140 years in business, it had only a handful of writing instruments, chiefly one mainstay model in chrome, silver, and gold. Cross sold at the three standard price points of high-end pens: ten dollars, fifteen dollars, and twenty dollars.

Then, in the late 1970's, the price of both gold and silver began to go up, pushing Cross pens and pencils up, too. The Bosses realized that soon their line would have a major gap—one set of pens at ten dollars, and then a void until twenty dollars. They'd long resisted new models, fearing they'd dilute their identity and hike up manufacturing costs, but this was different. That fifteen-dollar niche was a big chunk of the status pen business. The Boss brothers decided to ask R&D to come up with some new fifteen-dollar alternatives. In spring of 1980, the brothers settled on black—a matte, satin finish. They asked that it be ready for production in one year.

The job was given to Bob Harris, a Cross engineer reporting to Larry Farmer. He soon had a problem. He couldn't find a good-enough material to use for the black coating. There were dozens of possibilities, but none had the jewelry quality Cross was looking for. Harris had his people comb trade fairs and technical journals, asking leads from outside engineers. Finally, they found an inventor on the West Coast who had just what they wanted—corrosion-resistant black chrome, done in matte for certain airplane parts. It was hard and durable. Farmer and Harris made him an offer. They would work together to perfect it, then Cross would license the finished material for use in its factories, giving the inventor royalties.

"It'll be a good thing for you," said Harris, "and a good thing for us."

But the West Coast inventor held out. He wanted to do all the work himself, as a vendor. Harris tried to negotiate, but there was no give. "Take it or leave it," the vendor said. Harris was in a bind. This was his only option. Still, he worried that if he began contracting out key parts of the pens, it could jeopardize quality and supply, both essential for a premium product. He turned down the deal.

Now it was back to more trade fairs, more technical journals, and finally, he found another possibility, right in Cross's backyard. A Rhode Island vendor had been putting a matte black epoxy on wire racks used by industry. Harris began to look into it. He found that the vendor couldn't apply the finish as uniformly as Cross would like, but Harris saw promise. And if Cross could perfect this process, it would have a unique technology. Still, he knew it would mean a big investment. Instead of licensing the material, Cross would have to develop it.

"We went to finance to say this was going to cost some bucks," Farmer recalls. He wasn't worried. He smiles as he recalls why. "Finance reported to Ron," he says. "We knew what his answer would be."

They bought the best machines they could find, then started perfecting an electrostatic powder-coating process. They wanted it to put down a layer the thickness of a sheet of paper on the raw copper tubes of their pens and pencils. They got it down to a thickness of a few sheets, which some felt was fine, but Farmer knew it wasn't ideal. He asked for more money and more time, and got both. Finally, in mid-1981, Cross was back in the fifteen-dollar niche.

IF IT'S rare for American firms to export, it's rarer still for them to design or adapt products for foreign markets. We ship two-band radios to countries that use three-band; big, wood-laminate clocks to countries that like small, painted ones; and oversize appliances to Far East countries with tiny kitchens. We even ship cars to Japan with the steering wheel still on the left, although people there drive with it on the right. Though many U.S. companies understand it may be best to tailor, they don't feel it's worth it; the return wouldn't be quick enough.

John Lawler felt differently. For years, he'd known that in many European countries, fountain pens were more popular than ballpoints, especially as a status product. Cross hadn't made any fountain pens for decades, but in the mid-1970's, Lawler began to argue for bringing them back. In most American companies, management wouldn't be interested in big manufacturing investment for foreign markets alone. But this was Cross. By 1975, Lawler had convinced the Boss brothers to develop a new product solely for overseas sales. The company geared up a major R&D effort. It took seven years to perfect it. By then, 1982, some at Cross felt there could be a market for it in the United States, as well. They argued that it would be easier to introduce fountain pens at home. It's always better to launch on familiar ground, and besides, it was almost unheard of for a U.S. company to begin marketing a new product abroad. But the Bosses chose to do just that. Their priority was to push world sales, and the new fountain pen was key to that strategy.

It was a full two years later before they finally began selling the fountain pen back in the States. They were surprised to find the market bigger than they expected. It was a fringe benefit of export no one had thought about: By developing a product for overseas, they stumbled on a windfall of new sales back home.

Lawler found that the idea of foreign tailoring came up often at Cross. The company was so committed to adapting its products to overseas markets that it began sending engineers around the world to talk to customers—the same strategy used by Samsung and Volvo. "Not just salesmen," Farmer stresses. "Engineers."

At one point, an engineer named Bob Lozeau stopped in Thailand on just that kind of mission. He asked Cross's local distributor if there were problems worth looking at. The distributor said that, in fact, the pen sometimes didn't seem to write as evenly as it should. Unlike a salesman, Lozeau had the training to brainstorm the problem. He finally zeroed in on the cause: Thailand's hot, humid climate. It was causing the ink to absorb too much moisture, throwing off the flow. The plug on top of the ink cartridge, he knew, had been designed to breathe. That way, air could get in as the ink went down. Otherwise, a vacuum would form and pull the ink back from the point.

"Good design for the United States," Farmer recalls, "not a good design in Thailand." Or any other tropical climate.

It took a few months to come up with a solution, but he did: a nonbreathable silicon-grease plug that would seal the cartridge from the humidity, but ride the ink down to avoid a vacuum. The new plug is now in production. No more complaints out of Thailand—or out of the Rhode Island plant. The process turned out to be a bit cheaper and yet higher in quality than the old way. It was more than worth the engineer's plane fare.

Meanwhile, John Lawler worked to tailor Cross to local habits in his marketing, as well. He got each product's basic directions translated into six languages, and their ads into thirty. In America, the company tried to stress print ads in magazines, but Lawler learned he had to be flexible to succeed abroad. In Hong Kong, video is big, so he began to use it. In Egypt, he did wall posters. Lawler knows gold is popular in Latin and Spanish markets, so he stresses it there. He knows that bright colors are better for promotional materials in some countries, dark in others, and in certain places, he learned the hard way to be careful of too much white: It connotes mourning.

IN 1981, Ireland's program of luring new companies was having some trouble.[7] Some of the companies had proven to be opportunists. They came for government grants, and moved on to other countries once the grants ran out. Others stayed but provided only low-wage, low-skill employment. The government realized it had to fine-tune its economic-development programs, and got in touch with me to ask if I'd help with a strategy.

I flew over in the fall of 1981 and began by studying which plants were thriving and which seemed in decline. The Industrial Development Authority told me that would be easy to predict: Advanced-technology plants, like those in electronics and medical equipment, tended to be top performers, while traditional plants, like those in textiles, tended to have problems. But it wasn't that simple.[8] A number of electronics firms, I found, provided only unskilled jobs and paid low wages. Then I noticed a traditional company that was thriving in Ireland. It was Cross. The firm had just announced plans to expand.

Even though Cross was based in my new home state of Rhode Island, I'd just moved there and hadn't known of it. I drove to Ballinasloe to see the factory. The manager gave me a tour. Until then, I'd thought of a pen as the easiest of products to make; all you needed, I presumed, were a few parts, a few production steps, and low-skilled labor. The plant, however, turned out to be highly complex, with dozens of manufacturing stages. It helped explain how Cross had succeeded against potential low-wage competition. I'd already seen Volvo use the same strategy, and would later see Scharmann and Traub use it, too. Come up with a sophisticated design that requires high-quality, complex manufacture, and it'll be hard for low-wage rivals to duplicate.

The manager spent an hour or so showing me Cross's expansion plans. Then we sat down in his office to talk. I asked him how Cross was able to succeed at so high a price when the market was filled with decent pens costing a tenth as much. Part of it was image, he said, but only a small part. The real key was engineering. Give buyers superior quality, he said, and they'll pay a premium. I asked how Cross maintained that kind of quality. He went on to describe the strict testing, the right of all workers to reject any product, the nonstop investment in better production techniques. Then I asked why Cross was expanding in Ireland instead of America. Was it low wages? To push harder into the Common Market?

No, he said, costs were similar. And most of the new capacity would be going not to Europe, but beyond, to places like the Far East.

So why Ireland?

Government incentives were the key, he said. Not only would the company pay virtually no taxes on export profits, but the capital grants and leasing incentives would pay for most of the new plant and equipment. A dozen other countries I'd worked in had similar incentives— Scotland, Spain, Greece, Portugal.[9] America, I knew, had almost none.

THERE was a reason the Irish plant was starting to export beyond Europe—Lawler had been working as hard on small markets as big ones. At the same time Cross was investing in West Germany and France, he got pens into Burundi and Djibouti, into Sri Lanka, Bahrain, and Qatar.

He also pushed hard to get into one of the world's toughest export markets—Japan. He'd set up a small distributor there back in the late 1960's, but wasn't making much headway. By 1970, total sales were stalled around twenty-five thousand dollars. That's when he got a promising new inquiry. A big Tokyo import company wanted to take Cross on. The company had done its research. In its letter, the manager pointed out that Cross's current distributor was a small family operation, with few resources. He guaranteed ten times the sales.

Lawler flew to Japan to talk to him. He showed Lawler his facilities, took him to a fancy dinner, and stressed that he handled many major U.S. clients, Wilson sporting goods among them. Then and there, he offered to buy $150,000 in Cross products.

Lawler was sold, but out of courtesy, he went to see his current distributor, as well. This time, Lawler was served a low-key traditional dinner, with the family all around. The man's sincerity was obvious. He talked about being ready to push hard, but he'd need resources to do it. As they continued to talk, Lawler reminded himself of the value of staying with someone small and hungry. Despite the big distributor's come-on, there was still the risk of being lost amid all those other products. Too many distributors, Lawler was finding, just wanted to add another American name to their letterhead. If he showed his loyalty to his original rep, he knew he'd get back double the commitment.

But he had a concern. The family rep carried other lines, too. So Lawler decided to propose a deal. Would he restructure his company to focus exclusively on Cross? The rep said it was possible. He'd recently taken his son and nephew into the business; perhaps one of them could spearhead a new Cross-only subsidiary. Soon, they were close to a deal to have the nephew do just that. But the family said they'd need help in capitalizing it, money for advertising, displays, promotion, credit. Lawler said he'd discuss it with management back in the States.

In Rhode Island, they went back and forth and finally decided to go with the family. It wasn't much money at first—only a five-thousand-dollar equity investment for a 20 percent minority share. But in Japan, such gestures are important. The nephew was grateful, and proved a driven businessman. Cross steadily increased its investment. Lawler even made sure to tailor the product to meet local taste. He learned that the Japanese like fine-pointed refills, with black ink—easier to write in their ideographic language. It took some adjusting at the factory, but Lawler managed to get a line switched from Cross's standard blue medium to fine black for Japan. By the mid-1980's, Cross had achieved close to $4 million in Japanese sales, and was neck and neck for number one in the country's high-end pen market.

IN 1982, I went to visit Ron Boss for a study I was doing on Rhode Island's economy. We got on the subject of the company's foreign sales, a healthy 30 percent of Cross's total at the time. But Boss was concerned. Export had just begun to fall. Like everyone else, Cross had been hit by a tough pair of blows—a soaring dollar and the global recession. Other U.S. exporters were responding by pulling back. I knew of a number who'd closed their foreign distributorships as soon as they started taking losses, convinced it was better to stay home until the dollar dropped. Profit, they said, was more important than market share. They felt they could always go back in when things got better. I asked Boss what his own plans were.

He said Cross was indeed taking losses in several countries, but had decided to maintain its positions. "We want to make sure we don't lose our distribution," he said.

But wouldn't he lose some of it even if he stayed? Wouldn't the high dollar make his goods uncompetitive?

Possibly, he said, but management's plan was to keep prices as far down as possible. That would mean a profit hit, but at least the firm would hold on to market share. It was the kind of long-term outlook I usually heard only from Japanese or European businessmen.

I asked what he'd do if the dollar didn't come down soon. A company can take losses only so long.

One strategy, he said, was to go more aggressively into smaller countries to make up for losses in the big ones. Many of those countries, he pointed out, have currencies that are tied to the dollar, so when it's high, U.S. exports don't suffer. He also planned to balance the losses by cutting costs at home, improving factory efficiency. The main rule, he said, was to hold on to foreign customers no matter what. In the long run, he felt, it costs more to leave a country during bad times and later invest your way back in than to stay there and tough it out.

So Cross stayed. The years from 1982 to 1984 were hard ones. Despite Lawler's pushing, the company's overseas sales inevitably dropped as the dollar stayed strong. But Cross kept investing in distribution and promotion anyway. It paid off. When the dollar finally fell between 1986 and 1988, Cross's overseas sales machine was poised and in place. Soon, foreign volume bounded to record levels. Had the company pulled out during bad times, it would have never happened so quickly.

THE BOSS BROTHERS knew that even with a premium product, they still had to work hard to hold price within reach. They made it a policy to keep their prices going up slower than inflation. If they hadn't found ways to keep improving productivity over the previous decade, by 1980, Cross's fifteen-dollar pens would have been at forty dollars, their twenty-seven-dollar-gold-filled models at seventy-five dollars. Each year, Farmer spent several million dollars for new equipment, installing the kind of machines that allowed two operators to do the work of twelve. But it didn't mean layoffs. With sales expanding, there was always a need for freed assembly workers to run increased capacity. The workers welcomed the automation. They saw that it opened up skilled jobs. Instead of being on the bench, they were now being trained to run complex equipment.

By 1980, Farmer had mechanized most of the labor-heavy parts of the factory. Yet he had to keep improving productivity, especially as the dollar rose. It was a dilemma. How do you lower production costs if you've run out of obvious ways to mechanize? The answer, Farmer found, was to attack a much trickier level of factory inefficiency—indirect labor. In most plants today, indirect costs like material handling, inventory, rework, setup, scrap, and supervisors are much larger than the costs of people working directly on the product. Streamlining these costs is much harder than automating out direct labor. You can't just buy a faster assembly machine. You have to look for subtler shortcuts.

In time, Cross zeroed in on the more obvious possibilities, like cutting back on supervisors and using computers for design and manufacture. But Farmer was convinced there were even more costly inefficiencies buried beneath the surface. For example, he felt costs could be trimmed dramatically by cutting down on rejects. The problem was, he didn't know where to begin looking. Once again, he turned to Bob Harris, and together, they launched an exhaustive campaign of statistical tracking.

They started using charts to log the percentage of rejects in every corner of the plant. Over the months, trends appeared that showed them where the biggest problems lay. One area, for example, was the pen mechanisms; there were eight throwaways for every hundred—far too much scrap. Identifying the problem, however, turned out to be far easier than solving it. That took weeks of industrial detective work.

"It was a very long, arduous team effort," Farmer recalls.

By interviewing the workers, he was able to find the most common reason for the rejects. The problem, they said, was scratchy mechanisms—a grating feel when you twisted the pen to propel the point. But Harris knew a thousand things could be causing that; machines, operators, materials. The engineers double-checked all of those, and finally figured it out. It was the lubricant. A few years before, they'd lubricated the mechanism by hand with a special grease. Then they decided to automate that process. But you needed a precise amount of lubricant, and it seemed the machine wasn't consistent in applying it. The solution seemed obvious enough: tool the machine better. The engineers began to work on it, but didn't succeed. That happens, sometimes. Seemingly simple technical challenges turn out to be unsolvable. Finally, they decided to forget the machine. They'd try coming up with a whole new way of lubricating. It would cost money, but Farmer feels that if a manufacturing process becomes too big a fight, it's time to redesign the product, instead. The engineers began looking for alternative ways to coat the mechanisms, experimenting with dozens of options. They finally tried Teflon. It worked. The scrap rate, due to coarse mechanisms, went down from 8 percent to 1 percent.

The charts helped surface dozens of other bugs like that. It was a cumbersome process, but Farmer says it will go on forever. You can't just do it once and figure you've gotten the plant up to speed, he says. Plants don't work that way. Being a factory manager, says Farmer, is like being one of those carnival jugglers who puts a plate on a wand and starts to spin it, then another plate, and another and another. Finally, he's got all fifteen of them spinning, and his act is perfect. But just then, one of the first plates starts to wobble. To keep it going, says Farmer, he's got to run over and give it some "English." Then another starts to wobble. And another. If the juggler's going to keep the act humming, he has to keep moving. The charts are Farmer's way of finding out what plates are wobbling. And a factory, he points out, is a far more complicated juggle. The Cross production process has one hundred steps, necessary for a product of its quality. It's equally necessary, Farmer says, to keep monitoring them all with statistical quality control.

AS COSTS came down, Lawler kept pushing to hold ground around the world. In some areas, the high dollar was the least of his problems. Once, Cross did good business in El Salvador, for example, but the civil war began to change that. Lawler's representative there even had to stop using his car; anyone appearing to be of means, he explained, could end up a target of terrorists. Sales went down to five thousand dollars a year. Cross's profit was negligible, but the company stayed, and is still there. "People write with Cross pens in El Salvador," Lawler explains. "They need refills. They need service." More important, he adds, if things ever get better, the company's sales system will be ready to deliver. Were they to leave, there'd be no chance of success. That attitude, says Lawler, is important for any exporter who tries to get into Central or South America.

The markets there, he explains, are very tricky. They open, they close; tariffs go up, import restrictions change. Take Argentina, says Lawler. For fifteen of the last twenty years, it's been officially closed to Cross. Throughout, Lawler has remained ready anyway. He just keeps watching it, getting in whenever the door opens. If you have a local rep, he says, and understand how to put the export paperwork through, it's not hard. The thing to watch, explains Lawler, is a country's dollar reserves. Most developing nations need dollars to buy exports. When they end up short, the government starts barring outsiders from sending in product. But you don't give up, says Lawler, you just keep applying for permission. Lawler's local distributors do that for him, repeatedly applying to a country's central bank for approval to import Cross. When things are tight, they're told to come back next week, next month, next year. Often, approval is limited—maybe two thousand dollars' worth of pens instead of twenty-five thousand dollars' worth. Swings in profit, Lawler says, can be sudden. In the early 1970's, when Venezuela was booming with oil, Cross did over $1 million a year there. Then oil declined, the government went into debt, and dollars dried up. That meant Cross's business dried up, too—cut in half overnight. Lawler's reaction was to stay there anyway.

That kind of perseverance, he admits, would be hard to sustain if he weren't in so many countries. But he is—he's in 150, and that means he can almost always count on a sales climb on one side of the world to counterbalance a drop on the other. It's the same strategy used by Helmut Maschke of Scharmann. When U.S. sales fall, Maschke says, Russian sales often jump. The bumps smooth out. That, he explains, is why Scharmann stays in Russia. Lawler sees it the same way. India shows how far Cross is willing to go to maintain access everywhere.

FOR YEARS, India had been far tougher than almost any country; virtually a closed market. That only made Lawler want to get in all the more. But it was impossible. India was so short of currency reserves that it almost never issued import licenses. When it did, tariffs were often as high as 100 percent, which pushed Cross products way out of reach. Other rules were even trickier. At one point, India demanded that outsiders who do business there must share company secrets. Even major exporters, like IBM and Coca-Cola, wanted no part of that. Cross didn't either, but Lawler kept pushing. Even when the door to India was closed, he stayed in touch with potential local distributors. It's important, he says, to keep cultivating possible reps, so you can move quickly when things open. And the reps, he adds, often act as your local watchmen, letting you know when a market has new possibilities.

In the late seventies, one of Lawler's Indian contacts got in touch. Something new was happening, he said. The government was ready to try an experiment. No direct imports would be permitted, but if Cross was willing to assemble its product in a special region—a local free zone—it would be allowed to sell in India. The government felt the zone would provide both jobs and foreign currency. Lawler knew it wasn't Cross's style to let go of manufacture—quality control was too important—but he also knew there are two kinds of companies who export: those who adapt and those who fail. It would mean some special effort at the U.S. factory—getting pretested parts wrapped specially for assembly. "A bit of a pain," recalled Lawler. But in export, initial opportunities often are. Cross decided to do it.

Then, just when they'd gotten geared up, the program shut down. There'd been articles in local papers saying the free zone was being mismanaged, its products smuggled into the rest of India rather than exported through customs. The local partner who'd helped them get ready had to close up.

But Lawler still didn't give up on India. At one point, he took a trip to New Delhi to do a market study. He found what he was looking for— some high-end shops specializing in stationery goods. He took a tour of the rest of the city, and though there was a lot of poverty, there was a privileged class, too. It convinced him there would be enough customers there to justify the wait. He told his contacts to keep watching for opportunities.

In 1985, one of them got in touch. The free-zone program, he said, was back on track, this time with an added incentive. If Cross agreed to assemble a certain amount in the zone, the government would let it directly import a quarter of that amount from its home factory. Cross immediately started repackaging the parts. Then, to make sure quality wouldn't slide, Cross dispatched the manager of its Irish factory to train the new Indian assembly staff. Except for his getting sick from the food, it was a success. Cross's Indian sales were soon over two hundred thousand dollars. It wasn't a huge amount, but it was another foothold in a new part of the world. And as Lawler often finds, one foreign opportunity can lead to another. The free-zone setup, he now thinks, could be an entry to an even bigger market, the Soviet Union.

As long as Cross assembles in India, Lawler explains, that technically makes its pens an Indian product. The Soviet market is far likelier to open up to India than America. If it does, Cross would be qualified to go in from there. If you can't ship direct, Lawler says, then you go through the back door, but you go. And incidentally, he adds, he's heard that many Russians buy Cross pens while on the road. He thinks he can do well on their home soil.

WERE YOU to visit the Cross plant in Rhode Island before 7:00 A.M. or after 5:00 P.M., you'd find it quiet. The company runs only one shift there. It's by plan, not lack of demand. "You get the best people with one shift," Larry Farmer explains, "and when you get the best people, you get the best quality."

It's a philosophy that's taken a lot of extra investment. Instead of doubling its shifts, Cross has had to double its factory size. The company feels it's been worthwhile.

Cross now makes tens of millions of writing instruments a year. About 1,350 employees work at its Rhode Island factory. Although it doesn't seem the most exciting work, turnover is low. Among the regional labor force, Cross is a sought-after company. Workers pass along word of job possibilities to friends and family. Most who are hired become lifetime employees. Larry Farmer says it doesn't take much to earn that loyalty.

"We tell them thank you," he says.

For example?

"After Labor Day," he says, "we gave every worker a check and a note saying thank you very much from Brad and Ron. Not that people didn't want the money, but we got more comments about the letter."

Then there is the Christmas ritual. The two owners personally go to every worker—all 1,350—and hand them hefty annual bonuses that are keyed not to rank but longevity.

Every month, the company also holds employee meetings—a handful from each department. It's a forum to talk about anything from work rules to problems with the microwave ovens used to heat coffee. The twist to these meetings is that Ron Boss always runs them.

What does Ron Boss do when a base-level employee tells him she's not happy with the microwave?

"I get it fixed," he explains.

Frances Dowding began working at Cross seven years ago, after her children had moved out. The job has made things much better for her and her husband, a painter. Frances's salary has meant they've been able to enjoy their middle years more, taking trips to New York and Florida. In a sense, she is an American counterpart to the Korean workers in Suweon. Her standard of living springs from her company's success in the global market; her particular job is to oversee export packaging at the Rhode Island plant. Had Cross not stayed competitive, hundreds of Frances Dowdings would have seen their paychecks handed over to foreign replacements.

Anna Natale also makes her living by helping Cross sell to the world. She packs the pens in boxes for export. A pile of rejects sits near her station. As with all workers, she has the right to scrap anything she deems substandard. She picks up a pen to show an all but invisible nick.

Why does she bother to be so picky?

"We send out a quality product," she explains.

It's a commitment as deep as any you'd find among workers in South Korea or Japan. Ask Ron Boss why Cross urges its people to be so strict and he'll tell you it sets a tone. If you care about almost invisible nicks on the inner mechanism of one pen, it'll ripple out to excellence throughout the operation. But the only way to make it ripple everywhere, says Boss, is to include every worker in the checking system.

"You can't build quality at the end," he says. "You have to build it in each step of the way."

To an outsider, it might seem like repetitive work. Anna Natale sees it differently. "I love working here," she says. "If you're going to work for anybody, you have to work for A. T. Cross."

A half-dozen women around her look up and echo the thought. It's like being part of a family, they say, part of a team.

In a nearby department, a dozen workers pick up one refill at a time and write with each across a page. They're the people who hand-test every refill cartridge the company makes, rejecting those with even subtle problems. A worker named Lucille Bourgault takes a cartridge from her reject pile to show why she thinks it's substandard. She writes with it alongside a good one. There doesn't seem to be a difference.

"Look close," she says. "This one's a little lighter. We're very interested in quality."

Farmer mentions that Cross recently spent money to improve the printing of the company name on the refill cartridge. Ninety-nine percent of the time, that printing will be hidden, inside the pen, but Cross, says Farmer, feels even the invisible parts of the product should have a quality touch. It's why Cross polishes and plates the internal mechanism, also hidden. Ron Boss estimates the company could save $1 million a year by not bothering with inside grooming, but it doesn't interest him.

"If you're going to ask people to spend twenty-five dollars on a writing instrument," says Larry Farmer, "it better be perfect. Consistently, when I've reviewed that philosophy with Ron Boss, he comes down on the side of, 'Fine, we'll spend the money.'"

Farmer is proud of another aspect of the company's strategy: moving people from handwork to headwork. It's part of what drives its continuing push for productivity. Each new assembly machine means Cross can move a worker to a more sophisticated job.

As an example, Farmer walks to the department that does die cutting for the tiny corporate insignias Cross attaches to institutional gift pens—Coca-Cola, IBM, college seals, Airbus. Andy Rondeau, who works here, used to be a traditional die cutter. He'd get a company insignia, manually trace it, then set up the trace to be cut into metal for stamping. It was a skilled job, but mostly handwork. Today, he sits behind a hundred-thousand-dollar IBM CAD system, recreating the image not by tracing, but by touch points on an electronic tablet, hitting a keyboard as he goes.

Does he like this more?

"It's all brainwork now," he says. He adds that it brings him the fringe benefit of specialized knowledge, and in turn gives the company a fringe benefit, too: a better-used mind.

THOUGH GROWING, Cross remains a small, family-run company. But companies that size are as important to boosting our trade balance and living standard as those on the Fortune 500. They represent our richest untapped potential for export. And in the 1990's, export will be the key to enhancing our national wealth.

There is one unsettling twist to the Cross story. Today, the company exports more from its Irish plant than its American headquarters. Even when we have an aggressive, smart U.S. company that succeeds internationally, we don't always realize the benefits. There are a lot more Crosses out there. As with Singapore, Ireland is now home to a large number of U.S. factories: well over 400 plants employing almost one hundred thousand people, all built for export. Ultimately, the reasons come down to government policies. Ireland offers better incentives for export and plant construction than our own government.

The Boss brothers are committed to American manufacturing. They want to make their next expansion on home soil. We should make sure it's worth it for them. As a nation, we should work harder to make America the most attractive option for U.S. managers.

AFTER twenty-five years in the business, John Lawler reflects on how a small company can break into exports. First, he says, you have to be patient. Too many companies try to make a quick hit and then, if there's not enough payback, they give up in a year or two, Expect a marathon. It takes years to build a dealer network, years more to establish brand image. In some countries, it can be a seesaw. Trade doors can suddenly close, cutting your business by 90 percent. Stay anyway, keeping a foot in the door. In time, the door will open. If you're not there when it does, you'll be beaten by someone else.

Second, says Lawler, start by funding local distributors. As George Fisk said, they know the dealers; you don't. If you have no contacts, take a risk on someone. And don't hold out for big guys. Small and hungry is often better. Don't worry if your first orders are almost nothing. Your early priority shouldn't be profits, but getting a toehold. As you get bigger, explore building your own distributorships; you can better control your destiny that way. Then, just when you do begin to get profitable, it's often time to invest again. It's tempting, observes Lawler, to start coasting once the payback begins, but far better to turn that payback around. Open your own local distributorship, hire your own people, pour money into advertising. It will mean a few more years of little profit, but the only way to realize your best potential, Lawler says, is through relentless promotion and a sales force whose sole mission is to sell your product.

Meanwhile, don't get so wrapped up in big markets that you forget the rest of the world. Go everywhere, Lawler urges. In time, ten Burundis can bring you as much revenue as one Canada. If you can get into five new countries a month, do it. You don't make money in America by tiptoeing into three large cities and stopping. You go border to border. It's the same with the world. The goal is to cover it.

Finally—go. Travel. Walk the aisles of trade shows to look for new distributors; visit those you've already signed up to make sure they're doing the job. Meet with your own sales people. The more you visit, the harder they'll want to work for you.

GO INTO most office-supply stores and you'll see plenty of racks of Parkers and Sheaffers, more racks of Mont Blancs and Watermans. Cross usually has one small display. With its tiny product line, that's all it needs. Still, Cross today has over 50 percent of America's high-end writing-instrument market. It's the only major player in the business that's both owned by Americans and made in the United States. Sheaffer was bought by the Swiss, Parker by the British, and though Waterman was recently purchased by Gillette, its product is still made in France.

Each day, at the Cross plant in Rhode Island, the Bosses still fly the small government flag they received for progress in world trade—"E" for export. World sales are now the company's biggest area of growth. But as much as Cross is one of America's major export success stories, Lawler says the company has barely begun. That is the promise of the world market—its size.

France is a final symbol of Cross's commitment to seize world markets. By now, the company should have written France off as one of its frustrations. Nine years after investing in an independent subsidiary there, its progress remains slow. Cross has managed to double its business in France—from a half-million dollars to $1 million—but despite all of its investment, profits have been thin. Cross does better in some countries a third France's size.

Many companies would look at that and decide it's time to pull back. It could be argued that France is just too hard for certain foreign products, like premium pens. But Cross will not pull out. The slow going has convinced the company to do the opposite: invest even more. Over the next five years, Cross has decided to hire more salesmen and put several million dollars into new advertising.

"If you quit," says Lawler, "you may as well fold your tent and go home everywhere."

Even in tough countries?

"That's where you have to use your resources the most." The toughest countries, he says, also have the best potential. He's convinced you can always harvest that potential, but only with staying power. One or two years isn't enough. "It takes patience," says Lawler.

So Cross will stay. It's a strategy Lawler hopes to see other U.S. manufacturers pursue. American business, he says, has always been good at being aggressive and gutsy. He thinks that if we add one more trait—patience—we can succeed even in traditional products, anywhere in the world.

III

Competing in Future Technologies

THE U.S. TRADE BALANCE in advanced-technology products went negative for the first time in 1986 and was minus $3 billion in 1987.

Japan graduates more scientists and engineers each year than the United States despite having half our population.

The governments of Europe now spend more than twice as much as the United States government on research and development for commercial products.

7

Japan:
The Race
for the Sun

THE FLIGHT from London took eighteen hours. I landed in Tokyo at 9:00 A.M. on a Sunday, soon taking my place in the immigration line. It was the summer of 1974, my first visit to Japan, and I was confident it would be a productive week. I was due to meet both industrialists and government officials, and I had prepared well, reading histories and guides, asking colleagues how to behave, setting up an itinerary weeks in advance. I'd even read some classics of Japanese literature to understand the culture. I handed the immigration man my passport, then looked around the airport, ready to move on.

"Where's your visa?"

"What visa?" I said. No one had told me I needed a visa.

"You can't enter Japan without one." Then, in a matter-of-fact tone, he said I'd have to take the next plane back to London.

I told him that was impossible. I was here for an American business-consulting firm, and had a week of important appointments.

"I'm sorry," he said.

I asked to see his supervisor. I was sure this could be worked out. But the supervisor didn't bend. All right, how about the next-highest supervisor? Finally, an hour later, I found a sympathetic ear, the airport's chief immigration man. Maybe, he said, there was a way I could get into Japan after all.

I asked how.

He told me I could appeal directly to the Foreign Affairs Ministry for a visa—but only through my employer. No problem, I thought. The Boston Consulting Group had a Tokyo branch. I offered to get one of our Japanese staffers to make an appeal by phone immediately. Not possible, he said, the Foreign Ministry is closed on Sundays. I couldn't do anything until tomorrow. Fine with me. All I wanted at that moment was my hotel room. "Can I go?" I asked.

Out of the question, he said. I couldn't leave the airport without a visa.

"Wait a minute—if the ministry's closed until tomorrow, and I can't move without a visa, what do I do in the meantime?"

"We have to put you on the next plane to London."

"But if I'm in London, I can't go to the ministry tomorrow."

"Those are the rules," he said. "You must go back to London tonight."

There had to be a way to get around these people. I told myself I'd wait for the next shift; it's all a question of finding the right person. By 1:00 P.M., I was with the daytime supervisor. He seemed more flexible. After a half hour of negotiating, he finally said there was a possible loophole—a form I could fill out requesting transit status for one day. That would let me into the country long enough to get to the ministry on Monday to request my visa. The form was eight pages long and in Japanese. A junior official sat across from me and translated each question.

"Why did you come to Japan without a visa?"

I told him, but he said it wasn't a good enough reason and suggested another. Fine—anything that he thought would work. I'd obviously found a friend. It went that way for ninety minutes. I gave honest answers, he suggested more appropriate ones, I would agree, and he would write them down. Then we were done. We took the form to the supervisor who'd first suggested I fill it out. He studied it carefully. Finally, he said something to my form filler, who bowed deeply, then turned to me.

"Your request has been denied," he said. "Your answers are not good enough."

"But you suggested all the answers."

"I'm sorry, they are not good enough."

I had no choice but to surrender. No more appeals. The next flight to London left in two hours, at 6:00 P.M., and I had to be on it. I began to get ready, but then thought of one final possibility. A Japanese colleague, working for BCG in the United States, had given me the number of his younger brother, a deputy to a member of Japan's Parliament. I asked the immigration people if I could make one last call.

"Please be quick."

The colleague's brother was home. I told him my story. One hour later, he was at the airport speaking to immigration. Five minutes later, I was on my way to the hotel. The next day, the Foreign Ministry dispatched a car to deliver my visa to the BCG Tokyo office.

It taught me something I've never forgotten. When the Japanese bureaucracy wants to slow things down, there's no more frustrating bureaucracy in the world. When it wants to speed things up, there is no bureaucracy more efficient. During the next fourteen years, as I traveled to Japan some seventy times, doing consulting work for dozens of corporations, it was the same lesson, again and again. Always, the bureaucracy; sometimes nimble, sometimes immovable, all depending on Japan's best interests. Its skill, I found, stood out in one area above all others: steering the economy.

LONG BEFORE most governments saw the advent of a global economy, Japan's had already formed strategies to help companies compete in it. It gave incentives for investment, shared risk for new products, backed R&D, and underwrote export. But all the while, it was careful to let the free market work. My visits showed me how companies there competed as vigorously with each other as with the world. Steadily, I watched the country's economy progress. At first, in the late 1960's, Japan's main products were cheap radios and textiles, then steel and cars, and eventually semiconductors. It was done very methodically. All along, the key strategy was to emphasize efficient manufacturing. They borrowed our inventions—the automobile, the color TV, the VCR— and pushed for low-cost, high-quality ways to produce them. Soon they'd earned a reputation as the world's best manufacturers.

But Americans remained the world's best inventors. That was our economic weapon: creating new technology. Our university scientists, our corporate R&D labs, our government science support—none of it could be equaled. Even as the Japanese caught up to us in manufacturing, we stayed ahead in research. But today, something new is happening. Japan has taken another step in its competitive strategy. It has begun to challenge us in our last area of leadership, the R&D lab. Today, despite having only half our population, Japan graduates more engineers and scientists than we do. In the past decade, the Japanese have marshaled that brainpower to organize an extraordinary research drive, facing off against us over the industries of the next century. There are many battlegrounds—microelectronics, fifth-generation computers, advanced ceramics, biotechnology, superconductors. Many won't lead to high-volume products for ten to twenty years, much too long for most companies to keep up expensive R&D. Japan's bureaucracy understands that. That's why it's helping companies pioneer new commercial technologies—far more than our government is helping our own. That's why Japan has begun to match us not just in manufacturing, but inventing as well.[1]

The race, perhaps, can best be glimpsed through the story of a particular future technology, photovoltaics, the conversion of sun to electricity through silicon solar cells. The cells have only begun to emerge commercially—on calculators, outdoor lights, remote communication stations, and pilot power plants—but they hold the prospect of becoming a multibillion dollar industry, perhaps in a decade. Other future technologies will be bigger, but there's a reason why photovoltaics is an important story to tell. It's a unique symbol of America's potential to beat Japan, and also our potential to lose. It's one of the only cases where America launched a major government program to help private companies achieve commercial leadership. While that program was still in place, we were the world's solar pacesetter. Then it was stopped. And now we're falling behind. We're falling behind Japan.

TODAY, Paul Maycock looks back on his classroom years and describes himself as a typical student egghead—straight A's through high school, and a college major in physics. Industry noticed. RCA sent Maycock a telegram at Iowa State, offering him a job in its labs. Although he was due to go in the navy to pay back a scholarship, Maycock was able to pledge RCA several months. He arrived at the company's Camden, New Jersey, branch in the summer of 1957, the same summer the American occupation headquarters in Japan finally closed. He was looking forward to joining one of the nation's great research firms. He couldn't have been more let down.

RCA assigned him to the "Call of the Wild," a tape player that put out birdcalls to attract prey for hunters. His job was to make a transistorized model, getting rid of the old vacuum-tube design. After a week, Maycock told his boss he was bored. He was a physicist, not a circuit designer. Couldn't he get in on a project that was more groundbreaking?

Well, said his boss, if he didn't mind bad hours, there was a possibility. On Long Island, at the Brookhaven National Laboratory, RCA had a government-funded team working on one of the world's newest technologies—photovoltaic energy. America was about to launch its first satellite, and the government wanted it powered by cells that turned sunlight to electricity. Soon, Maycock was there. The solar cells, about a quarter-inch square, were made with what was then considered a wondrous new substance—pure silicon. The specific experiment was to see whether the cells would break down under the radiation of space.

Maycock was given the midnight to 6:00 A.M. shift, assigned to take down data all night. It was fine with him. At age twenty-one, he'd come East with the hope of associating with the best scientists, and now he was doing so. One of those overseeing the experiment was a man who would become one of the fathers of solar science—Joseph Loferski.

THERE WAS no question in Loferski's mind why America was the world's science leader: Government was committed to making it happen. He himself typified that commitment. His education was federally funded, and so was the riskiest research at RCA. Soon after he came to the company, government reached out to Loferski again. William Cherry, a Washington science administrator, called to ask if he'd come to the Brookhaven labs. Cherry's job was to search the country for top scientists and steer them into priority research. In this case, he wanted Loferski to help develop solar cells to power satellites. Loferski took the offer, eventually supervising the project that young Paul Maycock worked on. When it was done, Cherry called Loferski again, this time just to explore where government should go next with solar. The challenge, then as now, was efficiency—to make cells that would generate as much electricity as possible from a beam of sunlight.

Both Loferski and Cherry utterly believed in solar's potential. A shaft of sunlight covering a square yard of earth, they knew, contains 1,000 watts of power—enough to light ten 100-watt bulbs. But in the early 1950's, standard solar cells could barely convert one percent of that to electricity. The day they increased it to 15 or 20 percent, and reduced the cost of the cells, a few solar panels would be as good as a barrel of oil. Some physicists doubted it could ever happen, but Cherry was convinced. His mission was to make sure America led in developing this technology. Would Loferski be willing to keep pursuing it on government contract? It depended, Loferski said, on how much money was available. Money, said Cherry, wasn't a problem. The government was committed to solar R&D. The latest contract, to be funneled into RCA's research labs, would be for tens of thousands of dollars, a healthy amount at the time. Loferski signed on.

Although Cherry was with the Army Signal Corps, he didn't see the solar effort for defense alone. He felt it could evolve into a new industry. First, however, the technology would have to be made cost-effective. That probably wouldn't happen, Cherry knew, with a single breakthrough by a single Thomas Edison. Most scientific leadership is more complex than that. It grows out of a thousand breakthroughs. The nation that will lead, Cherry felt, is the nation willing to fund a whole range of research. Now, with solar, it began to happen in America. In the late 1950's, Loferski remembers going to an international photovoltaic conference in Tucson. There were no Japanese there, and only a few Europeans. The vast majority—almost a hundred researchers—were Americans. Almost all were supported by the government.

IT WAS in the mid-1800's that scientists first noticed the phenomenon of photovoltaics: Put certain materials in the sun, like treated copper, and you'd get a tiny electric charge. But no one knew how to harness it until 1955. That year, labs all over America were exploring new uses for silicon, the key to turning bulky vacuum tubes into tiny transistors. At Bell Labs, scientists were convinced silicon could be the key to solar-energy conversion, as well.

At the time, Morton Prince, now with the Department of Energy, was a young researcher working at Bell on solar cells. The challenge was to get the efficiency up from a fraction of a percent. The solution, if there was one, would be to change the silicon somehow, heightening its performance. But all Bell's experiments failed.

Finally, on a hunch, the Bell researchers wondered whether just the right spray of boron could do it. Prince remembers the day they tried it, putting a small silicon wafer in a glass ampule, painting on a source of boron, sticking it in a lab oven, and cooking it to 1,500 degrees Fahrenheit. The boron diffused nicely. They cleaned the wafer, soldered wire contacts on its back to catch the charge, and then it was time for the test. They hooked the wafer to a meter and simply walked over to a sunny lab window. They were praying for 5 percent efficiency—it would mark a terrific victory. The sun hit the wafer. Together, the team watched the meter. It went to six percent.

They'd done it. In America's most famous lab, on a day in December 1955, a month that saw the United Nations refuse to admit Japan, a group of Americans had opened the door to yet another new technology.

SOON Paul Maycock's summer at the Brookhaven solar lab was over. It was time to pay back his navy scholarship by doing a three-year officer's tour. Because he'd had superior grades, he was given the right to pick his billet. He knew where he wanted to go—and it wasn't the laboratory. Although a trained physicist, Maycock felt that only part of science is research. Another part, equally important, is to make sure there's support for it. At the time, the navy had just the job to let Maycock do that: giving out contracts to universities doing semiconductor work. Maycock took it. He found there was a lot of money to give out, $2 million. It was enough to let him feed a range of projects—semiconductors, fiber optics, photovoltaics and even the precursor to "Star

Wars": lasers for space weaponry. No other nation, he knew, had that kind of science support. Maycock himself was especially intrigued with solar. At the time, most of the projects were geared for space. Soon, he knew, America would have the world's first satellite in orbit. When it got up there, its energy would come not from nuclear or traditional batteries; it would come from the sun. He was proud that his favorite technology would be part of his country's most prestigious national experiment.

Then came a shock. Maycock happened to be doing a shift as watch officer in the Pentagon's command center one evening in 1957, when some of the sensors picked up a funny noise—a beep. Soon they figured where it was coming from. The Russians had beat them. They'd gotten up their own satellite first—one named *Sputnik*. Years later, Maycock would remember a Clare Boothe Luce poem printed on the front page of *The Washington Post* that mirrored the nation's fears: "Little slow beep. The Americans sleep—you know where to find them. Leave them alone, they'll quarrel at home, and you can mop up the world behind them." Most of America came to a consensus that week: If we're to lead in technology, we have to do two things. One, work harder. Two, pour more money into research and education. Maycock vowed to be part of making that happen.

THE AUTUMN of *Sputnik* found Japan still recovering from the war, too caught up in rebuilding the past to worry about researching the future. It had begun to do limited exporting, but mostly cheap clothing and toys. The country's living standard was less than a fifth of that in the United States. Its most advanced technologies were steel and shipbuilding, industries the United States had long since taken for granted. Photovoltaics was of no interest. Japan did almost no scientific pioneering at all. With few resources for lab work, the country's strategy was to borrow technology, not invent it. Between 1945 and 1970, Japanese companies bought twenty-five thousand foreign technology licenses. A full 80 percent of those came from one country, the United States.

IN 1960, in his lab at RCA, Joe Loferski got a letter from Brown University inviting him to join their faculty. It came at the right time; to move up at RCA would have meant becoming an administrator. Loferski preferred the lab, and Brown offered that. His only concern was whether there'd be enough money for experiments. Because of government, there was more than enough. The Defense Department had targeted semiconductors—silicon—as a crucial technology. That included photovoltaics. New equipment? No problem. Loferski was able to buy one machine for twenty-five thousand dollars and another for twenty thousand dollars, and no one blinked at the bill. Throughout the

1960's, research contracts kept coming; from NASA, the Defense Department, the National Science Foundation. The breakthroughs came, too. But suddenly, around 1970, things slowed down.

American science had delivered on solar's first challenge—space. Satellites using solar cells were being launched. The next step for photovoltaics was on earth; for power plants, for houses, for products. That was a challenge for industry. At the time, however, it wasn't cost-effective; it was far cheaper to generate electricity with coal, oil, or gas. With a payoff probably a decade away, private business wasn't interested, at least not without government help. And at the moment, that help was dwindling.

Loferski and his colleagues tried to argue for more commitment. To win in a new technology, they said—any new technology—you can't start research only when it's cost-effective. You need to begin years in advance. For that, Washington was essential. But the Defense Department had few solar projects on its table. The Vietnam War was taking up most of the budget. And there was no other government arm with big research money for future industrial technologies. America's solar effort began to slow.

THEN, in 1973, the world got a shock as jarring as *Sputnik.* OPEC suddenly hiked the price of oil, pushing the industrial West into crisis. All over the country, Americans found themselves waiting in gas lines. Paul Maycock, then working at Texas Instruments, felt solar energy was more urgent than ever. He decided to leave TI and take a job as director of solar planning for ERDA, the country's Energy Research and Development Administration. The job, he knew, would give him the power to turn the solar-research faucets back on. His key mission would be to usher in a new source of energy, but he saw another mission as well: to usher in a new American industry—new jobs and wealth. To Maycock, it was partly a matter of pride. Photovoltaics was an American invention, in his eyes one of the greatest. He wanted to make sure it would also be an American product.

THE UNITED STATES wasn't the only nation hurt by the energy crisis. Japan, which imported 100 percent of its oil, was devastated. In 1973, the Japanese government decided to act. It formed a research effort called Project Sunshine, aimed at developing alternate sources of energy. Yutaka Hayashi was one of the first scientists it supported. He'd just come back to Japan after spending a few years studying at Stanford in California. The facilities there, he'd found, were state of the art, and most of the research was government-funded. He was left in awe of America's commitment to science. Now, back home, Hayashi found the commitment in Japan a bit different. True, he'd gotten government research backing, but he'd been assigned to a crowded, underfinanced lab on the outskirts of Tokyo. Hayashi began his work by looking back overseas, toward America, the world's science leader. He gathered up all the U.S. solar literature from the previous twenty years and started going over it. What direction should he explore? Since part of the problem was the high cost of crystal silicon, commonly used for solar, Hayashi decided to focus on cells that used the least material possible— thin film cells. By 1975, Hayashi had begun to earn a reputation in the field, presenting a paper at the prestigious Institute of Electronics and Communications Engineers in Japan. Still, he knew he was playing catch-up. He had no illusions about where Japan stood in solar: far behind the United States.

WHEN THE Department of Energy was created in 1977, Paul Maycock found himself director of photovoltaics in a full-fledged Cabinet agency. He was convinced Washington now had the potential to do for solar what NASA had done for space. But he saw a difference. Maycock wanted this to be more than science leadership, he wanted it to be commercial, as well. He wanted to spur private business into developing a whole new industry. His plan was to help companies work not on defense projects, or theoretical research, but actual solar products. It wasn't just for the sake of America's energy needs, but also the economy. Eventually, Maycock saw solar becoming a huge industry, and he wanted its rewards to flow to the United States. That would take government's help up front, but unlike the space program, Maycock wanted solar eventually turned over to private companies. But how? What support do you give to start it? What incentives? Maycock knew where to look for a model—defense. For decades, America had led the world in military technology through a three-legged partnership: science, industry, and government. He and his staff began to craft a congressional act that would tailor the same approach to the technology of the sun.

The first step was research. That meant contracts to help scientists like Loferski unlock the secrets to high-efficiency solar cells. The second step was commercial readiness—funding for companies willing to develop solar products, principally power generation, which promised to be the biggest future gold mine. The final step was to create an early market for those products—a government market. Otherwise, they'd be too expensive to sell, and companies would have no incentive to start production. America, Maycock felt, wouldn't win the solar race if all it had were laboratory prototypes. It was essential to get photovoltaic factories built, to get photovoltaic production going. That way, industry would be poised for commercial sales once solar became cheap enough to compete in the marketplace. Maycock's decision was to have the government place early orders for demonstration projects. That would give companies a reason to start manufacturing. He and his staff sketched it all into a bill called the Photovoltaic Research, Development and Demonstration Act of 1978. It called for $1.2 billion of government money spread over ten years. It was groundbreaking—the first time in recent history that government had ever planned to create a new, non-military industry.

Maycock went to Congress to testify on the plan. There was no reason why America should be energy-dependent, he argued, and plenty of reasons why it shouldn't. "I hated the whole concept of buying oil from the Persian Gulf and spending $50 billion a year defending that part of the world," he would say later. "I didn't see what the point was when we could eventually have all the renewable energy we wanted." At the time, the energy crisis was still a hot national issue. The congressional vote was overwhelming—90 percent in favor. President Carter showed his support by having solar panels installed on the roof of the White House.

A year later, 1979, when the second energy crisis hit, Maycock's plan was already under way. He'd gotten thirty private companies, twenty-five universities, and four government labs all working on photovoltaics. He was careful to avoid redundant research. That was one value of government's role—it could act as referee to keep the players from duplicating efforts. One firm, for example, got a contract for slicing silicon, another for developing new coating materials, still others for increasing the cells' wattage. It wasn't anti–free market. Companies were still at liberty to pursue whatever they wanted with their own money. But Maycock wanted government's dollars to be used as efficiently as possible.

Maycock's next challenge was to make sure the companies talked to each other. If this was to work, the research knowledge would have to be shared. If all Maycock did was toss out fifty projects, each isolated from the others, the puzzle would never come together. That, he knew, was how technology research had traditionally gone in the United States. Communications was a weak point of the American R&D machine. The first breakthroughs on a new technology are usually made in universities, but since professors and industry rarely talk, it takes a long time for those breakthroughs to turn into products. The data usually doesn't surface for corporate engineers until the science periodicals publish it, sometimes a year later. That's fine if there's no competition, but if there is, especially overseas you risk being passed by. So Maycock set up a system to speed knowledge into the hands of companies. He scheduled regular meetings to bring government-funded experts together—twice a year for university researchers, twice for manufacturers, and once for everyone. Meanwhile, he made it the mission of his own staff to stay up on all contracts, passing more urgent news between the players, requiring companies to share breakthroughs with each other.

Then came a final government role. To make sure industry wasn't overlooking some of the puzzle pieces, Maycock's administrators surveyed the landscape of progress, seeing where there was more work to be done. If they found a neglected area, he'd offer a specific contract to coax a company to explore it. By 1980, the first year Maycock's program was up to pace, the government was spending $150 million on solar energy, enough to get private companies interested in it years before they normally would have been.

LATE IN 1974, I was having dinner in the coffee shop of Tokyo's Palace Hotel, home of one of the best plates of spaghetti in Japan. My dinner companion was a government economist. In the States, I was used to such officials dwelling on next month's producer-price index. The view here was a bit longer. My companion began outlining a national vision of stunning clarity—a stage-by-stage strategy of how Japan planned to move up the ladder of economic sophistication. Look back twenty years, he told me, to the 1950's. Everything Japan exported then was low-skill goods—mostly toys and shoes. By the 1960's, however, Japan moved up a level, to industries like steel, fertilizers, and ships. By this decade, the 1970's, they were moving into ever more complex goods, like cars and consumer electronics. I asked him about government's role. It certainly wasn't as spectator, I learned. He talked of how they'd given businesses loans, grants, and tax breaks to make each step possible. But he stressed that it was by incentive, not decree. The private sector was aided, not ordered.

"What next?" I asked.

"Next, we are preparing to move to knowledge industries like computers, telecommunications, machine tools, and semiconductors." Their plan, he said, was to be world-competitive in those by the 1980's.

"And after that?" I asked.

"After that, we will invent new technology instead of simply copying yours."

"Very ambitious," I said skeptically. Then I asked how could they beat giants like General Motors and Texas Instruments?

"They are, of course, very good companies, but they are too complacent. We will invest more. And our government will work with industry to catch up, and eventually win."

I was still skeptical, but also intrigued. The vision he'd laid out for me was devised by MITI[2]—the Ministry of International Trade and Industry. It's far more powerful than our own Department of Commerce. One of MITI's key functions is to target strategic industries, then support them with low-cost loans, tax breaks, R&D grants, and export help. For example, in the early 1970's, MITI decided that Japan needed a computer industry. It encouraged firms to enter the field and banks to lend them money. As further help, the government limited computer imports, organized a national research push, and offered financing for the computer producers. It set up a leasing company to help create a market for newly developed Japanese computers, even agreeing to repurchase outmoded machines as new generations became available. It also offered cheap financing to customers.

By 1979, as my dinner companion had predicted, I was seeing Japan making the same methodical progress in machine tools, telecommunications, and semiconductors as it had made in steel and ships. The next year, I decided to co-author a book on Japanese industrial policy and plans, and soon was giving speeches on the Japanese threat. But American businessmen seemed unconcerned. I remember a debate I had in Washington with the head of one of our leading electronics firms. "The Japanese are copiers," he said. "Their culture isn't suited for new-technology industries."[3]

But each time I returned to Japan, the progress was stunning. By the early 1980's, I was no longer skeptical of what my dinner companion had laid out for me that day at the Palace Hotel.

THE SECOND oil crisis in 1979 convinced MITI to redouble its push into solar energy.[4] It adopted a strategy similar to the plan Paul Maycock had just helped get through Congress. The Japanese increased funding for academic research, began to sponsor demonstration projects to give companies an early market, and organized scientific meetings to make sure everyone shared knowledge. But there was a difference. America was still spending far more on solar than Japan. America was still the clear leader.

FOR JOE LOFERSKI, who'd seen solar-research money dry up at Brown University in the early 1970's, Maycock's program couldn't have been more welcome. For the first time in years, Loferski got all the funding he asked for. He decided to focus not just on theory, but on products. In a sense, that was the influence of Maycock, who'd gotten everyone to see this as a commercial race. One of Loferski's bolder ideas was a system that would produce almost all the power needs of a house. At the time, there were two separate paths in solar, photovoltaic and thermal, which involved heating water by running it through sun-baked roof panels. Loferski designed panels that did both. With government help, he ordered three thousand separate silicon cells, then fabricated them into three-by-six foot modules. He went on to rig them to a prefab house. His goal was to make it affordable, not just a scientist's wonder.

At one point, as he got close to running through his grant, he turned to private sources, including a local utility. They gave him what he needed. Solar's future, Loferski felt, was more promising than ever.

MEANWHILE, Loferski's counterpart in Tokyo, Dr. Yutaka Hayashi, was still struggling on a shoestring. He had to hunt for discount equipment, asking science companies for used goods. For knowledge, he continued to look toward America, which was where all the breakthroughs were coming. One of the most interesting, Hayashi noticed, was the use of a new, potentially cheaper kind of thin-film silicon. So far, most solar cells were made of expensive bulk-crystal silicon. Now, RCA had gotten good results out of cheaper amorphous silicon. Its efficiency was lower than crystal—only a few percent as opposed to over ten—but its cost made it promising. If you could boost the efficiency of amorphous, Hayashi felt, it might be the best way to get affordable power. At the time, few in America thought you could do that. The American focus stayed on crystal. But Hayashi began to look at amorphous closer. So did a lab colleague named Dr. Kasunoru Tanaka. At the University of Osaka, a noted professor—Yoshihiro Hamakawa—focused on amorphous, as well. But the real momentum was coming from industry.

It began all the way back in 1967, with a Sanyo company researcher named Yukinori Kuwano. He was intrigued with the properties of amorphous, but back then knew it was out of the question as a commercial idea. That, however, didn't stop him from pursuing it at Sanyo. He began to surreptitiously gather supplies, adding requests for amorphous items at the bottom of equipment orders he'd put in for his other company work. He stored the surreptitious experiment in a surplus metal locker, breaking it out during free time. None of Dr. Kuwano's bosses formally approved what he was doing, but he knew he'd have the freedom to pursue it anyway. It's that way in many big Japanese companies. Although Americans see Japan's firms as regimented, with all employees strictly following corporate assignments, it's often quite different. Researchers are routinely allowed to do under-the-table experimenting, using company money. Indulging personal creativity, management feels, will often bring a payback.

So Kuwano was able to go ahead with his amorphous tinkering. His main progress was in making it into thin film. He didn't make much headway on its solar potential, though. That was RCA's breakthrough. But shortly afterward, the American amorphous research trailed off. Kuwano, however, began to commit more and more time to it. By now, his Sanyo experimenting was out from under the table and officially backed by the company. Not long afterward, other Japanese researchers, like Hayashi, Tanaka, and Hamakawa, were pursuing it. All the efforts, however, were scattered, and Japan's new amorphous converts knew it. They knew they could best move forward if someone was coordinating the work. Government alone had the ability to do that. In 1980, they persuaded MITI's Project Sunshine to start a serious program in amorphous silicon solar cells.

IN AMERICA, that same year, Maycock turned to the next stage of his program—getting industry into solar manufacturing. At Westinghouse, in Pittsburgh, the contract people received a Maycock RFP—request for proposal. Usually, those came from the Department of Defense, but Westinghouse noted this one was different; it came from the new Department of Energy. Specifically, DOE wanted designs for a factory line that would manufacture solar modules. The best proposals would win several million dollars. It seemed tailor-made for Westinghouse. Years before, in the early days of solar, the company had come up with a way to make photovoltaic silicon in ribbon form. At the time, it was too expensive to think of developing, so the Westinghouse people had shelved it. But now government was telling them it would share their risk if they got back in. They agreed. Charles Rose, who later would take charge of Westinghouse's photovoltaic program, was a key manager on the team.

Although new to solar, Rose had experience in shepherding lab work into manufacturing, having done it before with thermal power systems for submarines and space. This, Rose realized, would be his first government project geared not for defense, but the consumer. He knew some would say that's not the American way—the free market alone should determine what becomes a commercial product. He would agree with that, especially for products people are ready to buy. Government, he felt, shouldn't help industry develop a new line of cars. But this was different, a future technology. Government, Rose will tell you, had always been involved in future technologies—funding research for nuclear, space, a half-dozen others.

"Nobody went out and developed the transistor on his own," Rose says. Or computers. Washington poured hundreds of millions into those efforts. The payoff of those technologies, he explains, is now clear, both in defense and jobs. With global competition intensifying, he thinks it's more urgent than ever for government to help with new technologies. The country that waits for the market to drive research, he says, is the country that will be left behind—probably by the Japanese.

Maycock felt the same. That's why he'd sent out the RFPs. Rose had one month to send back a proposal. His team, which was supervised by Westinghouse manager Donald Roberts, went at it sixteen hours a day, seven days a week. "It was a high-burn period," Rose would say later.

The name of their process was called dendritic web. It was a way of making crystal silicon, but in ribbon form, like camera film, thinner than it had ever been made before. Thinner meant less silicon, and less meant cheaper. Rose knew amorphous silicon was cheaper still, but less efficient at the time; it only converted 6–8 percent of the sun to power. The crystal Westinghouse was using had the potential of going to 15 percent or more. The company's proposal was for a prototype line that would make large solar modules to power cities, towns, or institutions. Ultimately, the Westinghouse plan was for a factory that would make ten thousand modules a year, one every half hour. It asked the government for $3.3 million spread over two and a half years, which Westinghouse would match. The proposal was sent in. There were tense days waiting to hear. Rose and his colleagues knew a half-dozen others were bidding, too, and only two would be picked for this particular project. Finally, the call came. One of the contracts was theirs. Soon Westinghouse had joined a score of other American companies in stepping up solar research with government's help.

ACROSS the Pacific, Sanyo increased its solar budget. Beginning in the late 1970's, it had been joined in the race by several Japanese companies. Fuji Electric was one. But it wasn't much of an effort, at least in the eyes of Dr. Hiromu Haruki, Fuji's laboratory director. At first, he didn't see much hope for Japan's taking the lead in photovoltaics. He knew enough about solar to know America was far ahead. Still, it was probably worth a small program. He put a few workers on it. Then came the 1979 oil shock. Fuji asked Dr. Haruki to build up his program. At first, he hesitated. Was it worth pouring company resources into a technology that was years away? Soon, though, he found there was an incentive to do so. Project Sunshine—MITI's alternative energy program—had begun to offer major solar development contracts to companies. Haruki told his people to apply. At Sanyo, Kuwano's people applied, too.

FOR PAUL MAYCOCK, the start of the new decade was a heady time. Photovoltaic cells began to go commercial. Fifteen companies, almost all American, were bringing in sales in the tens of millions,[5] marketing systems for remote communications stations, desert pumps, offshore platforms, marine buoys, and even whole power systems for Third World villages. Some of the companies, like Westinghouse, were big ones, others gutsy entrepreneurs. "These people were visionaries who wanted to accomplish something," said Maycock. "They were the kind of entrepreneurs who never complain; they were optimistic even when they were close to bankrupt. Their nature was to risk."

Soon a number of Maycock's contract projects began to take shape.

There was a demo system that lit a school, another that lit a house. In Chicago, the ribbon for a solar-powered gas station was cut on the very day a thunderstorm knocked out power in the city. The sun came back out, and the station was the only one in the area able to pump gas. Then there was Maycock's favorite moment. In Arizona, a system gave power to fourteen homes in a remote Indian village. It cost ninety thousand dollars, but running cable from the nearest power plant would have cost more. Still, one of the TV reporters asked a village woman if it was worth all the money—the equivalent of sixty-five hundred dollars per house. Well, she answered, her husband just paid six thousand dollars for a pickup truck, and she didn't even drive; now she had lights for the kids to read by, a washing machine for clothes, a refrigerator to keep the milk cold. Yes, she said, there was no question it was worth it.

DURING those same years of 1980 and 1981, MITI began one of its biggest projects ever: the construction of a research city two hours from Tokyo, bigger than most major college campuses in the States.[6] It was named Tsukuba, nicknamed Science City. Its mission was not just to unlock nature's secrets, but to help Japan's industries develop products. There were other national labs around Japan, but the idea of Tsukuba was to put thousands of scientists from different disciplines together, able to feed knowledge back and forth. In one of the most impressive buildings, the electrotechnical lab, an entire section was mapped out for research into photovoltaics. Soon Dr. Yutaka Hayashi moved out of his crowded quarters near Tokyo, into a new lab in Science City.

The same spirit that created Tsukuba—the spirit of inventing technology instead of copying it—began to show itself in Japan's solar companies. Bolstered by government research money, Sanyo resolved to do some inventing of its own; it resolved to develop the world's first amorphous solar product. The assignment was given to Dr. Kuwano, who'd started his work in a surplus metal locker. But what product? What photovoltaic product could be mass-marketed immediately? He knew America's solar industry was pouring most of its dollars into power generation, but that, he felt, was next decade's market. The U.S. companies had chosen it because it's what they knew best—most were stepchildren of American oil and power companies—but Sanyo had other kinds of expertise. Specifically, consumer electronics. That's what Kuwano decided to pursue. The first product he had in mind was the calculator. The U.S. solar people found his choice puzzling.

"Americans laughed when we started development of solar cells for consumer products," he says.

But the choice reflected the strategy of many Japanese companies: If you want to win in a new technology, get into a mass product immediately. Though Kuwano knew calculators wouldn't be very profitable, they'd be an instant market, a reason for the company to move quickly from lab to factory. That, in turn, would give Sanyo expertise it could build on once the big-dollar products—like power generation— became feasible in the 1990's. The way to win an edge in a new technology, Kuwano felt, wasn't to spend years in the lab perfecting the ultimate product, it was to get a broad base in product, and to get it before anyone else.

AT WESTINGHOUSE, Charles Rose pulled together a team of engineers, took over a section of a company plant that had last been used to help with a NASA Mars mission, and went to work on his Department of Energy contract. Westinghouse's final goal was an assembly line, but first, the company had to design the end-result product itself—a solar module. The contract gave Westinghouse a three-month deadline for that. Rose's team met it, but he still decided they were going too slowly. Just because this was government money didn't mean his incentive was dulled. He knew a dozen other U.S. solar companies had contracts, too. This was a race, and Rose wanted Westinghouse to succeed first. The next deadline—nine months away—was to set up a prototype of the assembly line itself. Rose and his boss, Donald Roberts, decided to speed things up. With one engineer assigned to head off bottlenecks by putting together critical-path priorities on computer, the team finished in only three months instead of nine.

Soon, a camaraderie was built. This was more than a new product; it was a new source of energy. Westinghouse's production line would be making solar panels for electrical power generation, and the team saw a national urgency to it. Their first test would be the efficiency of their prototype solar panel. Would it deliver the power they hoped for? The day of the testing came. They put the module in a dark area enclosed by curtains. They set up a xenon high-intensity pulse light, filtered to match the sun. The test would be quick enough, just a flash. A technician gave the instructions to a computer console to trigger the light. For this to be practical, they knew they had to hit at least 10 percent efficiency. The xenon put out a burst. The computer console instantly displayed a power curve. It climbed all the way to 11.8 percent. That made it one of the most efficient manufacturable modules in the world. Westinghouse was ready to build its line.

BY 1981, Dr. Hayashi, newly settled into his Science City laboratory, marked his sixth anniversary of spending full time on photovoltaic energy. He'd only recently come to feel he was working at full speed. He'll tell you it often takes that long to master an area of research. That, he says, is why government is so important—it's far more able than companies to let specialists pursue basic science year after year. If a country is to develop a promising but unproven technology, Hayashi says, it needs to offer researchers the freedom to give all their focus to it. Now, Hayashi was focusing, chiefly on how to get more power out of amorphous. He took the classic trial-and-error approach, trying new ways to coat silicon chips, just as Bell Labs had done when it invented the first solar cell by adding boron.

At the time, many amorphous cells were made with a coating of indium oxide, but Hayashi knew it didn't work too well. Those cells were only 4 percent efficient. Maybe tin oxide would do better. He tried it, and it indeed delivered a little more, though not as much as he'd hoped. Still, he decided to stay with it.

"Of every thousand experiments," Hayashi will tell you, "one is successful." He tried different combinations, different ratios. He talked it out with his staff, at lunch, in the car, in the lab. One night, he was there late, after 9:00 P.M., working on a document, when an idea came to him. The standard way of layering on the tin oxide was to cook the cell in a lab oven at 400 degrees. Why not raise the temperature? The next day, he tried it at 450. He took out the finished chip and put it under a microscope. The surface had gone fizzy—crinkled. In solar cells, the accepted wisdom was that smooth is best. Had he been a corporate researcher, Hayashi says, he'd have thrown it out and started over. But he wasn't corporate. He was government. He had the luxury to follow every path, and his scientist's instinct told him not to give up. So he made a few more of the cells, then hooked them to a meter and exposed them to light. They actually gave better current. Unexpectedly, the texture had ended up trapping light instead of deflecting it. Maybe this would be a breakthrough after all.

Hayashi and one of his colleagues began giving a third of their time to tin oxide, a freedom they probably wouldn't have had as corporate scientists. Within a few months, they'd pushed the efficiency from 4 percent to 6.5 percent. Within a year, they had it to 8 percent, and moving toward 10. The government speeded their discoveries into the hands of industry. Soon Fuji and Sanyo were using tin oxide applied at high temperature in their experiments with power modules. In the life of solar science, it was just a small increment. But dozens of other Hayashis were producing other increments for Japanese industry. Without them, the country's Sanyos and Fujis would have needed years for each leap forward. Now, that was being compressed to months.

IN AMERICA, the government's late 1970's solar program grew chiefly out of the vision of one man—Paul Maycock. In a nation like America, a nation of individualists, the best policies often happen that way. Japan, a nation of consensus, believes in institutionalizing its visions.

Once the Sunshine Program was launched, it was driven by bureaucratic commitment, not a single visionary. Instead of having one Paul Maycock, Japan had a series of such men, assigned as officers on a ship whose course was already set. By design, the officers were rotated—a new head of solar technology for Project Sunshine was named every two years. Sho Marukawa had the job in 1987.

Like many members of MITI, he'd had impeccable schooling. In 1972, he graduated from Tokyo University, the nation's most prestigious college. At age twenty-four, he went directly into MITI. Could he have been paid more in private industry? Marukawa laughs. "It can't get much lower in this country than MITI," he says.

Does it mean a life-style sacrifice?

Well, he says, he'd rather not talk about the size of his house, or his hours—usually from 7:30 A.M. to 9:00 P.M. But he likes being part of planning for Japan's future. He explains that it's the only way to avoid crisis—especially in a nation that lacks America's resources. Japan, Marukawa will point out, has half our population—120 million people—squeezed onto only ⅟₂₅ our space. Geography has taught the Japanese to avoid waste. Look over the rooftops of downtown Tokyo and you'll see that almost half are used for recreation—tennis courts, jogging paths, athletic fields. It's a culture that seeks to squeeze the maximum from all they have. Marukawa's mission is to turn that philosophy toward the sun. His goal is to get affordable solar power by the year 2000. Now that it's still a technology challenge, his immediate call is to spur research. He talks of the conferences he organizes several times a year to get all those on government contract to share knowledge. He talks more of how his staff regularly visits solar projects, immediately passing on information to other researchers they feel would benefit.

For a bureaucrat, he speaks excitedly. It's amazing how much potential there is in solar, he says, adding that if all the sunlight that hits the earth's surface could be captured at 100 percent efficiency for only forty minutes, it would power the world for a year. He gives numbers to show how the Japanese are closing the price gap. It now costs them about $1.60 to generate one kilowatt-hour from the sun, and around 16 cents for oil. A decade before, a kilowatt from the sun cost one hundred times more. He is convinced the lines will eventually cross.

NOW THAT Westinghouse's prototype module had proved itself, it was time to put together the manufacturing line itself. But finding the hardware would be difficult. Charles Rose and Don Roberts would need wet-chemical-processing gear, cell-assembly equipment, and machines for web and crystal growth—none of which could be bought from a catalog. The company would have to design them. That kind of work, Rose and Roberts knew, would be enormously expensive. Take the machine for electrically interconnecting solar cells into a module. Rose figured it would cost almost nine hundred thousand dollars in 1981 dollars, but only a quarter of that was for parts. Most would be for the one-time expense of designing it. That kind of investment is worth it, says Rose, if you can get a return by selling the final product quickly. But if the market's still five or ten years away, it's too risky—unless you have government help. He adds that it need only be one-time help. With design out of the way, the next machine would cost them a quarter as much to build, which they could afford on their own. He also adds that the government money was not a free ride. Westinghouse itself had to buy the actual equipment. Soon they'd spent over $4 million on it. He felt it was worth the risk. Solar might not be big until the year 2000, but Rose was convinced the winners would be among those starting now.

IT WAS around that time, the spring of 1981, that I had a chance to glimpse the solar industry myself. Volvo's energy subsidiary had been approached by a Swiss inventor who'd come up with a solar cell that seemed to have promise. He wanted a few million dollars for the rights to it, a price Volvo was ready to pay. But first, Volvo wanted to know what kind of market solar was going to have. Management asked me to do a study.

I began in Europe, calling the technology people in a number of government ministries. They all said there was no question about who was ahead in photovoltaics: the United States. The oil shock had increased interest in energy alternatives—wind, geothermal, synthetic fuels—but the biggest excitement, I found, was photovoltaics. The Europeans saw this as a huge industry in fifteen years, and were envious that America was out front. There wasn't much question in their minds as to why; our Energy Department had the world's premier solar program. At a stage when leadership meant R&D, we were doing more of it than anyone else. Japan was clearly second, and likely to stay there. It was a rainy country, without America's sunlight. It was a crowded place, too, without much room to spread out solar modules. And though the government commitment there was good, America's was three times as good.

After my talks in Europe, I flew back home to explore with the U.S. industry, starting with a company called Solar Power in Massachusetts. Its president, Elliott Berman, was a classic American entrepreneur. He'd gambled on solar back in the early 1970's, and having just sold his company to Exxon, was looking forward to a big infusion of capital. Meanwhile, the government was already behind Berman—80 percent of his research was underwritten by Washington. Give the industry five or ten years, Berman told me, and solar will be cheap enough to start competing with oil in the Southwest. He wasn't worried about Japan. If America kept up its momentum, he said, the Japanese wouldn't have much chance.

I traveled west then, glimpsing models of solar's future. With government's help, Pacific Gas & Electric had covered a few acres of southern California with angled modules, cabling them together to make a prototype power plant, the kind that had the promise of feeding cities. Then I saw a builder in Phoenix—John Long. With the help of Maycock's program, he'd just finished putting up a miniphotovoltaic plant for a housing project. On cloudless days, it was enough to power the whole complex. He couldn't have done it without government—solar tax credits made it worthwhile. I saw a dozen solar firms, some entrepreneurial, some subsidiaries of huge conglomerates, all with one thing in common—absolute faith that America would win. I did hear one or two complaints about DOE's solar program—that some funding had gone to politically connected companies, for example—but the abuses were considered minor. Most said the program was a huge success. It proved, they said, how effectively government could help U.S. companies lead in commercial technologies.

By April, I'd finished the first half of my work, telling Volvo it would need a U.S. partner if it decided to go into the business. Because of government programs, the first big applications for solar cells would be in America. If the Volvo people wanted to develop their product, they'd need access to that market. They asked me to help them find a partner. I went out again three months later, in July 1981, to look.

Almost overnight, the mood had changed dramatically. The same people who'd been so exhilarated were now losing faith. They'd heard that the new administration in Washington was planning a change of course. There was nothing official yet, but the first echoes were bad. The White House was saying that government had no place in new-product development, and it considered solar an example. The fear of cuts—big cuts—was out there. The managers were getting cold feet, the researchers were demoralized. At one point, I was with the director of the Solar Energy Research Institute in Golden, Colorado. He went on for a bit about the country's solar vision, its projects, its promise. Then, suddenly, he stopped and leaned back. "But I don't know why I'm telling you all this," he said. "By next year, most of it will probably be eliminated."

And then what?

Then, he said, it would be all but impossible for any private company to keep the same pace.

Most of those I talked with were traditional businessmen, classic

American capitalists. You didn't have to convince them that the best of incentives is the free market. But solar wasn't there yet, they said. A market didn't exist yet. The technology was still in the lab. This was too soon for government to pull out.

Next, I went to the budget office in Washington, asking why it had targeted these programs for cuts. The main argument was ideological.[7] Government, they said, simply should not be funding R&D for nonmilitary projects.

Finally, I interviewed Paul Maycock, himself carried over as a member of the new administration's Department of Energy. I asked him about the talk of cutbacks. He acknowledged there might be some, but doubted they would be serious.

IN THE FALL OF 1981, Paul Maycock finished his solar budget for 1982. It came to $153 million. He knew that was a lot of money, but he was confident. Congress had already voted for the bill that laid it out. Besides, he saw this as the most promising kind of government money—investment in future industry. Unlike military programs, this all but guaranteed society an economic payback. He sent his numbers in. There would be a two-week wait before he got back a markup from the Office of Management and Budget—OMB's own proposal on what the solar money should be.

In October, the markup came back. At first, Maycock thought it was a mistake. OMB was recommending $27 million. That was a cut of over 80 percent.

BY THE FALL OF 1981, both Sanyo and Fuji had completed solar-cell-manufacturing plants, each making product for calculators. At that point, there was nothing comparable in the States. Some American companies had been making solar cells, but it was all batch processing, involving a lot of labor and no automation. In Japan, it was different—actual mass production. It was an unnerving lesson for the Americans, a reminder of how fast the Japanese were moving. Still, for Japan, it was more a psychological victory than an economic one. American companies remained far ahead in power-generation technology. Westinghouse was only one of many. Companies like Solarex, Arco Solar, Mobil-Tyco, and Motorola were even bigger. Almost all were being helped by government. All were convinced that if that help continued, America would still be the first to seize the sun's biggest prize—high-watt commercial solar.

IN MAYCOCK'S MIND, an 80 percent cut was unthinkable. He called OMB, preparing himself for a long, relentless negotiation. But he never got the chance. The OMB people told him they were sorry. It was pointless to discuss it. The decision had been made. Maycock did not give up. This would mean more than a scaleback; the nation's solar push was near top momentum on a ten-year plan; abort it midstream and most of what had been spent would be lost. He couldn't get a hearing with the new secretary of DOE, a former dentist, but did manage to see the assistant secretary. Maycock made his pitch. The $153 million is the law of the land, he said.

"There will be no appeal," Maycock was told. "Write it up as OMB suggests."

But what about the Japanese? Maycock asked. If we make these cuts, they'll be outspending us.

He was told it was no longer urgent. Oil prices were coming down. The energy crisis was ending. The administration felt industry should do solar on its own.

Maycock said he agreed—but it needed a few more years before it was ready to fly. "We're four years into a major government effort," he remembers saying. "Industry has hired a bunch of people. Contracts have been let. Phasing it down is one thing, but this will zero these people out."

He didn't succeed. There would be no adjustment.

Paul Maycock made a decision. At the time, he held a career senior-executive service post—a potential lifetime position. But in January 1982, he handed in his resignation, shifting his mission to Capitol Hill so he could lobby as a private citizen for the cuts to be restored. It was a long fight, and partly successful. He and others got the budget pushed back to $70 million. Still, the impact on his program would be devastating. The $70 million was less than half of what they needed. It meant contracts would be stopped all over the country.

IN THE EYES of MITI's solar people, the fall in oil prices was the third energy crisis. Now, they faced having to keep the country's sense of urgency despite good times. It was the job of Isao Kubokawa to see that through. He was the MITI man in charge of solar's budget in 1981. Like Maycock, Kubokawa knew a big cut would abort much of Japan's progress in the field. He gave most of his time to the budget fight. It would be wrong to call it a fight waged by a bureaucrat. That word doesn't quite fit people like Kubokawa in Japan, where civil-service work is the most prestigious of callings. It's a politically powerful calling, as well. In America, the president draws up the budget, then fights over details with a Congress spurred on by special-interest demands. In Japan, budgets are shaped somewhere else. Drive through the streets of Tokyo and you'll see that the most popular spot for public protest is not on the steps of the parliament building, it's outside the Ministry of Finance. That's who has real power over the budget. That's where Kubokawa had to make his appeal—to his fellow civil servants in Finance.

As Maycock fought a losing budget battle in America, Kubokawa geared up his Tokyo staff for their own fight. At first, he met his own share of skepticism. What's the urgency? Finance asked him. Oil prices are going down. The budget is tight. Why keep pouring money into solar now? Kubokawa stressed MITI's philosophy—energy is industry's blood, and in Japan, there's little of it. Our country isn't as vast and wealthy as America, he said. We can't respond to crises nimbly, we have to plan for them years in advance. The price of oil may be low today, but it's a nonrenewable resource, bound to go up again. That will mean more energy crises—well into the next century. Japan has to be ready, he said, and solar will be an essential part of the answer.

Finance asked why industry couldn't go ahead on its own.

Because solar's a long way from being profitable, Kubokawa said. It's still in the lab.

Finance made no promises.

Kubokawa came back again, and again, ultimately coming back dozens of times. Not supporting solar will cost more in the long term, he would say. If we stop midstream, we won't be able to start again by throwing a switch. Research doesn't work that way. We can't afford to be like America, he added. We can't simply forget 1973 and 1979.[8]

The decision finally came down. Kubokawa got everything he asked for, and more. The day his people got the word, they showed that Japanese civil servants perhaps aren't as restrained as Americans perceive them to be. There in the MITI office, they broke out a case of Suntory beer.

EARLY IN 1982, Charles Rose got the news. The government had decided to cut off Westinghouse's solar contract. Rose's first call was to the DOE program monitor to ask what could be done. The monitor told him he'd already tried to fight it himself. The termination was irreversible. Other photovoltaic companies, like Solarex and Union Carbide, were terminated, as well. The new philosophy, all were told, was that demonstration projects should be funded by companies alone. But Westinghouse didn't see a way to do that. This was a future technology with the payback still far off. It just couldn't sustain the same level of investment without government. At the peak of its momentum, the company had to slow the project to a crawl.

AS AMERICAN photovoltaic companies geared down, Japanese ones geared up. The calculator industry was ravenous for solar, swallowing everything that was produced. The Fuji factory went from a few thousand cells a month to a few hundred thousand, and then over a million. By 1983, Fuji was making 30 million cells a year. Sanyo was making even more. And soon, Sanyo was developing other consumer ideas: photovoltaic watches, radios, and car-battery chargers. In its most dramatic display, it permanently covered the nine upper floors of a Tokyo skyscraper with solar modules—wall to wall.

NOT LONG AFTER losing the budget battle in 1982, Maycock decided to fly to Japan. Now a solar consultant, he wanted to know if the Japanese were really catching up. He journeyed to Sanyo's photovoltaic headquarters on Awaji Island. He was surprised to find a fully operating cell-manufacturing plant. It was a continuous, automated process, pumping out two-foot-square panels to be cut for consumer products. Next, Maycock visited Fuji. The people there were more secretive, but he found they'd geared up mass production, too. The visit left Maycock troubled, and not just for the solar industry. It made him wonder about America's chance at other future technologies. Yes, in the past Japan had caught up with us in the battle of manufacturing, but in all cases, it was a me-too strategy. Even in semiconductors, we'd done the pioneering; they simply copied. This was different. In solar, the Japanese were innovating. They hadn't done that before.

Maycock had one other awakening during that trip. Like many Americans, he'd presumed Japanese companies don't see the free market as we do. He felt they were more inclined to act like soldiers, taking orders from government. He came back realizing the relationship among Japan's companies was just like in America: fiercely competitive. Pick an industry and you'll find a rivalry. They work with the government out of self-interest, he found, not some mythical patriotism. It convinced him that the outcome of this race would have little to do with cultural differences. It would come down to one question: Who had the best government backing? The answer was becoming disturbingly clear.

AT BROWN, Joseph Loferski got the same kind of news that Westinghouse and the rest of the solar industry had been getting. His money had been stopped. At the time word came in, he'd built one of the biggest university solar teams in the country—over a dozen people. Now, one by one, he had to tell them that it was over. The cutoff came just when he felt his life's work was coming to its peak. The year before, the nation's photovoltaic community had given him its highest achievement award—one named after the man who, as an agent of government, had breathed life into this new technology: William

Cherry. And now this. Although the cutoff meant stopping almost all his research, Loferski was convinced he could at least talk DOE into letting him finish the things it had already invested in—particularly his self-sufficient solar house. So far, he'd spent a half-million dollars setting it up. He asked if he could get a final fifty thousand dollars to test the system; otherwise, it would be all for nothing. They told him no. The house was mothballed; its potential would remain unknown.

FROM AFAR, in Tsukuba, Dr. Hayashi heard about the U.S. fund cut. In the solar literature, he began to read about researchers moving on to other fields. He did not celebrate. "It was quite sad for us," he said. He saw science as a brotherhood; now, he was losing part of the family. It would leave a hole in worldwide solar research. But there was reason to hope that the hole would be filled. Even as America was pulling back its dollars, Japan was spending more. The names in the international solar journals were becoming more and more likely to be Japanese. Before, when Hayashi wanted to keep up, he had to wait to read about the Americans. Now, he had only to call Osaka University, which was fast becoming one of the world's preeminent academic solar programs.

Today, Dr. Hayashi is in his fifteenth year of uninterrupted solar research. The knowledge he harvests continues to be fed to industry. In 1988, the sixth year of low oil prices, his staff was actually bigger than during the era of energy crisis. His lab is filled with the latest equipment to analyze the subtlest qualities of silicon and light absorption. "Quite expensive," he says.

Was it hard to get money for the equipment?

"Not impossible."

Ask, now, the same question of Loferski at Brown.

"What's going on in the laboratory is almost zilch," he says. He has received no DOE money in three years. At other universities, few of his colleagues have received much, either.

Morton Prince, who was at Bell Labs when it created the world's first silicon solar cell, is now with the Department of Energy. In a sense, he is a symbol of our potential. Many doubt our own bureaucracy can field minds good enough to steer sophisticated economic programs. But there are many like Prince, at the top of their fields, willing to commit themselves to public service. Still, he is now a bit frustrated. Although a government man, he speaks forthrightly about the solar budget, now under $40 million a year from a high of $150 million. "No," he says, "we don't think it's enough. None of us think it's enough."

SOON, three years behind schedule, Charles Rose hopes at last to see Westinghouse's solar manufacturing line completed. But it will be a smaller line. And many throughout the solar industry feel they've suffered losses that are hard to measure. When R&D is suddenly cut back, you lose momentum, and all the potential breakthroughs that come with it.

Westinghouse is still getting limited government support, but the restrictions on the money, Rose feels, explain why the United States has fallen behind. It's not like the previous money the company had gotten for a prototype line. The current dollars are for pure lab research. There's now a hard wall between the R and the D. In Japan, that wall does not exist. There, government money is not just for inventing basic technology, but designing prototype products and production facilities. Rose thinks if America is to compete, we have to reinstate the same rules. Past a certain point, he says, pure lab work won't help you win.

"If you want to be in the business," he says, "you have to get in the business."

MANY NOW FEEL the Japanese have caught up in American industry's key priority area—the manufacture of power modules. Companies like Sanyo, Fuji, Mitsubishi, and Kyocera are leading the challenge, all aided by the uninterrupted flow of government money.

"We lost three years that may well have cost us the window that the Japanese have moved into," Rose now says.

If the government money had kept coming?

"I think it would have been substantially different," he says.

In March 1988, Joseph Buggy, a Westinghouse senior manager, went to Congress to testify for an increase in the government's photovoltaics funding. Buggy pointed out that the manufacture of solar-power generation equipment cost about five dollars per watt. To be profitable for major use by utilities, costs have to get down to about one dollar a watt.

"The industry is in a critical phase," he said, "where the risks of development cannot be justified on the basis of conventional return-on-investment analyses. Foreign governments have recognized this, and because of the strategic value of photovoltaics, they have responded. Both the West German and Japanese governments now have photovoltaic R&D budgets that have surpassed ours for the first time. As you know, the 1988 U.S. photovoltaic budget was reduced from the 1987 level by about 15 percent. Meanwhile, U.S. industry has continued to 'go it alone,' but on a conservative basis that cannot hope to keep pace with foreign industry bolstered by government R&D support."

Charles Rose stresses that it's still a race.

"It's not over yet," he says. "It's not a battle lost."
But it is, he adds, a battle made more difficult.

IT SPEAKS WELL of America's corporate drive that so many of our companies remain in this race despite cutbacks. Westinghouse has not given up. America's biggest photovoltaic company—Arco Solar—continues to invest millions. There are a dozen other U.S. companies that are just as committed—Solarex and Chronar, Boeing and Solavolt. American industry is still resolved to make this technology theirs.

Dr. Kuwano, head of Sanyo's solar program, will himself admit that the race is not over. He knows Japan's factories are making more solar cells than America's, but the real profits, he says, will be in industrial applications, not calculators. By the mid-1990's, power generation will be 70 percent of the market. It's unclear who will win most of it. But Kuwano says Sanyo is poised. His strategy of rushing into solar-powered consumer products is paying off. Mass-producing cells for calculators and watches, he says, has given Sanyo invaluable expertise that's helping the company develop power-generation products.

Kuwano will tell you he's proud of Sanyo's commitment to solar, but he'll concede the company would never have made it this far without government. For a private business, he says, the risk of pouring so much so soon into solar would have been too high. If companies are to compete in any future technology, he says, they need help. He's grateful that MITI understands that.

THE SOLAR DIVISION of MITI's Project Sunshine is on the sixth floor of an eleven-story office building in downtown Tokyo. It's a messy, sprawling office that looks vaguely like an old newsroom. There are piles of paper everywhere, and file cabinets on top of file cabinets. Sho Marukawa, the MITI director who steered this divison in 1987, proudly showed photos of projects he has helped fund. Without government, he will tell you, most would never have happened. He has now moved on to a new posting in the United States. Was it frustrating for him to have to leave? To move on before solar truly blooms?

He says no. Japan is a bit different from America, he explains. In the United States, government commitments are often a product of the moment's passions. In Japan, there is a longer vision. He knows this mission will go on.

PAUL MAYCOCK sees solar at the same point where the transistor was in the mid-1950's—about to blossom. Today, worldwide, it's a $200-million-a-year business. In a decade, he predicts it'll be over $1 billion. "There is a knee on the curve where instead of having 20 percent compounded you have very explosive growth," he explains. The country that wins, he says, will harvest the best kind of jobs: engineers, programmers, technicians—jobs that low-wage countries can't easily take away.

Who will win?

"It's going to be awfully close," Maycock says. He stresses that even with limited government support, U.S. companies have done remarkably well. He considers us only a step behind the Japanese.

Where would we be if we had kept up the funding?

"I think," says Maycock, "we'd have been five years ahead."

In 1983, he explains, we were still out front, shipping 60 percent of the world's solar cells compared to Japan's 23 percent. In 1986, that turned around. Japan had 49 percent of the world market to our 27 percent. That same year, homeowner tax incentives for installing solar panels were eliminated, and those for commercial use were scaled way back. That will make it harder than ever to market what we produce. One other thing happened in 1986 that Maycock noted with disappointment. The solar panels installed on the roof of the White House by President Carter came down. All this comes, he says, in the face of our ever-increasing energy dependency. In 1987, we imported 40 percent of our oil and gas. It accounted for almost a quarter of our trade deficit—$41 billion. Soon it will get worse. By 1993, for the first time, America is expected to bring in over half of its oil from abroad.

PHOTOVOLTAICS is only one future technology, an important story because of what our government briefly tried to do with it. But there are other new technologies with even bigger stakes. Advanced ceramics has the promise of being the steel of the next century, replacing metals in car engines and airplanes. High-speed computers may well make those we have today obsolete. Biotechnology is likely to dominate the pharmaceutical industry. Advanced telecommunications and robots could each generate tens of billions a year in sales within a decade or two. Japan has targeted all those as even greater priorities than solar.[9] Hundreds of Japanese companies have invested in each field, many spurred on by government incentives. It's happening in a half-dozen other fields as well: opto-electronics, information technology, superconductors—industries that could mean as much to our children as computers do to us.

We haven't yet lost any of those races. Even competitors like Sanyo's Dr. Kuwano will concede we remain the world's leading nation for research. But somehow, Kuwano says, America has lost the drive to be out front in turning science into products.

"The United States is the leader of the world," says Kuwano. "Americans have more of a pioneer spirit than do the Japanese. But the United States seems tired."

Perhaps he is right, perhaps not. But the truth I've come to believe is this: For the first time this century, America is now in a race over the future, a race over tomorrow's technologies. And the Japanese are coming ever faster.

IN SPRING OF 1987, I met another MITI official for lunch at the Palace Hotel coffee shop. I hadn't been to the restaurant in two years, but as soon as I got the menu, the waiter asked if I wanted spaghetti. Things like that happen in Japan. My luncheon partner began discussing MITI's latest vision.

In the methodical way of the Japanese, they've charted out the exact point where they expect to pass us by as the world's technology leader—right around the year 2000.

Then he asked me a question. He said he respected America's achievements, but wondered what had happened to our technological will. Why is it, he asked, that except for military pursuits, we no longer seem to want to win? I wasn't sure what answer to give him. But after seventy visits to Japan, I'm convinced of something. Although the Japanese are good, we can be better. They may well win the technology race, but only if we let them.

8

Europe:
The Race for the Skies

FOR DECADES, one product has stood out as America's premier global business success—the commercial jetliner. Almost 80 percent of all those sold through 1985 in the non-Communist world were American-made.[1] By far, passenger jets have been our biggest export. In 1987 alone, they added $12 billion to our trade balance.[2] Some say that a jetliner is the most sophisticated product on earth. "I can tell you," one Boeing vice-president has been quoted as saying, "no nuclear reactor is near as complicated as a commercial airplane, by quite a little bit." Most have one hundred thousand kinds of parts, and well over one hundred microcomputers aboard. Building one takes thousands of subcontractors, thousands of engineers, and a total work force in the tens of thousands. To be a serious jetliner company, you need a half-dozen models, and it can cost up to $5 billion just to design each one. In so complex and expensive a technology, many felt, America couldn't possibly be challenged.

But it's begun to happen. The challenge has come from Europe—Europe as a combined force. Five nations have pooled their resources to form a manufacturing consortium dubbed Airbus Industrie. Its planes have wings from Britain, cockpit sections from France, tails from Spain, edge flaps from Belgium, and bodies from West Germany.

Ten years ago, the consortium was barely able to sell anything. The big American two—Boeing and McDonnell Douglas—seemed untouchable. By 1985, however, Airbus had climbed to 11 percent of the world market. By 1988, it had reached a full 23 percent,[3] passing Douglas to become the world's number-two producer. The latest Airbus, the A320, has proven the fastest-selling new jetliner in history. Even before its maiden flight, it received 294 firm orders, and almost 200 options. In 1986, Northwest Airlines alone made a $3.2 billion deal for 100 Airbuses.

In the next two decades, it's expected that at least eight thousand commercial jets will be sold around the world. That's a market of around $400 billion.[4] If America maintains its past leadership, we'll realize almost $350 billion of that market—around 80 percent. But if Airbus keeps gaining, our share could be closer to 50–60 percent, a potential loss of $150 billion in sales. That could affect our trade balance more than any other single manufactured product.

American plane manufacturers have charged that Airbus's headway has sprung from a single unfair advantage: government subsidies. There's no question that Europe's governments have bankrolled the consortium. But if America is to win this race, it's important that we realize the essence of the threat. It's not just a low-price threat made possible by subsidies; it's a technological threat. A quality threat. Our most sophisticated and supposedly untouchable industry is now facing a challenger capable of delivering high-quality engineering. Many U.S. pilots who've flown the Airbus planes will testify to it.

John Mulligan, now retired, was one of the first American pilots to test an Airbus. In 1977, he went to the consortium's Toulouse, France, headquarters for training after his airline, Eastern, leased several Airbus A300s, the first model. Having spent thirty-five years flying U.S. planes, Mulligan doubted a foreign machine could be anywhere near as good. Then he took the left-hand captain's seat for his first practice flight.

He noted that there were only two engines; U.S. widebody planes had three. He knew that was designed to save fuel, but he wondered about power. Then he took off. "I'd never been in an airplane with thrust like that," he says. Later, he would find the same performance in passenger flying. "That thing got off the ground fully loaded fast," he says, "and still more economically. We didn't use much more fuel carrying almost three hundred people than the Boeing 727 used carrying one hundred."

Once he got going, he found the plane more stable than any he'd flown. "It had a great wing on it," he says. Then there was the biggest difference—the piloting system itself. Everything was automatic. Unlike U.S. planes, this one went into complete autopilot once it got off the ground. All Mulligan had to do was give instructions electroni-cally. "Fly by wire," was the term. "It was great," Mulligan says. "We had autopilots in the other planes, but not as sophisticated as this."

Over the next five years, he flew Airbuses exclusively. Eventually, Airbus became the first producer to reconfigure the cockpit for two pilots instead of three. "Frankly," Mulligan says, "it wasn't good for the Air Pilots Association, but it cut down the expense enormously, and it was just as safe because these airplanes had such sophisticated equip-ment." After a lifetime of thinking American planes could never be rivaled, he came to a new view. "I wouldn't go back to flying anything I'd flown in the past," he says. Later, Mulligan would say there was an irony to Airbus's breakthrough technology. Most of it was American, developed for military or other electronic applications. It was our expertise, he says, but the Europeans were the first to adapt it to a com-mercial jetliner.

Airbus is just one product, one threat, but it's a symbol of some-thing broader. The Japanese aren't the only people challenging us in new technologies. Europe is, too—Europe as a combined force. And not just in airplanes.

I remember a time, not so long ago, when it was hard to believe the Europeans could pose any threat at all.

IN THE FALL OF 1971, I was watching television in my Oxford Uni-versity dorm room when a news spot came on about Europe's space program. I hadn't even known they had one. It turned out that it wasn't much. Two years into America's moon program, Europe, I was now seeing, was still trying to get its first small satellite up. Space was too expensive for any single European country, so a number of coun-tries had pooled funds to build a rocket. The result, the *Europa-2*,[5] had cost $700 million and was going to be the continent's first big step into the space age. But it didn't make it. That day the rocket had blown up. It was a marked contrast to our own performance. A few months before, three American astronauts had spent several days driving across seventeen miles of lunar surface.

Over the next week, the *Europa-2* fiasco was all over the British papers. One government official, interviewed on TV, showed classic British disdain. "What can you expect," I remember him saying; "when you marry a French head to an Italian body?" Many English officials said this should be the end of joint projects with neighbors. But others insisted Europe's only hope for technology breakthroughs was through cross-border partnerships.

Six years later, after I'd become a business consultant, I got another glimpse into the same issue. In 1977, Britain's National Economic Development Council asked me to look at the country's television industry. Thousands of Britons made their livings building TVs, but the industry was struggling. I soon found one reason why. It took the best British manufacturer three times as long to assemble a TV as most Japanese producers.[6] England was behind in product development, as well, and the reason was clear: Local companies were too small to afford the research. Collectively, the industry spent only a fifth as much as the Japanese on R&D, and most company labs were duplicating each other. The problem, I realized, wasn't just company size, it was country size. Britain's population was only 60 million, half of Japan's. Even if British firms combined, they wouldn't have the scale to succeed. The only way for medium-sized nations to compete in televisions was through low wages.[7] The only way to compete in state-of-the-art TVs was to be big enough for enormous investment. I saw only one hope for that: a multicountry consortium. Over twenty European companies in eight different nations made color televisions. Together, they could be as big a force as America or Japan.

That wasn't to happen for years, but meanwhile, the study helped me see Europe's potential. Other European studies I did in advanced technology areas like telecommunications showed me the same thing. Of course, I wasn't the only one to see it. Many in Europe had been talking about cross-border consortia for decades. In the 1960's, many European government leaders began to fear that America's massive defense and space programs were widening our technology lead. In response, Germany, France, and England each formed special efforts to seed industrial R&D.[8] France, for example, targeted aerospace, nuclear power and computers. The problem was that each country kept its efforts within its own borders. By the mid-1970's, the efforts were all failing—for the same reason I was seeing British TV firms failing. The countries—and companies—were too small to compete in big, advanced industries. It would be like our own big corporations trying to build on the resources of a few states instead of the whole nation. Several firms, like Philips, the Dutch electronics giant, did have facilities throughout Europe, but they ran each as separate companies. At the time, there were only two major attempts at Europe-wide technology cooperation: the space program and the Concorde. Both, however, were disasters, one technically, the other financially.

Then, starting around 1980, I gradually saw a change. My consulting firm has an office in Paris and another in Munich. In the past eight years, we've done about a hundred studies in dozens of European industries—telecommunications, specialty chemicals, textiles, office machinery. In all those and others, we've seen European companies finally forming cross-border consortia. It's now common to hear businessmen talk about pooling resources. The only way to compete with Japan and the United States, they say, is to build a bigger R&D and market base. Both Thomson of France and Philips, for example, have bought up enough European consumer-electronics companies to achieve world scale. They've even swallowed our own major players: Thomson bought RCA, while Philips bought Sylvania and Magnavox. West Germany's Siemens has built itself into a telecommunications giant the same way. Sweden's ASEA and Switzerland's Brown-Boveri have combined to form the world's largest power-generation equipment company. Sweden's Electrolux, having just bought America's White-Westinghouse and Tappan, is now bigger than any other world appliance maker.

But the new push isn't just driven by companies, it's driven by government. Beginning just a few years ago, Europe's governments started earmarking billions of dollars to spur the development of commercial technologies, something America still shies away from. Interestingly, the money isn't given out by individual nations, it's funneled through agencies whose reach spans all of Western Europe. There are four of them—ESPRIT, BRITE, RACE, and EUREKA—and they're similar to Paul Maycock's program; they work by giving R&D money to networks of companies and research institutes. Always, the networks cross borders. And the agencies share a common mission: to help Europe challenge the United States and Japan in the industries of the 1990's.

For years, European exports have mostly been in traditional industries—steel, cars, machines, and clothing. In advanced technologies, we've always held the edge. The Japanese have been our only serious competitor. That's changing. Europe today is poised to take us on in dozens of future industries—from robotics to biotechnology to information technology. The push has barely begun. We probably won't feel its full effects until the 1990's, but in a few areas, Europe has already shown how far partnership can take it. The most dramatic of those areas is aerospace.

THE IDEA of Airbus began at the height of American business supremacy, the mid-1960's. Over 90 percent of all jetliners sold around the world were American-made.[9] U.S. producers sold a third of all their planes overseas. They dominated Europe. But their models had all been designed for the U.S. market. What sold at home, it was felt, would easily sell overseas.

But in late 1966, Europe's three biggest air carriers—Air France, Lufthansa, and British Airways—met in London to talk about their own unique needs. They were concerned about the latest plans of American's plane makers. Boeing, McDonnell Douglas, and Lockheed were all working on the next generation of aircraft: widebodies. The European carriers welcomed widebodies, but no U.S. design was quite right for them. The new planes were all going to be powered by three or four engines and geared for long-haul flights of four to eight hours. For the Europeans, that wasn't cost-effective. Their most frequent routes were under two hours, and their fuel costs too high for more than two engines. When the London meeting was over, the carriers had come to agreement. They wanted a two-engine, short-range, low-cost widebody. Since they couldn't get that out of America, they would try getting it built in Europe. They realized no single European manufacturer was big enough to do it, so they decided to appeal to their governments for help.

IN JANUARY 1967, while still in his forties, Roger Beteille was in line to head up engineering for France's version of Boeing—SUD Aviation. He'd attended the École Polytechnique, the country's most prestigious technical school, then begun his career at SUD as a test pilot. He soon rose to be a key player in the Caravelle, France's most successful civil airplane. After that, he helped move the country into space by building SUD's missile and satellite program. Now, he was ready to run engineering for all divisions, a post he'd sought for years. But his bosses asked him to take on another project, instead.

They wanted him to create a widebody passenger jet. It wouldn't be for SUD alone, they explained; the company could never afford it. Beteille was told it would be a European project. The appeal of the big three carriers had worked. The governments of France, West Germany, and England had agreed to each give a million dollars to explore the building of a new airplane, a widebody geared for Europe. They'd chosen SUD to coordinate production, and the company wanted Beteille to get it started. He was intrigued, but cautious. He knew how hard it would be to challenge America in jetliners. He said he'd accept the job on one condition—that he could still have SUD's chief engineering post afterward. He wanted somewhere to go if the project didn't work. His bosses agreed. In July 1967, he became the consortium's first employee. Soon the plane had a name. It wasn't very poetic, but the politicians involved wanted to make jet travel accessible to the masses. It was dubbed Airbus.

Beteille's main challenge, of course, was a technical one—designing the plane itself. Then there was the financial challenge—making the plane economically successful. No one in Europe had ever done that, though many had tried. The continent's fourteen aircraft companies had built ten commercial jets since World War II, all business failures.[10] Few outside Europe had heard of the French and British models—Viscount, Comet, and Caravelle. World air travel was symbolized by U.S. plane names—707 and 727, DC-8, and DC-9. Beteille knew they were all excellent planes, tough competition. He also knew that in this new race, he was starting very late. The U.S. manufacturers already had tens of thousands of employees hard at work on widebodies. In Europe, Beteille's entire work force was himself. To build up a major corporation, Beteille knew he faced an initial overriding challenge—politics. He faced having to bring together three countries that had never been good at cooperating. The Concorde, child of a French-English marriage, was everyone's favorite example of that. The parents could hardly agree on anything. To avoid squabbles, they'd been forced to set up separate production and sales operations, a tremendous inefficiency. The Concorde had been bedeviled by cultural standoffs, as well. One French official refused to answer any letter he received in English, even though he was bilingual. The politics of Airbus, Beteille feared, would prove even more complex. In addition to France and England, he faced having to juggle a third parent, West Germany. And eventually Belgium and Spain, as well.

BETEILLE began by dividing up the engineering tasks. He visited each of the consortium's major contractors: Hawker-Siddeley in England, Deutsch Airbus in West Germany, and his own engineers at SUD. Each country, it was decided, would be given one part of the plane: the British the wings, the Germans the body, the French the cockpit section. Then Beteille turned to politics. To avoid infighting, he decided each partner would have to submit all ideas to the other two for criticism. And major decisions would have to be made by consensus. But Beteille knew that in business, diplomacy can only go so far. Past a certain point, he felt, you need authority. So he added one more rule: If there was a deadlock, he'd make the call. If it had been anyone else, the English and Germans might have seen it as a French power grab. But Beteille was known as a special kind of manager; he rarely gave orders without first making a convincing case.

"You can't run engineers like a dictatorship," he would say. "If you want to get the most out of people, you must persuade them that what you ask is right."

Now that he'd addressed both engineering and politics, Beteille turned to his next challenge, the marketplace. If this project was going to work, he had to first understand what kind of plane would sell. The most successful products, he felt, were those tailored to customer needs while still in design, so he began visiting airlines around the world, laying out his ideas, welcoming advice. He even visited U.S. carriers, most of whom told him there was no need for a twin-engine widebody. But he found one exception; Frank Kolk, the chief technical man at American Airlines. Kolk himself had pushed for a twin-engine widebody a few years before, convinced that if fuel costs went up and air travel got more popular, a low-cost, short-haul plane would be important. But the industry's principals had all told him he was wrong. With no Americans interested, Kolk was happy to give advice to the Europeans. Still, he was an exception. For Beteille, the message from America, the world's biggest market, was that no one would buy.

It put that much more pressure on him to build the right plane for the few carriers that did show interest, chiefly those in Europe. But even if he factored in the needs of every airline on earth, Beteille knew he could still miss. The problem was lead time. With jetliners, it can take ten years to go from initial design to finished product. And peak demand usually comes five years after that. Could he predict the tastes of so distant a market? There are few trickier industrial gambles than designing a commercial airplane. How many seats would carriers want? How much cargo space? What kind of distances? Even the carriers themselves could do little more than make educated guesses. It left Beteille, a man in his forties, faced with planning a jet for an aeronautics world that wouldn't exist until he was nearing retirement.

He faced another burden: entering a field where the standards were set by a giant that had more than half the world market—Boeing. Whenever Beteille would show novel ideas to airlines, such as new materials to save weight, the response would be the same: "But Boeing doesn't do it that way. And there must be a reason."

Beteille would move on to stressing his two-engine design, explaining how it would allow greater efficiency.

"If it made sense," the carriers said, "Boeing would do it."

Well, said Beteille, instead of three crew members, Airbus planned to simplify the cockpit so two could fly the plane.

"If two crew members were safe," came the response, "Boeing would do it."

At that point, Beteille would stress that Airbus planned to put tips on the wing edges for better stabilization.

"If tips were necessary, Boeing would do it."

None of that helped his confidence, but in each case, he went with the new idea. If all he did was copy Boeing, he felt, carriers would have no reason to switch. Why buy a me-too product from an untested newcomer? At the same time, Beteille understood the importance of staying compatible with the giant. He made sure his plane's aisles would accommodate standard meal carts, and the freight-unloading system would mesh with Boeing's ground gear.

During the fall of 1967 and winter of 1968, the design decisions intensified. Getting the three partners to agree wasn't easy. Beteille spent a lot of time on shuttle diplomacy. He can't count the times he flew from London to Munich to Paris and back. The broad decisions turned out to be somewhat easy—the plane would have 300 seats, weigh a lighter-than-average 140 tons, and get a heavier-than-average thrust of 48,000 pounds from its engines. The little things were much tougher.

"Details, details, and more details," Beteille would later explain. Getting everyone to break tradition by going with two engines, for example, was nothing compared to the fight over a few extra inches of passenger space. He remembers the fuselage team presenting its baggage door to be critiqued by the other teams—normal procedure in their consensus system. The door was similar to the one on Douglas's DC-10. But the critique teams wanted it improved. It should be idiot-proof, they said. They pointed out that luggage often arrives at the last minute, forcing ground crews to quickly open and close the door a final time. If anyone ever failed to latch the door right, the compartment could depressurize in flight, sucking down the passenger floor and causing a crash. The fuselage people resisted. It wasn't a realistic concern, they said. The only way to ensure that kind of safety would be to swing the door inward, costing valuable cargo space. The arguing went on all day. Beteille finally acted as arbiter, but was careful to make his case. He reminded everyone that Airbus's absolute priority was safety. He pointed out that ten years before, the beautifully engineered British Comet had several high-altitude breakups, which finished it off commercially. For a newcomer, a few quirky crashes could end everything. He prevailed. The teams agreed to go with the better door. Years later, a Turkish Airline DC-10 crashed because the cargo door had been left ajar. It forced other producers to retrofit their planes with better doors, something Airbus had done from the start.

The teams also fought about the idea of a two-pilot cockpit. The American widebodies were all going to fly with three, but Beteille felt it would save tremendous cost if they could design Airbus for a two-person crew. The doubters pointed out that airlines had said they'd never fly planes that way. It went against tradition. It went against pilot-union rules. Some feared it would go against safety. But Beteille again made his case. A two-man crew, everyone finally agreed, would be an important way to distinguish Airbus, avoiding a me-too design. They did make one compromise—they'd build in a third seat as an option. In fact, from 1973 to 1981, the consortium's first customers all used three-person crews. Then, in 1981, Indonesia's airline, Garuda, bought some Airbuses. They wanted to use native pilots, but couldn't find enough qualified ones. The president of the airline, himself a pilot, test-flew the Airbus to see if a crew of two was possible. The simplified electronic controls convinced him. He went ahead, and soon other airlines followed. Today, all Airbuses fly with crews of two.

There were dozens of decisions like that, from bolt size on door handles to choosing computers for the autopilot. To keep discussions moving, Beteille added a language rule at the critique sessions. All talks would be in the official jargon of flying—aeronautical English, required to make world air-traffic-control uniform. No French, said Beteille, no German, and no standard British—just American aircraft slang. Those who didn't speak it had to bring translators. That avoided the cultural standoffs that burdened Concorde. The arguments were still intense, but in Beteille's eyes, that was all right. "No one company would have thought of everything," he now says. "Together, we had a better chance."

SLOWLY, the design came together. They decided to call the plane the A300, a reflection of the number of seats. Now came the next step—organizing production itself. For that, Beteille would need just the right manager.

One of the key executives on Germany's Airbus consortium was named Felix Kracht. In December 1967, both he and Beteille happened to be in San Francisco on separate business. They met for the first time and spent a weekend together, discovering they had a lot in common. Both had started as test pilots, later moving into management ranks. Beteille was especially impressed with Kracht's willingness to gamble on new things—he'd been the first to navigate a glider across the Alps. For hours, they discussed the future of Airbus. Finally, Beteille decided to ask Kracht to coordinate the manufacture of the airplane. There on American soil, a Frenchman and German shook hands on a partnership that over the next two decades would help Europe take over 20 percent of the world's market in commercial aircraft. But a few months after that handshake, the Airbus project almost aborted.

IT HAPPENED over the most complex part—the engines. The world had three big producers of jet engines—Pratt & Whitney, GE, and Rolls Royce. Of course, the founding governments wanted Airbus to use Rolls Royce, the one producer based in Europe. At the time, all three producers were developing engines with forty-five thousand pounds of thrust for the new U.S. widebodies. Beteille's team, however, wanted something with more power. Since Airbus planes would only have two engines, he felt they'd need it. In the beginning of 1968, Beteille asked Rolls to develop a forty-eight-thousand pounder. Rolls agreed, but soon, Beteille began to grow concerned. Rolls was building a forty-five-thousand-pound engine for Lockheed's L-1011, and it was clear it had priority. Beteille understood why. In Rolls's view, Lockheed was a sure thing; Airbus wasn't. Still, it didn't make the frustrations easier. Engine development went terribly slowly, and then came the final straw. Rolls quoted prices much higher than Beteille had expected. Per pound of thrust, Rolls wanted to charge Airbus with two engines as much as

Lockheed would have to pay with three. Since engines would be the plane's biggest expense, this threatened to push Airbus way over its target cost. For a newcomer trying to break into a difficult market, high cost could be ruinous.

Privately, Beteille decided it was time to look for another engine company. Technically, he figured the switch would be possible; he'd redesign the plane to take an off-the-shelf forty-five-thousand-pounder from Pratt or GE. But politically, he knew that dropping Rolls would mean trouble. The British government, he felt, wouldn't tolerate losing a big contract for a local producer. The British might even threaten to leave the consortium, which could be crippling. Staying with Rolls, however, could be just as crippling. What to do?

Beteille felt he had one chance of holding onto the British without Rolls. His strategy was to first convince all three private production teams to take his side, including the one in England. Faced with that, the British government might come around. Beteille knew the ideal time to make the case: in December, when the three governments were due to give final approval to the whole project. That, however, was over six months away, which brought up a major problem. Airbus was now being designed around forty-eight-thousand-pound Rolls engines. If Beteille let that process go until December, it would mean starting a major plane redesign after a whole year's work. On the other hand, if he immediately called for a redesign around forty-five-thousand-pound engines, it would derail his strategy of first convincing allies to help persuade England. His solution was a daring one. He decided to set up a team of SUD Aviation engineers to begin a secret redesign around the replacement engines. They worked throughout the spring and summer of 1968. They stayed as close as they could to the main design, but some of their changes were big ones. For example, to get the plane's weight low enough for good thrust on 45,000-pound engines, they reduced the diameter of the fuselage and cut passenger seats from 300 to 250.

As they worked, Roger Beteille began the process of persuading the three production teams to back his engine change. If there was a most important person to convince, it was Henri Ziegler.

ZIEGLER, too, had graduated from the École Polytechnique. In 1927, a year before graduation, he still remembers rushing to Le Bourget Airport the day Charles Lindbergh landed, elbowing through the crowd and shaking the American's hand. Ziegler became a test pilot in the 1930's, organized parachute drops for the Resistance in the forties, moved on to help reconstruct Air France after the war, and then was named head of Brequet Aviation, a military aircraft company. In 1945, he was one of the first Frenchmen to see the need for cross-border cooperation in aeronautics. With the ink barely dry on the surrender documents and the hated Germans only recently gone from Paris, Ziegler wrote a bold memo to his government. In it, he proposed that France pool efforts with the Germans to design a civil aircraft. It wasn't a popular idea and didn't get far, but Ziegler didn't let go of it. Years later, in 1968, at age sixty, he was finally given the power to make it happen. He was named president of SUD Aviation. His immediate priority was a project that had been launched only a year before—Airbus.

If Roger Beteille was to succeed with his secret design, he knew he'd need the backing of SUD's new president. Ziegler was one of the first major players he sat down with. Beteille told him of the problems with Rolls. He doubted the Rolls people would deliver a decent engine anywhere near schedule, and even if they did, its price would make it hard for Airbus to compete. Beteille did leave one door open. When he was ready to shop for a standard forty-five-thousand-pound engine, Rolls would be able to bid against Pratt and GE. But it would have to win in a fair fight. And if Rolls lost, Beteille needed to be free to go with the Americans. Meanwhile, Beteille explained how he'd set up a secret team to do a second design. Would Ziegler back him?

In his younger days, Henri Ziegler had enjoyed the romance of test piloting, but left it for the production side of aeronautics because, in his heart, he was a pragmatist. Beteille's appeal spoke to that part of him. He was sold.

Through the fall of 1968, he joined Beteille in winning over allies. The two men traveled to Germany and Britain, visiting all the companies involved in Airbus projects. They laid out the Rolls decision, cajoling engineers, executives, and airline people. In the end, virtually all were persuaded.

THEN CAME the December 1968 government meeting. It took place at Heathrow Airport in London. French, German, and British officials filed into the room. Soon Beteille got to the point. He pulled out the secret design—minus the Rolls engines—and explained why it had to be. The British representatives heard him out, then gave their response: absolutely not. It contradicted the 1966 agreement. They would not support it. The two sides argued for hours, but it ended in deadlock. The meeting broke up with the project left in limbo. Afterward, things deteriorated even more. The British government was so angry it did what Beteille had most feared—pulled out of Airbus. Then it went even further, encouraging a local producer, British Aircraft Corporation, to design a plane to compete with Airbus. The British even tried to get French and German government officials to back their new plane, writing a white paper showing that it was better than Airbus in at least thirty ways. Beteille was shocked. He had no choice but to fight back, going to the same French and German officials with counterarguments on each of those thirty points. The lobbying war went on into 1969. Soon the newspapers began to ridicule the process as typical of European partnerships—one squabble after another. The press pronounced Airbus dead.

But in April, the project was resurrected. The German government sided with Airbus. So did the French government. So did the English Airbus private contractor—Hawker-Siddeley. All agreed to go with the alternate Airbus design. The one holdout was the British government. It would not rejoin the project. It would hold back its promised investment. But since Airbus no longer faced the expense of developing a whole new engine, Ziegler and Beteille felt they could afford to go ahead anyway. In May 1969, at Le Bourget in Paris, the same airport where Lindbergh had landed, the consortium came back together, minus Britain. The French and German governments each committed $400 million in loans. The private companies agreed to invest tens of millions more. Airbus was restarted.

But soon the engine war began again. What company would Airbus go with now? The players began to take sides out of self-interest. The French government wanted to use Pratt & Whitney, chiefly because Pratt held an interest in a local engine company called SNECMA. Meanwhile, Germany wanted to go with Rolls. The German government had agreed to do a certain amount of business with English companies in return for Britain having stationed troops to defend West Germany. But Beteille's priorities were again clear. He asked only one question: Who had the best machine at the best price? After exhaustive testing and negotiations, he decided on GE. Ziegler agreed. They prepared themselves for a long political fight, but it didn't happen. The governments looked over the deal, agreed GE was the best, and went with it. Facts were beginning to win out over politics.

THE DESIGN WORK continued into 1970. Meanwhile, Henri Ziegler decided Airbus needed a more formal company structure. The idea of an egalitarian consortium had been fine at first, the best way to get companies from separate countries to sign on. But now that Airbus was about to start production, Ziegler wanted a firmer hierarchy. Otherwise, he feared another Concorde: coequal players refusing to compromise. He also wanted to bind the manufacturers to the project and provide credibility to the eventual customers. He decided to turn Airbus into a corporation, with a central company overseeing design, marketing, and manufacture. It would be owned by the aircraft-production companies who were building the plane, and coordinated by its own supervisory board. Most important, while the parent aircraft companies gave up day-to-day control in the interest of efficiency, they agreed to financially guarantee all contracts. That way, customers would be assured they'd get their airplanes, parts and service. Airbus Industrie was formally incorporated in December 1970, with Henri Ziegler as its first chairman and Roger Beteille as its first managing director. At the time, it employed fewer than forty people, and had never produced anything except blueprints.

Over the next year, Airbus engineers worked to perfect Beteille's secret design—now the main design. It was dubbed the A300B. Meanwhile, Felix Kracht went on the road to set up a production system. That meant finding hundreds of companies to produce the plane's hundred thousand parts, then organizing ways to assemble them all. He, too, had politics to worry about. He knew that jobs had to be split among the partner countries. And more jobs, he felt, should be divvied out around Europe to give other nations enough of a stake to make them want to buy Airbuses. Then it got even more complicated. It wouldn't make sense for one piece of the plane to be farmed out to Belgium while its adjoining piece went to Italy, so Kracht had to give out contracts in clusters to allow companies to work regionally on subassembly. Through it all, like Beteille, Kracht had one absolute rule— quality and cost over politics. For that reason, the country with the greatest initial share of Airbus parts was the one with the best aircraft suppliers: the United States.

But Kracht leaned heavily on Europe, eventually finding suppliers to replace many of the American ones. Britain's Hawker-Siddeley would do the wings, Germany's Messerschmitt the rear fuselage, Holland's VFW Fokker certain wing segments, France's Messier the landing gear, and Spain's CASA the door and tail. Then came the decision on where the entire plane would actually be assembled. Concorde, because of politics, was split between France and Britain. That, however, was predictably inefficient, throwing off both cost and schedule. Kracht decided Airbus would be assembled in only one place. He chose Toulouse, home of SUD, by now renamed Aerospatiale. A political mess could have resulted, but Kracht was able to show it made the most sense technically. Everyone agreed. Again, pragmatism was winning over politics. In time, huge transport planes were landing each week in Toulouse bearing hundreds of parts for the first Airbus. The first European widebody began to take shape.

IN OCTOBER 1972, after four years and hundreds of millions of dollars, the A300B had its maiden flight. About fifty people gathered at Le Bourget Airport to watch. The plane flew perfectly. Later, Beteille would look back and comment that despite all the problems, everything up to then had been easy.

"The real challenge," he would say, "was persuading people to buy it."

On paper, he knew he had a good pitch—low price, 15 percent savings on fuel, state-of-the-art autopilot—but this wasn't a car. For an airline, taking on a new make of plane was an enormous—and expensive—decision. Most airlines had spent years building staffs to maintain Boeings and Douglases. Why should they add another logistics-and-spare-parts operation?

Then there was an even greater concern. If you gamble on a new brand of machine tool and it breaks down, you'll lose some money. If you gamble on a new brand of airplane and it breaks down, you'll lose a lot more. The Airbus was an untested jetliner from an untested company. How do you persuade customers to take a chance on such a thing? That job fell to a team that included Dennis Little.

IN 1968, Little felt he was in on the ground floor of aviation's future—he'd just been named chief sales engineer for the British Concorde. He was convinced airline companies would line up. Here was a plane that cut London to New York travel time from seven hours to three and a half. But as it turned out, no one lined up at all.

Actually, a half-dozen airlines took out options when Concorde was still under construction. At the time, 1968, the projected price was $20 million. But by 1971, cost overruns had driven it to $40 million. Worse still, it took as much fuel to fly the Concorde's one hundred passengers across the Atlantic as it did the 747's four hundred passengers. When fuel was ten cents a gallon, that didn't matter. By 1973, when fuel leaped to one dollar a gallon, it made the Concorde's costs prohibitive. Virtually every airline that had taken out an option decided to cancel. The consortium settled for selling a few Concordes to British Airways and Air France for a dollar apiece to get some use out of them. That was all the investors got back for their $2 billion investment.

In 1971, as it grew clear that Concorde was failing, Dennis Little got a job offer, this time from Airbus. He hesitated. He'd had enough of trying to sell planes built by European partnerships. Then he met with Roger Beteille, and right away, he saw this was different. Airbus, Beteille stressed, was driven by economic pragmatism, not politics. The planes, promised Beteille, would offer low price and low operating cost. They'd also have a dozen technological improvements, which Little knew was essential for a marketing man's pitch. Then there was the most promising news of all—Air France had already ordered six.

Little signed on. He soon got proof he'd made a wise choice. In 1973, just before the first Airbus was unveiled, Lufthansa of West Germany ordered three more. Little felt the initial orders were only the start. Once the planes were shown around the world, he was sure they'd sell themselves.

They began with some European demonstrations in the summer of 1973, and then, in September, came the real test. Forty Airbus employees got aboard an A300B and headed for a tour of the Americas. Their first stop was São Paulo. From there, they went to Brasilia, Mexico City, and on to Caracas. Next, they went to the United States. They gave demonstrations to airlines, to the press, to anyone who would listen. Everything was beautifully orchestrated, but Dennis Little began to realize no one was taking them seriously. The first U.S. stop typified the problem. In Miami, Airbus managed to get a local TV station to come by. Afterward, everyone thought it had been a major PR breakthrough. Then the evening news came on. The whole spot was an interview with an attractive stewardess from Iberia, the Spanish airline. The spot ended with a shot of the stewardess from the back and a wisecrack about Airbus's "Spanish tail," designed by CASA of Seville, being one of its best features. It seemed to be the same everywhere; Airbus was seen mostly as an amusement. "People just didn't believe the Europeans could build a good airplane," Little recalls. The trip ended without a single sale. So Little and his troops took another trip, this time to India, by way of Iran. Still no sales. In late November, they tried Africa. Again, nothing. Finally, they tried the Far East. The president of Japan Airlines told them to come back after they'd sold a hundred planes.

THE FAILURES only made the Airbus people push harder. Beteille himself began to give most of his time to selling. There seemed to be some interest from South African Airways, so he targeted them, going there eight times. In 1975, he finally succeeded. They bought four planes. When Beteille felt Indian Air had begun to show interest, he spent just as much time wooing them. Eventually, they gave him an order for three planes. He turned to the rest of the world, occasionally with French government help. At one point, a delegation of government ministers went to Korean Airlines. Soon KAL bought six planes. By the end of 1975, Airbus had thirty-two orders; still small, but enough to boost morale in Toulouse. It seemed that Airbus was finally breaking through. Then, in 1976, the aircraft industry went into a slump. Airbus went six months without a sale. Then a year. Then sixteen long months.

I remember visiting France around then as part of a study I was doing on helicopters. Every official I talked with mentioned Airbus. It's too bad, they said. It seemed as if it had promise, but it had turned out to be a failure. They all felt it was a good plane technically, but, like the Concorde, wasn't making it commercially. That, they said, seemed to be the failing of European projects. They predicted the governments would soon cut off Airbus's money.

In Toulouse, the response to the dry spell was to pour more investment than ever into marketing. Airbus pinpointed airlines that had a special need for large passenger short-haul planes—the A300B's niche—and pitched them hard. Alitalia was one, Singapore Airlines another, VASP of Brazil a third. Beteille's people spent a year trying to woo each. In every case, they failed. The airlines all had Boeing fleets. They knew Boeing technology, trusted its service, were confident it would be around in twenty years. With Airbus, they couldn't be sure. "Come back when you've sold more planes," they said.

Dennis Little still remembers the frustration. By the end of 1976, Airbus had ten "white tails"—unsold airplanes parked in its yard with no airline logos painted on. "We were rather like rats in a box with nothing to eat," he recalls. The company's biggest hope came down to one U.S. prospect—Western Airlines. Airbus management had been negotiating with Western for more than eighteen months over an eight-plane order. To Airbus, it would mean its first penetration of America. Western planned to decide at its January 27, 1977, board meeting. As the meeting approached, Little got good news. Western's engineers told him that Airbus had been the top performer in all their tests. They'd decided to recommend it. The day before the board meeting, he heard that the CEO himself would recommend Airbus. Little was ecstatic. Overnight, Airbus would be able to move 80 percent of its white tails. They'd have their first sale in over a year. The day of the meeting came with no official word, but there were leaks. Roger Beteille turned on the evening news to hear a French government minister saying Airbus had broken into America with a sale to Western. Beteille went to bed exhilarated. It was another four days before Western finally decided to go public with its decision. Beteille was awakened at 2:00 A.M. by a phone call. It was the president of Western, first telling him Airbus had indeed won the technical evaluation.

Then he said he was sorry. The sale had gone the other way. The board had decided to split its order between Boeing and Douglas. Beteille never found out why.

The Western deal had gotten such public buildup that the turndown set off a round of Airbus-bashing in Europe. A prestigious German magazine accused the French of mismanaging the sale. Meanwhile, in France, newspapers took broader aim, calling for a government inquiry into the funds being wasted on a plane that wouldn't sell. In Toulouse, it was a low point. It had been ten years since the decision to form a consortium, eight years since the first $400 million was authorized, and still no big breakthrough.

IN FEBRUARY 1977, Eastern Airlines decided it needed some new airplanes. It asked the big U.S. producers—Boeing, McDonnell Douglas, and Lockheed—to submit bids. Airbus's American representative heard about it and asked if his company could make a proposal of its own. Eastern wasn't encouraging, but told him he was free to try. Roger Beteille decided to make the pitch himself. Presentation day was March 4, 1977. He got to Miami twenty-four hours early to be fresh. Soon he was ushered in before Eastern's executives, including President Frank Borman. Beteille knew what was bound to happen; he'd been through it dozens of times. He'd make his presentation, then be thanked politely and ushered out with little encouragement. But this time, when Beteille was done, Borman seemed interested. Eastern was struggling financially, and Airbus's low price per seat, Borman felt, could help. So could its fuel and maintenance costs—15 percent lower than American-made planes. Borman wanted to know more. He asked Beteille to explain more specifically why he thought Airbus was technically superior.

Beteille went into his practiced answer. Airbus's fuselage was designed for less drag, which gave it more efficiency. Its two engines would make it cheaper to fly, but still give excellent takeoff thrust. It had an improved wing, making for better stability. It had a system to electronically correct for windshear. And its autopilot was the most sophisticated of any jetliner. When Beteille was done, Borman said he was still interested. If the planes checked out to be as good as Beteille claimed they were, he said, Eastern might buy some.

Over the next few months, Eastern put several Airbuses through an assortment of technical tests. The planes performed well in every one. But Borman had two other tests in mind. First, he wanted to see whether Eastern's service staff could easily maintain them. Second, he had to make sure American passengers would feel good about a European jetliner. Both those tests would take time. He asked Beteille if Eastern could take a few planes on loan to see? Beteille took the gamble. On May 2, 1977, he leased four Airbuses to Eastern for one dollar each. The planes went into service in August of that year for a six-month trial. The trial passed, but Eastern still wasn't ready. Could the airline keep testing? Beteille agreed. In April 1978, Eastern finally came to a decision. It would buy the four leased planes. There was celebration in Toulouse, and soon afterward, there came even better news. Eastern wanted to buy twenty-eight more planes. Airbus had made its first step into America. The breakthrough soon opened other doors around the world. By the end of 1979, Airbus's total sales were up to 111 planes.

EVEN AS the A300 finally began to sell, Roger Beteille knew it wouldn't be enough. To be a successful aircraft producer, a company needs more than one plane. The ideal, he felt, was a half-dozen. He took his first step toward a second model at a curious time—1976, the heart of the sales slump. Beteille saw it as a necessary risk. If a newcomer like Airbus was to keep winning buyers, it had to prove it would be around in twenty years. And unlike Boeing, it wouldn't be able to sell on reputation. Its only hope was to keep coming out with new, standout products.

Still, Airbus wasn't strong enough for a huge investment. There was no way it could start from scratch on a whole new plane. Beteille knew, for example, that the most lucrative market was the long-haul niche currently dominated by Boeing's 747, but for Airbus to compete there, it would have to redesign everything. That would be much too expensive. Instead, Beteille decided to slightly reconfigure his existing plane—the 250-seat A300. His idea was to shrink its size to a two-hundred-seater, and at the same time, stretch its range. That would let Airbus compete in a medium-haul niche. But that alone, he understood, wouldn't be enough. Since the competition had similar planes, the new Airbus would need an array of standout features to avoid a me-too image. The only way to woo customers from Boeing, he felt, would be with something different.

He knew there were new technologies available that none of his rivals were using, and now Beteille wanted to be the first. To save weight, for example, he began looking into composite materials that were lighter than the aluminum favored by other planes. He also decided to incorporate computerized fuel pumping to keep the plane's array of tanks at a perfect center of gravity. He resolved to make the wings more stable, to heighten engine efficiency, and to improve the autopilot.

He and his colleagues decided to call the plane the A310. Soon they were ready for the early design stage, and the process began again: meetings with airliners on what they wanted, more meetings with engineers on endless technical details. And then he was stuck. Before he could go much further, Beteille needed more money. That, he knew, would involve some tricky politics. Lately, the European press had been calling Airbus a waste of money. Now, in the midst of such headlines, Beteille faced having to ask his governments for more cash. It was clear he had little chance of succeeding. Then a possible solution fell into his lap.

In the summer of 1976, Airbus was unexpectedly approached by Boeing itself. The giant proposed that the two companies build a new plane together, one very close to what Beteille had been planning himself: a two-hundred-seat medium-haul jet. Boeing was calling it the 7X7. Beteille, intrigued, assigned a team to negotiate. Here was an easy way to have a piece of a second model. And if the plane sold well, it would give Airbus the resources to keep pursuing its own line. The talks went for three months, but then began to break down.

"Boeing was not interested in an equal partnership," Beteille would later explain. "They wanted to dominate." Though the idea still held financial promise, Beteille's instinct was to work out a shared deal or none at all. The talks broke off.

Then came another offer. It was from Boeing's rival, McDonnell Douglas. It proposed a joint venture on a two-hundred-seater of its own, to counter the 7X7. A new round of negotiations began. This time, things began to click. The two companies began working together, continuing for over a year, into 1978. Beteille began to see this as a real turning point. A plane like this would be a major doorway into America. Then the talks got complicated.

The Douglas people suddenly laid down a condition. They'd begun to worry that the partnership would end up giving Airbus too much expertise. They were especially concerned that Airbus might use that expertise to leap into the intercontinental market. At the time, Douglas was pushing hard for the long-haul dollar with a plane of its own, the DC-10. With the 747 already dominating that niche, the last thing Douglas needed was to face off against another player. So Douglas insisted that Beteille agree to stay out of that market. At the time, Airbus had nowhere near enough strength to develop a long-haul jet. But Beteille saw a time when intercontinental flight would be the biggest niche in aeronautics. If Airbus never entered that arena, it could find itself stunted. It might even fade altogether. Of course, severing the Douglas deal might make it fade sooner, but at least, if it survived, it would have a chance to be a world leader. Beteille cut the relationship.

It left him back where he'd started—trying to find the resources for Airbus to build a second plane by itself. At this point, he had no choice but to do what he'd tried to avoid: go directly to the French and German governments with his hand out. As soon as he did, the public resistance began. Opponents argued that Airbus was a drain on taxpayers with no prospects of profit. The A300's sales, they pointed out, were relatively small. And many of those sales were coaxed through political influence or cut-rate financing. Face it, the opponents said, Airbus wasn't competitive. Why pour more money down the drain?

But Beteille had supporters, too. Many in France and West Germany were concerned about more than short-term profit. They saw the United States still pulling ahead in the technology race. They felt that if Europe was to stay strong economically, it needed to develop advanced industries. They realized that a nation—or nations—can't do that overnight. If you cancel major industrial projects just because there's a slow return on investment, you'll never succeed. A private firm, Beteille knew, might have had a hard time seeing it that way. It's a rare company that can afford a ten-year or twenty-year lead time on breaking even. But Airbus's governments had a different priority: creating good, high-paying jobs for the future. If that meant no profit for a decade or more, it was still worth it.

In July 1978, Beteille won $1 billion in government money for the A310. Six months later, in January 1979, he scored another coup. The British government, realizing that they couldn't go it alone in commercial jetliners, decided to come back into the consortium. Then, four months later, Airbus crossed another national border. A Belgian aeronautics group joined up. The plane was truly becoming a Europe-wide effort. That gave Airbus new strength, and the second plane, the A310, gave it new promise. But Beteille remained worried. By 1981, he began to realize that a second model, though an ambitious undertaking, still wouldn't be enough.

Although the original A300 had continued to sell around the globe, it wasn't proving a blockbuster—so far, only a few hundred planes had been bought. And while everyone hoped the two-hundred-seat, medium-haul A310 would give Airbus a boost, Beteille knew it wasn't a big-volume niche. He'd chosen it because it was affordable, a reconfiguration of his first plane, but most predictions said the real money would be in two other areas: a four-hundred-seat long-haul plane, and a 150-seat short-haul model. Either, however, would take big investment—entirely new designs for Airbus. With the expense of building the A310, a third plane was the last thing Beteille should have been thinking about. But his focus was always ten years ahead. If Airbus was to compete in either of those big-money niches, he realized it would have to start now. Beteille launched the consortium into a third jetliner.

He chose the short-haul slot, a tough challenge, but easier than taking a leap to a jumbo jet, the industry's top-of-the-line machine. Specifically, he decided to build a 150-seater for routes of one to three hours. At the time, workhorses like the Boeing 737 and Douglas DC-9 served that niche, but both were over twenty years old. Beteille saw over three thousand 150-seaters being replaced by the end of the century, an enormous market. The Americans, he was sure, would eventually put up a fierce fight. But he felt there were ways to beat them. First, move fast; invest now. It didn't matter that Airbus was losing money and stretched thinner than ever; Beteille's best hope for a short-haul plane was to come out with a new one before anyone else. Then there was his other strategy, better technology. And not simply new bells and whistles—he wanted better engineering. In his first two models, Beteille had stressed the same thing, but the improvements were peripheral: a more stable wing, computerized fuel pumping, lighter materials. This time, he wanted to make a technological leap in the machine's very heart—the piloting system itself. His idea was to design the first passenger plane flown by electronic instructions given over computers rather than hands-on steering through mechanical pulleys and cables. In short, he wanted his new plane to have the most futuristic cockpit ever built into a commercial jetliner. That would mean a breakthrough in the most complex part of the most complex product on earth. To bring that off, he knew he'd need a huge increase in his consortium's R&D budget. It would put his profit payback further away than ever, but Beteille felt that in advanced technologies, the best way to ensure long-term success is to make research and development an absolute priority.

The start of 1982 was one of Airbus's most exciting times. The A300s were making slow but steady progress, occasionally breaking into new countries. The A310s would soon be ready to make their debut. And now Beteille was starting his third jetliner, one that had the promise of being the industry's technological standout.

That's when recession hit again.

An exciting time became a frustrating time. From 1982 to 1983, Airbus sold only twelve planes. In Toulouse, over twenty white tails backed up in storage. Hit by the same recession, industries around the world were beginning severe cost-cutting, and once again, there was public pressure for Airbus to do the same, to stop the drain on taxpayers. Beteille's strategy, however, was to take the same tough stand as the German machine toolmakers: Keep investing despite bad times, especially in R&D. Beteille wasn't running a clothing company, where you can slow and then speed production with the flick of a switch. This was an advanced-technology company. In that kind of business, he knew, if you cut back on research, laying off experienced engineers, it can take years to get back to pace. Beteille vowed not to let that happen. He vowed to keep pushing ahead with the design of his state-of-the-art 150-seater. But to do so, he would need his biggest government capital infusion yet, $2.5 billion.

He began to make the rounds, first to his governments, then his companies, pleading his case. The response was surprising. Despite bad times, he found that most shared his vision. Their one priority was technological progress. Their goal was to catch the Americans. They understood it would happen only through relentless investment. Airbus had now been at this seventeen years, a long time to wait for a return, but its principals understood the importance of patience. Japan had shown it in a number of industries, such as cars—one reason why that country was now booming. Airbus—and Europe—were ready to follow the same strategy. It helped that the A310, the second model, had just been launched. It symbolized the mission. Airbus was working, growing, delivering. It had spawned thousands of sophisticated jobs. Hundreds of precision-machine shops and electronics factories had started up in a half-dozen countries. Europe was building an advanced technology future. In March 1984, Roger Beteille got his $2.5 billion.

BETEILLE'S biggest question now was whether he could beat his rivals with his new 150-seat jet. He had enormous respect for America's plane makers, especially Boeing, but he felt each had the same weakness as many successful giants.

"Boeing dominated the civil aircraft market," he would say later. "It didn't have to advance too quickly."

Boeing preferred upgrading old models to developing new ones from scratch. Now, it had chosen to do just that for the 150-seat short-haul market. For twenty years, Boeing had served that market with its 737. And recently, instead of making a leap into a new plane, it had decided to upgrade the old one. It left Beteille an ideal opening. If Airbus could move quickly with its A320, and succeed, it would have the only state-of-the-art jetliner in that niche. He resolved to make it stand out as something truly special.

He formed a design team. One of his key designers on the project was Bernard Ziegler, the son of Henri Ziegler, who had recently retired as the first chairman of Airbus. The team's priority would be the cockpit. Almost all commercial jets, Bernard Ziegler knew, were still being driven the old way, by a direct-control yoke connected mechanically through a jack and servomotor. Beteille, Felix Kracht, and Bernard Ziegler, all test pilots, felt it was time to update that. Jetliners were becoming too complex for pilots to fly without computerized help, and it was showing. The three men studied worldwide accident reports, and found that over half were due to crew error. "What is crew error?" Ziegler would say. "It is not bad will. Just a crew not able to understand what is going on."

The instrument panels of major jetliners, Bernard Ziegler felt, had turned into a chaos of hundreds of switches and controls. The biggest problem was information display. Most planes had become festooned with over forty gauges and dials. It was hard to keep track of them. Ziegler's idea was to replace them with a half-dozen television screens, something Airbus had already incorporated into the A310. On the A320, the new plane, the designers decided to link the screens to a fly-by-computer system. Instead of a pilot guiding the plane by yoke, pedals, and levers, he'd be able to instruct the computer to do it electronically. It would make for far more precision.

The computer would also correct for other crew imprecisions. For example, if there was a bad calculation on the amount of fuel needed for a trip, it could mean an extra five tons would be put on board. That would wipe out all the weight savings Airbus was trying to gain by building the plane with new, lighter materials. A computer would make sure it didn't happen.

Beteille understood that if all those ideas had to be created in the lab, Airbus could never afford it. But the technology was already out there, mostly on military craft. Beteille's plan was to shop the world, searching for advanced features that could be transplanted into commercial passenger craft. Beteille's engineers began to hunt around, looking especially closely at the computer systems on fighter jets, America's F-16 and France's Mirage. Putting those features into the A320 would take more than a direct transplant. They'd each have to be carefully tailored for civilian use. Military planes, for example, have a ten-thousand-hour life; commercial ones go for sixty thousand hours. Military planes are maintained after every flight; commercial planes must go weeks between major servicings. Slowly, they worked through the details.

The goal was an autopilot that would constantly fine-tune the plane as it flew, controlling roll, rudder, and pitch for total efficiency. They also wanted systems that would electronically correct for sudden trouble, like bad weather, a stalled engine, or wing damage. Then there was the look of the cockpit. Early on, they'd agreed that the control yokes—the plane's twin steering wheels—were a problem. They blocked the view of the instrument panels. So Airbus got rid of them. Instead, pilot and co-pilot would have a simple sidestick at their outside elbows, and nothing between their chests and the panel.

By the time they were done, the A320 cockpit had a third fewer instruments than most other jets. That, however, didn't mean less information for the pilot. The half-dozen TV screens would still give far more than the old gauges could ever offer, but they'd do it on command—a few bits of data at a time instead of forty gauges constantly displaying figures. If the captain wanted to know flight pressures, altitudes, and speeds, the computer would instantly show them, adding how each would change in ten seconds. If a technical glitch developed, the computer would tell the pilot where it was, showing a diagram of the problem and ways to solve or minimize it. The pilots would still be able to control the plane by hand with the sidesticks, but unlike other planes, the A320's computers would correct for any human error. For example, say a collision threat forced a pilot to turn upward. In an ordinary jetliner, pilots worry that pulling too hard on the yoke could cause a stall. On an A320, the sidestick can be jerked to the limit, and the computer would still prevent a stall.

Beteille's team understood there was one problem with relying on a computer to fly the plane: What if it failed? To prevent that, they decided to put five computers aboard, each built in a different factory to make sure there wouldn't be common failures. Measurements that are fed into the computers would be taken on many different surfaces of the plane to ensure redundancy of inputs as well. To ensure that all those electronics wouldn't get knocked out by lightning, the Airbus team installed an electromagnetic protection system, this time developing a version of their own that rivaled anything on military planes.

Beteille's team gave just as much attention to the A320's mechanics. All other widebodies, for example, had traditionally bunched the hydraulic systems together. But if that part of the plane was physically damaged in flight, the designers feared, it would crash. So, beginning with the A300, the various hydraulic systems were spread around the body.

The same idea was carried into the A320. Later, a bomb was placed in the bathroom of a Thai Airline Airbus. While flying over Japan, it blew up, knocking out two hydraulic systems. But because the third had been segregated, the plane was able to land safely.

THE STRATEGY of rushing ahead with the A320 proved wise. Had Airbus tried to ride on its second plane, the A310, the consortium might have failed. The plane had only mediocre success—156 sold from 1979 to 1987, half of what the original A300 sold. The A320, however, was an explosive success. From its announcement in 1981 to the end of 1987—before its first commercial flight—Airbus got 294 firm offers and 182 options. No other jetliner had ever done as well. The most stunning order of all was from America's Northwest Airlines. It bought one hundred airplanes, a multibillion-dollar deal. Some U.S. politicians were miffed that an American carrier bought from overseas, but Northwest said it chose on merit alone. The A320's electronics, it felt, were the most advanced, its noise level the lowest, and its fuel use 50 percent less per seat than the older American planes in its fleet. For Airbus, it was a turning point. Up until then, its toehold in the United States was a token one. Now, all at once, its American sales had tripled. No other market was nearly as important. U.S. airlines bought fully half of the world's big passenger jets. And finally, Airbus had received a major American endorsement.

BY 1987, twenty years after it had begun, Airbus was ready to take the final step in its strategy. It was a strategy that began cautiously, in 1968, with Beteille's decision to build a mid-sized, mid-range plane, the A300. He stayed cautious with his next move—an upgrade to the longer-range A310. Only then did he make a bolder investment into the advanced A320. Now that it was succeeding, Airbus was ready for its biggest leap of all—a long-range jumbo jet, potentially the most lucrative niche of all. On June 5, 1987, the consortium put out one more appeal for money, this time for a staggering $4.5 billion. Beteille and his colleagues won it easily. By now, Europe's governments were committed to win in commercial jetliners. Immediately, Airbus began on its ultimate machines: first, a 328-seat long-haul model to be called the A330; second, a 280-seat ultralong-haul model to be called the A340. Already, they say, they have over 130 orders.

Henri Ziegler is now over eighty years old and retired in Paris. Roger Beteille is in his late sixties and retired in Cannes. I asked them each when they felt Airbus had become a success. They both gave the same answer: not quite yet. The real milestones, they said, will be the completion of the long-haul A330 and A340. Producing any widebody jetliner, they explained, is one of the hardest industrial challenges in the world, but it's not enough to succeed at one, or two, or even three. If you're going to compete globally, you need a full line of products. It took twenty years to do that, and the help of several governments, but Airbus, and Europe, are now almost there.

SOME INSIST that Airbus isn't a success at all. So far, it's swallowed over $7 billion in taxpayers' funds, and has yet to make money. But Roger Beteille will tell you that's typical for advanced technologies; it often takes ten to twenty years to turn a profit. He's right. Whether it's photovoltaics, supercomputers, or superconductors, a decade-plus lead time is becoming common. Often, there's only one way companies can sustain that investment long enough to become competitive—with the help of government. Nations that understand that will doubtless harvest the most jobs—and wealth—from future industries.

Some economists say Europe would have been better off if government had never bothered with Airbus.[11] Had the $7 billion been given back to the public as lower taxes, they argue, it would have spurred more fruitful investments. But as America has found during the 1980's, tax breaks don't necessarily lead to greater investment. Meanwhile, even before Airbus has become profitable, its government money has produced a rich harvest. Today, sixty thousand Europeans have high-skill, high-paying aeronautics jobs, most of which would probably have belonged to America if there were no Airbus. Jetliner sales have added almost $4 billion a year to Europe's trade balance. And Airbus's technologies are yielding other spin-offs: a new kind of carbon fiber for Austrian skis, flame-retardant nontoxic textiles for German car seatcovers, more reliable switches for German and French electronics applications.

Most important, Airbus is on the brink of being able to succeed on its own. Already, it's climbed to number two in an industry that may not have room for three players.

RECENTLY, for the first time in decades, Boeing's share of world jetliner orders fell below 60 percent. Airbus is now above 20 percent, and plans to soon pass 30 percent. Every time a $50 million airplane is sold by Airbus instead of Boeing, America loses about thirty-five hundred high-paying jobs for one year.[12] We also lose a minimum of $30 million of net exports. If Airbus wins only 10 percent more of the world's aircraft market, it will cost us $40 billion over the next two decades.

Boeing and McDonnell Douglas are still among America's best companies. Both are leaders in engineering, in manufacturing, in export. They've begun to fight back hard against the Airbus threat. Much of their focus, however, has been to charge the Europeans with unfair trade practices. Airbus has responded with charges of its own, bringing the press to call the debate "Air Wars."[13] In a sense, it echoes a wider trade debate unfolding between America and foreign competitors everywhere. It's a debate that raises a central question about the way modern nations are trying to compete: At what point do legitimate government incentives become illegitimate government subsidies?

The American plane makers say Europe's governments are going too far. They point out that Airbus has received over $7 billion in government loans since 1968, most of which won't be paid back. And that doesn't include the billions more to subsidize operating losses. That, U.S. plane makers say, is an unfair subsidy. Perhaps they're right.

The Europeans, however, counter that America's plane producers were also launched with government help. Most of our early commercial planes were converted military craft, designed and built with federal money. In addition, says Airbus, U.S. companies still get defense and NASA contracts, which indirectly help their commercial technology. That's probably right, too.

The Americans counter that Airbus parent companies get defense contracts of their own. Again, that's accurate. But the debate doesn't stop there.

There's also an argument over selling practices. The Americans say Airbus has distorted world trade by offering finance packages with no money down, low interest rates, and free leases. Worst of all, they've cut prices below cost.

To that, the Europeans say that the longstanding U.S. lock on 90 percent of the world jetliner market was tantamount to monopoly, and they had no choice but to offer good deals to break in. But it's more than good deals, the Americans say. Airbus's governments are supporting products that the market wouldn't. Had a private company launched the A300 and A310, it would have lost billions and canceled them. That's what Lockheed was forced to do with the L-1011. And so much money was poured into the A320, Americans say, that it can't possibly break even until it sells a thousand planes, a high target. Once again, possibly true. But the Europeans have a response: Boeing is also unfairly cutting prices on some of its models, leaning on the 747's monopoly profits to do it.

Finally, there's a debate over political influence. The Americans say Airbus's governments put pressure on other countries to buy, particularly those in the Third World. To win over Thai Airways, for example, they say Thailand was offered low-cost loans for building a sugar mill. To lure Indian Airways, the French offered technical assistance to clean up the Ganges and a speeded delivery of Mirage fighter jets. The Europeans, however, insist that's business as usual, pointing out that American embassy officials also push for aircraft sales. Besides, the Europeans say, the major airlines in West Germany, France, England, and Spain, all Airbus sponsors, have over two-thirds American craft in their fleets, while American fleets are still 90 percent Boeing and Douglas.

There's no doubt that Airbus is indeed playing by different rules. Boeing and Douglas are being forced to compete on their own against the combined power of six foreign firms backed by governments with deep pockets. But who is to say that America's rules are the only right ones to play by? Pressure from Washington may stop some of the subsidies, but that alone won't help America win this race. The fact is, Europe is in jetliners for keeps. The Europeans are going to see Airbus through. At this rate, some feel that in ten years, the consortium could climb from 20 percent of the market to 40 percent or even more. Whether or not we stop them will depend on one thing: not how well we do in the trade debate, but how well Boeing and Douglas do in developing new planes that are technologically better and more efficient than Airbus. To succeed, they'll need to launch the industry's most aggressive R&D effort. If they can't afford it, our own government should do what Airbus's governments are doing: help them. Help them invest. If we don't, an essential American industry could be jeopardized.

IT'S IMPORTANT to realize that Airbus is only one example. We face similar threats in dozens of other future industries. Nations all over the world are turning to government-company partnership as a key economic strategy. Europe is doing it more than ever. Across its landscape, it has begun to seed dozens of consortiums like Airbus. In the last few years, I've had a firsthand chance to see that evolve.

IN LATE 1982, I was in Sweden, having dinner with Bo Ekman, the Volvo planner who'd helped get "the Boston Report" started in Sweden. By then, both Volvo and Sweden had begun their turnarounds. But as we talked after dinner, Ekman said that something worried him.

As a country of 8 million people, Sweden was too small to pioneer new technologies. It had to wait for bigger countries to do it. That, he said, can hurt in a world where products need the latest features to compete. Since Japan was a leader in computers, for example, its car companies were able to work behind the scenes with that industry, designing new models around state-of-the-art dashboard microprocessors. Swedish car companies, on the other hand, had to wait for those microprocessors to come onto the general market, usually a few years later. That, said Ekman, wasn't good enough. If a nation is to compete, he told me, it has to be at the forefront of developing all the latest technologies. He saw one way Sweden could do that: through partnerships with the rest of Europe. Except for Airbus, however, few such partnerships were going on at the time. While Japan was organizing pooled R&D in dozens of new technologies, said Ekman, Europe was doing it piecemeal. Company labs were isolated, sealed off by national borders. And there was no agency—no European MITI—to link them together. The Common Market, said Ekman, focused mostly on trade issues. There was nothing that dealt with the commercial needs of companies. He felt it was time to change that.

Ekman knew you couldn't forge Airbus equivalents overnight. But as a start, he and Pehr Gyllenhammar, Volvo's chairman, came up with the idea of a continentwide network of industrialists. It wouldn't just be a fellowship group. Its goal would be to get companies to start working together on new technologies.

Gyllenhammar arranged to go from country to country to recruit his counterparts. But first, he wanted something to take to them—a report on how well Europe was competing globally. My consulting company's Paris office did the work. We were able to document that, in total, the continent was spending as much on advanced R&D as the United States or Japan, but it was scattered, with labs everywhere duplicating each other.[14] Europe, we found, was good at making products, at manufacturing, but not at inventing. Japan and America were far better at pioneering new technologies, and many European companies, we found, were getting worried about that. The automakers we interviewed, for example, saw a time when car engines would be made not with metal, but high-temperature ceramics. However, since Japan was the leader in ceramics research, its car makers would doubtless be the first to use the new kind of engine. That would give them an edge. We heard the same thing wherever we went. How, the Germans asked, could they continue to lead in machine tools if their Japanese rivals, drawing from a stronger national research base, should be the first to use new computerization and laser-cutting technology? The only way to keep Europe's economy world class, companies were realizing, was to bolster the continent's R&D—in as many areas as possible.

Gyllenhammar proved persuasive. In 1983, the European Business Roundtable was formed—over twenty top executives from a dozen countries.[15] They eventually began a range of shared projects, including $150 million in venture-capital funds to help pioneer new products. They also began to discuss a European version of MIT or Caltech, and an infrastructure program called "Missing Links." But the Roundtable is just one small effort, part of a new consciousness, one that's led to more concrete partnership programs that are about to pose major challenges to America.

One of those programs is called ESPRIT. It was founded by the Common Market in 1984 to seed research in computer technologies. During my business trips to Europe, I watched as ESPRIT got projects going in telecommunications, artificial-intelligence, computer-integrated office systems, and voice-activated microprocessors. More recently, it branched out into helping auto companies develop a system to diagnose engine problems. By 1988, ESPRIT had thousands of researchers in over three hundred companies working on over four hundred projects. Many of those companies had under five hundred employees, which is part of the vision: harnessing R&D talent in small operations. Europe has added two other programs to ESPRIT recently, BRITE and RACE. Like ESPRIT, they are designed to spur cooperative R&D in commercial technologies over the next decade.[16]

Not long after these got off the ground, an even bigger program was launched. This one, called EUREKA, was conceived by France as a kind of response to our "Star Wars" program. President Mitterrand, concerned that our stepped-up defense R&D would widen our technology lead, wanted Europe to begin a drive of its own. Its focus, however, would be strictly commercial. Industrial leadership, he felt, was just as important to national security as weapons leadership. But he stressed that no European country could do it alone. The only way to afford advanced-technology research, he said, was by pooling the resources of all countries. That was EUREKA's founding vision. Today, nineteen nations fund it. It supplies R&D money to companies throughout Europe, but only if they agree to work together. EUREKA-backed products are now beginning to come together the same way Airbus did— one piece from France, another from Germany, a third from Holland. Altogether, the program has committed $5.8 billion to about 170 projects involving 400 products. Some are broad technologies such as new designs for semiconductors, others are as concrete as an advanced fishing vessel.[17]

In December 1987, I got a telling glimpse of how these programs are working, and what they will mean.

IN MID-1987, Thomson of France closed a deal to buy RCA's consumer-electronics business. Because I'd been working as a consultant for RCA, Thomson asked Telesis, my firm, to stay on to help with the merger. One of our jobs was to find ways to pool the two companies' R&D so there wouldn't be overlap. One key area was high-definition television, the next generation of TV, which will have a much sharper image than today's sets.

The last time I'd looked at Europe's television business was when I did my study for England a decade before. At the time, I'd found that the industry was too scattered to compete, and saw little hope that things would change. Now, I was about to see that they'd changed dramatically.

One of my visits was to Thomson's main color picture tube plant south of Rome, in Agnani. I sat down to dinner with the plant's manager. Soon we got to talking about the sale of RCA. He was glad to see that Thomson, his employer, was strengthened by it, but felt bad that so great an American company had been taken over. He looked upon RCA as a legend, the inventor of the color picture tube, the firm that he himself was first hired and trained by. It puzzled him that the United States would sell so historic a company to foreign owners.

"We can't understand what's happening to America," he said. "Why are you letting your industry be bought up? Aren't people worried?"

I told him that day to day, things seem prosperous in America, so there wasn't a lot of concern.

Then we moved on to talking about the job of reorganizing company research. First, he wanted to know about RCA's facilities. He said he'd heard that even before the Thomson deal, RCA had tried to save money by selling its most sophisticated laboratory—the one in Princeton—and reducing research into the next generation of TV-tube technology. I told him that was true, then asked where Thomson stood on that kind of research.

Utterly committed to it, he said. I asked how much the company was investing.

Tens of millions of dollars, he said.

I told him that seemed surprisingly high, especially for a long-horizon project—something that wouldn't hit until the mid-1990's.

"Well," he said, "we get much of it paid for."

I asked what he meant.

Part of it, he said, came from the Italian government.[18]

What was it earmarked for?

The development of new factory automation, he said, adding that it was routine for the government to underwrite that kind of work. In depressed areas, he said, companies can even get help in directly buying factory equipment. Then the manager mentioned a second source of Thomson's research funding.

"The EUREKA program," he said, "is paying for part of our high-definition television program."

I quickly added the numbers he gave me and realized that it almost put Thomson's effort in the same league as Japanese companies. If they succeeded with this research, I knew they'd reap more than just a television payoff. High-definition screens had a number of other applications, including computers.

But what about other needed development work? To win in televisions, they'd have to work on more than just the screens. I asked whether Thomson was big enough to bring it off alone.

The manager said that Thomson wouldn't have to. The RACE program was providing some funds, and Thomson's major European competitor, Philips of Holland, was doing research in signal processing—the TV's actual circuitry. The arrangement allowed each company to put full strength in one area. Later, under the program, they'd share the results. Altogether, European government programs would be funding close to $100 million on television R&D. Only a decade earlier, I was convinced Europe's TV industry would soon be dead. Its strength was split among scores of isolated companies. Now, with government help, it had reorganized itself to be world-competitive.

FOR ME, Agnani was a glimpse into a new European reality. There are now hundreds of government projects like this, all focused on commercial products. I'm convinced that in the next five years, we'll soon be faced with a force from the West as technologically powerful as Japan. It will be a force supported by government. And our own companies will be faced with fighting back alone. Airbus shows the seriousness of the threat. If we can lose market share in one of our strongest technologies, others are vulnerable, too.

You could probably make a good case that EUREKA and ESPRIT are examples of unfair subsidies. But if we choose to fight back with trade negotiations alone, we'll only see more Americans lose good jobs. We'll pay the same price if we unthinkingly put up trade walls. We've been doing that with steel for twenty years, and it's yet to make us competitive again. A better response, I think, is to accept that all over the world, there's a new way of doing business, one we have to embrace ourselves. It's now standard for governments to fund commercial development. It's standard for companies to pool research. It's standard almost everywhere but America.

IN MARCH 1988, sixteen years after I'd seen the *Europa-2* blow up on TV in my dorm in Oxford, I heard another news report about the European space program. It was a launch of *Europa*'s descendant, a rocket named *Ariane*, built by the same kind of Europe-wide consortium that created Airbus.

The Europeans knew they were behind in space technology and would remain so. But they felt that America's decision to concentrate all its resources on the Shuttle was commercially unwise. Manned ships were far more expensive than unmanned rockets. You didn't need all that sophistication to launch communications satellites.

By 1985, the cost-conscious *Ariane* had begun to corner the world market for putting up satellites. When the *Ariane* took off in March of 1988, it carried with it an American satellite—the first to be launched since the Shuttle was grounded. After two long years, America was brought back into space by the expertise of Europe. I saw it as a symbol of a threat I've been watching evolve for years. In the race for technology's future, we will be challenged as never before.

9

Corning Glass:
The Battle
to Talk with Light

HE WAS one of about twenty-five American executives who came to talk to me about Japan in 1982. I'd given a number of speeches on how to compete there, and after each, more businessmen came by—from Cummins Engine, EG&G, Black & Decker. This time, it was a planner for Corning Glass. He explained that his company was having a problem with a new product—optical waveguides. After years of investing in them, Corning was finally seeing some customer interest. But Japan, the world's second-biggest market, wasn't letting Corning in. The planner wanted to talk about what Corning could do.

We spoke a bit about waveguides themselves—glass fibers created to replace traditional phone lines. The planner told me it was an extraordinary new technology, one that promised to be as revolutionary as the phone itself. It would allow communication by light instead of electricity, boosting information capacity hundreds of thousands of times. One hair-thin glass fiber—a waveguide—can carry six thousand telephone calls—as much as a four-inch-thick bundle of copper wires. The company's managers felt waveguides could soon be a $1 billion product, and Corning was out front, beating the Japanese. But not on Japan's home turf, and that was the dilemma. With Corning locked out, Japanese producers were able to build up their own waveguide industry without competition. Just as disturbing, the planner said, they were being showered with government money.

I told him it didn't surprise me. Japan had targeted telecommunications as a priority industry. Among other things, that meant protection from imports and R&D support. He wanted to know if there was a way our own government could stop them. I doubted it, but I did think there was room for Washington to do more of what Tokyo does routinely—R&D funding. We've done well with that in defense, I said, but not in commercial products. Our talk went on most of the afternoon. Afterward, he thanked me for the time and flew back to write his report.

It would be a long while before I heard about waveguides again, but three years later, in the summer of 1985, I got another call from a Corning planner. This time, he wanted the help of my consulting firm in developing a manufacturing strategy for the company as a whole. I told him it's better to approach it one business at a time, especially for a firm as diverse as Corning, which makes everything from kitchenware to nose cones for rockets. Since then, I've made about a hundred trips to Corning for a dozen studies.

One of those, in 1987, involved picking a few potential-growth products for the firm's technical businesses. To pinpoint possibilities, we looked for two things—a technological lead by Corning, and a large potential market. When we were done, the company's head of R&D, Dave Duke, asked if we could talk about my recommendations in depth. I met him in his office. Corning, I said, was ahead in the two products we'd targeted—both still confidential—but the Japanese were coming. If Corning was to win, it would have to invest heavily and quickly in development. I also advised Corning to build a plant even before the market took off. If the company wasn't ready to deliver the day customers came knocking, the market, I said, would all go to Japan.

At that, Duke all but leaped out of his chair and began to pace. He agreed; it was the only way to win. That, he said, is exactly what Corning did with optical waveguides.

Despite all my time with the company, I'd heard little about waveguides since my talk with the Corning planner five years before. I was curious how things had gone, but barely had to ask a question. For the next hour, Duke paced, going back and forth to a blackboard, laying out the whole story. It's one of the most impressive stories I know about how an American company stayed ahead of the world in a technology of the future.

THEY SPEAK at Corning of how their best product ideas came over the Gibson Bridge—the route to company headquarters across the Chemung River in upstate New York. Thomas Edison came across hoping Corning could design glass for his new light bulb. The company delivered, even creating the ribbon machine, capable of making tens of millions of bulbs a year. Another inventor crossed the bridge in search of a glass screen for something called television. Corning invented one, as well as a machine to mass-produce them. When NASA wanted ceramic heat shields for its first moon rocket, it, too, came to Corning.

Eventually, the bridge traffic began going both ways. Each year, the company would send a senior researcher to tour the world for ideas. In 1966, on such a mission, a Corning scientist named William Shaver stopped at the British version of Bell Telephone. He sat down with one of its executives to ask if there was anything Corning could help it explore. As a matter of fact, he was told, there was. The phone company had begun to worry that copper cable—standard phone wire—was becoming outmoded, unable to keep up with the boom in information flow. All advanced countries were facing the same problem. As far back as the 1950's, the streets under Manhattan were starting to fill with cable. There was a need for a new kind of phone wire, one that could carry more capacity in less space.

Essentially, that had been the challenge of the communication industry for a century—more capacity. It's what drove scientists to move beyond the telegraph, first to the phone and then the radio. From there, the challenge was to boost capacity with even-higher frequencies. AM carried thousands of cycles per second, FM millions, and television hundreds of millions. Soon, scientists learned how to use microwaves, which carried billions of cycles per second. Now, the British phone company saw a new opportunity—transmission by light. Its frequency was a staggering hundred thousand times higher than microwaves. But no one knew how to harness it.

THE BRITISH weren't the first to think about communication by light. Almost a century before, in 1880, Alexander Graham Bell managed to use light waves for a phone conversation.[1] He did it in Washington, D.C., between rooftops on Fourteenth Street. It was simple enough—he focused sunlight from building to building with a mirror, then talked into a mechanism that made the mirror vibrate. At the receiving end, a detector picked up a piece of the vibrating beam, then decoded it back into voice the same way a phone did with electricity. "I have heard articulate speech produced by sunlight," Bell wrote in his notebooks. "I have heard a ray of the sun laugh and cough and sing."

It was a stunning achievement, but Bell had a problem. If a cloud came by, it knocked the system out. The answer, Bell knew, would be to focus light down a closed tube. With the right kind of "light pipe," he felt, you could even bend a beam, just as electricity twists and turns along miles of telegraph line. The English physicist John Tyndall was the first to show that light could be channeled. In 1854, he shined light into a water-filled barrel, then pulled a plug on its side. As a spout of water came out, the light came with it, held within the stream. But by Bell's time, no one had figured out how to channel light much further than that. And even if someone did, there was no way to generate a precise light beam strong enough to stay focused over long distances.

Then, in 1960, the laser was invented. It was the perfect source. Now, all scientists had to do was develop a tube—a light pipe—that could carry it. Bell Labs soon began to experiment—literally with a metal pipe, its inside coated with mirrors. When that didn't work, they rigged it with lenses to keep the light focused. It was a little better, but if the pipe's temperature shifted in various spots, the focus was lost. To solve the problem, they put the lenses on mechanical sliders to adjust to the temperature, but by then, it was beginning to look like a Rube Goldberg machine; not the elegant solution scientists search for.

That's when the British phone company suggested the idea of using fiber optics—glass fiber.[2] It seemed ideal—the new fibers were hair thin, a perfect substitute for bulky copper lines. And they channeled light. You could shine a beam in one end, and even if the fiber bent, it would come out the other. But there was a major problem. The fibers didn't carry light very far. Fiber was fine for six-inch medical scopes, but useless for anything much longer. The glass wasn't clear enough. Essentially, that's much of what fiber optics comes down to—getting glass so clear that light keeps sailing through it. Fiber, in essence, is a hair-thin version of a window. The idea is to shine light in one end and get a good beam out the other. But if you took a yard-thick plate of window glass and put a flashlight at one end, you would barely see it from the other. If glass fiber was to replace phone lines, it would have to carry light far more than three feet, ideally up to a kilometer—⅝ of a mile. That's about the standard length of each segment of copper phone line, at which point the electricity fades and has to be boosted. It's inexpensive enough to do that every kilometer or so, but putting amplifiers every three feet to boost light on optical fiber would be pro-hibitive. Part of the challenge, then, was for Corning to invent a glass that was almost unimaginably clear—optical waveguides.

Engineers had come up with a measure to show just how far glass technology had to go. The goal for waveguides was to get at least one percent of a laser beam's light out the other end of a kilometer-long fiber. Then you'd still have enough to amplify. But conventional optic fibers were so opaque that laser light faded to one percent after only a meter—a thousandth of a kilometer. Since light loss was logarithmic, the experimenters were far more than a thousand times short of the goal. If you were down to a faint one percent after one meter, you'd have only one percent of that after two meters. In only five meters, you were already down to a hundred-millionth of a percent. At a kilometer, the percentage of light left was almost too small to compute.

The scientific measure for light loss is decibels per kilometer—a term derived from the name Alexander Graham Bell. A 99 percent loss after a kilometer translates to 20 decibels. That was Corning's goal. Few scientists believed it was possible.

ROBERT MAURER had the best of the physicist's credentials—a doctorate from MIT. When he graduated in the early 1950's, Bell Labs tried to recruit him, presuming he'd leap at an offer to work in the hot new technology of the time—semiconductors. Maurer wasn't interested. Everyone was going into that, and he didn't want to be part of a herd. Instead, he chose Corning. The industrial world, he felt, was moving toward new materials. Specialty glass struck Maurer as the perfect niche for the future.

A dozen years later, William Shaver came back to Corning with Britain's request for telephone fiber. Many at the company considered the idea a long shot. If you couldn't get light through a yard or two of window glass, how could you get it through a kilometer? But Maurer was intrigued. As a section head, he had his own budget, and felt he could afford to take this on. He brought the project to William Armistead, Corning's director of research. Armistead wasn't sure the problem was solvable, but he encouraged Maurer to give it a try. If a company doesn't gamble on the unlikely, Armistead felt, it'll never make breakthroughs. The same philosophy was built into the corporation's budget. Most materials companies spend no more than 2 percent of sales on research. Corning spends 6 percent. It's expensive, but the company considers it a good business decision. "We see it like this," one executive said. "If you make an honest contribution to technology, you'll make some money." So Maurer had the capital. Once he'd made the commitment, he knew he was in a race. Bell Labs was also working on waveguides, as were a dozen companies in West Germany, Britain, and Australia.

For the first year, the waveguide project was mostly a theoretical challenge. It began with Maurer, who worked on the physics of the problem. How well would certain fiber designs carry light? How would other designs keep light from scattering? Nothing seemed promising. He realized the chemical ingredients in the glass would be as important as the design. He decided to go see Pete Schultz.

Schultz, a Corning senior scientist, specialized in creating new formulas for glass. At the time, he was experimenting with possibilities for both optical glass and satellite mirrors. He'd enrolled in Rutgers

University in the early 1960's, not certain what he wanted to do. John Kennedy's call for a rededication to science—and space—spoke to him. He decided to get a doctorate in ceramic science, a key to rocketry. His personal specialty was glass. That's what brought him to Corning.

"If you were going to be a glass scientist," he recalls, "Corning was like Mecca."

Donald Keck, too, had an assortment of offers when he got his physics degree in 1967. Like Maurer, he wanted to get away from the herd. He hadn't given Corning much thought, but when its recruiter began talking about fiber optics, Keck was intrigued. He liked the idea of working with light. There was a particular moment in college that drew him to it. He remembers an old German professor who'd taught him electromagnetic theory. They were studying the speed of light—Einstein's theory. One day, the professor began to tie it in with a sweep of other physics formulas, concepts Keck hadn't thought were related. Now they wove together like threads in a fabric. "There was a glimpse at that moment where you kind of had a vision of the completeness of the universe," he remembers. "It was almost theological."

Before the Corning interview was done, the recruiter showed Keck something he hadn't seen before—a bundle of optic fibers. The challenge, the recruiter said, was to find a way to talk through these with light. That's what the company lab was working on. If it succeeded, it would change the way the world communicated. Keck said he'd be happy to come to Corning.

IT WASN'T a great lab. Later, Keck would say you have to picture a mad scientist bent over an old, cluttered table. "The Dark Ages," he recalls. "Low, triangular benches. Pieces of crude apparatus." It didn't matter. All he cared about was the challenge. His colleagues felt the same.

The team began to develop a rhythm. Maurer continued to work on the physics of the problem. Then Schultz, the chemist, would come up with formulas for creating the type of glass Maurer envisioned. Schultz would then work with Keck to draw the glass into a fine fiber—waveguides—and wrap it around a drum. The final step was measuring the fiber's purity. That was Keck's job, but waveguides were so new, he had to invent a way to do it. He crafted an apparatus that would hold a meter-long piece of fiber. Then he aimed a laser beam into one end of it. He needed a microscope to make sure the beam was in the fiber's core. At the other end, he rigged a gauge to measure what emerged. Finally, he came up with a formula to project a meter-long test to a kilometer. The first time he did it, he saw how far he and his colleagues had to go. Even with only three feet of glass, almost all the laser light was lost. The loss was in the thousands of decibels. Keck, Maurer, and

Schultz etched the goal in their minds—20 decibels—a long way to go, given the logarithmic nature of the measurement. Those first few months didn't bring them much closer.

ONE PROBLEM was the way the fiber had to be constructed. It couldn't be a uniform tube of glass, or else the light would diffuse out through the sides. It had to have two layers—a glass core to carry the light, and a glass skin to keep it contained. Without the skin—cladding, as they called it—the light would be like a stream of water spraying wildly through air, diffusing within inches. With a cladding, however, it would travel like water in a hose—channeled in the center. Since the core was the light's actual roadway, it had to be as clear as possible. Any impurity would absorb the light. The job of the cladding, however, was to keep the light beam reflecting back in. That meant it would have to be the opposite of the core—more like a mirror.

The big breakthrough, everyone knew, would be the core—the invention of a glass so free of impurities that light could sail through a whole kilometer of it. At the time, the purest glass in the world was a variety Corning itself had invented called fused silica. In the 1950's, the company had even put up a fused-silica plant to make products for the Defense Department's early-warning systems.

But it seemed out of the question for a waveguide core. Its first problem was its melting level—2,000 degrees Centigrade, more than three times the melting point of steel. For decades, the goal of the industry was to make glass melt ever lower, so it would be easy to work with. Science had gotten most kinds down to around 600 degrees, and for waveguides, most technical people felt it was essential to stay in that range. Spinning out precision-glass fibers at 2,000 degrees? It wasn't worth even trying.

But there was an even bigger problem with fused silica. If you used it for the core, there was no glass known that would work as cladding. The reason is that the main function of cladding is to act like a mirror. Picture the Lincoln Tunnel. Light comes into the core at the Jersey end, and if you're going to get it out the Manhattan end, you have to line the whole thing with long mirrors. But in a waveguide, it wasn't as simple as selecting any mirrorlike glass for the cladding. For a mirror effect to work, the cladding's refractive index—a physical property— had to be lower than that of the core. But fused silica happened to have the lowest refractive index of any known glass. If you used it for the core, the mirror effect wouldn't work. Anything you tried to use as cladding would leave you with the Lincoln Tunnel lined with windows instead of mirrors. Since the approach of everyone's research was to start with the core, which was the hardest challenge, fused silica seemed out of the question.

Corning's competitors, in fact, had focused on optical glass instead, the kind used for eyeglasses or telescopes. It was comparatively pure, though a long way from what was needed for waveguides. Still, various researchers worked hard to cleanse it. It was the basis of the whole race—the company that squeezed out the most impurities from optical glass would win. But no one seemed to be getting close. That's when Maurer decided to take a whole new approach. A backward approach.

While the rest of the world was starting with the core, he decided to start with the cladding. Its main requirement was a low refractive index. For glass, the lowest then known, of course, was fused silica. So that's what he decided to use. He dismissed its high-melting-point problem. Just because the glass business had been moving toward a low melting point didn't mean you couldn't defy that, and Corning did have experience working with glass at high temperatures.

But then Maurer came to a bigger problem. If he used fused silica for the cladding, he could no longer use optical glass for the core. That's because you couldn't use two completely different kinds of glass in waveguide fibers. If you tried that, temperature changes would make them expand and contract in different ways, breaking the waveguide. It meant he'd have to use fused silica for the core, too. In one sense, that had promise because it was so clear. However, to create the mirror effect, Maurer would have to mix chemicals into the core glass to make its refractive index higher than the pure fused-silica cladding. Later, he would admit it was illogical to do that. The rest of the world was trying to squeeze impurities out of core glass, and here was Corning, deciding to mix them in.

"Corning decided to be irrational," an executive would later explain. "To simultaneously say, 'Let's use it for the core because it's pure, then add stuff to it and make it less pure' is contradictory."

Maurer, however, believed in leaving the herd, so he went ahead. The question now was how could he get light through a core filled with additives? His hope was to find chemical additives pure enough to keep the glass from clouding too much. Few colleagues gave him much chance of succeeding.

MAURER MADE a point of ignoring skeptics. Once again, his research team began. Soon Keck had the first fiber sample on his measuring device. It didn't work. Neither did the next few. Some said it proved the fused silica approach was a waste of time. Maurer continued to allocate budget money to waveguides anyway. Nobody at Corning told him to stop. "It was not run like the German Army," he recalls. "You called your own shots." He did have to go through annual reviews, during which he'd put up slides showing how they'd gotten more and more light out of the end of the fibers. He'd make sure to show only the best experiments. "No reason to show all the bad ones," he would later say. If he had a most important backer, it was Armistead, the company research director. Both were ready to keep on risking, month after month. Maurer's own schedule was to give waveguides at least five years. Half of science, he will tell you, is patience. The other half is luck.

"If you have dozens of experiments going," he says, "maybe one or two will make it."

As time went on, waveguides began to look less and less likely to be among them. The research went from a year to two, and then three. In the science journals, articles were beginning to doubt it could ever happen. But at Corning, the team continued to have faith. Keck remembers the time well. It wasn't exactly like graduate school, where you discuss ideas over late-night pizza, but it was close. They'd brainstorm in the cafeteria, the elevator, the corridors. There were more than a few half-hour sessions as they stood by their cars with their keys in their hands. People who'd heard they were actually mixing chemicals into the core would tell them they were going about this backward. The idea is to get particles out of the core, the doubters would say, not put them in.

It only deepened the team's resolve.

"The world was taking the easy path," Keck recalls, "and Bob figured that was doomed to failure. He decided to run right against the best opposing linebacker. It was so simple it was brilliant."

Except that it wasn't working. Pete Schultz remembers the highs and lows. Each time they'd come up with a new formula, everyone was convinced it would finally get them down to the magic twenty decibel point.

"I think we got it," Schultz would tell Keck after drawing a new fiber.

A few days later, Keck would come back with the test results.

"It's four hundred dbs," he'd say.

"Ucch," said Schultz. "All right—why? What's the cause of the loss? What do we do next?"

Maurer himself knew that if his new approach was wrong, Corning would be left behind by Bell, or Europe, or possibly the Japanese. He does not recall losing sleep over it. "One thing you learn in research," he says, "is you have to live with failure."

THEY HAD one other headache as big as mixing a new formula for core—spinning it into fiber. Until then, everyone had been doing it the same way. They'd start with a big rod made of core glass, then surround it with a sheath of cladding glass, like a bun around a hot dog, and about that size. They held it vertically in a furnace, heated it, then began pulling out the melted end. As it stretched into hair-thin fiber, it kept the same scale as the hot dog and bun—thick core, thin cladding. That had been fine for things like medical scopes, but Corning's researchers realized they needed the opposite for waveguides—thin core and thick cladding to keep light in. But they soon ran into a problem—air bubbles. No matter how they tried the process, it left air bubbles where the cladding met the core. The bubbles acted like holes, allowing light to escape. They finally had to face it—if this was going to work, they needed a different method of making fiber. But there was no obvious alternative. They brainstormed ways to adapt every known glass-making process, but couldn't come up with anything. So Maurer told Schultz and Keck to forget glass technology. If all you do is think about what the industry's doing, you're locked in mentally. He urged them to look at other, unrelated areas of science. That way, they might find an idea worth transplanting. Keck and Schultz agreed.

"The most spectacular inventions," Keck would explain, "come when you take something from a totally different field and apply it to what you're doing."

Keck began to think. He knew IBM had developed methods of coating silicon chips with a method called sputtering. Why not try that? If the problem was that the hot-dog shaft of glass wasn't sealing well against the bun—why not get rid of the hot dog altogether? Why not just start with the bun—a hollow tube—and coat it with core glass through sputtering?

"Nah," Keck remembers being told by some colleagues, "that'll never work." No one in glass had ever heard of anything like that. Keck decided to try it anyway. "It sure helps to be naive and young," he explains.

He mentioned the idea to Schultz, who suggested a variation. Instead of using sputtering, he felt they should spray the inside of the cladding tube with superheated vaporized core glass. It was called vapor deposition, and Corning had perfected it in other areas. If you did it that way, Schultz felt, it would probably seal better, getting rid of the bubbles. At the same time, he pointed out, the spraying would allow the thinnest possible core, another key goal.

Maurer backed them, and not just because he liked the untried path. He had one other goal—creating a product the competition couldn't easily match. To achieve that, he felt, it wasn't enough for the product itself to be unique; you also had to come up with a unique way of making it. Maurer instantly saw that Schultz and Keck's idea would do that. It would give Corning a patented manufacturing process. It took months of trial and error, part of it science, part of it art. One breakthrough was the idea of hooking up a vacuum cleaner at one end of the glass tube to suck in the glass vapor uniformly. That was the art part. Or maybe the science part. They weren't sure. Whatever, it helped solve the problem. The fiber came out without bubbles.

Now, all they had to do was perfect the light-carrying range of the fiber itself. But neither science nor art seemed to be working.

KECK remembers one thing that sustained them through the frustration—leftover grad-school paranoia. Most scientists at Corning had worked under professors who'd been constantly worried that someone else would publish first, leaving their own work moot. Now, years later, Keck and his colleagues still had the habit of looking over their shoulders. Was Bell almost there? The Europeans? Japan? The more they failed, the harder they pushed.

Gradually, they were running out of formulas for making new kinds of core, so they turned to changing the way they cooked it. Maybe that would make it perform better. One day, they'd give it an extra braising at 300 degrees, the next day 400 degrees, then 1,000 degrees. They'd pump oxygen into the furnace. They'd try different ways of drying the fiber. Occasionally, Keck's measuring apparatus would tell him they'd made headway, but each time he'd look through the microscope to align the laser, there'd still be just a faint glow, a sign that the light was draining out. He knew that if he ever got it right, the core would hold on to much more light, and the microscope would show a far brighter glow. By 1970, the fourth year of Corning's research, many in the scientific community were beginning to face it; maybe this whole idea of optical waveguides was a dud. It was around that time that a paper was delivered at a meeting of the prestigious Institute of Electrical and Electronic Engineers saying glass-fiber waveguides were decades away.[3]

Donald Keck remembers doing one more routine sampling in August 1970. A new mix of fiber was drawn on a Thursday. He heat-treated it on a Friday. By the time it was done, it was late in the day, and Keck was anxious to get home for the weekend. He decided to make one more quick measurement. He put the fiber on the rig. He bent over his microscope and began to line up the laser. He watched as the pinpoint beam got closer and closer to the core. Suddenly, he got hit with a bright beam of light, right in the pupil.

"Good grief," he said, "what do I have here?"

It must have been a mistake. The laser was badly aligned perhaps, reflecting off something else. But he looked again, and it was the same bright beam. And yes, the laser was perfectly aligned, in the heart of the core. He looked at the fiber's other end—it showed a brighter spot of light than he'd yet seen. Finally, he realized what had happened. They'd done it. And they'd done it so well, the laser had burst down the core, bounced off the other end, and reflected back.

He looked to check the decibel level, the light loss—attenuation, in the language of the lab. Would it be under the magic twenty? He couldn't imagine it possible. But it was. Donald Keck's gauge told him light loss was under twenty. By now it was five-thirty. He rushed out of the lab. Maurer was gone, so he went to two or three other offices— no one. Then the elevator doors opened. It was Bill Armistead, Corning's head of research.

"Hey," said Keck, "you want to see something neat?"

The two went into the lab and shared the moment. Keck would say later that he could just about feel the spirit of Edison. Usually lab notebooks are fairly dry. On that day in 1970, Keck's entry is there for posterity.

Attenuation equals 16 db, it says. Eureka.

CHARLES LUCY first visited Corning while working as a civilian engineer for the navy. He crossed the Gibson Bridge as head of a project team working on an early-warning system for incoming missiles. They needed a pure, quartzlike material, and thought that fused silica, which Corning had invented in the 1930's, would fit. Later, in 1952, Lucy, an MIT electronics graduate, joined Corning. Like Maurer, he was convinced specialty glass would play a big role in future technologies, and he wanted to be part of it. He spent a few years in the lab, supervised the building of a fused-silica factory, and in the 1960's became head of Corning's fiber-optic business development group. He was a believer in waveguides right from the start, agreeing immediately to help sponsor Maurer's research.

After the breakthrough of 1970, it fell to Lucy to develop a market for waveguides. He began to show customers the product's first sample—a twenty-meter piece of fiber. He expected the telecommunications industry to stand in line for it. Soon he found that no one cared. No one wanted to buy it. After Corning had won the research race against every company in the world, it seemed the victory would be a hollow one: technical success, commercial failure. Lucy learned what the problem was when he paid a call on AT&T—the biggest potential customer of waveguides since it owned 80 percent of the nation's phone lines. Initially, the executives there were impressed by the new fiber. "You've done it," they told Lucy. Then they shrugged. They said it would be thirty years before the American phone system would be ready for waveguides. And when it was, they said, AT&T planned to have its own fiber.

Lucy asked himself what he should do now. His answer was to learn more about the potential market. "We didn't really know a thing about telecommunications," he would say later. He spent a few months traveling, meeting with phone-company executives all over the world. He came home a bit clearer on what Corning had to do. Most important, the company had to make it a finished product. At the moment, their waveguides were nothing more than raw glass fiber on big spools. To be ready for use, they had to figure out how to wrap it with cable. In addition, a range of new products would have to be developed to make the system work. They needed special lasers as light sources, connectors to bind lengths of fiber together, and devices called multiplexers to sort out signals.

Maybe phone companies still would hesitate, but without cabling and components, there was zero chance they'd even consider it. The first challenge, Lucy felt, was cabling. The problem was that Corning didn't know how to do it. No one did. He decided to turn to the country's copper cablers—the ones who wrapped phone line for companies like GTE. He presumed they'd be delighted to work with Corning. This, after all, was communication's future. Lucy began to knock on doors. The cablers told him to go away.

It turned out that most of them had just invested in new plants. With the information age exploding, they'd put all they had into expanded copper-wrapping capacity. The last thing they wanted to hear was that their new investments were obsolete. "It's kind of like if you were making buggy whips," a Corning executive would later explain. "The invention of the automobile doesn't exactly warm your heart." The most hopeful response Lucy got was from one cabler who told him to come back in the year 2000. Lucy had to admit they were perhaps being realistic. There were no guarantees that Corning would be able to sell big supplies of reliable low-priced fiber in the near future. Once phone companies bury cable and string it across the country, he knew, they want to be sure it won't go bad. Though waveguides were fine in the lab, they were unproven in the field. Why would cablers want to invest in something that could be twenty years away? Corning, however, had already done that, so Lucy pressed on.

He couldn't have been more frustrated. Corning's researchers, he realized, had proven perhaps too visionary. They'd come up with a miracle invention that was turning out to be far ahead of its time. It was as if Corning had invented the carburetor in the 1850's.

"There we were," Lucy would recall later, "all dressed with a technical breakthrough, and no place to go."

Corning had been through things like this with other products. A few years before, company scientists had invented biodegradable glass.

Management expected it to be a boom product, but no one wanted it. Now, it seemed Corning would have to make room on the same back shelf for waveguides. But Lucy wasn't ready to do that yet. If he couldn't find anyone in America interested in the product, he'd go abroad.

But as he traveled the world, he got the same reaction. No one wanted to touch waveguides. The fibers were uncabled, too short, too uncertain. The optimists were saying it was decades away, the pessimists never. The biggest disappointment was the British phone company, the people who'd started Corning on this in the first place. Now they told Lucy their biggest hope for waveguides had been for video phones, an idea that had been waiting for a new wire with more capacity than copper. Waveguides fit perfectly, but their latest surveys, they told Lucy, showed there wouldn't be much market for video phones until the next century. As much as Lucy believed in his product, he wasn't ready to wait that long.

"I was still a young man in 1971," he says, "and have always been willing to take the long-term view of new business development. But a thirty-year missionary phase was a little beyond even my planning horizon, and certainly beyond the company's."

The only way around it was to forget video phones and focus on what was already here—the telephone. He changed his strategy and went back on the road.

In 1971 and 1972, Lucy made fourteen trips to Europe and seven to Japan. As Corning's fibers got even longer and the decibel rate ever lower, he finally started seeing signs of foreign interest. They were faint, but they were there. That's when he discovered there was yet another obstacle to get past.

In most countries he visited, the phone systems were state-owned.[4] As such, they insisted on buying national products. Since they were the biggest potential customers—the only potential customers, really— Lucy found himself with nowhere else to turn. The markets weren't formally protected, but they were armored; there was no way to penetrate them directly. The only choice was for Corning to join forces with a foreign partner. Only then would the state-owned systems even look at Corning's product.

Few U.S. firms would have bothered. Instead of taking on the burden of a joint overseas effort, most would have simply licensed their technology to a local, then gone home and waited for the royalty checks. It's the standard way to squeeze profit out of patents. It's usually not good for America—it means jobs go overseas—but it's easy profit for the company.

Lucy, however, knew that profit from licensing is low—only a few percent on every dollar. He wanted more than that. Just as important, he didn't want to give this technology away. Waveguides were Corning's. The company had gambled on them, spent years inventing them. Now, he wanted to reap the benefits—to make them, market them, and harvest a full payback. It left him one strategy: to team up with foreign companies and try to sell from the inside. With no one in the States willing to buy, it was Lucy's only way of moving forward. He felt it was urgent that he make at least some headway. Back at Corning, the skeptics were becoming convinced that waveguides would never bring in a dime. Perhaps, thought Lucy, joint overseas agreements would prove them wrong.

In most companies, he might not have been allowed to keep gambling with an unproven product. But that's why he liked Corning. It let executives like him act like entrepreneurs. Waveguides were treated almost as if they were Lucy's business. He didn't need approval for every step he took. He had the freedom to go out on a limb.

He soon saw that joint agreements could be more than just a way to get access to foreign phone companies. They might also provide a way to get Corning's fiber fully finished as a product. The likeliest overseas partners were local cablers. With U.S. cablers telling Lucy they didn't want to see him, he now realized those in Europe might be his best chance for getting waveguides wrapped. "The keys to our success," he would later tell colleagues, "were on other people's keychains."

He began to knock on cablers' doors. Some had the same reaction as the Americans. "It smelled a little like technological upset of their copper game, which they needed like the plague," Lucy recalled. "It's natural—status quo is comfortable, change is a pain."

But some agreed to negotiate. He remembers bringing a reel of fiber to one of the first talks. Maurer was with him. When they got to the airport, they decided they couldn't bear checking it as baggage. "It was one of the early reels," Lucy explained, "one of our babies." To make sure it would be safe, they bought a separate seat for it, even belting it in. "I'll never forget the look on the face of the foreign customs guy," he recalls. "We were carrying this case like gold. We opened it up. And it was a piece of glass on a spool." It was even harder getting it back into the United States. The customs agent refused to let them pass until he'd looked up its classification. Lucy patiently explained there would be no classification for a few more years. It had just been invented.

In 1972 and 1973, agreements began to come together. First, there were cablers—Britain's BICC, France's CGE, Italy's Pirelli, and Germany's Siemens. He made deals with government technical agencies, as well, including CNET in France and CSELT in Italy. He even found a partner in Japan, Furukawa, a cabler for the national phone system there. The deal Lucy struck was simple. The partner would have to develop waveguide components and ways to cable fiber. In return, Corning would license them to use its patents and know-how to make waveguides in their own countries if a market ever developed. And there was one more condition—everyone would have to pay Corning an annual fee. Lucy, ever the entrepreneur, saw it as a way to get money to keep funding Maurer's waveguide research.

The deals were all simple partnerships, but Lucy did choose one company, Siemens, for a full-fledged joint venture. That way, he figured, Corning could gain direct experience in both cabling and components in case it needed to develop them back home for the U.S. market.

Lucy suspected that some of his new partners had shaken hands in self-defense. At first, they'd been afraid to touch waveguides, but now were more afraid not to, especially with state phone systems beginning to show some interest. An agreement, they felt, would at least give them some expertise in the unlikely event that the market took off. But they hoped it wouldn't.

"Their goal was to contain us," Lucy would say, "my strategy was to break out." To do that, he'd needed cabling and component know-how, development money, and a doorway into local markets. The partnerships gave these to him.

Giving patent licenses to its foreign partners, he knew, meant they could eventually start making their own fiber. But he also knew that if his own company kept improving waveguides, the partners would need Corning to help them remain state-of-the-art. As long as Corning remained the technical leader, it would hold on to a piece of the action anywhere it formed a partnership. With his new partner fees from abroad and continued R&D cash from Corning itself, Lucy was able to keep the waveguide research going strong. Soon, an engineering manager named Les Gunderson was appointed to oversee the practical development of waveguides and work with the R&D team. Technically, the progress was terrific.

But there were no sales.

No sales through 1973, through 1974, through 1975. Despite that, the Corning research team pushed harder than ever. Before the early breakthrough fiber had gained a single customer, the research team made it obsolete. They made fibers of ever-longer lengths, discovered a new additive for the core that was better than the original one, and began to work on a revolutionary new process for producing it. Early on, they made a major breakthrough with a fiber of astoundingly low light loss—only 4 decibels per kilometer. That would allow one waveguide to go twenty kilometers before needing a repeater—five times longer than standard copper wire. Pete Schultz remembers how obsessed they were with that particular breakthrough. Right afterward, a storm caused a catastrophic flood in Corning. The next day, Schultz was helping dig out a neighborhood when he ran into research director Bill Armistead, who was also at work. Both men were knee deep in mud, surrounded by devastation. Armistead looked up from his shovel.

"Peter," he said, "that fiber you made is fantastic."

But phone companies still refused to buy. Waveguides, they said, were expensive, untested, exotic, not worth the risk. Lucy's response was to keep pumping more money into Corning's lab. Meanwhile, he kept proselytizing, visiting phone companies around the world again and again. He even put together a small prototype line to produce samples.

"It was like after Wilbur and Orville took off," Corning's patent attorney, Al Michaelsen, would later explain. "You couldn't exactly sell tickets for a cross-country flight that day, but if you had vision, you'd understand the future."

By 1975, however, doubts at Corning grew. It had been five years since Donald Keck wrote *Eureka* into his lab book. And still all they were selling were samples. Some said it was time to stop wasting money and wait until the world was ready. But Amory Houghton, Jr., Corning's chairman, still believed in the fiber's promise. In 1975, he gave responsibility for waveguides to an aggressive senior executive named Lee Wilson, who also supervised Corning's electronic-components products. He told Wilson he was convinced waveguides would someday replace copper in phone lines; he wanted Corning to be the leader when that day came. By 1976, Corning had given waveguides a decade's work—and still no payback. Many firms might have considered the technology a washout at that point. But Houghton, Wilson, and Corning president, Tom MacAvoy, decided now was the time to make an all-out corporate commitment to it. If the product was going to work, they felt, Corning needed to build up a full business organization around it. They called in one of their best managers, Dave Duke.

DUKE had already had some practice creating a boom business from scratch. In 1970, new government rules came out requiring cars to have catalytic converters. Corning developed a ceramic honeycomb substrate that made the converters work. The demand was massive, and Duke was assigned to build up capacity to meet it overnight. He would later refer to that period of his life as "the war." But he succeeded, making Corning into the world leader. Afterward, he was put in charge of the company's Industrial Materials Business, a $100 million division with three plants and four sales groups. Then, in August 1976, he got a call from MacAvoy, Corning's president. He told Duke he had a great opportunity for him.

"You know those optical waveguides they're working on in the lab?" said MacAvoy.

Yes, Duke had heard of them—a great technology, but no market.

Well, said MacAvoy, Corning wanted Duke to develop it into a business.

Duke paused. Then he asked a question. "Tell me," he said, "this is still in the lab?"

"Right," said MacAvoy.

"How many people are on the business side of it?"

"Six."

At the time, Duke had a thousand people working for him. "Tom," said Duke, "what'd I do wrong?"

MacAvoy laughed. He told Duke he'd been picked because he'd done so well. Management believed waveguides could be one of the world's big future industries. Corning had won with them in the lab; there was no reason why the company couldn't win in the marketplace as well. Duke asked more about how far waveguides had gone. Maurer's people, he was told, had achieved a breakthrough product—kilometer-long fibers with only 4 decibels of light loss. But they just weren't taking off. Total sales were under $1 million, mostly samples. Competition seemed to be gearing up as well—ITT, AT&T, the Japanese. All had begun making fiber in the lab. Corning was ahead, but not alone.

Duke went to work. To help figure out how to sell the product, Lee Wilson had ordered a consultant's study on possible markets. The report came back. Its conclusion was a surprising one. It said it was unlikely that waveguides would be used for telephones anytime soon. Far better to try some special applications like linking computers to talk to each other. Duke and Lucy looked closely at the study data. It was prepared by one of the most prestigious consulting firms in the country. The report had cost Corning a lot of money. The two agreed how to respond to it.

They decided to ignore it. They decided to go after the telephone market after all. But as they both knew, the market wasn't interested. There seemed to be no magic tactic that could change that, so they settled for a strategy of relentless promotion. They put together elaborate marketing literature and flooded the world with samples. Back at Corning, they set up a training and demonstration program to prove to customers that waveguides were for real. All the while, they urged Maurer, Schultz, and Keck to keep improving the product.

Then Duke and Lucy made a bold leap; they decided to build a full-scale pilot plant that could produce five thousand kilometers of fiber per year. There were still almost no customers, but Corning wanted to start fine-tuning production anyway. The only way to lower the scrap rate and fine-tune the process was to get into test-manufacturing, a multimillion-dollar investment. "The real money-sucking phase," Lucy would call it. It was like building a chain of gas stations before the car was invented, but if waveguides were to succeed, the Corning team felt they had to be ready the moment the first big order came in.

SOON AFTER taking over, Duke met with Corning's Japanese licensee, Furukawa. Its people told him that Nippon Telephone and Telegraph (NTT), Japan's state-owned phone company was forming a coalition of three local companies to produce fiber for it—fiber NTT itself had developed. To Duke, it sounded like a terrific opportunity. He contacted NTT and asked if Corning's local subsidiary—a Japanese-incorporated firm called Corning KK—could join the group. Duke stressed that Corning was the world's technical leader. It could offer NTT more expertise than anyone else. The answer came back. It was a firm no.

Duke appealed to MITI—the Ministry of International Trade and Industry. But the people there said they were sorry. Even though it was government-owned, NTT's decisions were its own. It didn't sound right to Duke, but there was nowhere else to appeal. Corning was locked out. The next summer, Duke found out why.

He was back in Japan, attending a waveguide conference, when a MITI official took the podium. The government, he said, had targeted optical communications as a priority industry for the country. Then he began to lay out Japan's plan for becoming a world leader in the field.[5] Duke listened, alarmed. He'd known that NTT and its partners were working hard on waveguides, but he'd had no idea the effort was so big. The government was pouring millions into research. "They were going after everything," Duke would recall later. If Corning was to stay ahead, he felt, it was essential to take them on in their own backyard. Besides, if Japan was this interested in waveguides, it could prove the first big market.

After the conference, Duke made an appointment with NTT and asked if he could bid on future jobs. He was told that wouldn't be possible. If Corning wanted to see its technology in Japan, fine, but it couldn't sell it there. It would have to license it to a local firm, giving up all patent and marketing rights. It was one thing, thought Duke, to give fiber-making know-how to a joint partner to sell in its own country, as Corning was doing in Europe, but this was something else. NTT was insisting Corning hand over its inventions with no strings, even allowing the Japanese to sell it worldwide. In Duke's eyes, it was absurd. You don't give your secret weapon to the competition and then sign off.

The Japanese tried to reassure him. Corning, they said, would make good money on license royalties.

"We said no cotton-pickin' way," Duke recalls. "We want a piece of the action." His actual language was more restrained, but the result was a standoff.

Duke was somber as he flew home. "I remember coming back kind of shell-shocked," he recalls. "I'd seen what they'd done with cars, with consumer electronics—I was paranoid about the Japanese. I was scared to death of them." But it only made him want to fight harder.

At headquarters, Duke told his division chiefs what he'd found. The scope of Japan's waveguide plans left everyone alarmed. Corning was big—a $1-billion-a-year company at the time—but could it match a national, government-backed push?

Duke tried to rally his people. He told them size didn't have to matter; effort did. So did spirit. "It's time," he told them, "to decide how far we're going to go with this. Either we settle for a footnote as the inventor and take some royalties—which is no fun—or we retake the torch now. And keep it."

He went on to map out a new counterassault. This wasn't going to be another VCR story,[6] Duke said, not another case of America giving away its inventions. Waveguides were Corning's. And the only way to keep them was to win on three fronts: the lab, the factory, and the market. In turn, that meant three priorities—lowest cost, highest quality, biggest volume. Finally, he reminded everyone that it wouldn't work to merely stay even with the competition. Corning, he said, was smaller than its rivals, both here and in Japan. Look at AT&T, he said—it had more people, more money, and itself as a customer. When your competition's bigger, matching it isn't good enough. "I don't want to tie," he said. "If we tie, we lose."

SOON the message was given to the people in the lab. The boss was concerned. It left the lab concerned too. "It was a growing, gut-gnawing feeling that we needed to do something different," Keck recalls. "We really had to redouble the effort. Show them what we're made of."

They decided to focus on their manufacturing process. At the time, Corning had perfected what it called its "inside" technique—spraying the interior of glass tubes with silica vapor, then pulling them into fibers. It was clearly a good method, patented by Corning, but because it was close to well-known techniques in the electronics field, the competition had all copied its basic idea. Duke's instinct told him to find another way. You don't stay ahead by doing something the same way as everyone else. Besides, he felt the technique had reached a productivity limit. The tubes were only an inch in diameter, and spraying the inside was painstakingly slow. In addition, the tubes had to be replaced each time they were drawn down, slowing the process even more. If Corning was going to achieve a factory-cost leap, their research team had to find a way to make fiber faster.

In a sense, Schultz and Keck should have been the first to fight a new approach. After all, they were the main creators of the inside process. They'd watched it become the world's model. Now, they were being asked to make it obsolete. Later, Keck would say it didn't bother him. "The first way something's done is usually not the best way," he explains. Besides, he saw another problem with the tube method: It limited the theoretical length of fibers to four kilometers. The tubes were only big enough to feed out that much glass. Keck's ideal was for fifty-kilometer fibers, possibly even one hundred. To even dream about that meant a different process.

Late in 1977, the brainstorming began. They soon focused on an alternative they'd been tinkering with since 1971. They hadn't used it so far, because it seemed too hard to master. It was called the outside process, and the idea was to start with a rod, spray it with vaporized core glass, then spray cladding glass over that. At that point, the rod would be removed and the fiber pulled from the double cylinder of glass that was left. It had great potential. Production costs promised to be much lower than for the inside process. But there was a problem. The fiber that came out didn't work too well.

All that spray ended up filling the fiber with impurities, mostly water molecules. At most, a length of waveguide could stand twenty parts of water per billion. The outside process pushed it to several million parts per million. Now that Keck and his colleagues had decided to try perfecting it, the challenge of squeezing out the water fell to Pete Schultz. He and one of his key researchers, Bob DeLuca, began to look for ways to dry the glass vapor as it was laid down. There was progress, but it was slow. Some at Corning wanted to look for another approach, or stick with what they had. The old inside process worked fine, they said. But Maurer told Schultz's team to stay with it. Maurer's ultimate goal wasn't the thrill of discovery alone, it was the satisfaction of creating a leading product. If Corning was to do that with waveguides, it had to pioneer a low-cost manufacturing method that the competition could not copy.

IN 1978, Duke began to talk about taking another gamble. He wanted to move from the waveguide pilot plant to a full-fledged factory. There were strong arguments against it. The company had yet to receive a sizable order. The standard sale was for a few kilometers, a few dozen at the most. Many thought it could be a decade before the world would swallow what a new plant could deliver. But Duke was resolute. And he had a powerful backer—Corning's chairman, Amory Houghton.

Around the globe, both men were seeing hopeful signs. Phone companies in several countries were installing fiber test lines. There was a chance that one of them would take a sudden leap to an actual regional system and need fiber fast. Houghton wanted the company to be ready for that. It's rare for a U.S. firm to build a plant for a product that has yet to have a proven market, but Houghton, like Duke, was ready to gamble. Corning had been at this for over a decade. Far better, Houghton felt, to risk being saddled with an idle plant than lose a potential breakthrough order after all that investment. He decided to build.

They chose a spot where Corning had another plant with some extra space suited for conversion—Wilmington, North Carolina. Duke knew it would take months to get all the signatures needed to start the project. He and his boss, Lee Wilson, began to have visions of being surprised by a sudden order while waiting for the company paper work. So they didn't wait. By the time the last signature was put down by the last finance man, the plant was already half-built. By 1979, it was ready to operate.

MEANWHILE, Corning had been doing all it could to bring the U.S. market along. But it was frustrating. AT&T was set on developing its own waveguides, and worst of all, most cablers were still hoping the technology would just go away. A new plant wouldn't do much good if Corning couldn't get its fiber cabled. In 1974, Lucy had set up a small pilot cabling facility within Corning for samples. In 1976, Duke and Lucy came up with a plan to nudge the U.S. cablers along. If Corning could get a serious cabling operation going, they reasoned, it could convince the copper people that they had to act. But Corning had to approach this carefully. The point was to woo U.S. cablers as customers, not take them on as rivals. So Duke and Lucy decided to start up an operation just big enough to get the cablers nervous. For expertise, they chose to do a joint venture with Siemens, their German partner. Together, they formed a U.S. company called Siecor. Corning made its intentions very public, hoping the specter of competition would rouse the U.S. copper people.

It began to work. Cablers started to make inquiries. In turn, phone companies paid closer attention. But Duke found that nothing happens overnight. Unlike Corning, the cablers felt customers should come first, production second, not the other way around. Duke had only one consolation: With Siecor off the ground, the company was finally ready to deliver finished product, and in good volume.

BY 1982, the European joint-agreement strategy had begun to pay off. National phone companies started to place small orders for fiber, and Corning was there, ready to produce. By this time, Corning's European partnerships had been renegotiated by Lucy into full-fledged joint ventures, so they could move into production. To coax the market along, Corning also boosted its European marketing network. All of that, however, was still a gamble: Though annual sales were up to $10 million a year, Corning was spending much more to develop the business. So far, no profit. They welcomed these first customer nibbles, but all they were getting was five kilometers here, ten there, a hundred at the most. Three years after finishing its factory, Corning was still looking for a major order.

Then, in 1982, the U.S. government deregulated the telecommunications industry.[7] A company called MCI was one of the first to challenge AT&T with plans for a national phone network of its own. It decided to build that network with optical waveguides.

Duke wasn't sure what kind of scale the MCI people had in mind, but that fall he went to see them. He was with Al Dawson, head of Siecor, Corning's cabling joint venture. The two sat down with several MCI executives. There were routine introductions, a bit of small talk, and then one of the executives said something Duke could barely believe. As Corning knew, he said, MCI was planning to put in a waveguide phone system. They wondered whether Corning would be able to make them some fiber. Then they mentioned the amount.

Would it be possible to deliver one hundred thousand kilometers of it?

It was the breakthrough Duke had been hoping for—an order ten times bigger than anything Corning had seen. But now he was worried. Could they deliver that much quickly? And something troubled him even more than quantity. MCI was asking for a new kind of fiber with an ultrathin core—single mode, it was called. Though Corning had worked with single mode in the lab, it hadn't developed it for production. Lasers had only recently advanced far enough to produce an ultrathin beam, so it hadn't been practical. MCI, however, knew about the laser breakthrough and felt single-mode waveguides would be more efficient. That's what it wanted. Could Corning deliver? Could it deliver one hundred thousand kilometers of it?

Normally, it would have meant weeks of meetings back home to talk it out. But Duke didn't want to wait. He worried that MCI might look elsewhere if he hesitated. So, then and there, he gave an answer.

"Of course," he said.

The meeting continued. The MCI team began to talk price. They named their target. Duke knew it was terribly low for such a new kind of fiber. Again, that should have meant weeks of meetings back in Corning. But neither Duke nor Dawson wanted this to slip away. Dawson wrote a quick note and passed it to Duke.

"MCI price?" Dawson asked.

Duke wrote a note of his own and slipped it back.

"Hard," he said, "but yes."

Duke looked back at the MCI executives. The price, he said, was doable. The two sides shook hands. Duke rushed to a phone and called his lab.

"Guys," he remembers saying, "I just agreed to an order for one hundred thousand kilometers of single-mode fiber. Can you make it?"

The lab knew the way David Duke thought. More important, they'd begun to think the same way.

"Of course," they told him.

LATER, Donald Keck would say that normally, it would have been impossible to develop single-mode waveguides from lab to factory in such a short time. But Corning wasn't starting from zero. In 1971, the lab realized that single-mode would be the most efficient fiber. Unfortunately, lasers weren't yet thin enough for single-, so they'd gone multi-mode. All along, though, they knew it wasn't the elegant solution. Single-mode was more efficient. That's why, in 1979, the Corning team had begun experimenting with it again. Because of the laser problem, however, Corning hadn't planned on producing it until 1985, more than two years away. Now, they faced having to deliver in six months.

Despite what the lab team had told Duke by phone, they had a lot of uncertainty about this. Some began to think they should come out and say it—the company had overcommitted. Soon Duke came down to meet with them.

"I promised this," he told them of the order, "because I have faith in you guys." He kept up a pep talk for ten minutes. When he was done, there were no more doubters.

By gosh, you're right, Dave, Keck remembers thinking. We're going to do it.

Within months, they'd succeeded. They'd gone from a few prototypes to a finished, single-mode product. Keck was proud. It was far better than the multimode waveguides they'd been making. Those, he realized, had been like oversized pipes, the water spraying inefficiently out the end. These were like efficient hoses—the same amount of water, but this way, it raced out the end—clean, uniform, controlled.

Now came the next question—could they manufacture the fiber at unprecedented volume? It would have been impossible had they not gambled on the Wilmington plant three years before. Now they saw that the gamble, though visionary, hadn't been big enough. To give MCI what it wanted, they'd have to enlarge the plant. It would mean one of the biggest factory expansions in the history of the company.

Then came another dilemma. To make a profit at MCI's low price,

they'd have to make the plant more efficient. That would mean installing new equipment—the fourth generation of waveguide manufacturing. It represented the most advanced form of the outside process that
Bob Maurer had first begun to work on ten years before. The problem
was that this fourth generation was still being developed in the lab.
Normally, it would take months of testing before putting even one trial
machine on line. Now, Duke wanted to fill the plant immediately with
the new, unproven machines.

Most remember it as an argumentative time. Corning was known
for that, partly because of Duke's influence. He didn't want anyone to
be shy about his opinion. "People would say, 'You're wrong,'" he
remembers. "I'd say, 'I'm the boss.' They'd say, 'You're still wrong.'"

The debate went on for weeks. The pessimists said it was foolish to
go to the new outside-process machines. Wasn't the existing equipment—only eighteen months old—good enough? With an all-impor-
tant order to deliver, why launch a major plant expansion around
something that might not work?

The optimists, however, insisted that in so competitive a race, Corning would lose if it didn't gamble on the lower-cost new generation.

Finally, everyone sat down to make a final decision. The meeting
got heated pretty quickly. The doubters pointed toward the Japanese,
toward Bell, toward ITT. All were using the dependable inside process,
they said. The whole world couldn't be wrong.

That, however, only convinced Duke all the more to go with the
new way. Like Maurer, he hated staying with the pack. "I don't want
to be in a business where I'm just one of five guys doing the same
thing," he said. He again made the point about how it wouldn't be good
enough to tie. As competitive as waveguides were now, he said, the
business would be triply so in the future. This was like color TVs in the
sixties. If American companies had redesigned their products and factories then, while they were ahead, they'd have kept in front of the
Japanese. That's what was needed now—a factory leap. Most of the
researchers took Duke's side. A bit grudgingly, the others gave in.

"We could have been mortally wounded," Duke would say later.
"But I thought it was our only chance."

Bob Maurer, who tends to be unexcitable, does not recall losing
sleep over it. "You do the best you can," he says. "After that, to hell
with it."

Duke asked for factory expansion money. He got it, though not easily. The doubters were still calling for caution. "We had to scramble for
every nickel," Duke recalls. "Which was good. We had to make sure
we were right. If you're not forced to be disciplined, you can spend
money fruitlessly."

Now, he had to see through the actual work. With the catalytic converter, Duke had already gotten experience building a first-of-a-kind plant. For this team, he looked for people who were veterans of similar ordeals. "We brought in guys who'd been through the war before," he recalls.

He rented dozens of Wilmington condominiums and began to send his people there for months at a time, some for up to a year. A lot of those condos were filled with scientists. Since Duke didn't have the luxury of testing the prototype equipment in the lab, they'd have to do it on the factory floor. Dick Dulude, president of Corning's telecommunications group, was there when they gave the equipment a trial run.

"Some of it was pretty expensive," Dulude recalled later. "It got your attention when you finally threw the switch."

Soon waveguide fibers for the world's first national optical phone system started winding onto spools. Duke cranked up production to twenty-four hours a day to meet the order. It became clear they'd never have made the deadline had they stayed with the old inside process. The latest outside process was far faster. Corning was now making waveguides quicker than anyone else in the world. By shipment time, late 1983, they'd made enough to wrap twice around the equator. For the first time in sixteen years, they were making a profit.

By gosh, Duke remembers thinking, we're doing it.

ALL THE WHILE, Duke refused to give up on Japan. In 1982, he heard that NTT, the state phone company, was awarding contracts for waveguides. He flew to Japan and asked for specs so Corning could bid. NTT said he couldn't have them. By now, Duke had realized that if you're going to compete abroad, you have to be as serious about fighting trade barriers as making good product. Duke complained to the U.S. Special Trade Representative Office about the NTT turndown. In turn, the trade representative complained to MITI. It worked; MITI agreed to let Corning bid. Duke went back to NTT. Yes, the officials there told him, you're now allowed to bid. Duke asked for the specs. Sorry, NTT told him, we can't give you the specs. Duke asked why. Because, they explained, those belonged to the Japanese companies who'd worked with NTT in developing them.

"But if I don't have the specs," said Duke, "how can I bid?"

You're free to bid, the NTT officials told him. But you're not allowed to have the specs.

Duke came home empty-handed. It went like that year after year. "To me," says Dick Dulude, "it was a classic case of Japan, Inc., really stonewalling us while they developed their own fiber technology. I don't know if it was MITI or NTT. But from the outside, it sure looked organized."[8]

Even from the inside—in Japan—Duke had seen evidence of that.

He saw some stories about Corning's effort in the local newspapers. "If we let Corning come in here now," one company executive was quoted as saying, "it's so technically strong, we'll never be able to develop the Japanese industry on our own." Duke found out one other thing that disturbed him. Corning had been trying for years to get its waveguide patents approved in Japan. The process seemed endless. By now, most other countries had accepted the patents. Japan was still rejecting them. He vowed he would not give up.

THE MCI order caught the world off guard—AT&T, the Japanese, everyone. Duke knew they would all scramble to catch up. Corning had the football, and the other players were going to want to take it away. No one else, however, had a full-scale, single-mode factory. No one had the outside production process. No one else had Corning's quality, either. Its fibers were now longer than anything made by the rest of the world.

Soon, GTE Sprint and U.S. Telecom followed MCI, asking Corning for substantial orders—one hundred thousand kilometers each. Others lined up, as well, the numbers going from hundred-kilometer bites to tens of thousands. Overnight, Corning had moved from trying to create a market to trying to keep up with it. Suddenly, Duke saw demand ballooning to over a million kilometers a year, maybe more. At the time, plant capacity was three hundred thousand. Soon he was thinking about yet another factory leap. In late 1983, he asked for more expansion money. This time, it was the largest expenditure request in Corning history—$100 million. The goal was to boost plant capacity to 1.5 million kilometers. The money would also go to yet another generation of factory equipment. It didn't matter that the current machines were unmatched; Duke felt the time to improve is when you're ahead. Despite the proposal's size, this time, there wasn't much arguing.

In 1984, eighteen years after Maurer's first experiments, fourteen years after Keck wrote *Eureka* in his log book, waveguides had finally become a sizable world industry. And Corning Glass and its partners had the biggest piece of it.

But the company's fight was hardly over.

ASK DAVE DUKE today about the biggest headache of the waveguide story, and he'll give you a curious answer. Not the research battle, not the factory gamble, not even the fight to break into Japan. The biggest headache, he says, was the legal struggle—the struggle to keep competitors from stealing Corning's inventions. Many have tried.

It began in 1976. By then, all the big American communications companies were experimenting with fiber, trying to push samples onto the few customers who were buying. One of those customers was the U.S. government. It chose to buy from ITT.

But the ITT fiber, Corning found, was an exact duplicate of its own. Corning's waveguide people, led by Lee Wilson, debated a lawsuit, but hesitated.

"It was a hard decision for Lee," Duke recalls, "because there wasn't much of a market. A few hundred kilometers, a couple hundred thousand dollars a year." Many at Corning urged the company to forget about it; no reason to get into a major brawl over pennies. Better to spend the money perfecting the product. Corning's attorneys decided on a middle ground—try negotiating. Maybe ITT would come around.

But ITT took a hard line, insisting it wasn't violating patents. This was their own design, the ITT people said, their own manufacturing process.

The decision on what to do next was more philosophical than financial. There probably wasn't much money at stake here, but there was something more important—Corning's birthright. Over the years, Corning had prospered through the genius of its technology. It had harvested huge profits on patented products like Pyrex^R ovenware and photochromic eyeglass lenses and Corelle^R tableware. At the time, waveguides didn't seem as if they'd be as big, but if Corning was to prosper in the future, it had to defend its patents even in small cases.

In July 1976, Corning filed suit against both ITT and its customer, the U.S. government. With waveguide's small market, the lawyers figured it would be a small fight. It wasn't. ITT countersued, charging Corning with trying to build a monopoly. That was a common enough tactic; Corning wasn't surprised. What did surprise the Corning people was what happened next. Instead of negotiating, ITT fought relentlessly, first for months, then for over a year, eventually for five long years. For much of the time, the battle was at fever pitch, each side producing a thousand documents a week. It even went global. When ITT charged that Lucy's European joint agreements were a conspiracy to monopolize the world market, Corning's people had to fly overseas for depositions. Altogether, the company's top executives ended up spending 210 days being cross-examined by ITT's attorneys.

Finally, a trial was scheduled for August 1981. A month earlier, there came another surprise. ITT settled. It admitted it had infringed Corning's patents and agreed to pay big penalties. Soon afterward, the government settled, too, paying $650,000 for buying infringing fiber. It had been a tense, exhausting five years. The ordeal had left Corning drained. But at least it had won. The legal battle was over.

And then it happened again. This time, it was a Dutch-owned firm based in Massachusetts called Valtec, owned by Philips, the huge electronics conglomerate. Valtec, too, was now pumping out copies of Corning's fiber. No one was ready for another five years of a thousand documents a week, so Al Michaelsen, Corning's patent attorney, headed to Philips to talk out a solution. "I said, 'Here are the patents,'" Michaelsen recalls, "'here's your product. We say you're infringing, and it's as clear as the sun comes up in the morning.'"

He wanted to make sure this wouldn't turn into a standoff, so he gave Philips room.

"If you think you're not infringing," he recalls saying, "tell me why. If you can convince me, we'll go away. But let's talk, let's not go into a multimillion-dollar litigation."

But Philips wouldn't yield. Its lawyers fell back on the familiar defense. This was Philips's own design, not Corning's. Philips had no intention of stopping production. It left Corning facing a hard decision. Was the company ready for this again? Another legal war was the last thing anyone wanted to face. But they couldn't help coming back to the unavoidable question: What's the point of having patents if you don't defend them? They sued Philips. Philips countersued. It cost another difficult year, but, finally, Corning won again. Philips settled, agreeing to stop production.

And still the waveguide legal struggle wasn't over. While fighting the infringements, Michaelsen had to carry on a parallel fight to win patents around the world. The only way to do that is one country at a time. He found it's never easy.

In the United States, the procedure is straightforward. You file a patent application, and only one office decides whether you get it—the government examiner. Overseas, the rules are different. There, once the examiner is convinced, your application's published. Then, anyone can fight it. Each time someone files an opposition, it's like a lawsuit. Michaelsen was overwhelmed at the number of opposers he had to take on. In Japan, West Germany, England, Holland—over fifteen companies tried to knock Corning's patents out. West Germany was especially tough, Japan the toughest of all. The officials in Japan denied almost every one of Corning's patents. "Unless you've been through it," says Michaelsen, "it's hard to imagine the magnitude of the undertaking and the time and money that are consumed." It went on for years.

In the midst of it, yet another legal battle began at home. One of Corning's Canadian customers called to say he was seeing some new fiber up there that looked remarkably like Corning's. Duke's people arranged to get hold of a sample and did some tests. Though it wasn't identical, it was a close copy, violating a number of patents. This time, the fiber was being made in Japan. The company was Sumitomo Electric.

Again, some at Corning argued that they should just ignore it. Corning wasn't big enough to keep pouring millions down a legal rathole. This was the way the business world worked—competitors were always trying to skirt the edges of each other's patents. Better just to get on with the next generation of product than fight over the current one. "Our resources were stretched to the limit," Michaelsen recalls. "You only have so many troops." Some even suggested licensing Sumitomo. That way, they could at least get a royalty. But Duke pointed out the long picture. Few materials companies, he said, put as much into research as Corning: over $100 million a year. Out of all that, he said, the firm might get one major breakthrough a decade. The only way to continue a high level of research was to get the maximum possible profit from each of those breakthrough products. Waveguides were one.

But he knew that suing would be especially tricky in this case. It would involve going after a Corning customer—Canada Wire and Cable, which was wrapping the copycat Japanese fiber. It's never good business to sue a customer. Duke and his people seesawed back and forth. But finally, they chose to fight. It came back to the question of birthright.

"This was our invention," Michaelsen recalls. "We worked hard to create it. It wasn't right that someone was trying to take it away from us."

Still, the last thing Michaelsen wanted was a drawn-out lawsuit. Once again, he tried to negotiate. "There is nothing I know that consumes more resources than patent litigation," he says. Unless Sumitomo flat-out stonewalled them, he resolved to work it out.

Sumitomo stonewalled. Corning sued.

It was as draining as Michaelsen expected, but eventually, in early 1984, they won that one, too. The Japanese were forced to stop shipping into Canada. But that didn't end it. Duke isn't sure why the Japanese are so relentless—perhaps it's a question of survival, perhaps strategy—whatever, they soon came back at Corning again, this time on American soil. They began to export fiber, still made with Corning techniques, into Corning's backyard.

Instead of taking them on in a courtroom, Duke and Michaelsen chose a different strategy. They protested to the International Trade Commission. It can be even harder to win there than before a federal judge, but there was an advantage. If the ITC went with Corning, barring Sumitomo, the ruling could be used in the future against all copied fibers from any country. Corning would no longer have to fight importers case by case.

Both sides began to give evidence, and soon things began to look bad for Sumitomo. Then, suddenly, with testimony still unfolding, the

Japanese pulled a surprise move. In early 1984, they opened a wave-guide-research facility in North Carolina. At least that's what they insisted it was for—research. Corning saw it a bit differently.

"I said one thing," recalls Dick Dulude. "That's the biggest research center I ever saw."

He turned out to be right. Sumitomo suddenly announced it had converted the center to a factory. Then Sumitomo stopped importing, arguing that the ITC case was now moot. Now that the company's fiber was local, it wasn't a trade case anymore. The case went forward anyway. Corning won only half of it. The Japanese fiber, the ITC said, indeed violated Corning's patents. However, Sumitomo's sales were so small, it was deemed that Corning wasn't badly injured. At this point, though, the real problem was Sumitomo's North Carolina fiber. Corning tested it and found it violated the same patents. Once again, Michaelsen met with Sumitomo's people to negotiate. Once again, they refused to give. Once again, Corning sued, this time in U.S. District Court. After three grueling years, in October 1987, Corning won. Sumitomo was ordered to pay attorney's fees. It was also ordered to stop production. The day after the ruling, the North Carolina waveguide production closed down.

THROUGHOUT the legal battles, Corning's research team pushed on in the lab. It was the one part of the up-down struggle that stayed constant. No matter what else was going on with waveguides, the lab never stopped improving them. Eventually, the team developed a fiber of staggering length: one hundred kilometers—sixty-two miles. If you filled the deepest ocean trench on earth with that glass, you'd be able to see the bottom almost as if you were looking through air. Duke was confident some of the fiber would soon end up exactly there—along the bottom of the oceans, linking continents by light. His nightmare was that once in place, three or four miles deep, the fiber would go bad. He wanted to make sure the product was flawless, so he asked his manufacturing people to invest in still-better equipment. His particular concern was the drawing process—sixty-mile pieces of fiber had to be pulled out at a tolerance no more than a micron, a hundredth the width of a human hair. Duke asked if the drawing towers could be made better. His people told him Corning already had the best in the industry. Make them better anyway, said Duke. It ended up costing millions more.

"It used to drive me nuts," recalls Dick Dulude. "The rest of the world was building simple towers of stainless steel, and we had these massive, stable ones."

They began to go through new factory generations at almost unprecedented speed. Even the most aggressive companies revamp their machinery no more than every four or five years. As of late 1987, Corning was revamping an average of once every eighteen months—five times in eight years.

"And six is standing here ready to go," Dulude said in mid-1988. "And we have some concepts worked up for seven."

Corning moved to push the technology on other fronts, as well. One weekend, after a fairly dull conference in Washington, Don Keck and Dave Duke went out to a seafood restaurant together. Of course, all they talked was fiber. Keck remembers Duke asking him if he had any ideas about what Corning should do next. As a matter of fact, said Keck, he had.

Go ahead, said Duke.

The industry needs more than fiber alone, said Keck, it needs the stuff that makes fiber work: better lasers, repeaters, connectors. He mentioned things that were only theories—like splitters that would cut microscopic beams of light, filled with information, in two directions. Keck felt other companies weren't pushing that hard enough, and thought Corning could do better. He didn't have to talk Duke into it. Soon Corning poured millions into the idea—exploring a range of fiber components. In time, they'd even developed Keck's light-splitter.

Ask Keck, now head of optics and physics research for Corning, if it isn't time to relax for a while after eighteen years of breakthroughs, and he'll give you a ready answer. No company is easier to beat, he says, than a contented one. Each time something comes out of your lab, he says, your first goal should be to obsolete it. "If you don't," he says, "someone will obsolete it for you."

They've now got the decibel level of Corning waveguides down from several thousand to less than .3, and Keck is working on 160-kilometer fiber—100 miles long. Much of that drive springs from his scientist's soul. He likes inventing things. But he'll smile and tell you that it also comes from another part of him as well, the part that rubbed off from Dave Duke, the part that enjoys beating the competition.

THE PRICE of Corning's first fiber was several dollars a meter. It's now below twelve cents. The market has gone from a few thousand dollars a year to close to $1 billion. Despite being blocked by Japan and limited by AT&T, Corning and its partners have by far the biggest part of the market. Globally, Corning now has a presence few American businesses can match. In most countries, you'll find Japanese cars everywhere, American cars nowhere. But look closely at the world's phone systems, and it's the opposite. Corning's technology is everywhere, Japan's mostly limited to its own soil.

Soon the fiber market is expected to expand again. The biggest market is still untapped. Eighty percent of all telephone wire doesn't run from pole to pole, but from pole to home. Corning sees those links eventually going to waveguides. It would increase a household's capacity for information thousands of times, making it possible to do such things as shop by TV, select movies for house-by-house feeds, and install video phones. For Corning, it would increase the potential market by billions of dollars a year. The company's lab is already gearing up for it, developing new, ultraflexible fiber that can be looped over ducts, around corners, through walls.

DUKE will tell you he's still paranoid about the Japanese—that's his word. "They're tough," he explains. "The only way you win is to be just as tough."

Part of that, he says, involves lobbying Washington for help. He points to what he calls a typical unfair trade practice: For a long time, Japan's state phone company bought fiber from local companies at three times international prices, allowing them high profits for investment and for selling the same fiber around the world below market prices. You have to fight that kind of thing, says Duke.

But he also believes that American business can't fall back on trade accusations as an excuse. Corning's main push in Japan, he says, is to win through direct competition. For example, he says, Corning has begun to develop products tailored to local needs, and recently opened a Japan-based sales and service organization to offer on-the-spot service. Meanwhile, Corning's people continue to go there four or five times a year to keep pitching. In 1988, it finally paid off. For the first time, a small length of Corning fiber was placed in a Japanese phone cable. It was a modest victory, but any foot in that door, says Duke, is essential. Japan, he points out, is the world's second-biggest market. If an American business is going to make it globally, it has to sell there, no matter what the frustrations. He's convinced there's got to be a way, just as Corning found a way in Europe.

"You have to sell the way the customer wants to buy," says Duke. "If he wants to buy French products, you have to make yourself look pretty darn French."

Duke knows his global fight will only get tougher. First, in the early 1990's, Corning's original patents will run out. Then there's the low-wage threat. The Koreans recently announced plans to make fiber.

Duke will tell you Corning already has a strategy of staying ahead of them in place: the Wilmington plant. It's the kind that low-wage countries can't equal—automated enough to outproduce them, and sophisticated enough to demand highly skilled workers. As for the patent problem, Corning has a strategy for that, too: keeping R&D an absolute priority.

Ask Duke what he's proudest of, and he won't point, as Edison might have, to the invention itself. That's essential, but America's biggest challenge, he feels, is to learn how to parlay its inventions into leading products. That's his greatest pride. Ask him if there's a secret to getting there, and he'll point to something unlikely, attitude.

"We did it by wanting to be the best," he says. "We had a passion. We were working day and night. But we were winning. And that's contagious."

DUKE finished telling the fiber story. As we sat together in his office, I told him it was exactly the kind of aggressiveness Corning would need if the other products we were looking at for the 1990's were going to be winners, too. But there was a difference, I said. Corning would now be facing a more competitive environment than ever—tougher than what it faced in waveguides.

He asked what I meant.

In future advanced-glass products, I said, Corning will probably never again have the kind of five-year lead it enjoyed when it first invented fiber. At best, it'll be more like five months. "Look at your competitors in Japan and Europe," I said. "They're much closer to you on these new products than the Sumitomos were back in 1970."

The customers would be more aggressive, too, I said. Most will be far readier to adapt new technologies than the phone companies were with fiber. Corning would still have to do what Lucy did—go out and proselytize—but everyone else will be proselytizing, as well. More important, I said, your competition will be tailoring products even before they finish inventing them. It's becoming a common strategy to work with customers while you're still in the R&D lab. Look at waveguides, I said. You spent years inventing fiber before you started to cable it. That won't work anymore. In the future, if you wait that long to make something market-ready, you'll wake up to find your rivals already there. The only way to beat them will be to get customers advising you in the lab while you're still experimenting.

Then we talked about manufacturing. That, too, I said, was going to speed up. You invented waveguides in 1970, and didn't build your first full-scale pilot plant until 1976. Admittedly, that was in advance of the market, and unique for its time in America, but from now on, I said, it'll be dangerous to wait that long. Japan and other countries are moving too fast. To win, you have to start test manufacturing when you're still in the lab. And it'll be necessary, I added, to keep to your waveguide strategy of avoiding the herd. It can take years to win patents, but if you invest early in unique factory processes and constantly upgrade them, you can keep an edge right from the start.

Finally, we talked about government support. Foreign companies were getting far more of it than companies here at home. I told Duke he'd have to look closely at that, sizing up just how well armed his competitors were before taking them on. One new technology under way at Corning is advanced ceramics. Unfortunately, I said, Japan has a huge government-funded program on that. There was no way Corning could match the Japanese across the board with its own resources, and so far, our government was funding mainly defense-related ceramic applications. That meant Corning would have to pass on some promising potential commercial applications. It was too bad, I said. If our own government gave companies as much support, they wouldn't have to limit themselves like that.

I SAID GOOD-BYE to Duke and headed back to the airport. On the way, I got to thinking about how the waveguide story would be viewed by many big U.S. corporations. Of course, they'd applaud its success, but I think most would have never allowed their own people to have done what Corning's did. Building a factory before there's a ready market is rarely done in button-down corporate America. Neither is taking years of losses or pushing for factory redesigns every eighteen months. But that's just the kind of behavior—risky, entrepreneurial behavior— that high-technology corporations will have to do more of to compete.

The waveguide story reminds me of a quote attributed to Fred Bucey of Texas Instruments. "No great breakthroughs," he said, "have ever been achieved by reasonable men." It's almost the definition of an entrepreneur—someone willing to take unreasonable risks. But most small entrepreneurs don't have the resources to invest in many of the big-technology industries of the future, only global corporations do. If ours are to win, their managers have to start acting more as Corning's acted—like entrepreneurs who just happen to be part of a company that sells $2 billion a year.

Today, many of America's new phone lines would probably be made of Japanese fiber had Corning not let managers like Maurer, Lucy, and Duke follow their instincts. There are men and women like them in all our major corporations. We have to start letting them take more chances, accepting frequent failures as the price of occasional success. But if companies are to risk on the same scale as our world competitors are now doing, they'll need help.

It took Corning almost seventeen years to move waveguides from lab to profits. Companies throughout the Far East and Europe often have government help to get through that difficult phase. If America were to start funneling as much government R&D money into commercial projects as we do into military ones and as our competitors do, I'm convinced waveguide stories would be common.

In the next decade, there won't be time for our companies to catch up with new technologies once the market takes off. Most will find themselves in the same situation as Dave Duke was when he went to MCI. That day, either Corning was ready or it wasn't. If Duke had been forced to say he needed another year or two, MCI and other phone companies would have had no choice but to call Tokyo.

Corning, however, was ready, all because a few visionaries were allowed to take unreasonable risks. That's why nations everywhere are now talking by light over American fiber.

Postscript

In July 1988, I took part in a Washington conference on foreign competition, held in the Rayburn Building on Capitol Hill. Its focus was the electronics industry, and it included the CEO of Tandy, the head of Atari, the chairman of the American Electronics Association, and the American inventor of the VCR, who'd seen his idea turn into a huge Japanese industry.

I'd been on similar panels before, and had always seen the participants dismiss the specter of foreign competition. This time, it was different. Everyone agreed that overseas companies were threatening to swamp the American electronics industry, especially in semiconductors and televisions.

Eight years earlier, dozens of U.S. firms were making 85 percent of the world's memory chips, and semiconductor executives said there was no way Japan, or anyone else, could challenge our lead. By 1988, however, there were only a handful of American memory-chip companies left. Our global market share had shrunk to 15 percent. Japan's share, meanwhile, had soared past 75.

Television was even worse. America, once the world leader in electronic appliances, was barely in the running anymore. We made almost no VCRs, video cameras, or compact-disc players. There were no longer any strong American-owned television makers: RCA had been bought by the French; Magnavox and Sylvania by the Dutch. And soon, said the conference panelists, a lucrative new technology would be emerging: high-definition TV, a hundred times clearer than current models. They pointed out that these new TVs would be integral to many of our key industries, from machine tools to computers. Most important, high-definition TV promised to be the heart of a new kind of product that would be part of almost every home in the modern world: a communications and entertainment center that would allow people to order products, send electronic mail, select movies, shop for groceries, make bank deposits, and maybe even vote. Within a decade or two, said the panelists, it would be one of the single biggest products on earth, worth tens of billions a year in sales. And now they asked a question: Would America have a piece of that wealth? In this important new technology, would we be there?

They saw only one way that it could be possible.

"No matter how hard we try on our own," one executive said, "we can't compete by ourselves." What the electronics industry needed, he said, was a Washington-backed strategy to combine the strengths of America's companies, universities, and government labs. The competition had been doing that for years, he said; if the United States didn't do the same, we'd lose more than the electronics race, we'd lose a piece of our living standard.

The foreign electronics challenge worried me deeply, but I left that conference more hopeful than I'd been in years.

IN THE PAST, conferences like that usually ended with the participants resisting any mention of government involvement. I remember being on a semiconductor panel in 1979, a time when the United States still dominated the world memory-chip market. When it was my turn to speak, I pointed out that MITI had plans to push harder into electronics than most Americans realized. It had organized a powerful, four-part strategy: home-market protection, government investment help, pooled national research, and assistance in export. The Japanese were building huge electronics conglomerates, better able to invest than our own small entrepreneurs. If we didn't match that kind of effort, I said, Japan could catch us in five years. But the others on the panel—executives and economists—felt I was being alarmist. The Japanese, they pointed out, were good copiers, good manufacturers, but they weren't good at new-product development, especially in advanced technologies.

Over the next few years, I attended a score of similar meetings, covering industries from machine tools to aerospace, and the outlook was always the same. Government should fight dumping by foreign companies, but it shouldn't do what MITI was doing. American industry didn't need government strategies; it didn't need research consortia. Companies would do fine on their own.

Overseas, the attitude was different. By the early 1980's, the Japanese were building competitive strategies in a dozen new technologies—computers, advanced ceramics, biotechnology; the list got longer each year. Europe's companies, with the help of government, were doing the same. Even low-wage nations, like South Korea and Singapore, were doing more than we were in offering incentives in areas like R&D, training, and plant investment. It seemed that almost everyone in the industrial world but America was taking a new approach to doing business.

By the mid-1980s, when Japan and Europe were becoming more competitive through government-backed R&D and worker training, our only competitive policy was a lowered dollar. To some extent, it worked. Our goods became cheaper, easier to sell abroad. But today, it has still failed to turn around our massive trade deficit. Price alone doesn't always make for export success. In many industries, like machine tools, engineering and marketing are more important. In other industries, like microwave ovens, even a drastically lowered dollar won't bridge the price gap with low-wage rivals. To compete, high-wage countries obviously need more complex strategies. Some have mastered those strategies. Despite a soaring yen and a high mark, the Japanese and Germans continue to sell America billions more in goods than we sell them.

Meanwhile, our cheap-dollar policy has had a disturbing side effect: It's made our assets cheap, a temptation for foreign takeovers. Today, when you buy Carnation milk, Q-tips, a Brooks Brothers suit, or a set of General Tires, the profits flow overseas. Even the corporate royalties from the voices of Bruce Springsteen and Michael Jackson now go to Japan's Sony, which bought CBS Records. True, foreign buyouts bring new investment into America, often creating better productivity the first few years, but in the long run, most foreign owners tend to move high-paying and high-skill jobs closer to their national base. Research and development goes too, as does the production of key components. And if jobs have to be cut in a recession, owners are more likely to cut overseas. Any worker will tell you that the boss calls the shots according to what's best for the owners. If a company is French, decisions will be made in the interests of France. Allowing our economy to become absentee-owned won't make us more competitive. It will, however, make us more dependent on the whims of foreign nations.

If a low dollar and foreign investment won't solve our problems, what will? The answer, I think, is to look closely at world business success stories—like those in this book. Most share the same four elements: technological leadership, a skilled work force, strong exports, and a solid local production base able to take a long-term view.

OVER THE next decades, a few dozen basic technologies will be essential to the economic growth of nations. We can't predict which will be the biggest, or emerge the fastest, but if we're going to protect our living standard, we have to be strong in all of them—from biotechnology to superconductivity. The Japanese and European governments are investing in all these areas. Our government isn't.

Spend time in Japan and you'll see government efforts similar to Paul Maycock's photovoltaics program in dozens of future technologies. It's the same in Europe. Everywhere but here, governments are supporting commercial R&D. They're even going beyond the lab, doing all they can to help companies develop new products. In America, if you need money to invest in an unproven product, you have to raise it on your own. In nations like Japan, France, West Germany, and Sweden, government itself gives new-product grants or loans. It also encourages companies to pool their efforts through research consortia.

It wouldn't cost a lot for America to increase its own investment in new technologies. We could, for example, get much of the necessary R&D money simply by shifting some of our defense-research budget to commercial projects. I've spoken with many military people who'd support that. They're afraid that if we don't revive our besieged industries, especially electronics and industrial machinery, we may soon have to go to Japan or Germany to produce our more sophisticated weapons.

AS THE world's technology becomes more sophisticated, workers have to be more sophisticated, too. Instead of tightening the same bolt every ninety seconds, they'll be running computerized equipment. Even Third World nations like Singapore are preparing for that, investing as much in factory employees as factories. In America, however, most of our training programs focus on management alone. That's valuable, but it's not enough. We have to see what nations overseas have seen for years: that the industrial future will depend on the skills of hourly employees.

In West Germany, companies are able to bolster those skills through a national apprentice program, something that could prove a good model for the United States. We'd have to tailor it to our more informal culture, but a few years as a company apprentice would help many young Americans start their careers with directly relevant skills.

As for veteran employees, Singapore is leaping forward with one of the most advanced training networks in the world. That, too, could be a model for us. Most American industries, I think, would welcome working with state governments to set up special training institutes. Unlike Singapore, we already have a powerful base: a strong system of community colleges and technical institutes that could help with customized classes. Finally, we could give companies incentives to set up both in-house training and adult-literacy programs. Every dollar invested in worker skills almost always pays back in productivity.

BUT AN R&D and training push won't be enough if U.S. companies don't sell globally. Because of our huge home market, few bother trying. The result is that many American manufacturers have been surprised by rivals who build strength abroad, then attack the United States with first-rate products. It's essential to help our own companies fight back on foreign turf.

One problem is protectionism by foreign governments. As a consultant, I've seen many superior U.S. products—like Corning's waveguides—hindered by countries using quotas, unfair approval processes, and a dozen more subtle roadblocks. If we countered with blanket protectionism, it could throw the world into depression. But there are still ways to fight back. Washington could prepare lists in advance of foreign products to retaliate against. That way, we could hit back surgically if a trading partner tries to put up walls. If we do it quickly and consistently, foreign governments would eventually stop putting up trade walls in the first place.

We also need to match the export-financing help that foreign governments offer their companies. France helped Aerospatiale compete with Bell in helicopters by offering low-cost loans to world customers. While working to eliminate such subsidies, our government should nevertheless guarantee it will match them when they occur. No U.S. company should be at a disadvantage because of export help for a competitor.

FINALLY, there is a need—a crucial need—for a strong, American-owned production base. Most Japanese and European leaders are determined to have robust local firms in all major industries. They work hard to keep from losing them. America doesn't. Soon it's likely there will be no American-owned company in consumer electronics—a $100 billion world market. We're losing our position in machinery, too. One reason foreign firms have boomed in both those fields is that quick profit wasn't their first priority; production was. If you look for a payback first, and quality manufacturing second, your payback may never come. But make quality manufacturing your priority, and a long-term payback is far likelier. Every chapter in this book is about a world success story; none of the companies could have achieved it if they hadn't been willing to wait three years or more to break through.

"American companies can regroup," said Ernst Ehmann of Traub. "But it can't be done in a year. It will take a long-term strategy. If the U.S. companies have to continue to show a profit increase every three months, then it's going to be very difficult."

One reason German companies are freer to invest in long-term plans is the nation's banking system. Banks there aren't just lenders, they often own equity, too, giving them a stake in seeing companies grow, long term.

In Japan, large manufacturing companies tend to stay focused on production and marketing even in tough times. During the mid-1980's, Japanese electronics companies chose to keep semiconductor prices low despite billions of losses so they could keep building world market share. Their smaller, stock-market-dependent U.S. rivals couldn't afford the stakes, so the Japanese came out the winners, and are now making good profits.

The threat of hostile takeovers is another source of pressure on U.S. managers, forcing them to emphasize high stock prices over high investment. Companies that invest aggressively in five-year growth plans are becoming takeover targets because their profit temporarily goes down. Our system, therefore, is becoming one that discourages long-horizon investing. Sometimes, hostile takeovers are healthy, a means of ousting bad management. But too often raiders are merely looking for quick profit. They buy into a company overnight, then offer top dollar to other stockholders, trying to get majority control. That draws in arbitrageurs who buy stock and then sit on it, looking for quick profit as raider and company try to outbid each other. Whoever wins, the company usually ends up so saddled with debt it's unable to invest in new growth, and often has to sell off pieces of itself to survive. Meanwhile, America's competitiveness disappears into the pockets of short-term speculators.

One way to limit the problem is with a sliding scale on capital-gains taxes. Those who hold stock for over five years would pay low capital gains while overnight speculators would pay high. That would encourage a longer view. Another idea is to give voting rights to long-term stockholders only. That way, raiders and arbitrageurs wouldn't be able to buy into a company one day, then force it to sell the next. It would leave our corporations freer to emphasize production over quick profit.

But there's no victory in stressing production if it ends up overseas, which is where many strong U.S. companies are building plants. It's inevitable, and healthy, for certain firms to go abroad, but in too many cases, it's because foreign governments offer better incentives than we do. We can easily match those incentives. But it's not as simple as helping with factory investment alone. To keep American firms on home soil, government has to support all the pillars of competitiveness: R&D, training, export assistance.

I STILL HEAR the argument that it's not government's place to get so involved in business. But in small ways, it has already begun to happen. Because of foreign competition, the United States has formed a joint government-business R&D project in semiconductors. Some states have been particularly aggressive, starting product-development funds and research consortia, and have even passed laws to limit hostile take-overs. But to compete in the big technologies of the next decades, we need help on a scale only Washington can provide.

We have no MITI of our own to guide that help, but I'm not sure we need one. It could be just as effective to create a coordinating group like the National Security Council to take a strategic national industrial view. Its mission would be to encourage an organized industry response when it sees America falling behind in crucial technologies or skill areas.

Even our competitors, I think, would welcome a more coherent U.S. industrial strategy. Overseas businessmen have often told me they don't want a rapid U.S. economic decline and the unstable world it would bring. For years, they've wondered whether America would find the will to move forward. On and off, I've wondered the same thing.

But recently, I've begun to see signs of hope. I've attended a dozen meetings this past year where people ranging from Defense officials to Congressmen have called for more government-business partnerships to meet the foreign threat. The July electronics conference in Washington was a symbol of it. Industry leaders who'd once dismissed industrial strategy as unnecessary were now insisting it was America's best chance.

When it was my turn to speak at that conference, I tried to play the skeptic. The public, I said, is wary of government involvement. It's not our ideological tradition.

It's no longer a question of ideology, the electronic executives said. It's a question of whether America will be a leading economic player in the next century. Again, they pointed to a product that promises to be one of industry's biggest by the year 2000: home entertainment and communications centers, to be built around high-definition TVs. And they asked: Are we as a nation going to be part of it? Are we going to be there? Everyone agreed it will be worth tens of billions of dollars a year. Everyone agreed that if Washington doesn't help industry invest in it, all that wealth will go to our rivals.

We're not quite as far behind in other industries, but more than ever, our foreign competitors are gaining. They're gaining in aerospace and superconductors, in cars and factory automation, in computers and advanced materials. They're gaining in those and a dozen other technologies that will be the wellspring of the next century's prosperity. To compete in each, we have to compete in all, since many depend on each other. But we can't do it without the economic strategies that are now common almost everywhere in the industrial world but the United States.

There was a question I kept hearing at that July conference that now keeps coming back to me. It's a question about America's share in the technologies of the future, the industries of the future, the wealth of the future.

Are we going to be there?

Notes

Introduction

1. The process of making steel has many steps. Coals are blended and purified to make coke, which is then combined with iron ore in a blast furnace to make a purer form of iron called pig iron. This is then combined with steel scrap and other materials in a steelmaking furnace. The molten steel that emerges then goes through various stages of semifinishing in rolling mills that make round or rectangular shapes called slabs, billets, or blooms. Finally, these shapes are rolled and drawn a varying number of times to produce wire, sheets, bars, rods, pipe, and other finished steel products. Increasingly, the semifinishing stage is eliminated for many products, as molten steel is continuously cast and flows directly into semifinished billets or slabs with no intermediate casting as an ingot.

By the mid-1970's, Japanese mills had already built a significant productivity advantage over their U.S. counterparts in the following ways:

- Every doubling in size of a blast furnace can result roughly in a 30 percent reduction in the cost of pig-iron production. In 1977, Japan had twenty-five blast furnaces capable of producing over 2 million tons of iron annually; the United States had none. In fact, most U.S. furnaces were under 1 million tons in capacity.
- Basic Oxygen Furnaces (BOF) are more efficient than open hearths; and continuous-slab or billet casting is more efficient than the production of ingots

and the subsequent rolling of the ingot on slab, bloom, or billet mills. Japanese companies adopted both basic oxygen furnaces and continuous-casting technology faster than did their U.S. counterparts. By the mid-1970's, 78 percent of Japanese steel was produced on BOF furnaces compared to 58 percent of U.S. steel; and 51 percent of Japanese steel was continuously cast, compared to 15 percent of U.S. steel. In addition, the Japanese BOF furnaces were on average 30 percent larger than those in the United States. They also operated more efficiently due to more automated-material batch feed, better process control, which meant a lower amount of time and energy per batch, fewer supervisory personnel per ton of steel produced, and less maintenance due to shorter periods of downtime. The Japanese furnaces went down as often as U.S. ones, but required less time to repair.

· Japanese rolling mills (hot-strip, cold-rolling, plate, bar, rod, etc.) ran at faster speeds and had higher uptimes than those of U.S. producers. They also had lower scrap rates due to better process-control efficiencies. The major reason was that they were of newer design. The following table shows relative average ages of selected Japanese and U.S. steel rolling mills in 1978.

	U.S. % OLDER THAN		JAPAN % OLDER THAN	
	25 YEARS	20 YEARS	25 YEARS	20 YEARS
Plate Mills	45	54	5	20
Hot Strip Mills	16	32	—	10
Cold Strip Mills	29	54	—	15
Wire Rod Mills	17	18	—	5

· The most significant productivity difference came in overheads and indirect labor areas, such as material handling, rework, internal transport costs, maintenance, and setup. As the following chart shows, Japanese plants were bigger:

Capacities of Integrated Japanese and U.S. Steel Mills

MILLIONS OF METRIC TONS	U.S. PERCENT OF PRODUCTS	JAPANESE PERCENT OF PRODUCTS
Over 8	0	70
Over 5.5	20	81
Over 4.5	31	85

Japanese plants were also newer on average. Japan started eleven new plants after World War II compared to only one new plant in the United States. Because of their scale and modernity, Japanese plants were able to amortize overhead more fully and realize the advantages of better layout. Most U.S. plants expanded through incremental investments, resulting in a more cumbersome product flow than Japanese plants. At J&L facilities, semifinished product was shipped for miles around a mill following a zigzag path from one station to another. In Japan, the flows tended to be in line. Aside from the extra material handling labor, at J&L, large "scarfing" areas existed to take rust that accumulated in storage off of the semifinished steel.

My comparisons on this trip were between J&L facilities in Aliquippa, PA, and Cleveland, Ohio, and facilities of Nippon Steel in Kimitsu and Oita and NKK in Fukayama.

2. The two major raw materials used in steelmaking are iron ore and coal. In 1974, it cost J&L $19.85 per ton of ingot steel for iron ore at its Cleveland plant, and $17.82 for coke. The iron ore came mainly from mines in northern Michigan and Minnesota, and the coal mainly from mines in West Virginia and Pennsylvania. Like most major U.S. steel companies, J&L owned some of its own mines.

Overall, at the time, the cost of mining iron ore in Australia with high iron purity and low overburden ratios (proportion of rock dug up to iron ore) was about 40 percent of that in Minnesota. In 1974, it cost $3.50 per ton to transport iron ore from Minnesota across the Great Lakes to Cleveland, and $6.50 per ton if it needed to be sent from a lakes point by rail to Pittsburgh. Using supertankers, the Japanese steelmakers were able to send iron ore an average of 5,800 miles from Australia or Brazil to Japan for $3.80 per ton in 1974. In fact, the Australian iron ore could be landed at U.S. ports more cheaply than ore from Michigan and Minnesota. The Japanese mills were all located at deepwater ports to receive the huge supertankers. U.S. mills, with a few exceptions—Sparrows Point and Burns Harbor—did not have deepwater ports, and therefore could not easily secure the cheaper ore.

Coal was a traditional strength of the U.S. steel industry. The United States was the traditional source of low-volatile coal, the best material for coke. As late as 1970, Japanese steelmakers imported 42 percent of all the coal they used from the United States, which tacked on a fifteen-dollar-plus penalty per ton of coal for shipping and profit versus what U.S. steelmakers paid.

But by the time I did the study for J&L, and to a much greater extent by the late 1970's, Japanese companies had found ways to reduce their dependence on high-cost U.S. coal.

New sources of coal in large open-pit mines were developed in Australia and western Canada during the late 1960's and 1970's. Their cost of production was one-third that of U.S. underground Appalachian mines. In particular, U.S. low-volatile mines were becoming more expensive to operate. Most U.S. low-volatile mines were in four counties in West Virginia—McDowell, Wyoming, Raleigh, and Miner; Buchanan County in Virginia and Cambria and Somerset Counties in Pennsylvania. I visited a number of mines in these counties.

In the United States, about 87 percent of low-volatile coal was produced in underground mines. Mining under these conditions has to be one of the most difficult and dangerous jobs in the world. You descend through a hole in the ground, then board a flatcar where you ride in a prone position for thirty minutes to an area deep in the mountain where the only lights are on your hard hat. The height from ground to ceiling is four to five feet, and heavy machinery digs out the cave wall as you move ahead. Progress is slow. This compares to open-pit mining, in the open air, which is more like a large construction project.

In an underground mine, the height of a seam of coal plays a key role in the cost of extrusion—the thinner the seam, the longer the production time.

One ton of coal may represent a block seventy-two inches high and seventy-two inches wide. An operator can move eighteen feet or three tons of coal in each pass in such a seam. If the seam is only thirty-six inches high, he can only move two tons of coal per pass. In the early 1960's, only 45 percent of the small mines in these counties were under fifty inches. By 1975, 91 percent of the small mines were operating at under fifty inches.

The problem faced by Japanese steel producers was that the lower-cost Australian and Canadian coal was also lower quality. To reduce their dependence on high-cost, high-quality U.S. coal, they developed new methods of coal blending. They discovered that the value of different types of coal depends on their strength and fluidity. The Japanese developed methods to use to greater advantage the lower-grade coals by blending them precisely to achieve an acceptable strength and fluidity mix. (The methods of blending coal are best described in the Matsuska and Miyazu charting methods.) This allowed them by 1973 to reduce their U.S. dependence down to 25 percent and to go down below 20 percent by 1977.

The following chart shows the results of this work:

Value Mix of Coals Blended Index of Price

	U.S. MILLS*	JAPANESE MILLS**
1965	100	88
1970	100	82
1975	100	71
1978	100	69

*U.S. Steel and J&L Steel plants mix.
**Yawata, Oita (1978 only), Amagasaki, Wakayama, Muroran, Kimitsu mix.

In addition, improvements in Japanese blast-furnace technology enabled the Japanese to use less coke per ton of pig iron produced, as the following chart indicates.

Coke per Ton of Pig Iron Produced (kg)*

	U.S.	JAPAN
1965	610	807
1970	636	478
1975	611	443
1978	597	429

*Same plants as previous chart.

Finally, Japanese companies devised a materials advantage from their use of better methods to gather not just bulk steel scrap from their processes for reuse, but also to recover iron and steel "fines," which are given off by most steel processes. The recycling of these fines improved overall raw-material yields, and also made pollution control more effective.

All things considered, Japanese iron-ore and coal costs were slightly lower than those at U.S. mills when I did my initial studies.

3. The massive capital investments that allowed Japan to overtake the United States in steelmaking efficiency occurred between 1966 and 1972, when the Japanese steel industry increased its assets by over 23 percent a year, compared to only 4 percent a year for U.S. companies. During this period, the Japanese companies replaced outmoded equipment such as open-hearth furnaces that had been installed in the 1950's and 1960's. This growth occurred despite the fact that U.S. companies had a higher return on assets during the period. The Japanese companies incurred a marginal debt-to-equity ratio of about eleven to one during those years, allowing a satisfactory return on equity and guaranteeing the continued improvement of their competitive productivity.

Financing of Steel Investment

	JAPANESE BIG 5* (1968–1972)	U.S.** BIG 8 (1966–1973)
Asset Growth Per Year	23.6%	4.2%
Average Return on Assets	1.8%	3.8%
Average Return on Equity	20.0%	6.5%
Marginal Debt-to-Equity Ratio	11.6:1	1.7:1
Overall Debt-to-Equity Ratio 1972	6.3:1	6.82:1
Cash Sources of Financing:		
Debt	91	63
Retained Earnings	1	37
New Equity	8	0

*Nippon Steel, NKK, Sumitomo, Kawasaki, Kobe
**U.S. Steel, Bethlehem, National, Republic, Inland, J&L, Youngstown, Wheeling, Pittsburgh

While it is correct to say that Japanese companies outspent their American counterparts during the 1960's and 1970's, this is not the primary reason that they overtook the U.S. industry in productivity. In fact, even though the Japanese did spend more, U.S. industry was spending at a sizable rate as well. Over the twenty-nine years between 1950 and 1979, U.S. companies invested over $60 billion (in 1978 dollars).

Part of the U.S. industry's problem was poor investment choices. It tended to invest to overcome specific production bottlenecks in old facilities, and thereby to increase capacity. Because of relatively low capital-cost outlays per additional ton of steel, these "round out" investments usually showed better discounted-cash-flow (DCF) rates of return, and were less risky than totally new (Greenfield) plants.

But this type of investment typically created a number of problems. If the new facility—say a hot-strip mill—did not fit at the site of the old hot-strip mill, it was placed somewhere else at the plant, complicating product flows. Often these round-out investments met their direct labor-reduction targets, but created significant extra costs for material handling, inventory, scrap rework, maintenance, and setup. In addition, because the new line was often too large for the older lines that fed it or used its output, it was underutilized, which inevitably gave rise to calls for additional round-out investments to overcome the newly formed bottlenecks.

Thus, U.S. steel companies made small, incremental investments to obtain "cheap" capacity rather than making the larger, more aggressive, and riskier investments that could have led to superior productivity overall. The U.S. companies sought to keep the return on investment—ROI—up by keeping the "I" low, but this strategy left whole plants uncompetitive. In the long run, this philosophy was self-defeating.

4.

Integrated Steel Mills
Built Since 1950

U.S. PLANT		JAPAN PLANT	
Plant	Capacity (MM Metric Tons)	Plant	Processed Capacity (MM Metric Tons)
Bethlehem Burns Harbor	6	Nippon Steel:	
		Kimitsu	14
		Yawata	12
		Sakai	4
		Nagoya	7
		Oita	12
		NKK:Fukayama	16
		Kawasaki:	
		Chiba	7
		Mizushima	10
		Sumitomo:	
		Wakayama	10
		Kashima	15
		Kobe: Kogogawa	10
	6		117

5.

Major Third World Steel Mills
Being Built or Expanded
in Mid-1970's

Korea	Pohang
Venezuela	Acero
Mexico	Hylsa, Ahmsa, Sicartsa
Brazil	Tubarao, Itaqui

6. I projected demand of 850 million tons for 1980, with supply exceeding 1 billion tons. Most industry experts were projecting a 1-billion-ton demand by that year. In fact, demand was below 800 million tons, and capacity did exceed 1 billion tons.

7. See, for example, "Projection 85," a comprehensive if inaccurate forecast prepared by the International Iron and Steel Institute in 1973, or numerous articles by Father William Hogan of Fordham University such as "Steel Capacity Warning," *Metal Bulletin Monthly*, June 1973. It was Father Hogan's work that served as the basis for most industry estimates.

8. Throughout this unpleasant history of America's steel decline, industry officials and experts have consistently seen silver-lined clouds. In July 1968, the president of Republic Steel said in *Business Week*, "The most frequently heard suggestion for solving the steel import problem is that the domestic industry

should regain its former commanding lead in steel technology. This suggestion stems in part from the mistaken belief that the industry has been too slow to adopt new technological developments. The fact is that American steel technology is superior to any other country."

In the December 18, 1971, *Business Week,* the president of Bethlehem Steel said that "the long range threat of foreign steel competition seems to be diminishing."

In 1973, when the boom in steel demand caused the Japanese to prudently withdraw and raise prices, the president of the American Iron and Steel Institute predicted in an interview I had with him that American buyers would not so easily buy Japanese steel again.

In a 1975 *Wall Street Journal* article, the president of Jones & Laughlin Steel Company, despite the warnings in our report, said, "The steel import situation has changed dramatically and perhaps permanently during the past two years. . . . In this period, both European and Japanese competitors have experienced sharply increasing costs for labor, raw materials and energy, which have in conjunction with the double devaluation of the dollar raised the cost per ton of foreign steel delivered to the U.S. to about the same levels as American steel. . . . The era of cheap foreign steel has gone the way of cheap foreign oil, never to return."

Current pronouncements about how the lower dollar has made U.S. steel competitive again should be viewed in this context.

9. In 1977, imports moved to over 20 percent of U.S. consumption, and U.S. steel companies' losses mounted. A special White House task force was organized, which came up with a "trigger price" system to protect the industry. This system worked by preventing foreigners from selling in the United States below a certain price.

Despite this protection, the industry has downsized dramatically. In 1987, its production was 79 million tons, compared to 121 million tons in 1973. Some investment in modernization has taken place, though studies we have conducted cast doubt on assertions that the United States is now competitive. Some U.S. minimills, which produce with electric furnaces and continuous casters, can for certain products achieve competitive cost levels, but they represent only 20–25 percent of the industry's production. The massive dollar devaluation has brought profits to the industry once again, but it is a much smaller industry, which is still of questionable competitiveness.

10. Volkswagen officials approached BCG in July of 1975 and asked for a quick study to be done by September 1975. They were considering a U.S. facility because the German mark was rising rapidly against the U.S. dollar and because labor was scarce in West Germany. Although our study was brief, we expressed serious reservations about a U.S. plant. We agreed that the mark would probably rise further against the dollar, but doubted whether Volkswagen could obtain adequate scale in the United States to fight the Japanese push in small cars. Volkswagen management went ahead anyway, using substantial financial incentives from the state of Pennsylvania to build a plant in 1977. The plant did not succeed, and was eventually shut down.

11. In 1975, Japan's automobile production was about 4.2 million cars, and its domestic market was only 2.5 million cars. Leaving 1.7 million cars for export. In 1965, Japan had produced about 1 million cars and exported only about one hundred thousand. Beginning roughly in 1970, the domestic Japanese market growth slowed due to saturation of the first car-buyer market, a shortage of space, and high fuel costs. As a result, competition in the domestic market became fierce, and the push to export increased. By 1980, Japanese companies produced 7.3 million cars and exported 4.2 million of them, 1.8 million to the United States.

12. Our calculation in 1975 showed that Nissan, for example, could lower its U.S. price for its Bluebird (510) four-door sedan by $600 in the United States and still make more money on that sale than it made on its Japanese domestic sales of the same model (on roughly a twenty-eight-hundred-dollar FOB price).

13. *World Motor Vehicle Data*, Motor Vehicle Manufacturers Association of the United States, Inc. (Detroit, Michigan: 1987), pp. 385–395. Exact calculations are difficult, because one must estimate actual sales prices per model and also determine what volume of certain foreign brands are produced in the United States and what volume of certain U.S. kinds are sourced from abroad.

14. The Japanese government's role in the car industry began in the 1930's, when for military and for foreign-exchange reasons, the government passed a law that forced the market leaders, General Motors and Ford, out of Japan. After failing to encourage Zaibatsu to enter the industry, the government provided incentives for Toyota and Nissan to do so.

In the immediate postwar period, the car industry was in disarray. Toyota, the largest producer, had to be saved from bankruptcy in 1949 by the Bank of Japan. The bank opposed development of the industry, but MITI was in favor. The Korean War resolved the issue by creating an export market for Japanese-produced cars. Thus, in 1952, MITI developed a policy to protect and help fund development of the industry, and to help it acquire needed technology.

The government played a significant role in the industry in the 1950's and 1960's. Government intervention in the car industry was characterized by three major policy goals: discouragement of foreign capital in the Japanese industry and protection against car imports, attempts to bring about rationalization of production, and assistance with overseas marketing and distribution expenditure. Recently, the Japanese government has played only a minor role to assist in arranging voluntary export cutbacks and in the industry's research-and-development program to develop an electrically powered car and a ceramic engine.

The government devised a comprehensive and imposing set of protection measures that discouraged foreign investment in the car industry. These laws specified that no repatriation of earnings or capital would be guaranteed from foreign investment in marketing facilities. Repatriation would be guaranteed for investment in production facilities only if it "contributes to the development of the domestic industry."

MITI's purpose was to discourage import marketing investments while leaving the door open for selected joint ventures with foreign producers who had superior car-parts technology. Admission of large American and European motor-car assemblers was ruled out. Two instruments—quota and tariff—were used to protect the industry. Quotas were applied throughout the mid-1960's, and prohibitively high tariffs through the mid-1970's.

The imposition of import quotas and tariffs created for Japanese producers a market opportunity that they were not technologically prepared to exploit. Domestic producers turned out only 4,317 passenger cars in 1951, and these were uncompetitive in price and quality with Western imports. Parts technology and production methods were undeveloped. Most manufacturers agreed with MITI on the necessity of importing foreign technology.

MITI controlled all foreign-licensing agreements. To make technology agreements more attractive to the licensor, it guaranteed the remittance of royalties from Japan. The policy stipulated, however, that continued remittance would be guaranteed only if 90 percent of the licensed parts were produced in Japan within five years.

MITI had struck a compromise. Obtaining operational foreign technology required substantial imports of foreign "value added" in the form of parts and subassemblies. By making remittance conditional on the transfer of parts manufacture to Japan, however, MITI served notice that knock-down imports would be permitted only for a limited period. Domestic manufacturers were thus given additional incentive to develop manufacturing capability for their licensors' parts. Import controls were not, however, relinquished; quotas and tariffs on parts were retained.

A year after the policy was agreed on, six domestic manufacturers had negotiated agreements for knock-down assembly of foreign cars in Japan under license. Of the six, Nissan was the only one then producing passenger cars. Hino, Mitsubishi, and Isuzu were traditional truck manufacturers. MITI approved the applications of these four, while rejecting those of two others, Fuji Auto (no relation to Fuji Heavy Industries, now producing cars) and Nichiei. MITI considered those firms too financially weak to survive, and did not want a fragmented industry. Nissan and Isuzu cooperated with Austin (UK) and Rootes (UK) respectively. Hino cooperated with Renault (France) and Mitsubishi with Willys (USA). Toyota and Prince, two of the three major passenger car producers of the period, used domestic know-how exclusively. The four licensees rapidly developed their own technology, with the result that assembly of European cars in Japan did not last very long. The Isuzu-Rootes agreement was the longest, running until 1964, but producing less than $1 million in royalties over twelve years.

In the past three decades, the government has used a variety of financial-assistance programs to aid the car industry. The Japan Development Bank extended reconstruction loans to car producers from 1951 to 1955, financing roughly 9 percent of their total investment. Special accelerated depreciation rates were extended to car producers, permitting rates of up to 50 percent depreciation in the first year. Finally, during the 1950's, direct subsidies amounting to roughly $1 million were awarded to the Automobile Technology Association, representing manufacturers. After this initial financial assistance, the major investment role played by the government (primarily MITI) was to encourage rationalization, both of the parts industry and of the car industry itself.

The car industry has from its inception been highly competitive internally. As a result, MITI has often met opposition from producers when it advocated mergers and associations within the industry. MITI's attempts at industry rationalization have been most effective in the parts industry, where it had the cooperation of the major car producers.

The structure of the car-producing sector in the Japanese economy resembles a series of pyramids, with the products flowing from the bottom to the top. At the top are the vehicle producers—Toyota, Nissan, etc.—which manufacture engines and design and assemble vehicles. Each assembler is supplied by an affiliated group of primary-parts manufacturers. These firms, roughly three hundred in number, usually sell exclusively to one assembler. (It should be noted, however, that several large, independent parts manufacturers have now emerged.) The bottom layer comprises the small-parts subcontractors who supply, both exclusively and nonexclusively, the primary-parts firms. There are several thousand small subcontractors, many of whom are affiliated through ownership, technology agreements, or simply captive arrangements with primary-parts manufacturers or the assemblers themselves.

This system gives the assembler a stable yet elastic source of supply, as demand fluctuations are felt by the marginal subcontractor. Labor costs at the subcontract level are usually lower than in the large firm.

The chief problem in the 1950's was the large number and small size of the primary-parts manufacturers and subcontractors. A low production scale precluded economies of scale and modern production technologies. The firms were financially weak. Both MITI and the major car producers recognized that the production efficiency and technological progress of the industry would be inhibited if this structure remained.

MITI had taken a serious policy interest in the parts industry since the early 1950's. In 1952, MITI directed budget monies originally allocated to the car assemblers' development to immediate subsidies for specific parts producers. Over the next few years, it recommended that the Japan Development Bank extend long-term credit to large, viable parts suppliers of the four major car producers. At least ten parts manufacturers participated.

In 1956, MITI used a major piece of new legislation to implement a more thorough financial assistance and rationalization program in the parts industry. An Auto Parts Committee including MITI Heavy Industry Bureau officials, presidents of various parts manufacturers' trade associations, and senior officers of the Automobile Industry Association, representing the car manufacturers, was formed to coordinate the program.

This ad-hoc committee was responsible for taking the initiative to develop operational programs acceptable to all its constituents and formally proposing them to MITI. The car-parts program was planned in five-year intervals, and formally lasted until 1971.

The committee worked between 1956 and 1966 to modernize facilities and concentrate production among fewer producers in forty-five of ninety-five parts categories. Mergers, although encouraged, were not explicitly directed. Using criteria heavily influenced by MITI, the committee approved borrowing for large, specialized exporting firms. Within the constraints of the affiliated system, MITI wanted to develop a small group of large, specialized parts firms capable of competing with American suppliers.

The ten-year program from 1956–66 was reasonably successful. Nearly $50 million in low-interest long-term loans were extended by the Japan Development Bank and the Small Business Finance Corporation over the period. Market-share concentration occurred, and costs were reduced.

Price reductions over this period were critically important to Japan's subsequent export penetration of the United States market. Annual percentage-price reductions from 1960 to 1965 averaged roughly 30 percent.

Despite gains in industry concentration and efficiency, however, the primary-parts manufacturers in 1966 remained largely one-product or two-product companies. (The criteria used for the advancement of loans had, in fact, encouraged specialization.) In addition, Japanese parts manufacturers were smaller than their American counterparts. MITI thought that larger, horizontally integrated parts manufacturers would improve Japan's competitive position and would reduce the need for domestic firms to seek foreign technology through joint-equity ventures.

Consequently, the rationalization program that MITI approved for the third five-year period (1966–71) emphasized horizontal combination, even across affiliated group lines. The government offered financial assistance either to mergers or to jointly established research efforts by parts producers. MITI hoped to create large "unit system" subassembly producers. The program was not successful. Despite annual production growth rates of 25 percent to 40 percent during this period, which made low-cost, long-term lending sources extremely attractive to these capital-constrained single-product companies, borrowings were not heavy, and government-program budgets were not fully utilized.

Nor was the horizontal-consolidation phase of the program successful. A number of subcontractors merged into primary-parts manufacturers. For example, two large Nissan affiliates in the lighting-equipment area merged, and a three-way clutch venture including Toyota and Nissan affiliates was considered. But there was little impact on the primary-parts manufacturers who were the real targets of the program.

The major reason for the relative failure of MITI's efforts was that the car producers themselves, especially Nissan, were reorganizing their affiliates during this period. This inevitably caused some tensions. The vertical nature of the affiliate system did not easily accommodate the horizontal total-market orientation of the government's program.

Overall, the consolidation and modernization of parts suppliers during the 1950's and 1960's was essential to the emergence of a world-competitive industry. It is clear that government played a crucial role in this effort, although its wishes did not always prevail. By the early 1970's, the industry had attained competitiveness, and MITI moved to a "hands off" policy vis-à-vis the parts industry.

A further way in which the Japanese government has aided the automobile industry is through export assistance, including some financial support and direct functional assistance. Such aid was directed toward the development of overseas marketing-and-distribution capability for Japanese car producers.

In 1949, six car manufacturers established an Export Promotion Association to perform basic overseas market research. The Ministry of Commerce and Industry subsidized the research and the preparation of catalogs written in English—perhaps Japan's first car-export marketing step.

Long-term export credit offered by the Export-Import Bank of Japan dates from 1950. The bank historically emphasized heavy-equipment industries with large export-financing requirements, including cars, ships, and locomotives. Its lending was typically supplemented by commercial bank credit, with terms advantageous to the borrower. Since the early 1970's, however, preferential export borrowing terms have been disappearing.

The first tax assistance came in the form of an export income-deduction provision in 1953. This system, which provided a maximum deduction of 8 percent of net export income, was initiated by MITI and approved by the Ministry of Finance. Fewer than 150,000 passenger cars were exported under this tax exemption, and the Japanese discontinued the practice in 1964 in compliance with GATT regulations.

In the same year, a series of more indirect financial incentives was established, including measures that permitted exporting firms to establish tax-free reserves for overseas marketing development and investment. Most notable among these income reserves was that for "overseas market cultivation," which allowed a firm to shield 0.5 percent of its export sales from tax. In addition, an accelerated depreciation schedule tied to export performance was instituted. A manufacturer who increased his export business relative to competitors or to the previous year's performance qualified for special accelerated schedules on export-related capital investment. For the rapidly growing firm, these reserve and depreciation measures become a permanent and not insignificant source of funds. Suspension of these special provisions was announced in 1972.

A more detailed discussion of MITI's attempts to rationalize the car industry can be found in Ira Magaziner and Hout, *Japanese Industrial Policy,* Policy Studies Institute (London, 1980).

15. The company was Titan, a subsidiary of Grupo Alfa based in Monterrey. Titan was originally founded to provide boxes for the Garza Sada Brewery in Monterrey, and then branched out to sell throughout Mexico.

16. The term *maquila* is derived from the verb *maquilar,* which translates as "to do work for another." In colonial Mexico, *maquila* was the toll paid by the farmer to the miller as payment for processing grain. The current usage describes the Mexican corporation being paid a fee for processing materials.

The program was introduced in response to the termination of the Bracero Program by the U.S. This had permitted the free flow of labor from Mexico to the United States for agricultural and other low-wage work. The aim of the Maquila Program or Border Industrialization Program, as it was initially called, was to expand manufacturing employment along a 12.5 mile-wide strip from Brownsville, Texas, to San Diego, California. Therefore the industries in the northern region would assist in replacing the employment opportunities that were no longer available in the American Southwest.

As with other export-processing zones, the conditions for industry development have been due to both exporting-country and importing-country actions. The Maquila Program is a Mexican program that is augmented by separate U.S. tariff legislation that exempts the U.S. content of the imported goods from tariff.

The Maquila Program was initiated by Mexican law, under 1965 legislation. The program allows for the duty-free importation of plant and machinery, and raw materials and components "inbound" for production. Additionally, the customs procedures for the maquila industries are expedited.

The legislation was extended in 1972 to allow maquila to be established in any part of the country, except in already industrialized areas, such as around Mexico City. At the end of 1986, some 93 percent of the maquila were located in northern Mexico. Officially, the name of the program changed to the Mexican Industrialization Program.

Another change to the legislation, in 1973, allowed foreign investors to own 100 percent of the Mexican maquila company. The Foreign Investment Law generally requires a minimum of 51 percent Mexican ownership.

The program generally provides for all of the production to be sold as exports. However, under certain circumstances, usually where there is no competing product manufactured domestically, up to 20 percent may be sold within Mexico. Generally, the 20 percent domestic sales will be allowed for maquilas operating in the interior and south of Mexico.

The reason that most firms set up maquila is to employ cheap labor for assembly work, and to avoid high tariffs on reentry to the United States. Most of the maquila products enter the United States under Customs Codes 806.3 and 807.0, which were established in 1930. In 1966, the existing U.S. codes were amended to complement the Mexican legislation. However, the changes were minor.

By mid-1987, there were about eleven hundred firms in the Maquila Program. By majority ownership, some 67 percent are American, 30 percent Mexican, 1 percent Japanese, 1 percent European, and fewer than 1 percent from other countries. The value added is estimated to total $1.3 billion for Mexico in 1987. This consists mostly of wages; the maquilas buy only 1.3 percent of their raw materials locally.

The industries are heavily concentrated on the nineteen-hundred-mile border with the United States, which runs along the Rio Grande from Tijuana to Matamoros. The largest industry grouping is in Juárez, where the maquila industries provide employment for some 90,000 workers, over one third of the work force.

Throughout Mexico, the maquilas employ some 280,000 workers, about two thirds women. In the past five years, the proportion of men in the work force has doubled. Most of the workers employed have no more than a high-school education.

The minimum unskilled wage in June 1987 was approximately seventy cents. This is made up of about 77 percent cash wage and 23 percent statutory benefits. Companies generally provide additional benefits such as productivity bonuses, subsidization of meals, transportation allowances, and savings plans. The unskilled fully loaded labor cost averages under a dollar. Although there is a large cost differential between the American and Mexican unskilled workers, the difference narrows at higher skill levels.

Total labor costs are not comparable on a wage basis only. In addition to the noncash benefits detailed above, the indirect labor-related costs will often be higher at the Mexican plants than comparable American-located plants.

There will usually be a number of U.S. management people at the maquila plant, whose salaries will include allowances for relocating to a border city. There are also additional travel costs for technicians, engineers, and company management that add to the labor-related costs. A final factor is the usual requirement for additional indirect staff, such as quality controllers and supervisors for the less skilled work force.

Although gross statistics on the Maquila Program are relatively available, individual companies are often shy about their participation in the program, fearing that public exposure will adversely affect their reputation with unions, workers, and certain members of Congress in the United States. Most maquilas will trade under a different company name and are reluctant to give interviews on their Mexican activities.

The major U.S. firms in the Maquila Program are General Motors with some twenty-three plants, General Electric with fourteen plants (more than fifteen thousand employees), and Zenith with seven plants (more than twenty-four thousand employees).

Juárez has a predominance of large companies in its two hundred foreign-owned plants. In the six large industrial parks in Juárez, the Mexican park owner will typically provide water, sewer, and power hookups. Often the factories are owned by the industrial park and leased to the maquila firm.

The Japanese firms are concentrated in the less-unionized Tijuana area, where there is still a forty-eight-hour work week. There are twelve Japanese firms, with eighteen plants, employing about eight thousand workers there.

In addition to the cheaper wages in Mexico, the Japanese companies have powerful reasons for shifting more of their production offshore, particularly their assembly and finishing operations. When the United States imposed trade sanctions on Japan for dumping semiconductors on U.S. markets, the products made in maquila were exempted. Nor do the exports to the United States of Japanese-made products appear as imports from Japan if they are finished in Mexico.

The potential for Japanese firms to sidestep trade regulations by using the maquilas has not gone unnoticed. The Subcommittee on Commerce, Consumer and Monetary Affairs held hearings on the subject in June 1987.

Not all the Japanese or U.S. firms use a high proportion of U.S. components in exporting via the U.S. customs 806.3 or 807.0 regulations. A number of firms choose to import components from overseas countries and assemble in Mexico. For example, some Matsushita products, marketed under the Panasonic and

Quasar brand names, use mainly Japanese components and have low U.S. content.

The Koreans are recent entrants to the maquila program, led by Samsung, Goldstar, and Daewoo.

The Maquila Program has grown rapidly since 1982, at least partly due to the effects of the debt crisis, which forced wages down and caused the huge devaluation of the peso (twenty-fivefold fall in value). Since 1982, the border cities have doubled their manufacturing output and absorbed almost 1 million immigrants from further south.

The Maquila Program is only the Mexican program for export-zone processing. Many others have been long established throughout the world. U.S. imports under tariff items 806.3 and 807.0 have grown from $0.9 billion in 1966 to $36.5 billion in 1986, an average annual growth of over 20 percent per annum.

There has been a change in the firms that have moved to Mexico. Initially, it was the labor-intensive firms only: clothing, toys, luggage, furniture. Then the more capital-intensive firms started moving their labor-intensive operations: electrical appliances, electronics, automotive parts.

In 1986, the electrical goods and electronics sector accounted for 32 percent of maquila firms and 44 percent of maquila employment. The transportation equipment sector is the next in terms of employment, with 20 percent, followed by textiles and apparel, with 10 percent.

There has been a heated debate within the United States on the benefits of the Maquila Program. The AFL-CIO and a number of politicians have charged that the program is merely an export of U.S. jobs, and a way to circumvent U.S. employee health and safety regulations.

Supporters like the Border Trade Alliance, a coalition of U.S. frontier-state politicians and maquila-related interests, counter by emphasizing the linkages between the maquila and U.S. firms and suggesting that the alternatives for U.S. firms are to migrate to the Far East, or to close down.

U.S. labor unions and members of Congress have charged that more than three hundred thousand jobs have been exported to Mexico by firms seeking lower wages and fewer restrictions on health and safety. Other estimates put the job losses at 1 U.S. job lost for each 2.5 Mexican jobs created. This would imply that some 110,000 jobs had been lost to date.

Organized labor representatives contend that wages are kept low by Mexican government policies that discourage trade unionism, and tax laws that encourage U.S. firms to relocate. The U.S. customs tariff provisions 806.3 and 807.0 come in for particular criticism.

Supporters of the Maquila Program reverse the argument and point to the U.S. jobs that have been saved by U.S. companies continuing to supply components to Mexican plants, and by U.S. companies being able to stay in business by utilizing Mexico's low-wage assembly. They identify the Maquila Program as a response that U.S. firms can make to competitive threats from overseas firms with access to low-wage manufacturing.

They also point out that even the high estimates for job losses represent a tiny fraction of the estimated 11.5 million American jobs lost between 1979 and 1984 due to plant shutdowns or relocations.

Maquila Plants in Operation

NUMBER AT YEAR END

	1982	1983	1984	1985	1986
Border	516	562	678	742	915
Mexican Interior	72	44	44	47	72
Total	588	606	722	789	987

Source: U.S. Department of Commerce

Maquila Employment

EMPLOYEES AT YEAR END

	1982	1983	1984	1985	1986	1987
Admin./Technical	21,860	29,210	36,547	39,488	49,800	
Production Workers:						
Females	77,032	103,568	116,469	122,085	146,700	
Males	23,601	40,350	49,602	55,971	71,800	
Total	100,633	143,918	166,071	178,056	218,500	
Total Employment	122,493	173,128	202,618	217,544	268,300	

Source: U.S. Department of Commerce

17. A Telesis study done in 1983 for a client considering expansion in Mexico, which involved interviews of a sample of one hundred companies operating in Juárez, Reynosa, and Matamoros.

18. By 1975, imports had risen to 15 percent of all goods and by 1980, to 20 percent. The trend has continued. In 1988, imports were well over 25 percent of all goods sold in the United States. The trend can be traced through yearly issues of the U.S. Commerce Department's *International Economic Indicators.*

19. *Metals Bulletins Handbook.* Brazil also was increasing output, going from 15 million tons in 1967 to 27 million tons in 1970, to over 60 million tons by 1976.

20. This figure includes export sales of helicopters and parts from the United States; co-production in foreign countries—most notably a major operation at the time in Iran; sales to foreign militaries paid for either in part or in total by the U.S. Defense Department; and sales to offshore oil operations around the world, even if the buyer was an American-based company.

21. The state-run oil company Pertamina went bankrupt in 1976 and had to be reorganized. The purchasing operations were the source of much of the problem. It was not uncommon for bid prices to be moved upward to allow for personal skimming by officials.

Chapter 1

1. The idea of cooking with microwaves originated with Raytheon managers involved in the production of magnetron tubes for radar installations during World War II. They worked on the concept beginning in 1942 and received

their first microwave cooking patents in 1949. Raytheon introduced the first microwave-cooking oven, the Radar-range, in 1953. The original versions were as big and heavy as refrigerators and cost as much as some automobiles. Raytheon licensed its invention to Tappan and Litton, who in 1955 began selling home models.

2. This estimate is based on internal production figures from Samsung and from GE internal sources. Publicly reported industry-association data is not accurate in market-share breakdowns, as companies do not necessarily report accurate figures to these associations. Korean-made microwaves are sold under many labels, including GE, J. C. Penney, Montgomery Ward, Whirlpool, Sears, Emerson, Samsung, and Goldstar.

3. In 1988, Samsung surpassed Matsushita, Sanyo, and Sharp in total number of units produced, though its total sales valued in dollars may still be slightly smaller at the retail level due to mix and high retail prices in Japan.

4. Korea did not begin to offer color-television transmission until four years after the production of color televisions commenced at Samsung, Goldstar, and Lucky (now part of Goldstar).

5. The study was commissioned by the National Economic Development Office in Great Britain, an industry-, labor-, and government-sponsored organization with separate councils for a variety of industries. Britain's television makers were suffering and wanted to understand the new competition they were facing from Japan and Korea. They asked for a strategy on what they could do to become competitive again.

6. In 1960, Korea's GNP per capita was less than 10 percent of that of the United States.

7. Every five years, the Korean government publishes a detailed economic plan. As part of that plan, targets for growth by industrial sector are set, and specific proposals are made on how to reach the goals.

8. The Pohang steelworks in South Korea was, at the time, one of the world's most modern and efficient mills. It was built with technical assistance from Nippon Steel and NKK of Japan.

9. In the years from 1952 to 1967, fewer than ten thousand microwave ovens were sold in the United States, most of them made by hand assembly at Raytheon and sold to restaurants and airlines. Litton tried to introduce them for home sale during this period with little success. Both Raytheon and Litton had over 75 percent of their revenues at the time in defense industries.

10. The microwave oven was first demonstrated in Japan by Raytheon in 1960 at a trade show. Japanese consumer-electronics companies led by Toshiba and Sanyo took an interest in the product and began building copies of the restaurant model shown by Raytheon. By that time, the New Japan Radio Company (NJRC) was the only maker of magnetron tubes in Japan left over from World War II. The other companies that had made radar systems ceased doing

so when the American occupation authorities prohibited military work by Japanese firms.

NJRC continued funding nonmilitary uses for microwave tubes in medical heat therapy and civilian communications. NJRC and Raytheon linked up and traded technology in the sixties. Spurred on by Sanyo and Toshiba, a scientist at NJRC named Keishi Ogura developed a low-cost magnetron for consumer application in 1964.

By 1968, Japanese companies were exporting consumer microwave ovens to the United States. Raytheon bought Amana to try to sell to U.S. consumers, but the Japanese market took off quicker, spurred by lower-cost product designs and Japanese cooking tastes, which fit the microwaves' capability.

In 1968, thirty thousand microwave ovens were sold worldwide. By 1975, 2.2 million were sold, with 1.3 million sold in Japan and nine hundred thousand in the U.S. By then, all the major Japanese consumer-electronics companies had developed products, and a number of them, including Toshiba and Matsushita, were producing their own magnetron tubes. As the ovens' volume and quality grew their costs for the tube decreased. NJRC, the Japanese inventor of the microwave tube for cooking, now partly owned by Raytheon, was surpassed, stopped making tubes in 1980.

11. In the mid- and late 1970's, Raytheon-Amana and Litton dominated U.S. microwave-oven production. General Electric entered the business in the early 1970's, but had only 7 percent market share in 1973, well under its more than 30 percent share in electric ranges. GE did not invest seriously in the business until the late 1970's. Whirlpool, White/Westinghouse, and Maytag, America's other large appliance companies, did not enter the microwave business at all in the 1970's.

12. Japanese producers had 30 percent market share in the United States by the mid-1970's. Raytheon and Litton dominated, with over 60 percent of the U.S. market at the time. The Japanese share decreased to 25 percent in the late 1970's due to the rise of the Japanese yen and trade pressure that forced the Japanese companies to begin opening assembly plants in the United States. Characteristically, U.S. producers and the business press hailed the demise of the Japanese threat at this time. By 1982, however, the Japanese share of the U.S. market was back up to over 45 percent, and Raytheon and Litton's combined share was down below 25 percent.

13. Almost all of the world market growth from 1975 to 1980 came in the United States. The U.S. market grew from nine hundred thousand units in 1975 to 3.2 million units in 1980. Meanwhile, the Japanese market declined from 1.3 million units in 1975 to nine hundred thousand units in 1980. The competitive battleground clearly shifted to United States territory.

14. During this trip, I spent two weeks in intensive meetings with government and industry leaders discussing South Korea's economic development. They were avidly interested in the new concepts of economic development we were discussing with Swedish leaders, and anxious for me to comment on their plans. I was impressed with the close cooperation that existed between the gov-

ernment and large industrial leaders, though some industrial leaders were not completely happy with the degree of control exerted by the government. There was a clear common understanding of growth priorities and a sharing of investment.

When I returned to the United States from this trip, I met with a Department of Transportation team studying the world automobile industry. They were mostly interested in Japan, and hopeful that the high yen (190 to the dollar at the time) would make Japanese small cars uncompetitive.

I told them this was unlikely, and then mentioned that Hyundai was likely to be the biggest threat in small cars in a decade. Despite my descriptions of South Korea's plans, the U.S. officials were unimpressed.

The chart on p. 327 illustrates the type of plans that the Korean officials laid out for me on the evolution of their industrial structure. These plans have been largely carried out.

15. Samsung's desire to push ahead and develop a microelectronics industry in the late 1970's was highly controversial within the government of South Korea. Many felt it was necessary if the nation was to become a developed country and build a successful electronics industry. Others felt that South Korea could never compete in this fast-moving, expensive new technology and would waste billions of dollars trying. Samsung did go ahead, and was followed by others. South Korea is not on the cutting edge of integrated-circuit technology, but is now a low-cost, fast follower whose companies supply IC's to many U.S. companies today, including on an OEM basis to U.S. IC makers.

16. These figures were derived from a Telesis survey of producers. In addition to Matsushita and Sanyo, Sharp had 14 percent share, Toshiba 7 percent, Hitachi 2 percent, and Mitsubishi 1 percent. Altogether, Japanese companies had about 60 percent of world production.

17. Amperex is actually a subsidiary of the Dutch electronics giant Philips. Its magnetron facility was relatively new in Rhode Island, but did not have the scale, cost levels, or technology to be competitive.

The prices Amperex needed to be profitable were 30 percent higher than those quoted by their Japanese competitors. GE and other U.S. manufacturers did not want to purchase from their competitors in Japan, but could not suffer the 30 percent price penalty that purchasing from Amperex entailed. They switched to the Japanese, and Amperex had to shut down.

18. Telesis study for GE. GE's share had risen from 7 percent in 1975 to 16 percent by 1980, and had then declined.

19. Telesis study for GE.

20. Interviews with Matsushita for Telesis study for GE.

21. The share of other U.S. manufacturers had gone from 50 percent in 1976 to 42 percent in 1979 to 30 percent by 1983. Meanwhile, the Japanese share of the U.S. market climbed from 27 percent in 1976 to 38 percent by 1980 to 48 percent by 1983.

22. Telesis analysis.

Korean Development Pattern for Potential Export Sectors

	1966–1971	1971–1976	1976–1981	1981–1986
Infant industries	Electronics assembly Shipbuilding Steel Fertilizer	Commodity-car assembly Consumer electronics Special steels Precision goods (watches, cameras) Plant construction Metalworking	Components for cars, ships Machine tools (MC) Final machinery assembly Simple instruments Assembly of heavy electrical machinery Semiconductors for watches & calculators	Machinery components for cars, ships Machine tools (MC) Final machinery assembly Simple instruments Assembly of heavy electrical machinery Semiconductors for watches & calculators
Industries attaining competitiveness		Electronics assembly Shipbuilding Steel Fertilizer	Commodity-car assembly Consumer electronics Special steels Precision goods (watches, cameras) Plant construction Metalworking	
Self-sustaining industries		Textiles Clothing Shoes	Electronics assembly Shipbuilding Steel Fertilizer	Commodity-car assembly Consumer electronics Special steels Precision goods (watches, cameras) Plant construction Metalworking

Sources: Korean Economic Planning Board, five-year plans.

23. GE sent over a number of quality-control and manufacturing engineers who helped Samsung develop its testing and production techniques. It took well over a year of joint work before GE felt that an acceptable quality level had been met. This assistance probably cut years off of the time Samsung would have required to become a high-quality, high-volume microwave-oven producer on its own.

24. Interviews with Samsung management in Suweon in July 1988.

25. The distribution, marketing, and selling elements of the price, as well as part of quality control and engineering and profit, stay with GE in the United States. The exact proportion is confidential, but it is less than half of the selling price.

Chapter 2

1. The Singapore Economic Development Board puts out a publication entitled *Leading International Companies in Manufacturing and Technical Services in Singapore.* The 1987 edition lists companies and products. These figures are derived from a phone survey done by Telesis of U.S. firms listed in the publication. The numbers are approximate.

2. Singapore's GNP per capita as a percent of the United States GNP per capita was 15 percent in 1960; 18 percent in 1970; 38 percent in 1980; and 52 percent in 1988. The figures are calculated from IMF data.

3. Technically, the small, oil-rich sultanate of Brunei on the island of Borneo has Asia's highest living standards, but its economy is an anomaly.

4. Britain's GNP per capita is currently 69 percent of that of the United States compared with 52 percent in Singapore. If the GNP per capita growth rates of the past ten years continue in both countries, Singapore will be richer by 1995.

5. The first British settlers arrived in Singapore in 1819, but the official settlement of the territory came in 1826, when the British East India Company formed the Straits Settlements, which included Singapore, Penang, and Malacca. Singapore became a crown colony in 1862.

6. Singapore does produce about thirty thousand metric tons of vegetables per year, and lesser amounts of fruits, nuts, sugar cane, and eggs. In addition, well over one hundred thousand metric tons of fish are landed in Singapore each year, though only twenty-five thousand tons are reputed to come from Singaporean fishing vessels. Collectively, only ten thousand Singaporeans out of over 1.2 million are employed in agriculture, forestry, fishing, mining, and quarrying, and Singapore produces less than 2 percent of its own raw-materials needs.

7. Literacy figures are hard to compare across countries due to different definitions. These figures are rough, and come from figures compiled by the Singapore EDB and the U.S. Department of Education in 1984, with similar

definitions of functional literacy—eighth-grade reading levels and basic ability to add, subtract, multiply, and divide. While the exact numbers are disputable, the orders of magnitude are indicative.

8. International Labor Organization annual employment statistics.

9. The British government implemented a decision beginning in 1968 to close down all of its military bases "east of Suez." Singapore was one of its biggest.

10. Annual report, Singapore Economic Development Board.

11. The average remuneration for all Singapore workers in manufacturing in 1979 was only two thousand dollars per year. The most prevalent jobs were the manual insertion of electronic components into circuit boards, manually attaching lead wires to integrated circuits, hand-assembling motors, transformers, and coils, and sewing. Typical factories employed long lines of women doing these tasks.

There were, of course, exceptions. But few companies had yet made major capital or skill-upgrading investments in Singapore in the late 1970's.

12. In 1983, I directed a study of Rhode Island's economy, during which we interviewed state economic development officials in over thirty states. Every one of them talked about skills development as being essential to successful economic development. The programs they put in place, however, usually involved little expenditure, and were simple training courses to make potential workers ready to take a job in a new or existing factory. Rarely did the courses go beyond teaching five-to-ten-year-old skills to those out of work, or teaching the basic procedures of a company that was opening a factory to those who would be employed at the factory.

Besides Singapore, Sweden, West Germany, and the Republic of Ireland had skill-development programs that I observed that went beyond general platitudes. In Japan and South Korea, aggressive skill-development programs also exist, but they are run and funded primarily within large companies.

13. The craftsmen centers take high-school graduates as apprentices for two years of intensive training, followed by two years of on-the-job work in selected companies where their skills can be practiced. Even while in the center training course, attempts are made to simulate the factory production environment. By the end of 1987, over 6,000 trainees had completed their first 2 years of training, and were placed in over 350 companies.

The Japan-Singapore Technical Institute provides a crucial but often overlooked need—a training program for maintenance technicians. One of the biggest hesitancies that companies have about putting sophisticated operations in a developing country involves the inability to get machines properly maintained.

The Institutes of Technology provide two- and three-year diploma courses for high-school graduates and people already in the work force. All students in these programs carry out industrial projects for companies in their second and third years that typically last for three to six months. There have been over 700 graduates of these 3 institutes, who are now employed in over 150 companies. They are all expanding enrollments, so that by 1990, the annual graduating classes will be triple their current levels.

14. The main purpose of the CUT program is to introduce new technologies into the existing workplace by taking people already in industry and providing them with courses on the latest world developments in factory automation and operation and product development. These courses are quite sophisticated in areas such as IC, design, robotics, CAD/CAM, and CNC technology. Since mid-1983, over four hundred specialized courses have been organized under this program, with over four thousand participants from industry.

15. The SDF, founded in 1979, has as its goal to encourage companies to invest in skills development. While the EDB institutes can be effective for limited worker groups, the upgrading of the mass of workers must be done by employers themselves. The SDF has encouraged them to do so through the use of financial incentives. Over $80 million was spent last year on programs for over ten thousand workers.

The SDF also tries to educate employers in how to do good training. It publishes booklets and has meetings with managers and supervisors to offer assistance. The SDF also has encouraged industry associations and various trade groups to set up their own training centers. There are now eleven of these centers in areas such as banking, contracting, insurance, hotel management, retailing, and textiles.

The SDF also has developed a program to encourage more employer-based training activities for junior-level workers. This program, called Core Skills for Effectiveness and Change (COSEC), includes training in personal effectiveness, communication, problem solving, work economies, and computer literacy. The aim is to help workers to adapt and respond flexibly to changing business environments. Pilot COSEC programs have been organized in the retail and banking sectors.

16. The National Computer Board was set up in 1981 to promote the use of information technology in Singapore and to develop a strong information-technology industry for internal use and export. The board has established a number of Applied Research Centers, including the Information Technology Institute (ITI) within the board, the Institute of Systems Science (ISS) within the National University of Singapore, and in cooperation with America's Grumman Corporation, the Grumman International Nanyang CAD-CAM Research Center (GINTIC).

The board also operates a Software Technology Center within the Singapore Science Park, and maintains an office with the EDB in Boston.

The board is the focal point of a government-sponsored effort begun in 1980 to computerize in the nation. The government identified computers and information technology as keys to productivity and overseas competitiveness in 1980. To set the pace of computerization, the government itself embarked on a massive program to computerize the civil service. Then it developed fiscal and other financial incentives for companies to computerize. For example, companies purchasing computing hardware can write off their equipment in one year, and there are grants and low-cost loans available for local companies wishing to purchase computers. The government will even provide assistance to small and medium-sized companies that wish to computerize by financing their use of consultants to assist their computerization.

Since 1980, the board has also encouraged the training of information-technology professionals. The number has grown from only eight hundred in all of Singapore in 1980 to over seven thousand in 1988.

17. This figure is based on estimates of total personal computer sales in the United States from the Electronic Industries Association and sales projections made by Telesis for one of our clients.

18. The Singapore government has a number of tax incentives designed to encourage companies to do research and development in Singapore. Companies that undertake R&D can have "pioneer status" (tax holidays) for longer-than-average periods of time; an investment allowance of up to 50 percent in addition to normal capital allowances for R&D-associated fixed investments is possible; R&D operating costs including manpower, materials, and utility costs can receive a double deduction; and companies can set aside 20 percent of income as an R&D reserve to be spent tax free within three years.

In addition, a number of grant programs are available. For example, companies with at least 30 percent local ownership can receive a dollar-for-dollar grant to assist with the direct manpower, materials, prototyping, consulting fees, and equipment required to develop new products. There is also a research-and-development assistance scheme that contributes to R&D efforts associated with the Science Park. As of March 1988, over seventy projects had been funded to the tune of over $15 million. While many of these have been for local Singapore utilities and agencies, foreign companies are increasingly taking advantage of the funds. Seagate Technology received a grant to work with the Department of Electrical Engineering and the Department of Mechanical and Production Engineering of the National University of Singapore on a fast random-access compact-optical-disc storage device, for example.

The venture capital fund is relatively new, but has already invested over $5 million.

Chapter 3

1. GE also manufactured and sold electric ranges, washers and dryers, dishwashers, disposal units, and microwave ovens in 1979.

2. At the time, GE was divided into six sectors. The consumer sector included GE's major-appliance, lighting, small appliance and audio, air-conditioning, and television businesses which at the time had about $6 billion in total sales. The major-appliance business was the sector's largest.

3. Japan's refrigerator and compressor producers had concentrated on their own home market in the 1970's. The only exception was in small six-cubic-foot-and-under models, where the Japanese, Italians, Yugoslavs, and more recently the Koreans dominated world markets. U.S. producers had pulled out of these small-size markets long ago. In 1979, Sanyo set up a plant in California to assemble these small refrigerators.

Matsushita's compressor move to Singapore was the first sign of a Japanese company moving into world markets in large refrigerators.

4. The only exception was the United States, where Whirlpool, Tecumseh, and White, GE's traditional competition, were all as high-cost as GE.

5. Telesis study.

6. Telesis study.

7. In my consulting work, I have seen many examples of companies ceasing the manufacture of key components to source from abroad at lower prices, only to find substantial price increases a few years later when their factories are irrevocably closed.

For a product like compressors, which require major investment, the barriers to reentry are prohibitive.

8. Tennessee, like many other states, offers training money to firms that expand or modernize plants in their state. In this case, state grants ran over $1 million.

9. Refrigerators must work harder in hot climates, so it is not surprising that the problems began to occur there. The problem was serious mainly for larger compressors.

Chapter 4

1. In early 1985, when the last of these particular machines were purchased, the deutsche mark was valued at 2.6 to the U.S. dollar. By the time of my visit in late 1987, it was valued at 1.7. This means that a 1-million-mark machine would be priced at $384,000 in 1985, and the same machine would sell for $588,000 in 1987, a 53 percent increase. In the case of these particular machines, the German manufacturers had absorbed some of the currency change as lower profits on dollar-denominated sales, so annual prices had gone up only 40 percent.

2. These figures are derived from the *Industrial Statistical Yearbook* for 1984, Volume 2, published by the United Nations in 1986. They are for the category titled Nonelectrical Machinery Excluding Transportation Vehicles. The figure for the Soviet Union is a rough estimate, since a comparable industrial-category breakout is not given.

1983 Production Nonelectrical Machinery

BILLION $

USA	188	Canada	8
USSR	120	Sweden	5
Japan	103	India	5
China	73	Spain	3
Germany	53	South Korea	3
France	30	Yugoslavia	2
UK	26	Other	20
Italy	13	Total	652

America's 1983 share of 29 percent as represented in these figures declined from an estimated 35 percent share in 1977, and according to a recent Telesis estimate declined further to 23 percent by 1987.

3. Each year, the Verein Deutscher Werkzeugmaschinen Fabriken (VDW) in Germany prepares an estimate of world production, export, import, and consumption by country for machine tools, excluding parts and attachments. In 1986, they estimated world production at DM 63.5 billion, or slightly under $30 billion.

4. The 1977 world production of machine tools was $15.1 billion. U. S. companies produced $2.3 billion, or 15.2 percent (National Machine Tool Builders Association Annual Report, 1977; VDW Annual Report, 1977).

5. The United States produced $2.7 billion of machine tools in 1986, or just over 9 percent of total world production. Our performance in 1987 was even worse (VDW Annual Reports, 1986, 1987).

6. National Machine Tool Builders Association, U.S. Department of Commerce *Current Industrial Reports,* and IM146 and EM522 reports. In 1977, imports at $401 million were smaller than exports at $427 million; by 1987, imports ran at almost five times exports.

7. In May 1986, President Reagan decided to pursue Voluntary Restraint Agreements (VRA) with the four largest machine-tool importers of 1985: Japan, West Germany, Switzerland, and Taiwan.

The first agreement was reached with Japan, in December 1986. The Japanese pledged to voluntarily limit exports of six types of machine tools to the United States for the period of 1987 through 1991. Shipment volumes were essentially frozen at 1981 levels.

Limits were set on the three best-selling tools: machining centers, numerically controlled lathes, and numerically controlled punching/shearing machines. The quotes and expected market-share results for these machines were set at:

TYPE	UNITS	EFFECTS
Machine Centers	2,800	decrease of 22% from 1985, Japanese share of U.S. market; cut to 52%.
NC Lathes	3,200	decrease of 17% from 1985, Japanese share targeted at 57.5%.
NC punching/shearing machines	250	Japanese share estimated at 19.3% of U.S. market.

The Japanese acceptance of these restraints was contingent upon similar agreements with the other three targeted importers.

Also in December 1986, Taiwan signed an agreement similar to Japan's ("frozen at 1981 levels"). West Germany and Switzerland refused a formal agreement, but are voluntarily maintaining lower export totals.

8. In 1977, Japan produced $1.2 billion of machine tools, or 7.7 percent of total world production. In 1986, Japan produced $7 billion worth of machine tools, over 24 percent of world production (VDW Annual Reports).

9. In the machine-tool industry for example, German wages plus benefits averaged about $17.62 (at DM 1.8 to the dollar) while U.S. machine-tool workers averaged $13.63, in 1987 (*Maschinenbau-Nachrichten,* July 1987, p. 7).

10. U.S. Commerce Department Trade Statistics for 1987.

11. Germany had a positive trade balance of over $50 billion in 1987 in steel, automobiles, machinery, and chemicals.

12. Germany produced $3 billion of machine tools in 1977, or 19.8 percent of world production (VDW Annual Report).

13. VDW Annual Report. Germany's share of world production is the same today as in 1977, while ours dropped from 15 percent to 9 percent.

14. The Federal Republic of Germany has a population of 60 million people, compared to the United States at 240 million. Our consumption of machine tools varies from 1.5 to 1.8 times West Germany's consumption, and our production is less than half of West Germany's. The small consumption difference relative to the difference in population raises questions about the modernity of America's metal-using industrial base, and the production differentials raise a question about the competitiveness of our machine-tool industry.

15. The industry's close association with the military has been both beneficial and at times disastrous to the continued well-being of the industry. During wartimes, the industry benefited from massive increases in demand, an example being during World War II, when some eight hundred thousand machine tools were produced. However, at the end of the war, approximately three hundred thousand U.S. government-acquired machine tools were dumped on the domestic market. This had a severe dampening effect upon the vitality of the industry, and it had not yet recovered when the Korean War once again heightened demand for machine tools. Additionally, these wartime experiences with government management and allocation procedures left a legacy of suspicion among machine-tool builders that still persists.

One major benefit to the industry has been the development and diffusion of state-of-the-art technology, carried on outside the industry mostly as a result of Department of Defense initiatives. Perhaps the most important was the technological shift to numeric control (NC). The U.S. Air Force funded research, and in the 1950's placed orders for large numbers of NC machines with many major machine-tool companies to ensure that the new technology diffused throughout the industry. The Manufacturing Technologies Program of the Department of Defense (ManTech), dating from the early 1950's, played an instrumental role in the development and diffusion of NC and CNC technology, and now spends an average of $225 million annually on R&D in manufacturing systems, robotics, and flexible manufacturing systems.

16. The Japanese share of world production in 1977 was 7.7 percent, but in 1970 their share was less than 2 percent. Though they were still small, the German government and many German company executives were aware of their progress and their plans to increase share dramatically in the future.

17. Cycle time in this case refers to the total amount of time required to

take a raw part and finish machining it. It includes actual times for various machinery steps as well as setup times.

18. In 1977, there were 1,250 machine-tools producers in the United States, including job shops, according to the NMBTA. By 1983, the number had dropped to about nine hundred, with almost all the net losses coming from 1981 to 1983. Since 1983, the number has dropped even further, to about 650 in 1987.

19. The most famous action was taken by Houdaille Industries, which filed what is most certainly one of the most thorough trade complaints in U.S. history. With their lawyers, the Houdaille people developed a document of well over one thousand pages in length detailing how the Japanese government assisted its machine-tool industry and how Japanese companies were allegedly competing unfairly in the U.S. market. Because I had written a book on Japanese industrial policy and was knowledgeable about Japan, I was contacted no fewer than ten times by various representatives of Houdaille for advice, as were many other "Japan experts." The NMBTA also made numerous complaints. All of these complaints fell on deaf ears until 1986, when the president, allegedly for defense reasons, pursued the voluntary restraint agreements.

20. In addition to owning equity in industrial companies, German banks commonly hold the proxy rights for shareholders who don't attend the annual meeting *(Hauptversammlung)* of a publicly held company *(Aktiengesellschaft,* or AG). In West Germany, it's illegal for a corporation's management to hold these proxy rights as it would in the United States. Instead, the average shareholder gives his proxy to the bank where his/her stocks are deposited. (The term for this is *Depotstimmrecht* or "deposit voting rights.") This practice is a consequence of Germany's "universal banking" system, in which the banks are also the dominant traders on the German stock exchanges and serve as stockbrokers for the general public.

The combination of their equity holdings, the proxy rights, and long-term creditor relationships give the German banks—especially the four major national banks—a substantial influence over long-term investment decisions. Though bankers have less influence in smaller companies, their involvement is still much greater than in the United States.

At the annual meeting of a publicly held corporation, the banks generally see their interests as the firm's long-term viability, since that will assure the continued payment of dividends to the shareholders—either themselves or the customers they represent—as well as the continued payback of present and future loans if they are among the firm's creditors. They attempt to elect members of the supervisory board who will share their perspective.

If a bank serves as one of the long-term creditors *(Hausbanken)* for a corporation, then this bank will typically have one of its officials elected to the supervisory board by the shareholders. This Hausbank representative is an important voice for capital on the board, since German law does not allow anyone from the firm's executive management board to sit on the supervisory board while he is still in office.

Officially, a Hausbank is not permitted to receive confidential information about the firm through its representative on the supervisory board. Nevertheless, the involvement of the banks as owners, proxies, and/or creditors gives them a close familiarity with the corporation's management and internal business. This involvement accounts for the active participation of German banks when there's a need for restructuring a troubled German corporation, or even a troubled industry, as in the current coordination of capacity reductions by the German steelmakers. In both situations, the banks are concerned that the company or industry regain a strong competitive position, and they are willing to suffer losses for a number of years if they expect future profits when the restructuring is complete. Even aside from future profits, banks may be willing to accept losses as part of a restructuring plan, since their investments in the firm may already be so great that they couldn't afford to let the firm go bankrupt.

This long-term relationship between the German corporations and their national banks serves as a hindrance to mergers and acquisitions that are not in German industry's long-term interest. German managers don't spend their time worrying about "raiders." Hence, German corporations don't complain about another law that prohibits them from holding significant amounts of their own stock, since they don't need to have these reserves as a defense against unfriendly takeovers, as do corporations in the United States. As a result, of course, German firms can use more of their corporate assets for productive investment. Finally, the tight-knit organization of the German banking system enables German industry to quietly but strategically limit the extent of foreign ownership in its manufacturing base. Germany's complicated laws regarding the operation of financial institutions also make it somewhat difficult for foreign banks and insurance companies to enter the German market.

21. The graphic simulator was also a significant step in marketing the CNC lathes to Traub's traditional customers, the small and medium-sized jobbers. These jobbers resisted the transition to the CNC lathes. The main reason was that they didn't like the high price compared to the conventional machines, but that wasn't all. The computer control was too mysterious, because there was no way for the operator to assess what was happening to the workpiece as it was being machined. The only method of following the process was to analyze a plotted graph that was located away from the shop floor. This limitation held many machinists back from learning about CNC and prevented them from applying their skills once they did, since they still couldn't follow the workpiece and make whatever adjustments were necessary.

The development of a CNC graphic simulator solved many of these problems. This potential sparked the interest of the German Ministry of Technology, which had already been running various programs to support Germany's transition into computer-integrated manufacturing. The ministry agreed to underwrite 30 percent of the personnel costs that were needed for the simulator's research and development.

Besides the eventual contribution of the graphic simulator to Traub's sales, the simulator has become a standard training tool for German machinists and apprentices who are learning how to use CNC. In December 1987, Hekeler estimated that thirty thousand to forty thousand people across Germany had been trained with it. IG Metall has also held up the simulator as a model of how technology doesn't have to be designed to de-skill workers. On the contrary, the simulator enables a skilled operator to enhance the effectiveness of the machine. And to become a skilled operator, the apprentice must now be trained in CNC programming as well as the traditional machinist's curriculum.

22. The DGB (Germany's Central Trade Union Confederation) adopted the thirty-five-hour work week as official union policy in 1977. The concept is a response to the modern production technologies that improve productivity but require fewer employees. The idea is that a shorter work week would cause a sharing of the economy's jobs, since employers would need to have more workers to cover the gap. The total weekly paychecks, however, are to remain the same, which means that employment costs would rise. According to the DGB, these additional costs would be paid from the additional profits achieved through the more efficient, less labor-intensive production technology.

Even though the DGB made the thirty-five-hour week official policy in 1977, it was not until 1987 that it received unanimous support. It had originally been adopted over the objections of several unions because of a push by IG Metall. During the following ten years, two camps rose up around the issue: IG Metall, the Print and Paper Workers' Union (IG Druck and Papier), and a cluster of other unions in favor of the shorter work week versus the Chemical Workers' Union (IG Chemie), the Construction Workers' Union (IG Bau-Steine-Erden), and a cluster of other unions who wanted to deal with national unemployment through early-retirement plans. The debate was resolved last year when the early-retirement camp conceded that although the employers are paying for early retirements, there is no reason for them to hire replacements. In contrast, the shorter-week approach increases the actual manning necessary for production.

Not surprisingly, industry has been the strongest opponent of the thirty-five-hour week. In 1954, it had been willing to shorten the work week down from forty-four hours to forty, but that was during the postwar *Wirtschaftswunder* ("Economic Miracle") when the German GNP had been growing at a real annual rate of 7–10 percent. In the late 1970's, with the economy slowed down, industry made a shorter worker week the basic issue that could not be negotiated. It came out during the 1979 steelworkers' strike over a shorter week that the Federal Confederation of Employers' Associations (Bundesvereinigung der Deutschen Arbeitgebervergande—BDA) was orchestrating resistance to any negotiations over a less-than-forty-hour week by making it the basic issue in what was called the *Tabu Catalog* ("Taboo Catalog")—a "secret" handbook of negotiating dos and don'ts passed to each of the individual employers' associations.

The first major breakthrough for the thirty-five-hour week came when IG Metall struck over the issue and won a 38.5-hour week in 1985. This was followed by the 1987 IG Metall auto, machinery, and electronics contract for a further decrease to thirty-seven hours, which is to be carried out in two steps over three years. The separate negotiations in the steel industry in early 1988 have gone one step further, with an agreement for a 36.5-hour week. IG Metall intends to move down to thirty-five hours as part of the 1990 contract.

During the 1987 negotiations, IG Metall asserted that 80,000–100,000 jobs had been maintained or created through the 38.5-hour week. This is a controversial issue that has been contested by business and conservative government leaders. These opponents of the thirty-five-hour week say that the shorter work week will actually cause unemployment in the long run by making German goods noncompetitive due to high labor costs and forcing German employers to rationalize even more jobs through automation. During IG Metall's 1985 strike, Chancellor Kohl went so far as to call the thirty-five-hour week "idiotic, stupid, and foolish" *("blödsinnig, dumm, und töricht")*.

23. One enters almost every job in West Germany (with the exception of teaching) through the apprenticeship *(Lehre)* system, unless it's the type of job that in the United States would require an American master's degree in the humanities or a bachelor's degree in the natural sciences. In total, about 60–70 percent of German students go into apprenticeship programs.

West Germany has three separate kinds of schools from the time a student is ten years old. Each of the three schools is geared toward different career tracks that a student is expected to take in the future. Hauptschule is the school for those going into basic apprenticeships at age sixteen. Realschule is for those who will go into more "advanced" apprenticeships at age sixteen and perhaps into technical college thereafter. (Zebbities was in the Realschule.) Gymnasium was previously for those students going directly into a university or technical college, but now it is also attended by many of those going into the most advanced nonindustrial apprenticeships. Gymnasium students are usually eighteen or nineteen by the time they successfully complete the *Arbitur*—a difficult set of written exams required for graduation.

The German school system, like many other government programs, varies considerably between the *Lander* ("states"). Although the three kinds of schools have traditionally been kept separate, there has been movement in some of the Lander toward the Gesamtschule ("united school"), where the three kinds of schools are combined under one roof—somewhat like a U.S. high school with an intensive vocational department and honors program. This approach is being pushed most in the regions where the Social Democrats are in power. A trend throughout West Germany is the upward shifting of educational expectations. Hauptschule, which used to be considered a solid education, is now seen as a bit remedial. Realschule, which used to be considered as an advanced education, is now seen as standard. And Gymnasium is continually more popular for people who want the high-level business positions for which the *Arbitur* is a prerequisite for entering apprenticeship.

Along with the advantages of the German training and education system, there are certain disadvantages. Ten-year-olds are separated and tracked toward a career type. There are ways to switch between schools or to requalify for entering an apprenticeship, but they are not generally taken. Fifteen-year-olds are put in the position of deciding their long-term career path. Those who can't enter the apprenticeship system because they had poor grades when they were thirteen to fifteen may stay in the category of *Hilfsarbeiter* ("helper") for the rest of their lives, since one can only enter more skilled jobs with certification from an apprenticeship. There is increasing social prejudice and status consciousness on the basis of one's qualifications.

Nevertheless, it is clear that the apprenticeship program plays a crucial role in providing Germany with a skilled work force.

24. Because of the low dollar, U.S. machine-tool production and exports are up significantly in 1988 over 1987, but production will still be at less than half the German rate. With a few noticeable exceptions, most inquiries are price-based. A similar phenomenon occurred in 1978–80, when a low dollar temporarily allowed U.S. companies to increase exports of unsophisticated price-sensitive machine tools. In the long run, the U.S. industry will have to increase the sophistication of its products and establish sustained positions in world markets to achieve major export growth. Opportunistic price-driven sales of unsophisticated products will eventually lose out to competition from low-wage countries such as Taiwan and South Korea.

25. *Maschineenausfuhr der BR Deutschland,* published annually by the Verband Deutschen Maschinen und Anagenbau e.v. (VDMA).

26. Sweden has taken over $100 million of German machine-tool exports each year for the past few years, for example.

27. The overriding reason behind the differences in job turnover for machinists in 1969 and 1987 was the different economic circumstances. Germany in 1969 was experiencing the *Wirtschaftwunder,* with a 7.9 percent real GNP growth and a 0.9 percent unemployment. In March 1988, Germany had 9.6 percent unemployment, and the city of Mönchengladbach had 10.6 percent unemployment.

It can be said, however, that Scharmann's training program attracts good candidates. Fifteen-year-olds (or at least their parents) are most interested in finding apprenticeships where the training has a reputation for high quality. This can be judged from a publicly available record of the percentage of each firm's apprentices who pass the final exam. Another issue is whether the apprentices get hired when the training is over, since no employer has an obligation to do this. Scharmann has a good reputation in both areas, and in this sense is sought after.

Another important factor in the low turnover rate of trained employees is that they have good benefits and job security where they are. When a person isn't worried about losing his job, he doesn't have to spend his time "keeping options open." A number of managers in Germany have also told me that they'd look down on a fellow manager who tried to jockey his career between firms. He might be successful for a few years, but sooner or later he'd be recognized as a wheeler-dealer type, a *"Karriere Vogel,"* which directly translated means "career bird." Germany also doesn't have the "headhunter" phenomenon of job brokers calling up to lure skilled employees away to other firms.

28. Union members account for approximately 40 percent of the German work force. This is a decline from the 1950's, when the figure was approximately 45 percent, but an increase from 1969–70, when the figure dropped to around 35 percent. Total DGB membership as of December 31, 1986, was 7.768 million.

German unions and courts interpret the right of association in Germany's basic law *(Grundesetz)* to mean that union membership must be voluntary (i.e., no closed shop). The pressure to join the union comes from one's fellow workers, since it is understood in the metal industries, for instance, that IG Metall is responsible for the wage and condition gains that are received by union and nonunion workers alike. Anyone who does not join gets labeled a *Trittbrett Fahrer*, which refers to someone who used to ride on the stairs of a streetcar (before the days of automatic fold-up stairs) without actually coming inside and paying the fare.

German labor acts within a two-tier legal structure that does not exist in the United States: The Works Council at the plant level, and worker co-determination on the supervisory board at the firm level.

The Works Council *(Betriebsrat)* at the plant level is comprised of employees and given the right by the Works Constitution Act *(Betriebsverfassungsgesetz)* of 1972 (and previously 1952) to co-determine with management all matters concerning the structuring, organization, and design of jobs, operations, the working environment, manpower planning, and personnel management, as well as in-plant training. In firms with several plants, a United Works Council *(Gesamtbetriebsrat)* is also formed at the firm level to carry out the same functions for the firm as a whole.

The Works Council must be consulted on any firings, and has the right to call for and then negotiate a Social Compensation Plan *(Sozialplan)*, paid for by the employer (with varying degrees of assistance from the government) whenever significant layoffs occur.

The Works Council members are elected directly by the employees, and are released from their jobs without a loss of pay to serve their Works Council functions. Since the position requires substantial knowledge of labor law and corporate finance, council members are also released without a loss of pay for specialized training—often subsidized by the employer. Furthermore, depending on the number of workers being represented, a certain number of Works Council members are released from their jobs to conduct their Works Council duties full time (e.g., in a plant with 1,000–2,000 employees, the number of full-time Works Council members would be 3). Apprentices also have a nonvoting advisory role in the Works Council through their elected representatives *(Jugendvertreter)*.

Works Councils were first enacted through German law by Germany's Weimar government in 1920, under pressure from a Worker Council movement and mass strikes in 1919. Since the Works Council is essential to the running of plant operations but independent from the direct control of union officials, it serves to keep the unions responsive to the employees on the shop floor. An indication of its effectiveness in this regard is that IG Metall sometimes has a difficult time "getting its way" when it tries to implement its policies within the plants, since an idea will not be accepted until it has Works Council support.

IG Metall criticizes the Works Constitution Law to the extent that it works in the employer's interest by enabling the employer to bypass IG Metall and negotiate with the Works Council. For example, IG Metall fights against overtime because it decreases industrywide employment by allowing employers to avoid hiring and then training additional full-time, benefit-receiving workers.

The employees on the shop floor, however, will often favor overtime, because it means more money in their paychecks. Since the Works Council will make the day-to-day decisions about overtime, the fact that it is under pressure from its constituents on the shop floor will work to the employer's advantage.

Co-determination *(Mitbestimmung)* by employee representatives on the supervisory boards (similar to boards of directors in the United States) in firms with over two thousand employees is a second means of worker power-sharing in Germany.

A typical firm of between two thousand and ten thousand employees will consist of six employee representatives and six shareholder representatives. In practice, this means that the shareholders and management will retain a majority, since the employee representatives must include one representative from the managerial staff. The other employee representatives include (in this example of a twelve-member board) at least one representative from the salaried employees, one representative from the wage employees, and two trade-union representatives. The remaining representative will come from whichever group—management, salaried or wage employees—is the most numerous. (This almost always means the wage-earning employees in such a large firm. Of the 3.6 million employees who voted in the metal industry Works Council elections, for instance, roughly two thirds were wage-earning employees.)

The election of shareholder representatives is conducted at the firm's annual meeting. Elections of the employee representatives are conducted in four separate votes corresponding to the representation outlined above: 1) wage employees elect their representative(s); 2) salaried employees, including management, elect their representative; 3) management elects its representative (who by law cannot be a member of the executive management board *(Vorstand)* due to the legal separation between the management board and the supervisory board); and 4) all employees elect the trade-union representatives.

The chairperson of the supervisory board is elected by a two-thirds majority. This chairperson is given the right to cast the deciding vote in the case of a tie. As the above election procedures show, the shareholders and the management clearly have the decision-making majority.

A stronger form of co-determination functions in the coal and steel industry. Under this system, the management/shareholders' voting power and the employees' voting power are equal. However, the chairman, who traditionally comes from the employer side of the board, has the deciding vote in the case of a tie.

Furthermore, the personnel director *(Arbeitsdirektor)*, who serves as a member of the management board, is nominated by the employee representatives and is himself a union member. This is especially significant given the capacity reductions in coal and steel, since it is the personnel director, along with the Works Council, who develops the parameters of the Social Compensation Plan before a pit or plant is closed. On the whole, however, the importance of this co-determination system is decreasing substantially because it only covers a few large companies, and even these have been able to alter their conglomerate structure so that their nonsteel divisions are covered by the standard co-determination system described above.

The principle of co-determination was fostered in the British-occupied industrial Ruhr region in part because of the British Labor government's interest in the concept. Furthermore, the industrialists in the Ruhr region were on the defensive about their role in the war, and were anxious to work together with the unions to avoid being dismantled by the Allied powers. The position of industry leaders became more secure, however, once the British and American zones were joined in 1947 and the Americans replaced the British as the dominant influence. American policy put a priority on preparing West Germany for the Cold War, and relaxed the pressure to remove former Nazis from power or to reorganize German industry. This change from the British to the American interests also helped shift the center of German political debate toward the "free market," which had the effect of undercutting the strength of the German unions.

Co-determination at the firm level was enacted into law for the coal and steel industry by the Allies in 1947 and then by the new German government in 1952, but it was never extended to the rest of the German economy. Instead, a one-third-employee co-determination system was adopted for companies over five hundred employees, which was modified in 1976 to the partial co-determination system currently in use. Co-determination was achieved to a greater extent by the legal creation of Works Councils through the 1952 Works Constitution Law, although the labor movement was disappointed that the law drew the councils away from the union and toward the firm. At the level of government planning, the union goal of state planning agencies never materialized. Nevertheless, the DGB does have a significant role in the governing boards and committees for social insurance and other social programs, as well as state-run enterprises (e.g., the post office and telephone system, the railroad).

Basic collective-bargaining agreements are made by the unions and the employers' associations at the industry level. Each industry's employers' association and union is divided into geographic regions (typically twelve), which negotiate separately. The practical details of these agreements, which have usually covered wages annually and conditions and job classifications triannually, are then interpreted by the Works Councils.

German collective-bargaining law binds the employers within the employers' association and the union members they employ to follow the industry contract. Although only around 40 percent of all German workers are unionized, 90 percent of German workers end up being covered by these union contracts. This is accounted for by the fact that 80 percent of all employers belong to employers' associations, and if they gave their nonunion employees anything below the union contract, they would simply be pushing these employees to join the union.

There is an unwritten law upheld by unions and employers against labor conflicts during the life of a contract. This concept is called *Friedenspflict* ("peace obligation"), and is considered a main factor in the relatively few strikes in West Germany. Furthermore, even though there are no federal laws governing how unions must arrange strike votes after a failed contract negotiation, most unions have self-imposed bylaws requiring a 75 percent approval from membership within the given bargaining district. Once a strike or lockout begins, however, federal law strictly governs the way it must proceed.

Chapter 5

1. Sweden's investment as a percentage of GNP actually was slightly higher in the first half of the 1970's than in the 1960's, but productivity and export growth in the first half of the 1970's were less than half the rate of the 1960's.

2. The tools we were developing to analyze the structural evolution of an economy were based on the corporate-strategy audit. It is typical for a corporate-strategy consulting firm to go into a conglomerate and spend a few days looking at the strength of the company's various businesses in a cursory way to construct a portfolio based on business size, market growth, and competitive position. This is then used diagnostically to decide what areas are most important, which require the most attention in a study, and which will be users and generators of cash. A complete business strategy cannot be developed on the basis of an audit, but key leverage points for management study and action can be identified.

A national economy like Sweden's is really a collection of individual businesses. For an economy to prosper, it must have a competitive advantage based on productivity or price in a large number of its businesses. This advantage allows a higher value added per hour of work in the economy, which translates to a higher living standard. This higher value can be achieved either by improving productivity or price within existing industries or by shifting industrial structure toward activities that allow higher productivity or price.

In a small country, there are usually a few hundred businesses that comprise a significant share of the economy exposed to world trade. It is often possible to audit competitive position in these, and thereby to evaluate the structural strengths and weaknesses of an economy. It is also possible to categorize other businesses in the economy according to surrogate measures such as average wage, growth, value added per employee, skill levels, etc., to allow generalizations for policy purposes.

Key to the strategic appraisal is to make evaluations at the level of a business, not an industry. Since no public data is organized that way, a detailed interview process is necessary to conduct a strategic economic audit. The data I used in my initial meetings with Volvo and the Swedish Ministry of Industry was from public sources, but showed conceptually the type of analysis we would do.

3. In 1987, Sweden exported Skr 281 billion and imported Skr 252 billion. Sweden's GNP per capita in 1988 stands at 3 percent higher than that of the United States, and its government accounts were roughly in balance.

4. In 1987, Volvo sold 106,539 cars in the United States; Mercedes sold 89,918; BMW sold 87,839; Audi sold 41,322; Renault sold 13,991; and Peugeot sold 9,419. In total, Volvo produced 400,000 cars; Mercedes produced 540,000; BMW 430,000; and Peugeot and Renault about 1.6 million autos.

5. The Uddevalla shipyard received funds in 1972; Götaverken in 1972, 1976, and again in 1977; the NJA Steel Company received funds in 1971, 1972, 1973, 1974, and 1977. The government was approached in 1977 for assistance by at least five forestry companies, three specialty-steel companies, the LKAB

iron-ore mining company, and five shipbuilding companies. The state subsidies took the form of equity infusions in state-owned companies, special grants, and low-interest loans, and loan guarantees.

6. Target wage increases are negotiated centrally in Sweden, with specific negotiations carried out within these general guidelines by specific companies and their unions. The 40 percent figure is a rough estimate of actual final negotiations that we received during our study from the SAF, the Swedish Employees Federation.

7. Passenger-car production fell from 29,984,208 in 1973 to 24,958,731 in 1975. Demand dropped even further, as 1975 was a year of significant inventory building.

8. The idea was a good one. For decades, companies would cut back production and investment during recessions, only to be caught short and lose opportunities for sales and growth when the boom eventually came. For workers, periods of no work alternated with periods of overtime. The idea was to flatten out the cycle of building inventories during the recession that would be ready for sale when the recovery came. Instead of paying companies to keep unneeded workers or paying unemployment compensation to the laid-off workers, the government helped finance the inventories. In addition to promoting stability, the Swedes thought it would enable them to gain market share when the recovery came, since they would have products in inventory while competitors would be caught short.

Unfortunately, the Swedes picked the wrong recession to try out their ideas. The oil-crisis-induced downturn was longer-lived than usual, and structural changes in the world economy meant that even after the recovery came in world demand, many Swedish companies were no longer competitive in their traditional products. The policy wound up leaving many companies short of cash, and postponed the nation's awareness of structural economic problems by making it seem as if there were no economic problems in 1974 and 1975.

9. The Swedish krona went from 5.5 to the U.S. dollar in 1973 to 4.8 in 1976. For periods during 1977 and 1978, it strengthened even further, to 4.2.

10. The direct costs of mining iron ore in Sweden were more than four times those in Australia, despite the high degree of automation in the Swedish mines. In addition, the Australian and Brazilian mines were more than twice the size of the largest Swedish ones, allowing a better spreading of overheads. The Swedish ore was magnetic, which meant it was easier to separate, but separation was not a major cost element. The Swedish ore also was high in phosphorous, which meant that it had to be discounted in many markets.

There were a few segments in which Sweden could remain competitive. Within the Baltic area, Sweden's cost disadvantage was minimal, since large, oceangoing supertankers had to unload the ore onto smaller ships, incurring significant extra cost. The Swedish ore, being magnetic, could be purified to 72 percent and was thus well suited for direct reduction applications. Swedish pelletizing technology was also advanced, though this advantage, we felt, might eventually disappear.

The iron-ore industry in Sweden would not disappear, but we felt it could eventually shrink.

11. The Koreans entered the shipbuilding industry in the early 1970's, and quickly built up their productivity. By 1975, they had easily surpassed the outmoded British shipyards, and were approaching the levels of German yards, which, unlike their Swedish counterparts, had not invested heavily. (See Exhibits 1 & 2, below).

Exhibit 1

SHIPBUILDING PRODUCTIVITY, 1967–1976

Output per
Man-Hour
(Compensated
Tons)

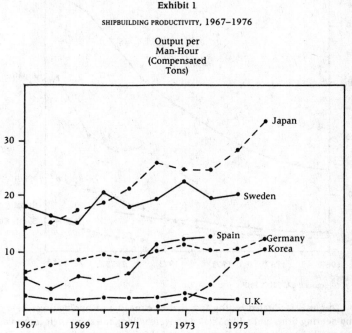

Sources: Industri, Sweden, Ministry of Transport, Japan, Department of Employment, U.K., Statistisches Bundesamt, Germany, Instituto Nacional de Estadistica, Spain, Gotaverken

12. Sweden was caught by the same trends I had seen in 1973. Developing countries had increased their share of world steel production dramatically. Whereas developing countries made up 11 percent of non-Comecon world commodity-steel production in 1966 and 13 percent in 1974, by the early 1980's, they represented over 22 percent of world commodity-steel production.

The movement of developing countries into world steel trade was precipitated by the fact that steel was perceived as essential to industrialization by many developing countries, on a par with basic infrastructure such as utilities, roads, and communications.

As a result, precious capital and foreign exchange were used to purchase steel mills. In almost all cases, steel mills were publicly owned or funded in significant degree by governments.

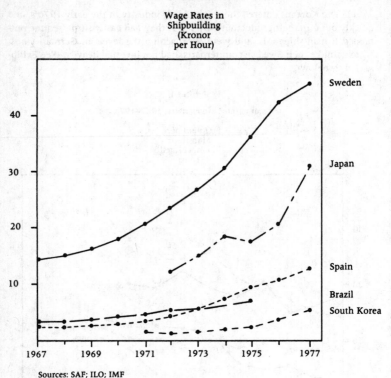

Exhibit 2

WAGE RATES IN SHIPBUILDING

Wage Rates in
Shipbuilding
(Kronor
per Hour)

Sources: SAF; ILO; IMF

This was facilitated by the fact that steelmaking technology was held by engineering firms and millmakers who were willing to export their technology and machinery. Japanese, European, and U.S. engineering firms provided the technology for numerous mills being built in developing countries.

Once developing countries entered the commodity-steel business, their operating costs were usually competitive with those of European and North American mills. In steelmaking, scale, plant layout, and level of technology were the key determinants of competitive productivity. Newer plants tended to be more productive on a purely operating-productivity basis than older ones. The mills purchased by developing countries typically incorporated the most up-to-date technology and were of a scale (3–6 million tons per annum) to be competitive with most European and U.S. plants (though Japanese plants still tended to be considerably larger, 10–15 million tons per annum).

Overall, the output per man-hour at many developing-country mills were not quite as good as in the United States and West Germany, but given their lower wage rates, the developing countries' productivity was sufficient to give them an overall labor cost advantage.

	1977 LABOR COST (KRONOR PER HOUR)	MAN-HOURS PER TON SHIPPED*
United States	56.5	10
West Germany	48.9	12
Brazil	7.0	19
South Korea	4.0	17

*In peak year of production: 1974 for the U.S. and Germany, 1977 for Korea and Brazil.

Sources: American Iron and Steel Institute; Korean EDB; Brazilian State Planning Board; Steel companies.

But because developing countries considered steel as part of general industrialization and because of the government role, these mills were rarely evaluated on a return-on-investment basis. Foreign currency to recoup the import of all of the capital equipment required for the mill was usually considered as more important than profits in won or cruzeiros. Even in times of world-demand recession, it was more acceptable to cut price than to leave the new national steel mill partially idle.

This was not to say that all steel products would be affected or that no barriers existed to this competition. Some steel businesses are potentially sheltered by their transport, value, and distribution characteristics. For example, steel reinforcing bars can be defensible due to their relatively low value and the small size of the average customer purchase; in the American reinforcing-bar business, regional minimills in the southern part of the country have been able to compete successfully against large, fully integrated mills in the North. Certain general bar products can be protected by the variety of product grades and customers.

Sweden's mills were small by world and even European standards. While some rolling mills were competitive in technology and scale, the blast furnace, steelmaking, and plant sizes were subscale. The plants tended to have awkward materials flows, sometimes requiring intershipments among plants. The Swedish industry had an additional disadvantage in raw materials, due to the lack of deepwater ports and the relatively high cost of Swedish iron ore compared to that of Brazil and Australia.

Moreover, Sweden's customer/product focus was suboptimal. Exports of steel had long been oriented toward shipbuilding markets in Europe. The Swedish industry was unable to supply the flat-rolled grades required by the domestic automobile industry.

Despite these difficulties, we believed that Sweden could continue economic steel production, particularly for the home market. With appropriate marketing and finishing investments to create defensible segments, and with a rationalization of the industry, it would be possible to preserve much of the industry's employment. Some decline, however, was inevitable.

Sweden's steel industry was unique in having a high proportion of its total production in special steels, including high-carbon, alloy, stainless, tool, and high-speed steels. These steels were traditionally made in small-batch electric-furnace processes. In the late 1960's, the Japanese began to introduce higher-scale production processes for stainless and high-carbon flat-rolled products.

These large mills changed the nature of these businesses, making scale a key requirement for a low-cost position.

Specialty steels seemed to promise higher growth, greater profitability, and greater defensibility against developing countries than did commodity steel. During the 1970's, most European countries (including France, West Germany, and the United Kingdom) and many American producers, as well as the Japanese, expanded their specialty-steels production very rapidly.

In recent years, Sweden's production in special steels had been growing more slowly than that of major competitors in Japan and West Germany. (See Exhibit 3, below.)

Exhibit 3

STAINLESS STEEL PRODUCTION GROWTH

(Index)

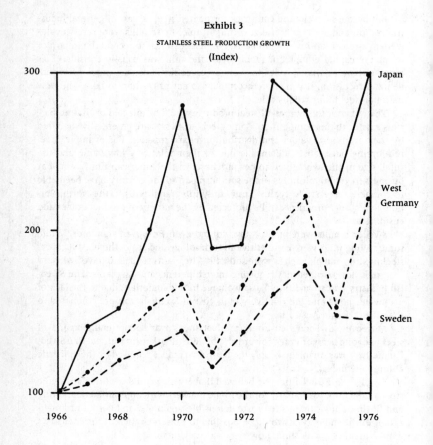

Sweden maintained productivity advantages in high-speed steel and some tool steels where it had large world-scale and significant customers within Sweden (for rock drills and saw blades, etc.), and where world volumes were not great enough to attract large stainless and alloy producers. In addition, certain products within stainless, high-carbon, and alloy steels were not as amenable to large-scale production because of the variety of grades.

For these products, run length could be a significant element in competitive productivity. Therefore, the existence of a number of mills that in some cases duplicated product made the Swedish industry less efficient than it could have been.

Nevertheless, because of its technical know-how in production, selling, and applications engineering, Sweden's specialty-steels industry remained competitive in many of these products.

For these reasons, we indicated that if the specialty-steels industry rationalized in the near future, it need not contract as much as commodity steels, despite the lower proportion of potentially sheltered businesses in this industry and despite its dependence on exports. This in fact occurred.

13. Competitive productivity in forest-products industries begins with the cost of wood. Wood costs are primarily a function of the annual growth increment of the tree, which yields benefits in cutting, short transport, and silviculture; the diameter of the tree, which affects cutting and short transport; and the terrain, which affects the methods that can be used for cutting and haulage.

Historically, Sweden's main competitors in the European market for pulp and commodity papers were the other Nordic countries and the northeastern United States and Canada. In terms of growing cycle, diameter, and terrain, Sweden's forests were competitive, and Sweden developed technology that allowed its industry to be more productive in cutting and transport. These advantages even allowed Sweden to ship pulp to U.S. markets.

The forest industry has moved increasingly toward the southern states in the United States and toward British Columbia in Canada. As a result, Sweden's competitive position has deteriorated.

For a long time, this deterioration was hidden from the Swedish industry as the dollar remained at artificially high levels. It was not until the dollar devaluations in 1971 and 1973 that the full extent of Sweden's disadvantage became apparent to the industry.

Swedish trees have an average growing cycle of about eighty-five years, compared to twenty-five to thirty years in the southern United States and sixty-five years in British Columbia. The average diameter of pulpwood cut in Sweden is less than in the southern United States, which in turn is less than in British Columbia. Both Sweden and Canada suffer a disadvantage relative to the southern United States in terrain; in Sweden, the rocky terrain hinders cutting and transport; in British Columbia, the mountainous terrain makes infrastructure costs high.

In sum, the cost of wood delivered to the pulp mill in Sweden was significantly higher: about 170 kronor per ton, compared to 80 in the southern United States and 90 for British Columbia.

Wage rates in this industry were higher in Sweden than in the United

States, as well; furthermore, wood owners' rents were higher in Sweden than in either competitor country. But even if these differences were removed, Sweden's industry still suffered a significant cost disadvantage.

While Sweden was at the limit of its renewable production capacity, forests in the southern United States and western Canada still had room for expansion. In addition, massive new sources of wood were being opened up in Latin America (primarily Brazil), West Africa, and Asia (primarily Malaysia and the Philippines). These forests could be extremely productive, since they were composed of fast-growing, large-diameter trees. Moreover, the wage rates and rents paid for their development were significantly lower than in Sweden. Infrastructure costs were often publicly funded.

Brazil, for example, in 1974 represented only 2 percent of pulp production in the world. But Brazil was building over 12 percent of all plants then under construction, and a much larger proportion of those that represented actual capacity additions, since many of the North American and European plants were replacements of old mills. The estimated costs of wood at the pulp mill in Brazil range from forty to sixty kronor per ton, significantly less than in even the southern United States.

Two other factors are important in determining overall competitive cost position in the making of pulp and paper: the manufacturing process costs and the transport to market.

Manufacturing costs in pulp and papermaking are heavily dependent on the scale of the mills and the type of technology used. In these respects, Sweden was competitive with the United States and Canada. Sweden's paper mills and its pulp mills that produced for export were only slightly smaller and older on average than those in the United States and Canada. Sweden did enjoy a significant cost savings on transportation to European markets, averaging some 160 kronor per ton.

Thus, the major source of Sweden's disadvantage was wood cost; the major source of advantage was transportation cost; processing costs were roughly comparable.

As a result, Sweden's competitive position differed significantly among forest end products. In pulp and paper grades that had a high wood content per ton of finished product, Sweden was at a net disadvantage; those with lower wood per ton of final product offered a better opportunity. In chemical pulps and kraft papers, Sweden tended to be less competitive.

Sweden's forest-products industry was under severe competitive pressure. Almost 80 percent of Sweden's pulp exports were in chemical pulps, and over 40 percent of its paper exports were in kraft paper. The problems would persist, since they resulted from the continuing shift to more economic sources for the European pulp and paper markets. Sweden's high wood cost meant that it was a marginal producer in some of these products.

Individual companies with an appropriate product mix or strong distribution structure or those who owned hydroelectric power or forests could remain profitable, but these represented a limited part of the industry. When there was a severe shortage in the business, as in 1974, the industry as a whole could be profitable, but on trend its performance was not likely to be satisfactory.

Forest Products Segmentation Hypothesis

	Wood Usage (Cubic Meters per Ton)	Cost Disadvantage to North America in European Market (Kronor per Ton)		
		Wood	Transport	Total
Less Defensible				
Bleached Sulfate Pulp	5.2	522	(162)	360
Kraft Paper	5.1	432	(176)	256
Kraft Liner	4.4	441	(171)	270
More Defensible				
Newsprint	3.1	99	(86)	13
Sawed Timber	2.0	63	(162)	(99)
Coated Paper	2.0	63	(171)	(108)

Source: BCG analysis

Sweden was competitive in certain paper grades, but a large-scale shift of activity into these areas could be difficult. In many of these products, the prime competitors would be European paper companies, and there were distribution barriers and trade barriers that limited Sweden's volume potential. Similarly, while research and development produced new grades of specialty papers in which Sweden could be competitive long term, such opportunities could not replace all of the uncompetitive tonnage.

Overall, we believed that Sweden's forest industry could be profitable by shifting its mix and by rationalization, but we did not believe it could provide Sweden with a growth in exports.

14. Sweden had many companies with potential for growth. We listed twenty-eight in the engineering and chemical sectors as examples. "The list" became a source of public debate, with companies not on the list complaining that we had overlooked them. In fact, as it turned out, the companies on this list did indeed provide 80 percent of Sweden's export growth in the 1980's.

COMPANY	Percent of Total Eng. & Chemical Exports	Percent of Total Eng. & Chemical Employment
AGA	.3%	1.4%
Alfa Laval	3.3	1.5
ASEA	10.3	7.6
Astra	1.5	.7
Atlas Copco	2.4	1.3
Bacho	.3	.7
Berol Kemi	1.8	.3
Bofors	1.4	.4
Boliden Kemi	.5	.3
Bulten Kanthal	.7	.9
Datasaab	.7	.6
Electrolux	3.6	5.2
L. M. Ericsson	6.3	6.0
Husqvarna	1.5	1.2
KMW/KAMYR	2.2	.5
Kabi	.5	.4
Kema Nobel plus Supra and Unifos	1.3	1.5
Kockums (machinery)	.9	.3

COMPANY	Percent of Total Eng. & Chemical Exports	Percent of Total Eng. & Chemical Employment
Perstorp	1.0	.6
Pharmacia	.7	.3
Saab-Scania	7.2	7.0
Sandvik	5.2	2.3
SKF	2.7	2.5
SMT-Pullmax	.3	.2
Svenska Flakt	1.4	.9
Swedish Match (machinery)	.5	.1
Tetra Pak	.5	.3
Volvo	17.6	9.6
	76.6%	54.6%

Sectors: Metalworking, Mechanical and Electrical Engineering, Transport Equipment, Chemicals and Pharmaceuticals.

Sources: Annual reports; SCB; BCG analysis

15. In 1980, the Swedish trade balance (with imports on a CIF basis dipped to negative Skr 11 billion. During the late seventies, the trade balance had typically been about negative Skr 5 billion.

16. Volvo's car business lost money in the late 1970's, though if its profitable spare-parts business is included and its partial ownership in the DAF Company in Holland (which produces Volvo's 300 line) is excluded, it stayed about break-even during the period.

17. The accounting systems of most companies track direct costs of material and labor in excruciating detail, but allocate overheads—usually larger than direct costs—without much regard for where costs are truly incurred. As automation has reduced the direct costs of most products dramatically, these overheads have become much more important determinants of competitive cost differences among companies.

Correctly understanding how these costs differ among products is crucial to successful product development and pricing strategies. Volvo was one of the early companies to grasp this.

18. I was continually impressed during my work in Sweden with how knowledgeable Swedes were about world events. Swedish union leaders and rank-and-file workers had a grasp of international economic and business affairs that exceeded that of most U.S. business leaders I have met. Sweden's high level of education and its emphasis on training no doubt play a role. Also, Sweden's high living standard, which filters down to line workers, gives them the resources to travel abroad, which also contributes to this worldliness. Finally, the political debate in the country revolves around issues and tends to play an educational function.

Like most small countries, Sweden's economic debate can become insular and homogeneous, and can benefit from outside stimulation. But the Swedes realize this, and are constantly bringing in outsiders like ourselves to trigger debate. They are also consummate participants in international organizations to broaden their perspective.

19. This study, entitled *The Engineering Industries and Swedish Industrial Policy*, was co-sponsored by Sweden's Federation of Engineering Companies (Sveriges Mekanförbund) and Sweden's Metalworkers Union (Svenska Metallarbetareindustriförbundet). It provided four case studies of industries that could expand—materials-handling machinery, cutting tools, offshore engineering, and energy-generation equipment—and discussed impediments to their growth.

It then made more specific recommendations of what types of policies could promote growth in these sectors and in the engineering industries in general than had been possible in our first report. This report hit again at the money being wasted by the government on shipbuilding and other declining industries.

The report helped bring the industry association and union together, and they subsequently cooperated on a number of other projects. It reinforced the need for a change in government policies, and in so doing, was one more step in the consensus-building process.

20. The government had spent about Skr 19 billion (about $4 billion) in direct grants and equity infusions to support bankrupt companies from 1976 to 1980, with over half coming in 1979 and 1980. In addition, it had provided over Skr 27 billion (over $7 billion) in loan guarantees, mainly for the shipbuilding and steel companies, many of which had to be nationalized during the same period. These massive expenditures in a government budget already in serious deficit made support programs for growing industries and for R&D and training hard to fund adequately.

21. Most nations, including the United States, spend between 2 percent and 3 percent, including what is spent for defense.

22. Created in 1979 as an autonomous public foundation, the Industrifond provides loans for large industrial-development projects that have good prospects but that because of resource constraints or high risk might not otherwise be undertaken by a company. The fund may lend up to 50 percent of a project. The loans are conditional and may be written off if a project proves unsuccessful. The fund is paid back in various ways when a project is successful. Over the years, the fund has operated in the black and has stimulated many high-growth investments that might not otherwise have occurred.

23. The effective tax rate for most Swedish companies is close to zero. The Swedish government believes that taxing companies is not productive for the economy. It is far more important to have them invest to create wealth for the economy. The reserve funds ensure that a certain portion of a company's investments are made in ways that both company and government find useful. It is a very effective system, which encourages investment in the economy, enhances public purpose, yet gives Swedish companies a competitive advantage vis-à-vis foreign competitors that are taxed.

24. Sweden has one of the strongest training programs of any country in the world. Six percent to 7 percent of the government budget, which corresponds to 2.5 percent of GNP, is utilized for labor-market policy. This equals 5 billion U.S. dollars for a work force of 4.4 million people. Almost 70 percent of

the budget goes for active training and placement programs, and only 30 percent for unemployment benefits or handouts. In the United States, over 90 percent of the labor-market budget is for handouts.

The philosophy behind Sweden's efforts was expressed in a recent speech by Allan Larsson, director general of Sweden's Labor Market Boards (AMS).

> Changes caused by new technology, international trade and by the other factors always include the risk that individuals lose their jobs and become unemployed. Therefore the government has to make an important choice of strategy. The choice can be expressed in two questions:
>
> —will the market solve the problem and the government just pay handouts?
> —or do we need political measures to make the market operate so that unemployment can be reduced or prevented?
>
> This is a choice between a handout strategy and an employment strategy. Sweden has for many years given priority to the employment strategy. This means that jobs, training and other measures of vocational preparation have highest priority, while handouts—for example unemployment benefits—are only regarded as the last resort.
>
> There are both economic and social reasons for making such an effort. Work is an important part of a good society: Everybody who is willing and able to work should be given the chance to do so.
>
> Unemployment is a waste of resources, and most active measures already pay off in the short run in terms of government finances and are highly profitable in the long run.

The Swedish government runs a sophisticated national employment service to match workers and job openings. About 50 percent of new job openings are filled by this service in the country. But in a changing economy, many workers need counseling and training before they can be placed.

About 130,000 people, or about 3 percent of the work force, receive some sort of training paid for by the government each year. Most, about eighty thousand to one hundred thousand each year are trained at one of eighty AMU schools originally established by the government, but now run by a private, nonprofit board that has regional centers around the country. This board can be paid by AMS to train workers it has identified as needing help, or it can contract to local companies to carry out their training needs.

Making the AMU autonomous, decentralizing its organization and encouraging it to sell training to companies, are relatively recent changes.

The labor-market board (AMS) also provides incentives to stimulate the demand for labor where and when it is necessary. This program is most often used for teenagers, who are guaranteed at least a four-hour-a-day job, and for disabled persons. About 75 percent of the funds go for disabled workers to create employment alternatives instead of early retirement and other social programs. The incentives make their work economic for a company, give society the benefit of the productive capabilities they do have, and allow the people to live productive lives.

Overall, the beefing up of Sweden's traditionally strong labor-market and training policies probably played a bigger role in Sweden's restructuring than any other single factor, and understandably is the major contributor to its low unemployment rate.

25. An AMS employment office was established in Uddevalla a year before the shipyard closed. More than 30 placement officers and counselors were placed there to serve the 2,340 workers laid off.

About 75 percent of the workers were retrained and found new jobs, and about 25 percent retired. The training in automobile assembly for Volvo took fifty to sixty weeks per worker. In addition, AMU provided training in plastics molding (a forty-week course), electronics and computer technologies (fifty- to sixty-week courses), tele-electronics (fifty to sixty weeks), and a variety of other disciplines.

Training in some courses, such as small-business economics, took place in a nearby college. With government assistance and funds, forty-seven new companies were also formed.

26. Volvo's return on investment in cars in 1987 (despite the effect of the low dollar), was twice that for any U.S. company.

27. Sweden has 81 percent of its adults in the labor force, a bigger percentage than any other industrialized country (the United States is 74 percent). Of those in the labor force, less than 2 percent are unemployed in Sweden, a smaller percentage than that of any other developed country (the United States has averaged 6–7 percent).

Chapter 6

1. Recent estimates by the U.S. Department of Commerce are that between twenty-five thousand and thirty thousand U.S. firms are engaged in exports.

2. This figure is derived from a Telesis survey of Fortune 1,000 companies that identified the top two hundred exporters in the group, added up their total exports, and related them to total U.S. exports. If any non-Fortune 1,000 companies are bigger exporters, then U.S. exports are even more concentrated than this. Only manufactured goods and manufacturing companies were included in the survey.

3. This is derived from a Telesis study of the exports of the fifty largest companies in a variety of countries. To some extent, these differences are due to the size of the home market of each country. But this in itself would not account for the magnitude of the difference.

4. The Johnson and Nixon administrations were concerned about America's declining trade surplus, which eventually went negative in 1972. They established programs to help finance exports and to encourage small companies to export. Some, like the DISC program, provided monetary incentives, and oth-

ers, like the "E" awards, were to provide recognition to companies who made the effort.

5. Ireland's industrial-development schemes are among the most elaborate offered anywhere in the world. Ireland will provide capital grants that can reach 40–60 percent of the total capital cost for plant and equipment for a new facility. It will also provide grants for research and development and for training. Through tax-based leasing and interest subsidies, the Irish government will provide favorable financing for working capital, and often for the portion of fixed-asset investment that a company makes itself. The government normally imposes a 10 percent tax on corporate profits, but this can, in effect, be easily reduced to zero through various depreciation and tax-credit schemes.

These incentives, plus Ireland's membership in the EEC and the excellent marketing efforts of the Industrial Development Authority of Ireland, have resulted in hundreds of U.S. companies building plants in Ireland. Most of them do not ship product back to the United States like the plants in Singapore, but they do substitute for U.S. export.

6. Under the Domestic International Sales Corporation (DISC) Act of the Internal Revenue Code, certain domestic corporations that sold products on foreign markets were treated for tax purposes as if they were foreign corporations. The effect of these provisions was to allow deferral of federal income tax on the corporations' current income. Although deferral was normally limited to half of the profit attributable to the DISC, liberal pricing and costing regulations enabled companies to defer tax on more than 50 percent of their profits for foreign sales. By 1980, these tax deferrals were costing the government about $1.4 billion per year. DISC was eventually eliminated because there was no evidence that it really stimulated new exports as opposed to just rewarding companies that would have exported anyway.

7. Ireland's industrial policies had been very successful at bringing foreign companies to the country. The Irish government, industry associations, and unions were concerned about two issues, however: 1) Ireland's wages and income were still low, and the jobs being provided by the foreign companies might disappear if wages and income rose; 2) the industrial development programs were expensive, and Ireland's government budget deficit was large. For these reasons, they wanted an independent evaluation of Ireland's industrial-development programs and recommendations for changes of direction. They were aware of the Swedish study I had led a few years earlier, and therefore asked my new company, Telesis, to perform the study.

Overall, our findings were positive about Ireland's industrial policies, but we did recommend a refocus of resources into indigenous-industry development and the assistance of overseas marketing and a concomitant cutback on incentives to foreign companies providing only low-skill assembly jobs in the country.

Our report was controversial and triggered an even greater national debate than in Sweden, and eventually led to changes in Ireland's industrial-development policies.

Ireland's inability to face up to its macroeconomic problems, however, has hindered its overall economic progress. Good macroeconomic policies are not sufficient in today's competitive world without good industrial-development policies; but as Ireland has discovered, good industrial-development policies are not sufficient either, unless good macroeconomic policies are in place.

8. A major pitfall of most economic analyses of industrial development is a reliance on industry aggregate data to make projections. Thus, economists often speak of the whole electronics industry as high skill, high wage, and the whole textile industry as low skill, low wage. In fact, comparable parts of both of these industries are high skill. They are those parts with a high design content (whether fabric or computer architecture) or high potential for automation. Similarly, many textile and electronics assembly businesses are low skill.

The Telesis approach to analyzing an economy relies more heavily on a business-by-business analysis of key competitive variables. For example, a chemical business that involves making industrial cleaning compounds has more in common with the electronic-process-control industry than it does with a commodity-chemical business such as chlorine production. The key to competitive success in cleaning compounds and electronic-process control is the application of engineering-tailoring products efficiently to specific customer needs, whereas in bulk chemicals, manufacturing scale and cost is key, as it is in the production of some electronic components, such as resistors and capacitors.

Grouping together resistors and process-control systems as electronics, and cleaning compounds and chlorine as chemicals, is not helpful for analytic or policy purposes.

9. The provision of tax holidays, capital grants, training grants, R&D incentives, etc., has been a common feature of industrial-development policies around the world. The theory is to help fund investment that would not otherwise occur, and thereby to receive the ongoing economic benefits of industrial operation. These incentives are used in particular to attract multinational companies to locate in countries that are not yet fully industrialized, such as Ireland, Portugal, or Brazil, or to locate in depressed regions of industrialized countries such as Scotland, Wales, or Northern Ireland in Great Britain; or Berlin in West Germany; or the southern regions of Italy.

As a general rule, incentives by themselves are usually not enough to attract and retain most companies. But if the incentives are backed by good infrastructure: investment in education, roads, parts, airports, etc., they can make a difference.

Chapter 7

1. Japan's public and corporate funding for R&D has increased dramatically during the 1980's. Japanese companies spent about $19.8 billion in 1981 compared to $35.9 billion for U.S. companies, or about 55 percent of U.S. levels. By 1986, the last year for which figures have been calculated, Japanese companies were spending $41.6 billion compared to $58.2 billion for U.S. companies, or about 71 percent of U.S. levels. Telesis estimates that in 1988 Japanese com-

pany spending on R&D will be close to 90 percent of our levels, even though their economy is only half our size.

The U.S. government spends far more on R&D than the Japanese government, about $59 billion in 1986, compared to about $12 billion in Japan. But this is misleading. About 70 percent of the U.S. government funds are spent on defense R&D, an additional 12 percent on basic health-care research, and 16 percent for space exploration. The remaining $7 billion provides support for basic research primarily in areas as diverse as the environment, housing, and energy. Very little goes to support potentially commercial ventures. In Japan, about 80 percent of the R&D funding, or about $9 billion, goes to research and development in commercial areas.

In addition to R&D funds, Japanese government policies are far more aggressive in subsidizing prototype markets for new products either by purchasing the products directly, as in solar-power generation plants, or superconductive train systems, or by stimulating private purchases through tax incentives, as in machine tools, or through special leasing schemes, as in computers.

2. MITI is the most important institution in Japan's industrial policy-making process. Formed in 1949 by the combination of the Ministry of Commerce and Industry and the Board of Trade, it includes all but a few major industries in its jurisdiction. MITI is notable for the variety of roles it plays—broad policy architect, *ad hoc* working-level problem solver, formal regulator, regional-policy arbiter, and informal administrative guide. In some industries, it has a strong statutory authority.

Other ministries play roles similar to MITI's in some major industries. Telecommunications producers and Nippon Telephone and Telegraph Corporation are supervised by the Ministry of Post and Telecommunications. The Ministry of Transport oversees railway equipment producers and operating companies. Pharmaceuticals, one of Japan's developing industries, responds to the Ministry of Health and Welfare. These industrial ministries are in general more conservative and protective internationally of their constituents than MITI is today.

But MITI's influence is pervasive in shaping overall Japanese industrial policy. The ministry has been assigned responsibility for:

- shaping the structure of industry and adjusting dislocations that arise in transition
- guiding the healthy development of industries and their production and distribution activities
- managing Japan's foreign trade and its commercial relations
- ensuring adequate raw materials and energy flows to industry
- managing particular areas such as small business, patents, industrial technology, etc.

The breadth of this charter, in both function and spirit, gives MITI a comprehensive perspective across industries and policy areas.

MITI has responsibility for developing industries as well as regulating their excesses. Difficult trade-offs are made, and various policies integrated informally within one ministry culture. Thus, it considers the whole range of potential government measures—tax, antitrust, special lending, price and capacity controls, export and import measures, environmental regulations, raw-material price-setting and procurement, technology subsidy, dislocation subsidy, regional policy—that influence an industrial sector's performance and its effect on other sectors.

MITI does not employ all these tools in every industry, nor does it act independently of other agencies. In fact, the treatment of various industries differs enormously; many experience little or no special "policy intervention" for long periods, while a few (like petroleum refining and computers) are highly coordinated or subsidized. Moreover, MITI is neither autonomous in determining policy nor can it directly finance its own program. The Fair Trade Commission limits MITI's structural initiatives, the Diet and Prime Minister's Office circumscribe MITI politically, and MOF passes judgment on its budgets. Nevertheless, MITI remains the focal point in industrial-policy determination, lending it continuity and consistency. There is no pretension of zero-base budgeting, no sudden upheavals after elections. Policy changes are usually a long time coming (which is sometimes a weakness) but well rooted when they emerge.

Much of the leverage MITI and other agencies exert over industry stems from the pervasive practice of administrative guidance. Administrative guidance occurs when government officials guide industries and firms in desired directions by informal means, and without statutory authority. Ministries justify the practice by invoking the broad statutory mandate of laws under which they were established, which call on the ministries to promote, regulate, and guide those industries under their jurisdiction. Japanese academic thinking leans toward the view that specific statutory authority is not required for administrative guidance. Ministerial officials summon representatives of a firm, an industry, or the industry association to their offices and express their wishes or expectations. These may be expressed in the form of a request, a recommendation, or, occasionally, an admonition. Compliance is technically voluntary, but the officials do not hesitate to use the various carrots and sticks available to them—which are often totally unrelated to the issue at hand—to assert their will.

Administrative guidance is a fundamental part of the government-business relationship in Japan. Businessmen generally understand that in the long term it is in their best interest, even though on particular occasions the issue being pressed by the ministry is an unpopular one. MITI, for example, will suggest that a company participate in an unappealing foreign-investment project or delay a capacity addition to accomplish a broader end. Firms vary in their rate and spirit of compliance, but all regard administrative guidance as justifiable and part of the price business pays for the valuable services of an economic bureaucracy that in general guides the economy well.

MITI's structure is well suited to its broad policy role. The Minister's Secretariat and four bureaus—Industrial Policy, International Trade Policy, International Trade Administration, and Industrial Location and Environmental Protection—develop and coordinate policy across industries. Three bureaus—Basic Industries (steel, chemicals, fertilizer, etc.), Machinery and Information Industries, and Consumer Products Industries—develop programs, implement general policy, and solve problems at the individual-industry level. Finally, there are nine regional bureaus that reconcile policy to local issues and develop MITI's extraordinary industry data base. The acuteness and soundness of MITI policy are attributable to the interplay among these horizontal policy bureaus and vertical industry bureaus, with their broad powers, comprehensive data base, and first-rate career staff. Japan has thus far avoided the proliferation of layered agencies that single-issue politics has brought to America's industrial policy.

The Industrial Policy Bureau has played the major role in guiding overall industrial development. It is this bureau that has emphasized the shift toward more knowledge-intensive businesses. Within the bureau, general divisions work out actual policy details: the Industrial Structure Division projects the desired future structure of industrial output and designs broad measures toward achieving it; the Business Behavior Division studies tax measures and labor issues; the Price Policy Division is responsible for seeing that appropriate industries are adequately financed. This last division makes recommendations on which businesses and projects gain access to low-interest funds through MOF's Fiscal Investment and Loan Plan (FILP).

The Industrial Structure Division does the staff work on basic structure policy. The five explicit criteria used in their deliberations are:

- the rate of growth the industrial sector is capable of sustaining, given financial, labor, and other direct constraints
- the desirable structure of the industrial sector in terms of input-output balance, socioeconomic limits like regional balance and environmental protection, the need for productivity increases, etc.
- international competitiveness
- corporate vitality, particularly adequate profitability and reinvestment rates
- the optimal rate of structural change that would meet economic targets while keeping dislocations tolerable

A number of advantages accrue to MITI's organization. MITI officials can negotiate solutions to a problem intramurally, where there is "give and take" on both sides. An example is MITI's adjustment in the metal flatware industry, hit hard by yen revaluation in the late 1970's. Steel is a major cost element to this industry, but flatware is a small customer to steel producers. MITI was able to negotiate raw-material price relief for the flatware industry and make it up to the steel companies somewhere else. The more issues under a ministry's jurisdiction, the greater potential for consistent and rational policy, but also a higher quality of staff will be demanded. The staff of MITI based in Tokyo itself is remarkably small—fewer than twenty-five hundred professionals. The small ministry size and its broad range of responsibilities give its professionals a breadth of experience and close relations with one another.

Japan's industrial policy process is often misunderstood. In sectors of policy interest, MITI collects a good deal of market and competitive data, gives administrative guidance to firms, and issues a log of paper in support of a policy. Communication between MITI and individual producers takes place frequently, and at several levels. Some observers of this process have mistakenly concluded that MITI is dictating investment rates in the industry. This is not MITI's intention. Market prospects, not ministries, stimulate investment in growth businesses, and ultimately discourage investment in declining ones. MITI understands that it would be counterproductive to force wary producers to invest. Nor can a ministry know any particular business sector well enough to design or direct a specific series of investments. Instead, MITI tries to develop a shared perception of a business's future and designs incentives and subsidies to accelerate the desired course.

Nor does MITI normally have the power to dictate investment choices to business. Indeed, the autonomy of the individual firm sharply limits the government's ability to change industrial structure. What is industry development for MITI is risky capital investment for the firm that, although interested in sector structure, is more directly interested in its competitive position. Unless its survival is at stake, a company will accept the incentives and subsidies available to the industry but balk at measures that threaten its autonomy. For example, in the 1960's, Japan's motor-car companies welcomed the government's import protection, low-cost lending, and tax deferrals, but rejected MITI's attempts to merge producers and keep minority foreign-capital investment out of the industry. In the 1970's, the key mainframe-computer producers—Hitachi, Fujitsu, and Nippon Electric—remained independent competitors despite MITI attempts to consolidate the industry. In electronic calculators, Sharp and others successfully deflected MITI's attempt to shut off U.S. integrated-circuit imports, which threatened Japan's fledgling high-cost production. While serving MITI's longer-term structural aims, this import ban would have seriously damaged calculator producers' cost position. More recently, aluminum producers have resisted MITI's plan for permanent-capacity retirement by formula allocation. The producers want short-term relief only, in order to preserve long-term strategy flexibility.

Although conflicts do arise between MITI and reluctant companies, the ministry has many tools of persuasion. It has carrots—it can provide access to funds for investment—and it has sticks—it can hold up building permits, regulate raw-material imports, and provide material incentives to competitors. However, MITI's greatest strength appears to be its understanding of the competitive stages through which an industry moves and its ability to fashion appropriate policy.

MITI's policy objectives vary according to the competitive position of a business. For businesses in the early, rapid-growth phases of development, such as computers and machinery, policy calls for protection from foreign competition, concentration among producers, government support of the industry's cash flow, and stimulation of new technology. Today, real protection is available only to a few industries, but MITI remains aggressive on the other fronts. For businesses that are already internationally competitive—motor cars, steel, consumer electronics—government assistance recedes as it is no longer necessary. Finally, for businesses in competitive decline, MITI becomes active again, this time trying to bring about capacity reduction and rationalization.

The process of discussion and debate between MITI and the companies in response to developments in the marketplace creates a dynamic decision-making process. MITI aptly refers to Japan as a "plan-oriented market economy."

There are three broad industrial policy concerns of MITI and the other industrial ministries: investment rate and structure of producers, technology development, and export-import measures. Below is a general survey of measures brought to bear on these concerns.

Investment rate and structure of producers: Japan has adopted policies generally favorable to capital investment—no capital-gains tax on securities, central bank permanent control of interest rates, a strong antiinflation commitment, and a minimum of administrative barriers. A relatively high growth rate in the economy as a whole also helps sustain high investment.

MITI, however, does not always favor investment by all competitors. In the rapid-growth development stage of an industry, MITI prods an industry to concentrate; conversely, in no-growth, declining sectors, MITI promotes capacity retirement. In both cases, MITI's objective is to accelerate market forces and bring about more stable competition among a few relatively low-cost producers. In Japan, the key concern has been putting capital together, not splitting it apart.

Historically, the government has protected rapid-growth industries from imports with formal barriers at the same time that it has sought to eliminate marginal producers. The success of these consolidation efforts was mixed. MITI exercised strong authority in the most fragmented industries, like sewing machines and car parts, where concentration brought unquestioned benefits in larger scale and lower costs. But in industries where marginal producers were still large companies—motor cars, petroleum refining, and chemicals—MITI failed to bring about mergers and absorptions. Group banks provided easy access to low-cost capital, while high growth concealed weaknesses and postponed the shakeout. MITI has usually managed to enforce a capacity-expansion queue in the capital-intensive, heavy-process industries, in part through foreign-exchange control of their raw materials. Even here, however, mavericks like Idemitsu in refining and Sumitomo in steel have been able to elude control.

Today, only a handful of fast-growth, high-technology industries, such as computers, telecommunications, and railway equipment, are protected from imports, and primarily through closed procurement rather than duties and quotas. In telecommunications and railway equipment, investment is stimulated and competition allocated directly by operating public corporations that buy the equipment.

There is open competition, however, among Japanese computer producers, and government has done its utmost to support investment in this business. It finances most leasing and software to preserve the producers' capital. The Japan Development Bank grants low-interest loans to producers to finance the generation of new equipment. And the tax laws generously cushion producers from the loss on the trading in of old machines; accelerated depreciation of capital investment is also given. MITI has tried for years to consolidate the mainframe industry into two or three equipment-compatible groups, but centrifugal forces have prevailed. Six Japanese mainframe manufacturers remain, and even given the increased rationalization among them, they divide the market very thinly. Fujitsu and Hitachi, the two leaders after IBM, together have less than 40 percent of the total market.

As it encourages investment and formally or informally protects knowledge-intensive growth industries, MITI discourages investment in and protection of declining industries. Today, some large declining industries—aluminum smelting, shipbuilding, synthetic textile fibers, etc.—post major structural problems. These industries are high cost internationally, have excess capacity, and have large outstanding loans.

In May 1978, the Japanese Diet passed the Structurally Depressed Industries Law, enabling MITI to develop a stabilization plan using government funds. The procedure specified by the law is typically Japanese. Industries become eligible for assistance only if two thirds of the producers petition MITI, which then decides whether to grant their request. This condition helps the ministry to bring about a working agreement among the producers, whose cost positions and proposed solutions usually differ significantly. The major creditors, like the Industrial Bank of Japan, sit on *ad hoc* committees with MITI to study the nature of the problem in a particular industry and ways to solve it. The law establishes a government-loan-guarantee fund when the producers borrow heavily because of massive scrapping or mothballing of capacity.

Concerns for industry structure and investment will occur in growth and decline phases only. In both cases, industry consolidation at optimal scale is the major goal. Currently competitive industries receive little attention.

Technology development: A second concern of Japanese industrial policy is technology development. This concern has grown as Japan has moved toward more knowledge-intensive industries and as it has approached the frontiers of technology. There are some major government financing efforts—notably in energy and semiconductors—but the government mainly uses a variety of incentives for private development.

The government's own research-and-development effort is small, in part because the Japanese have been so successful in exploiting the basic research of American and European government and university laboratories, and in part because large national applied-research projects are managed by government laboratories but performed on contract by working groups of corporations. MITI's Agency of Industrial Science and Technology has sixteen associated research institutes that organize and manage long-term, large-scale projects to develop system technologies for commercial use. Some current examples are VLSI semiconductors, high-performance jet engines, water desalination, and natural-resource recycling. These projects run for five to eight years, can cost hundreds of millions of dollars, and are typically performed and co-funded by *ad hoc* associations of several large corporate and university laboratories. They are exempt from the Antimonopoly Law.

For industry in general, government uses a variety of more modest incentives and supporting tools for corporate research and development. These include tax credits, grants, loans, and sponsorship of associations. Some are available to all corporations, while others are tied to particular MITI objectives.

There are three principal corporate tax incentives for technology development. One stipulates that 25 percent of any year-to-year increase in research-and-development expenditures over the previous year is a tax credit, up to a limit of 10 percent of total corporate tax. In 1978, manufacturing companies realized a 15-billion-yen benefit through this credit. The second is accelerated depreciation on research-and-development facilities and hardware, which can often mean a 60 percent write-off of the original purchase price in the first year. The provisions try to conserve the cash flow of high-technology businesses. As growth of an industry slows, these incentives, appropriately enough, become ineffective, and more cash flow is exposed to tax. The third is a lower tax rate on income received from technology licensed overseas—worth 10 billion yen to the manufacturing sector in 1978.

The government, in cooperation with other institutions, also directly funds research and development. Such grants can take one of several forms. Most common is a matching grant. Ministries receive applications in designated research-and-development areas from either companies or associations formed for that purpose. Many associations are groups of small companies that could not finance new technologies on their own. Often the technology issue is straightforward: for example, developing a continuous textile operation to replace a vertically fragmented one. For small business, MITI or the trade association sponsors these arrangements. Matching programs are not, however, a major funding source of Japanese corporate research and development; they typically account for less than one percent of the total. A parallel matching-grant program is run separately for small business.

Motor-car and boat-racing tax proceeds also benefit research and development. MITI guides the direction of these funds to various industry associations, which then distribute the money to specific projects in rationalization, research, and export promotion. They are separate from the government's official budgets, and help to finance sectors and products that are not household words in Japan. In 1978, racing subsidies to the machinery industries, for example, were 7.3 billion yen.

Loans for technology development form a traditional element of Japanese industrial policy. The Japan Development Bank makes loans under various program headings—commercialization of new technology, developments of prototypes, and commercialization of new technology for small enterprise. These loans are project-related and simply represent low-cost funds; hence, they are a marginal incentive. Loans are provided primarily to manufacturers, and sometimes to users of the qualifying machinery. These programs have grown throughout the 1970's. The government lent a total of 30 billion yen to all Japanese industry in 1976.

Overall, the government has increased its commitment to research and development over the decade rather substantially, mainly in the form of a few large, high-priority projects. This is consistent with the restructuring toward more knowledge-intensive industries.

Export-import measures: The third major concern of Japanese industrial policy has been international trade. Through the early 1970's, the Japanese government stimulated exports, restricted manufactured imports, and assisted large-scale raw-materials imports—classical behavior for an island economy poor in natural resources and prone to experience trade deficits. The tax system, through special reserves and accelerated depreciation, effectively shielded significant portions of export revenue from taxation. The Bank of Japan discounted short-term export bills at less-than-market interest rates, and cheap long-term credit for export-related investment was available from the Japan Development Bank and the Long Term Credit Bank of Japan. High duties and quotas blocked imported manufacturers where Japan thought itself uncompetitive. Assistance was given to overseas projects in mining, forestry, and the like, with financial guarantees and government-to-government assurances in order to strengthen supply security in basic materials.

The story is quite different now. Broad export incentives are gone. The tax system retains incentives only for exports by small and medium-sized companies, and for overseas investment. Export-related accelerated depreciation—worth 55 billion yen to the manufacturing sector in 1970—was eliminated in 1972. Export bills now carry only a quarter of one percent discount off domestic bill rates, and this subsidy works primarily to bolster Japan's declining exporters of textiles, plywood, flatware, etc.

Although MITI no longer directly assists exports, certain government policies and practices do aid selected knowledge-intensive industries. Japan's Export-Import Bank aggressively finances and insures exports of plant systems—a rapidly growing part of trade. Large Third World development projects that Japan finances and supplies enjoy top priority and receive official economic aid. The country's utility monopolies in power generation and telecommunications protect and support designated key products and provide a large production volume on which to base an export effort.

The Japanese home market for manufactures is now essentially open, and foreign producers' market penetration depends on marketing effort and the suitability of the product far more than on government-approved barriers. There are three major exceptions to this pattern. One is government-operated monopolies, such as telecommunications, railway, cigarettes, and some computers. Closed procurement is the tool. Ministries other than MITI typically oversee these barriers, and are under considerable international pressure to liberalize them. The second relates to machinery imports, where the structure of Japanese industry keeps imports to a minimum: heavy-industry companies are often part of large Zaibatsu containing chemical, steel, electrical equipment, and other companies that buy machinery from within their own group.

The other exception is Japan's political wards, such as agriculture, retailing, and unskilled labor-intensive manufacturing, where large, competitively vulnerable constituencies command protection. This residual protection is similar to that in other advanced countries. By and large, however, the appreciation of the yen and the migration of labor-intensive production to developing countries is opening the door to imports. A large number of Japanese industries—textiles, aluminum, chemicals, and metalworking—are under increasing pressure as international product specialization shapes trade patterns.

3. This was a common refrain in the early 1980's. Many U.S. businessmen, policy officials, and media analysts saw our entrepreneurial small companies as untouchable by the Japanese. There were many pseudosociologists of Japan with themes about why Japan's collectivist culture did not allow for the creativity and freedom necessary for invention and entrepreneurship.

These arguments have proven baseless as Japanese companies have shown themselves quite capable of pioneering new technologies and products in the 1980's.

4. In 1980, MITI increased funding for Project Sunshine through its Agency of Industrial Science and Technology. More important, the New Energy Development Organization was established by the government and the private sec-

tor, at MITI's initiative, to take the lead in the construction and operation of pilot plants for Project Sunshine. In addition, specific government funding for photovoltaics and related projects increased from under $10 million in 1979 to $30 million in 1982 within AIST alone.

5. They included Solarex, Arco Solar, Solar Power (Exxon), RTC, Motorola, Solenergy, Mobil Tyco, and TRW. A dozen others were doing serious research, including GE, RCA, Boeing, Hughes, Lockheed, Motorola, Honeywell, Rockwell, Martin Marietta, Bechtel, Spire, Chevron, United Technologies, Varian, and Westinghouse.

6. The Agency of Industrial Science and Technology runs sixteen research institutes around Japan. Beginning in 1988, it consolidated nine of these in Tsukuba. They include the National Research Laboratory for Metrology, The Mechanical Engineering Laboratory, the National Chemical Laboratory for Industry, the Fermentation Research Institute, the Research Institute for Polymers and Textiles, the Geological Survey of Japan, the Electrotechnical Laboratory, of which photovoltaics is a part, the Industrial Products Research Institute, and the National Research Institute for Pollution and Resources. Together they make up perhaps the largest research center in the world, with several thousand scientists.

7. I was amazed at the lecture I received, unsolicited, from an OMB official who quoted Adam Smith, literally, to tell me that the only legitimate research functions of government were for defense and navigation. He allowed as how the government would probably continue to fund some basic civilian research, though many in OMB also felt this was inappropriate and a waste of money. When I asked him about international competition, he was clear and definitive in saying that if foreign governments were, in fact, assisting companies with applied research and development, it was because they were misguided socialists whose economies would suffer because of too much government interference. The marketplace on its own could spend what was needed for R&D.

8. Being 100 percent dependent on foreign oil, Japan was hit particularly hard by the oil price increases of 1973 and 1979.

9. My company, Telesis, has had the opportunity to investigate Japanese developments in a number of new-technology areas in conjunction with our normal corporate work. The companies themselves have played the biggest role in Japanese R&D expansion, virtually doubling their R&D budgets over the past five years. But government programs have also increased at roughly 5 percent per year for commercial research and development.

As one MITI friend described it to me, Japan has gone "technology crazy" over the past five years. In the areas we have examined, the main impact of Japanese government involvement is to create motivation and engender cooperation. MITI in particular prods companies into investing in various R&D programs by organizing research consortia, providing funding, and engaging in discussions with the companies.

The following charts from AIST documents illustrate the breadth of Japan's commercial R&D efforts.

AIST selects technical themes that are of particular importance and urgency to the nation as a whole. These involve resource and energy problems, social development, and the improvement of public welfare. Government funds are employed to promote R&D through closely coordinated industrial and academic organizations.

A total of twenty-four projects have so far been undertaken, and some have already been completed.

PROJECT NAME	PERIOD (FY)	OUTLINE OF PROJECT
C1 Chemical Technology	1980–1986	R&D on processes for producing basic chemicals such as ethylene glycol, acetic acid, ethanol, and olefins from C1 compounds like carbon monoxide that are obtained from natural gas, coal, tar, sand, etc., as alternative raw materials.
Manganese-Nodule Mining System	1981–1989	R&D on an efficient and reliable hydraulic mining system in which manganese nodules are collected by a towed vehicle for commercial-scale mining to help ensure a stable supply of nonferrous mineral resources.
High-Speed Computer System for Scientific & Technological Uses	1981–1989	R&D on high-speed computer systems for scientific and technological applications (processing of image information from satellites, simulation of nuclear fusion, etc.) that present computers cannot handle with adequate speed.
Automated Sewing System	1982–1990	R&D on an automated industrial sewing system, involving processes such as preparation, making up, and finishing, to address the diversification and rapid change in the domestic apparel market.
Advanced Robot Technology	1983–1990	R&D on advanced robot technology for systems to support people working under difficult or dangerous conditions.
Observation System for Earth Satellite-1	1984–1990	In cooperation with STA, R&D on an observation-sensor system for earth-resources satellites, composed of a synthetic aperture radar and visible and infrared radiometers.
New Water Treatment System	1985–1990	R&D on a new wastewater treatment system using a high-concentration bioreactor and separation membrane, for water reuse and energy recovery (e.g., methane gas from anaerobic bioprocess).

PROJECT NAME	PERIOD (FY)	OUTLINE OF PROJECT
Interoperable Database System	1985–1991	R&D on technology for interoperable information systems with such features as distributed databases and multimedia technology, to form an infrastructure for the "information society."
Advanced Material-Processing & Machining System	1986–1992	R&D on advanced processing equipment (high-power excimer laser, high-density ion beam, high-performance machine tools), processing technology using advanced processing units, and development of total system.
Super High-Performance Electronic Computer	1966–1971	Large scale supercomputer system.
Desulfurization Process	1966–1971	(1) Efficient removal of SO_2 contained in the gas exhaust from power plants or other plants that consume a great deal of heavy oil. (2) Direct removal of sulfur from heavy oil.
New Method of Producing Olefin	1967–1972	Economical production of olefins by direct cracking of crude oil instead of naphtha.
Remote-Control Undersea Oil-Drilling Rig	1970–1975	Remote-control oil-drilling rigs for use underseas.
Seawater Desalination & By-product Recovery	1969–1977	Economical large-scale production of fresh water and economical by-product-recovery technology.
Electric Car	1973–1977	Various types of electric cars to replace ordinary vehicles in urban areas.
Comprehensive Automobile Control Technology	1973–1979	Integrated control technology to help relieve traffic congestion, reduce automobile pollution and traffic accidents, etc.
Pattern-Information-Processing System	1971–1980	Computer technology for the recognition and processing of pattern information such as characters, pictures, objects, and speech.
Direct Steelmaking Process Using High-Temperature Reducing Gas	1973–1980	Direct steelmaking technology to help solve the pollution problems that accompany present-day methods and to reduce dependence on coal as a raw

PROJECT NAME	PERIOD (FY)	OUTLINE OF PROJECT
		material. The new technology aims at a closed system using heat energy from a multipurpose high-temperature, gas-cooled reactor in the steelmaking process; this new reactor is scheduled for development in the near future.
Olefin Production from Heavy Oil	1975–1981	Technology for manufacturing olefins from heavy oil (asphalt), which is difficult to desulfurize.
Jet-Aircraft Engines	1976–1981 (Phase II) 1973–1975 (Phase I)	Research and development of a large scale turbofan engine for use in commercial transport in the 1980's.
Resource Recovery Technology	1976–1982 (Phase II) 1973–1975 (Phase I)	R&D on technical systems for the disposal of solid urban waste, centered on resource recycling to promote the efficient utilization of resources and facilitate the treatment of solid urban waste.
Flexible Manufacturing System Complex Using Laser	1977–1984	R&D on a production system capable of flexibly and rapidly producing mechanical components for small-batch production of diversified products from metallic materials.
Subsea Oil Production System	1978–1984	R&D on a subsea oil production from small-scale oilfields that is possible without any adverse effects on the fishing industry, and that is effective for oil production in deep waters (over 300m in depth) and suitable for use in the seas surrounding Japan.
Optical Measurement & Control System	1979–1985	R&D on an optical measurement and control system permitting massive volumes of data, including picture images, to be measured and controlled in adverse environments.

AIST also is sponsoring a series of projects that deal with revolutionary basic technologies essential to the establishment of the new industries that are expected to flourish in the 1990's.

The fields covered are new materials, biotechnology, and new electronics devices. From these three fields, the following thirteen special categories, which have all theoretically or experimentally shown potential for application in new industrial technologies, have been selected. Under this project, research and development in these categories will be conducted until the materials are ready for practical application.

PROJECT NAME	PERIOD (FY)	OUTLINE OF PROJECT
(1) New Materials a) High-Performance Ceramics	1981–1992	Development of very strong and rustless ceramics with high-dimensional accuracy at elevated temperatures, and technologies to permit their application as materials for gas-turbine components.
b) Synthetic Membranes for New Separation Technology	1981–1990	Development of synthetic membranes for new separation technology, which can separate and refine freely mixed gases or liquid mixtures by utilizing differences in the property of matter.
c) Synthetic Metals	1981–1990	Development of synthetic metals and polymeric materials that are light in weight, resistant to corrosion, and conduct electricity like metals.
d) High-Performance Plastics	1981–1990	Development of high-performance plastics, polymeric materials that are light in weight but as strong as metal.
e) Advanced Alloys with Controlled Crystalline Structures	1981–1988	Development of very strong alloys, light in weight and with excellent heat resistance, by single-crystallization, grain-refining, and particle-dispersing techniques.
f) Advanced Composite Materials	1981–1988	Development of advanced composite materials that are lighter than aluminum alloys and stronger than steel, with strength and hardness to suit specific purposes. They could be used as structural materials, if high reliability is realized.
g) Photoactive Materials	1985–1993	Development of photoactive materials, which characteristically exhibit a reversible change in the structure of arrangement of molecules in response to a light stimulus. These materials are essential to the realization of optical innovations such as high-density optical memory.
(2) Biotechnology a) Bioreactor	1981–1990	Development of bioreactor systems capable of saving substantial amounts of energy and resources currently consumed in the chemical industry.
b) Large-Scale Cell Cultivation	1981–1989	Development of nonserological culture media and culture methods for mammalian cells in order to establish large-scale and high-density cultures.

PROJECT NAME	PERIOD (FY)	OUTLINE OF PROJECT
c) Utilization of Recombinant DNA	1981–1990	Investigation of DNA-recombination technology for the purpose of developing new microorganisms for practical use in industry. Research materials are host-vector systems permitted in the guideline for DNA-recombination experiments or safe systems that have been newly developed.
(3) New Electronic Devices a) Superdevices	1981–1990	Development of superlattice electronic devices that have an extremely fine structure tailored to atomic scale and utilize new electronic effects arising in such an artificial structure.
b) Three-Dimensional ICs	1981–1990	Development of three-dimensional ICs characterized by a three-dimensional arrangement of active elements and made up of alternately stacked semiconductor layers for active elements and insulator layers for separation.
c) Bioelectronic	1986–1991	Bioelectronic devices are new functional devices for future computer elements. The project aims at understanding neural systems and biological information processing, and at the same time at fabricating well-organized molecular systems.

Japan is also putting much effort into raising the standard of its medical and welfare services, and there is an urgent need for more advanced apparatus in this field. Often, however, the development of technology for medical and welfare apparatus is hampered by large risks. Since the 1976 fiscal year, AIST has addressed this problem by carrying out R&D aimed at the rapid development and marketing of reasonably priced, high-performance apparatus in this "high risk" category. Research work is conducted at AIST's national research laboratories or on a consignment basis at the Technology Research Association of Medical and Welfare Apparatus (administered jointly by MITI and the Ministry of Health and Welfare). By the end of fiscal 1985, R&D had been completed on seven types of apparatus for medical care and eight for welfare use. Eight of these pieces of apparatus are already in use.

The following are completed R&D projects funded by AIST:

A. Medical equipment technology:
(1) Multichannel automated biochemical analyzer
(2) Automated differential blood-cell analyzer
(3) Artificial heart for clinical use
(4) Portable artificial kidney
(5) Laser scalpel

      (6) Positron computer technology
      (7) Liver-function technology
  B. Welfare equipment technology:
      (1) Modular-type motorized wheelchair
      (2) Braille duplicating system
      (3) Goit pattern analyzer for the handicapped
      (4) Multifunctional bed for the bedridden
      (5) Middle-ear implant
      (6) Guide device for the blind
      (7) Vocal- and speech-training device
      (8) Active artificial leg
      (9) Three-dimensional working chair

In addition, the following activities are currently being researched:

R&D THEME	PERIOD (FY)	OUTLINE OF PROJECT
A. Medical equipment technology		
1. General Equipment		
(a) Supporting system for early detection & treatment of neurological & psychological problems	1981–1986	Early detection of nervous-system problems of newborns and babies and treatment-support system.
(b) Blood treatment system for immunorelated diseases	1983–1987	System for treatment of autoimmune diseases, such as serous maesthemi.
2. Cancer-related equipment		
(a) photochemical-reaction system for diagnosis & therapy of cancer	1984–1987	Cancer diagnosis & treatment system utilizing laser-induced photochemical reaction.
(b) Immunochemical cancer-diagnosis system	1985–1988	Diagnostic system enabling early detection of deep cancers.
(c) Hyperthermia system for cancer therapy	1986–1989	Device capable of warming the cancer tissue selectively at a certain temperature for treatment.
B. Welfare equipment technology		
1. Book reader for the blind	1982–1988	System of comprehending words in books & reading them out loud.
2. Transfer supporting system for the handicapped	1983–1987	System for caring for & moving bedridden physically handicapped persons.
3. Automated body-temperature adjuster	1984–1987	System of aiding the automatic body-temperature-adjusting function of physically handicapped persons.
4. System for processing prosthetic sockets	1986–1989	Device to produce prosthetic sockets by determining the forms & properties of the cutting sections.

These programs are indicative of AIST's efforts. In addition, extensive industrial R&D is conducted through the Ministry of Post and Telecommunications, the Ministry of Transport, the Ministry of Health and Welfare, and a variety of other agencies. In addition, more basic research is carried out by the Ministry of Education and the Science and Technology Agency.

The fundamental issues in all of this are not related to the amount of money spent, though that is large and increasing, but rather to the coordinating strategic role played by the government in setting a national agenda for technology development, and in the fact that most of the R&D effort is devoted ultimately to producing commercializable products by industry. It is applied commercial research and development, not only basic and defense-oriented research like in the United States.

Chapter 8

1. See table, "Commercial Jet Transport Aircraft Deliveries," pp. 374–375.

2. U.S. export and import statistics 1987, from the U.S. Department of Commerce.

3. Based on firm orders. Includes A300, A310, and A320 sales.

4. A recent publication by Airbus Industrie presents unit projections for commercial jet-aircraft demand as calculated by Airbus, McDonnell Douglas, and Boeing. This publication was presented on September 16, 1987, at the Annual Aerospace/Defense Conference of Drexel Burnham Lambert. It arrives at a market of roughly four hundred aircraft per year, to which we applied a $50 million average price tag, which is probably conservative. The $400 billion figure is derived by multiplying eight thousand aircraft times $50 million.

The following is excerpted from the Airbus presentation: "The Airbus econometric model, driven by trends in real GNP and real air fares, predicts that, over the period 1986–2005, world air traffic will grow at an average annual rate of 5.5%." This puts its expectations somewhat below those of Douglas, which projects much higher growth outside the United States, and in extremely close agreement with the midpoint of Boeing's high and low econometric forecasts. Boeing's aircraft demand forecast is actually based on a "baseline" growth forecast of 5.3 percent through the year 2000, which Airbus calculates as extrapolating to 5.1 percent through the year 2005; this gives a forecast size of the world air travel market within 8 percent of the Airbus forecast.

Average Annual Increase
1986–2005

Douglas	6.3%
Airbus	5.5%
Boeing—high	6.9%
—low	3.9%
—baseline	5.1%

Commercial Jet Transport Aircraft Deliveries

	1958	'59	'60	'61	'62	'63	'64	'65	'66	'67	'68	'69
707	8	77	91	80	68	34	38	61	83	118	111	59
727						6	95	111	135	155	160	115
737										4	105	114
747												4
757												
767												
DC-8		21	91	42	22	19	20	31	32	41	102	85
LC-9/MD-80								5	69	152	203	121
DC-10												
L-1011												
880/990		14	33	33	16	4	2					
U.S. Manufacturers Subtotal	8	112	215	155	106	63	155	208	319	470	681	498
Comet	7*	19	20	14	13	2	2	1		1		
Caravelle		18	39	39	35	23	22	18	18	20	15	11
Trident							12	10	11	1	11	9
VC-10							13	12	7	10	9	2
BAC-111								34	46	20	26	40
F-28												10
Mercure												
A300												
A310												
BAe 146												
VFW-614												
Concorde												
Non-U.S. Manufacturers Subtotal	7*	37	59	53	48	25	49	75	82	52	61	72
Total	15*	149	274	208	114	88	204	283	401	522	742	570

*Plus 33 Comets delivered 1952–1957

Part of this traffic growth will be absorbed by increases in average load factor and aircraft productivity. On these items, Boeing forecasts a rate of load-factor increase less than half that predicted by Douglas and Airbus. The other forecasts are broadly similar, and result in Douglas projecting a total fleet-capacity growth substantially higher than Airbus, and Boeing forecasting a rate identical to the Airbus prediction.

Average Annual Increase 1986–2005

	RPMS	LOAD FACTOR	AIRCRAFT PRODUCTIVITY	ASMS
Douglas	6.3%	0.5%	1.2%	4.6%
Airbus	5.5%	0.5%	1.0%	4.0%
Boeing	5.1%	0.2%	0.9%	4.0%

Each manufacturer uses its own method to determine what proportion of the forecast capacity growth will be provided by increased frequency of service,

'70	'71	'72	'73	'74	'75	'76	'77	'78	'79	'80	'81	'82	'83	'84	'85	Total
19	10	4	11	21	7	9	8	13	6	3	2	8	8	8	3	968
54	33	41	92	91	91	61	67	118	136	131	94	26	11	8		1,831
37	29	22	23	55	51	41	25	40	77	92	108	95	82	67	115	1,182
92	69	30	30	22	21	27	20	32	67	73	53	25	23	16	24	628
												2	25	18	36	81
												20	55	29	25	129
33	13	4														556
53	45	32	29	48	42	50	22	22	39	23	78	43	51	44	71	1,242
	13	52	57	47	43	19	14	18	36	40	25	11	12	10	11	408
		17	39	41	25	16	11	8	14	24	28	14	6	4	2	249
																102
88	212	202	281	325	280	223	167	251	375	386	388	244	273	204	287	7,376
																112
9	4	5	3													279
2	13	11	7	4	6	9	7	4								117
1																54
22	12	7	2	4	2		6	3		3	2	2	1	2		234
11	10	13	19	9	22	17	13	11	13	13	12	10	16	17	12	228
				6	4									1		11
				4	9	13	16	15	24	39	38	46	19	19	16	258
													17	29	26	72
													10	11	18	39
			1	4	5											10
			1	6	2				5							14
45	39	36	31	27	45	49	49	33	37	60	52	58	63	78	73	1,428
333	251	238	312	352	325	272	216	284	412	446	440	302	336	282	360	8,804

and what proportion by increased aircraft size. Douglas forecasts a significantly lower growth in aircraft size than Airbus and Boeing. Consequently, the Douglas forecast growth in number of aircraft is much higher. The Airbus and Boeing forecasts appear remarkably close.

Average Annual Increase
1986–2005

	REQUIRED CAPACITY	AIRCRAFT SIZE	NUMBER OF AIRCRAFT
Douglas	4.6%	1.1%	3.5%
Airbus	4.0%	1.6%	2.4%
Boeing	4.0%	1.7%	2.3%

Where the three companies differ is in the treatment of aircraft retirements. Unlike Boeing and Douglas, who apparently apply fixed rules regarding the ages at which various categories of aircraft are retired from service, Airbus makes a detailed study of each airline, using knowledge of the individual airline's past, present, and anticipated future retirement policy. Where no specific airline policy is apparent, it assumes a maximum service life of twenty years with each aircraft's first operator. Upon retirement from its first operator, it assumes that an aircraft will become available on the used market as a candidate to fill the needs of other airlines in competition with new aircraft.

To compare the Airbus retirement forecast with the Boeing and Douglas forecasts, therefore, it is necessary to deduct the 809 aircraft that Airbus predicts will return to the fleet as used aircraft. This results in a forecast that 79 percent of the aircraft in service in 1985 will have been permanently retired by the end of 2005. Despite some ambiguity in its definition of permanent aircraft retirement, the Douglas forecast appears to imply that some 10 percent fewer aircraft will be retired over the twenty-year period. Boeing's retirement rules imply that only 60 percent of the 1985 fleet will be retired over this period. Although Boeing does not fully explain the basis of its assumptions, they appear to reflect a judgment that widebody aircraft and new-technology derivatives will prove more durable than older-technology aircraft, and perhaps that the economic characteristics of new aircraft will not be sufficiently attractive to displace a number of existing types. Remembering that the oldest widebody has been in service for only eighteen years, and that the structural condition of many early 747-100s makes it questionable whether they will—as assumed by Boeing—remain in service for another nine to twelve years, Airbus believes that Boeing's forecast of retirements may be unduly conservative.

Through Year 2005

	1985 FLEET	RETIREMENTS	% OF 1985 FLEET RETIRED
Douglas	5,733	4,092	71.4%
Airbus	5,765	4,557	79.0%
Boeing	6,672	4,002	60.0%

From these projections, each manufacturer derives a forecast of the numbers of aircraft that will be required worldwide to accommodate the increase in passenger traffic over the forecast period. As expected, Douglas forecasts a much higher number of aircraft than does Airbus. Despite its lower traffic-growth forecast, Boeing predicts a larger year 2005 fleet than Airbus. This is because the Airbus forecast is limited to the 204 airlines that currently operate aircraft of at least 100 seats, whereas the Boeing forecast covers 360 airlines, including many that may be expected to grow into this category over the next twenty years. In fact, Airbus, with the A320 as its smallest present product, very specifically has not attempted any systematic forecast of total demand for aircraft in the hundred-seat category.

	1985 FLEET	2005 FLEET	NEW AIRCRAFT REQUIRED
Douglas	5,733	11,407	5,674
Airbus	5,765	9,350	3,585
Boeing	6,672	10,514	3,842

Combining the forecasts of new aircraft deliveries to accommodate traffic growth and to replace aircraft retired from service, and even though the methods and assumptions used by the various forecasters are sometimes quite different, the Airbus forecast is only 298 aircraft, or less than 4 percent, higher than the extrapolated Boeing forecast. The extrapolated Douglas forecast appears some 20 percent higher.

With the major and obvious proviso that all of this assumes no cataclysmic change in the world's social or economic order, it is evident that all three major airframers agree that over the next twenty years, with deliveries of large commercial aircraft averaging around four hundred units per year, commercial-airplane manufacturing will remain one of the world's great growth industries.

1986–2005

	FLEET EXPANSION	REPLACEMENT AIRCRAFT	TOTAL
Douglas	5,674	4,092	9,766
Airbus	3,585	4,557	8,142
Boeing	3,842	3,002	6,844

5. The *Europa-1* had also met an unhappy fate. After the *Europa-2* blew up, the European space effort was temporarily abandoned. It was Europe's first large attempt at technical cooperation, and its failure was a huge blow to those who promoted European unity.

6. The British television manufacturers ranged from a high of 7.3 hours per set down to 4.6 hours. The Japanese companies ranged from 2.2 hours down to 1.2.

7. The Koreans and Taiwanese were developing successful color-television industries by copying Japanese or U.S. designs and capitalizing on low-wage labor. But even they were ultimately vulnerable to larger companies basing some assembly in low-wage countries and using scale and technical sophistication to succeed.

The UK had ten television producers for a market of 1.5 million units, compared to Japan, which at the time had eleven producers (six main ones) for a 9.6-million-unit production.

8. Efforts to promote French technological development began in 1958. An interministerial committee was established to direct government R&D aid, and a special supporting agency, DGRST, reporting to the prime minister, was created to coordinate the activities of different departments.

In 1960, to give a clearer picture of the national public effort for R&D, the government instituted a centralized budgeting procedure, *enveloppe recherche.* This budget excluded such major expenditures as military and aircraft R&D; nevertheless, it rose from 0.5 percent of gross national product in 1958 to 2.6 percent in 1967.

Following the U.S. model, the growth of French R&D expenditures occurred mainly in "Big Science" projects like the Concorde, the Plan Calcul, and the Force de Frappe. These were expected to contribute to the country's political independence and simultaneously improve the position of French industry.

At the end of 1959, the government created the "Concerted Actions" as a means to reorient traditional scientific institutions to serve national needs. In 1962, the various "Concerted Actions" in space were reorganized into the National Center for Space Studies (CNES).

Finally, military research was reorganized and centralized via the newly created Direction for Research and Testing (DRME).

In the late 1960's, the French government tried to refine its policies. France was the first European country to introduce a scheme of cooperation between business and government on R&D projects.

The Aid to Development program, introduced in 1965, subsidized the development cost of industrial projects. This assistance was to be repaid in case of commercial success. An analogous "predevelopment" program was also established, but funding was relatively insignificant. Two sectors were initially selected: heavy electrical equipment and machinery. This scheme served as a model for other European governments (the BMFT in West Germany and STU in Sweden).

In 1967, a special agency, ANVAR, was created to offer support at the market-introduction stage of the innovation process. The focus was to be on small firms or investors. Special tax advantages were given to newly created venture-capital firms, and risk credit could be provided to innovative firms through a letter of agreement.

Thus, France developed a set of aid mechanisms to cover the entire innovation process, from basic to applied research, product development, and market introduction.

IN THE LATE 1960's, three factors changed the nature of the German economy. First, the upward movement of the deutsche mark converted the strength of German export sectors into a higher standard of living for the people of West Germany.

Second, the share of the national income devoted to wages and social benefits increased. Higher labor costs had to be reflected in higher-skilled or more knowledge-intensive production if German industry was to remain competitive.

Finally, developing countries with internationally low wage rates were entering new businesses and threatening many low-skilled, labor-intensive, or simple-technology businesses in West Germany.

These three factors together increased the need for industrial restructuring toward higher-value businesses. The new government that came to power in 1969 recognized this, and a new economic policy was developed.

Beginning in the late 1960's, the German government made a deliberate decision to use its R&D support to improve the competitiveness of German industry. Noncommercial programs were now coordinated by a separate agency, the Ministry of Education and Science, created in 1969, and the BMFT, Bundesminister für Forschung und Technologie, was formed to pursue the broad goal of supporting German high-technology industries in order to secure long-term employment and ultimately raise the country's standard of living.

The BMFT used a sophisticated decision-making process to allocate its resources. Public appropriations by the Bundestag were authorized each year for such general programs as "Securing of Energy" or "Humanization of the Workplace." These programs were generally planned by BMFT officials after discussions with industry, universities, and unions. They were designed to meet a series of expectations from different parts of the society. Although they evolved around broad policy issues like energy sources or working conditions, these programs were convenient "packages" for specific actions at a finer level of detail.

The BMFT's emphasis on technology development, rather than general science promotion, brought it very close to the problem of industrial restructuring. For each program, individual projects proposed by companies were screened by a committee composed of government officials, industry representatives, independent consultants, and labor representatives. The final decision was made by the BMFT, and a project leader was chosen from outside the government to act as a link between the different parties involved.

Projects were evaluated on the basis of their technical merits and, more important, their long-term impact on German business position. While government R&D support was initially motivated by a desire to narrow the technological gap between West Germany and the United States, and later to match or respond to government policies in the United States and Japan, project selection was increasingly focused on improving the competitiveness of German industry in key-technology businesses.

THE UK EFFORT was older but smaller than those in Germany and France, representing only 1.2 percent of GNP. The UK developed a complicated network of government agencies that provide R&D assistance. The National Research and Development Corporation (NRDC) was established in 1949. Various national laboratories and research centers carry out basic and applied research; research associations provide technical information and advice in specific industrial sectors.

Although there were a large number of agencies involved in government-funded research and development, the bulk of R&D expenditures is concentrated in three sectors (and controlled by a small number of agencies). Aircraft, space, and nuclear together accounted for 91 percent of government R&D funding.

9. Before Airbus, there had been ten European commercial jets developed, but collectively they had sold fewer than fourteen hundred airplanes, well below the number sold by the late 1960's for the Boeing 727 alone.

10. The Comet with 101 sales, the Trident with 117 sales, the Viscount with 438 sales, including prop planes, the VC-10 with 54 sales, the Vanguard with 43 sales, the Britannia with 82 sales, the BAC 111 with 200 sales, the Caravelle with 278 sales, the Mercure with 10 sales, and the Concorde with 16 given away.

11. Many economists argue that society would benefit more if the governments simply lowered taxes instead of spending the $7 billion. The economists' arguments hinge around the theoretical assumptions that a) the money lent by the governments to fund the Airbus development would have in fact been

invested by a myriad of individuals rather than consumed; b) those investments would have yielded a better return than the Airbus investment in discounted cash flow; and c) such a measurement accurately reflects the long-term returns to society from invested capital.

All three of these assumptions can be questioned. Most individuals consume more than they invest, so returning the funds to private individuals through a tax cut would likely cut the amount invested. Presuming that alternate investment would yield higher returns in the long run is an open question. Rating all investments equally ignores the fact that some provide infrastructure for others. Jet aircraft is one of those, as it provides a market for many advanced materials, electronic systems, and software. Without those key baseload investments, others could not take place. Decentralized investment decisions are usually best, but not in all cases.

12. These figures are derived from a U.S. Department of Commerce study quoted in a pamphlet issued by Boeing entitled "Foreign Government Targeting of Hi-tech U.S. Industries: Example: Commercial Jet Aircraft" issued in October of 1985. The figures in this report correspond to ones developed by Telesis.

13. Over one hundred articles have appeared in *Business Week, The Economist, The New York Times, The Financial Times,* and *The Wall Street Journal* alone from 1985 to 1988. In addition, countless advertisements have appeared from both sides, and intensive lobbying has taken place on both sides of the Atlantic Ocean.

14. In 1979, for example, U.S. government and industry combined spent $56.5 billion on R&D, Europe spent $39.5 billion, and Japan $18.2 billion—but if only civilian R&D is considered, Europe spent $28 billion, the United States $27 billion, and Japan $17 billion. The issue for Europe is that West Germany alone spent $12.5 billion, and France and the United Kingdom $7.9 billion each.

15. The roundtable was initiated by Volvo, Philips, Ciba-Giegy, and Siemens, and came to include over twenty companies by mid-1985.

16. In the past five years, there have been several major initiatives to promote international cooperation in research and development in European industries. The primary objectives are to combine scattered research efforts and prevent duplication, spread risk, and consolidate scarce financial and technical resources so that European industries can continue to compete on a world scale. The technical and financial demands of research in advanced technologies have increased to the point that few companies have the resources to pursue full-scale research programs on their own.

The majority of cooperative R&D programs have been initiated by the European Economic Community (EEC), which spends over $1.1 billion on R&D annually. The EEC pursues its own basic research, as well as promoting cooperative "shared cost actions" in areas ranging from biotechnology and energy research to advanced technology. Of the cooperative initiatives within the EEC, there are three major programs:

ESPRIT—European Strategic Program for Research and Development in Information Technology, promotes cooperative projects in precompetitive
information technology. Budget (1988–92): 3.2 BECU.

BRITE—Basic Research in Industrial Technologies for Europe, which sponsors
applications-oriented R&D in traditional industrial sectors. Budget:
800m ECU.

RACE—Research and Advanced Communications in Europe, an initiative promoting select projects with the specific goal of establishing an advanced Integrated Broadband Communications network in Europe by
1996. Budget: 1.1 BECU.

Each of these programs sponsors cooperative projects in precompetitive
R&D on a cost-shared basis, with the EEC providing 50 percent of the costs and
the remainder being borne by the research partners. Participation is open to all
industrial firms, research institutes, and universities within the EEC. Each project must include at least two industrial partners from different member nations,
in order to ensure the industrial relevance of the project.

Proposals for cooperative projects are submitted by the parties in response
to periodic "calls for proposals," which the commission makes according to a
specific research agenda. The proposals are then evaluated and selected according to their strategic significance. (The ESPRIT program and particularly RACE
outline detailed project goals, and proposals are designed to meet these needs.
BRITE, being more application-oriented, is less focused, and its calls only outline general areas of possible research.)

Almost all of the cooperative R&D programs are still in the early stages of
development. ESPRIT, the oldest, began in 1985, and the first phase of RACE
started at the beginning of 1988. For most projects, it is thus too early to assess
results, and the full impact of the programs will not be visible until results reach
the market phase—not until well into the 1990's. However, the preliminary
results, particularly from the first ESPRIT phase, seem very promising.

Despite the resources that have been devoted to them, the cooperative projects still represent a very small portion of total R&D spending, and the primary
impact of all of these programs will not be the specific results that they produce.
It will rather be in the general spirit of cooperation that they are fostering.
Already, there has been a significant increase in cross-boundary and cross-
industry cooperation in Europe beyond that within the formal programs, in
areas extending from basic research to product marketing. Between 1983 and
1986, international cooperative commercial agreements in Europe increased
more than 700 percent. Previously, almost all cooperative marketing agreements were initiated outside Europe, with U.S. companies.

Several notable initiatives have been made by private companies, as well.
Bull, ICL, and Siemens recently collaborated to create a large joint-research laboratory (ECRC), a project that would have been inconceivable in Europe prior
to the launching of ESPRIT and other initiatives.

Combined with this acceptance of the value of collaboration is a growing
recognition by European governments and the community of the importance
of public support (particularly financial support) in helping industries maintain
a competitive position.

ESPRIT (European Strategic Program for Research and Development in Information Technology)

Information technology is one of the fastest-growing areas in industry. In 1985, the IT market in OECD countries totaled 440 billion ECU, and the market is expected to grow at a rate of about 15–25 percent per year. World R&D activity in IT is also expected to increase to $90 billion by 1990, up from $35 billion in 1986. Besides its own significance as an industry, IT also directly affects many other economic sectors through its impact on communications and factory automation. Competitiveness in IT is therefore basic to the success of an industrialized economy.

The ESPRIT program in information technology was initiated in 1982 in response to a recognition of the industrial importance of IT, as well as of the fundamentally weak position of the European IT industry, which suffered from limited resources and scattered markets. The program has three objectives:

- to provide European IT industry with the basic technologies it needs to meet the competitive requirements of the nineties
- to promote European industrial cooperation in precompetitive R&D in Information Technology
- to promote internationally recognized standards

Following an initial pilot phase, the first phase of ESPRIT began in 1983, with a total budget of 1.5 billion ECU (50 percent financed by the EEC).

Support for the program was high, and ESPRIT succeeded faster than expected almost from the start. Two major calls for proposals in 1984 and 1985, and a smaller one in 1986, resulted in a total of 227 projects being funded for the 4-year period (or about 1 out of every 5 proposals submitted).

Participating in these first-phase projects are 536 organizations, with an average of 3 industrial firms and 5 partners total per project. The number of participants includes nearly 200 research institutes and universities, and 146 small or medium-sized companies (SMEs). Projects are thus not limited to large companies, and over half include the participation of at least one SME. Large companies are the most dynamic, however, and their influence is magnified through multiple participation. Eleven major European corporations participate in over fourteen projects each. (Philips in fifteen, Bull in twenty-eight, Thomson in twenty-six, Siemens in twenty-two, etc.)

Projects average three to five years in length, and by the end of 1986 ESPRIT projects were employing nearly three thousand researchers annually.

The Project Areas
ESPRIT sponsors projects in five main areas of research:
   Three basic technologies:

- advanced microelectronics
- software technology
- advanced information processing

   Two applications areas:

- office automation systems
- computer integrated manufacturing

I. ADVANCED MICROELECTRONICS

The primary goal of ESPRIT in microelectronics research is to ensure that European industries remain competitive in the design and production of semiconductor components—the fundamental units of IT technology. Advances in integrated circuits have largely been responsible for the massive economies in size and cost, and improved performance of IT products in recent years. Europe has consistently lagged behind the United States and Japan in this area.

The main thrust of research is focused on advanced development of current silicon-based semiconductors by creating chips of high complexity and transmission speed. The goals are the achievement of:

- submicron circuitry complexity, which would allow the production of individual chips with up to several million circuits. (Current advanced technology uses chips with a complexity of several microns.)
- high-speed switching (with speeds measured in picoseconds, or 1/1,00,000 microsecond)

Other projects are exploring the potential of compound semiconductors such as gallium arsenide for capabilities beyond the reach of the current technology.

The research in basic components is supported with work in:

- Computer Aided Design (CAD), to solve problems in the design of complex chips
- optoelectronics, especially in its potential in data transmission
- advanced display technologies, for larger displays and more compact solid-state office work stations than currently exist
- innovative projects in packaging, device modeling, and special processing materials and techniques

A total of forty-three projects are supported in this area, representing about 25 percent of the ESPRIT budget.

II. SOFTWARE TECHNOLOGY

In contrast to its position in microelectronics, Europe has a promising technological lead in certain aspects of software technology, which the EEC hopes to consolidate into a strong market position through ESPRIT. A comprehensive software development program is also necessary to support a major effort in IT. The ESPRIT projects seek to develop a scientific system for software engineering, as well as methods for software design within the broader context of complex system development.

The aim of research is to improve: a) the productivity of software development; and b) software product quality. This effort includes projects in the development of:

- software design methods and tools, system development
- support methods to simplify software production management (to help manage development teams, large amounts of documentation, and computing facilities involved in software development)
- a "common environment" for the management of software production data (the stepping stone to industrial integration of the project results)

- evaluation and demonstration projects on the uses of the software results in industry

This area includes forty-seven projects, representing about 20 percent of the program budget.

Strong progress has been made in development support projects. The next major thrust will be to promote the rapid transfer of results into industry.

III. ADVANCED INFORMATION PROCESSING

The primary challenge in design of the next generation of computers is to go beyond data and text manipulation to the development of systems that are able to process knowledge, to understand and analyze a variety of forms of text, including speech, video signals, etc.

The ESPRIT effort focuses on four areas:

- knowledge engineering (methods for computer knowledge acquisition, representation, and processing)
- external interfaces (understanding and processing of speech, computer vision)
- data and knowledge bases (for storing complex knowledge)
- advanced computer architectures (development of high-performance computers and systems)

Most of these projects are fairly advanced and long term, but some encouraging results have been achieved in knowledge engineering. Future projects will need to focus on design and integration of systems into industry.

The area includes forty-five projects, and about 22 percent of the ESPRIT budget.

IV. OFFICE SYSTEMS

This area focuses on the application of advances in microelectronics, software technology, and information processing to produce office systems that are user-friendly and capable of managing complicated multimedia data (including text, drawings and photographs, and speech). The development of complete office systems, as well as methods for integrating components for various producers, is considered an essential vehicle for introducing advanced IT achievements into industry.

Forty-three ESPRIT projects cover four areas:

- efforts to design new methods to improve user productivity and office management
- development of major new human-machine interface technologies (document representation and information manipulation)
- advanced technologies for communication between office systems (especially optical technologies)
- applications systems for storing multimedia information

These projects represent slightly over 20 percent of the total budget.

V. COMPUTER INTEGRATED MANUFACTURING

Although CIM represents a relatively small portion of the ESPRIT budget (13 percent, for thirty-six projects), the area is critical to the program in several ways. Computers are making rapid inroads into all areas of manufacturing through methods such as Computer Aided Design, Engineering, and Manufacture (CAD/CAE/CAM); flexible assembly and design; robotics; computerized testing; and quality control. It is an area where application of new IT advances can make a significant impact on the market, as well as providing the rapid channeling of ESPRIT results into industry. It is also an area that is heavily dependent on the ability of a wide variety of machines to communicate with each other, and the need for the development of common design rules and standards makes CIM particularly well suited for a cooperative approach.

There are two basic approaches in this area. Much of the EEC effort focuses on the design of open systems for communication between machine subsystems and the development of design standards. A further initiative is directed at the development of actual computer manufacturing systems in areas of particular strategic importance. These areas include:

- CAD/CAE/CAM
- flexible and manufacturing systems
- subsystems and components
- CIM systems applications

Significant inroads have been made, particularly in open systems design, where a number of projects have produced marketed results, and a few have been incorporated into manufacturing lines.

ESPRIT II

Following the success of the first five years of the ESPRIT program, the second phase of ESPRIT is being launched this year. ESPRIT II has a budget of 3.2 BECU, or more than twice the resource power of the first phase. Participation is being expanded to include partners from EFTA countries, although these partners will not be eligible for matching EEC funds.

The program is designed to continue and expand upon the successes in ESPRIT I, with increased emphasis placed on technological application and transfer of the new advances. The major goals will be:

- to provide the IT industry with full systems capability based on state-of-the-art semiconductor technology. The projects will place special emphasis on custom or application-specific integrated circuits, a small field in which Europe has acquired a particularly competitive position with the help of ESPRIT I.
- to provide powerful, cost-efficient, and reliable information-processing systems, emphasizing total systems design, parallel designs, and knowledge engineering
- to promote the integration of IT into industrial and business applications
- microelectronics and peripheral technologies
- information-processing systems
- IT application technologies

However, the fundamental emphasis and distribution of the projects will remain the same. Resources will be fairly evenly distributed among the three areas, with slightly more support given to IT applications technologies.

There are two significant new initiatives under ESPRIT II. In addition to the general precompetitive efforts, the program will be sponsoring a small number of Basic Research Actions, collaborative projects in fundamental research. The subprogram is directed at universities and research centers, for whom the EEC will provide up to 100 percent support. Industries may, but are not required to, participate. The object of the projects is to maintain a strong base for the industry in fundamental IT. Project areas will include:

- molecular electronics
- advanced systems design
- artificial intelligence and cognitive science
- application of solid-state physics to IT

Another new initiative in the opposite direction will be the support of several ambitious and carefully targeted cooperative projects involving a number of large IT firms. These Technology Integration Projects (TIPs) will require large-scale industrial involvement and commitment. (The commission is giving no indication of the scale involved at this time.) Some sample TIPs include:

- High-Speed Silicon Integrated Circuits; Nonvolatile Memories Macrocells (multifunction IC)
- Parallel Architecture for High-Performance Computers
- Industrial Automation (including batch and continuous manufacture)
- Multimedia Integrated Workstations

The first call for ESPRIT II proposals closed in March 1988, with a strong response and an unexpected number of high-quality proposals. The level of response was so high that the funds allocated for the initial call were increased from 600 to 780 MECU. Project funding was also squeezed so that a quarter of the proposals were accepted, at one sixth of the proposed funding. It is presently unclear whether this response will bring an increase in overall program funding at a later time.

RACE (Research and Development in Advanced Communications in Europe)

RACE differs from the other EEC R&D programs in that it is organized around a very specific goal: to lay the foundation for an EEC-wide Integrated Broadband Telecommunications Network by the mid-nineties, thus paving the way for the European communications infrastructure of the next century. Such a massive and technically complex project necessarily requires close collaboration on an international scale. R&D cooperation in RACE is therefore more a means to an overriding end than a primary objective in itself. Nevertheless, the benefits to the EEC from cooperating on such a scale are expected to be great.

Integrated Broadband refers to a telecommunications network that combines computers, satellites, optic cables, and digital switching to allow the integration and transmission of a wide variety of different signals (including telephone, television, video, computer communications) over the same communications system. It will greatly improve present forms of communication, while also making possible future services such as video phones, home banking, and dial-up TV video libraries.

To design such a system, RACE brings together members of national governments, telecommunications services, the IT industry, and new specialty-service sectors. The program will promote research in critical technologies, systems design, and development. Standardization efforts will also play a major role at all levels of the RACE program.

Aside from its primary objective, the more general aims of RACE are:

- to promote the continued competitiveness of the European telecommunications industry
- to ensure network operators are as well prepared as possible to meet future technological and service challenges
- to enable a basic minimum of EEC states to introduce commercial IBC systems by 1996
- to offer users world-competitive telecommunications services
- to help create an internal EEC market for IBC-related telecommunications equipment, based on common standards

The RACE program was formally adopted in 1986, following a one-year pilot-definition phase. The program has a total budget of 1.1 billion ECU, half of which will be provided by the EEC, and half by the national governments and telecommunications services.

Work on the first forty-three projects began early this year, following a call for proposals late in 1987. The projects combine partners from network operators, industries, and research laboratories all over Europe, including five non-EEC countries. They have a budget of 360 MECU.

Program Structure
The RACE program is divided into three concurrently running parts:

I. IBC DEVELOPMENT AND IMPLEMENTATION STRATEGIES
The goal is to reach agreement on strategies, functional requirements, and systems definitions for the introduction of IBC, and to identify technological and standardization requirements. Projects will be directed toward the system definition process (i.e., role of satellite systems in IBC network, international transmission of high-definition television, and Europe-wide provision of mobile telecommunications).

II. IBC TECHNOLOGY R&D
Precompetitive research projects in areas critical to the development of low-cost IBC equipment and services. Key research areas include:

- optical switching and transmission: technologies that allow the transfer of large amounts of information at high speeds (especially work in Asynchronous Transfer Mode techniques)
- application of advanced technologies to systems development (projects will include some long-term research in optical signal processing, but will mainly

explore the potential of silicon, gallium arsenide, and indium phosphate, for mass production of cheap components
- development of software to control high-level information flows, and to develop more efficient ways of encoding complex signals such as images and voice
- development of evolutionary systems and subsystems, multipurpose terminals for home or office use that can manage a variety of information forms. In this area, RACE includes R&D on high quality videophone and HDTV technologies, digital videotape recording, and multipurpose terminals

III. FUNCTIONAL INTEGRATION

Projects in pilot demonstrations of integrated broadband systems, to assess system characteristics and their potential for future evolution. Development of tools to test and verify systems.

Program Timescale

MID-1988: Initial estimates about the configuration of the IBC system; the number of users, their distribution and calling rates, etc.

MID-1989: Firm decisions about first IBC network; introduction and evolution strategy

MID-1990: Definition of systems architectures

END 1991: Agreement on IBC systems architecture, based on internationally developed standards

END 1995: Commercial introduction of IBC

BRITE (Basic Research in Industrial Technologies for Europe)

The BRITE program supports projects in basic technological research for traditional "sunshine" manufacturing industries (motor vehicles, chemicals, aeronautics, textiles, plastics, furniture, food and drink, etc.). Manufacturing makes up a critical part of Europe's economy, providing about 30 percent of the GNP and employing over a quarter of the population. The increasing need to introduce high technology, however, both into new products and into production methods, has created structural weaknesses in various sectors of the industry. This is particularly true in industries with a rapidly expanding demand, such as instruments and chemicals, and those that are experiencing a relative decline (clothing, textiles, motor vehicles). Success in both of these areas largely depends on the use of technological improvements to capture the top end of the market. The BRITE program is directed at addressing these needs.

BRITE has targeted research in new materials and production technologies (especially production technologies and pilot and demonstration projects for products made from flexible materials), as critical to industrial development in the next decade. Main emphasis is placed on technologies that will improve industrial productivity, product reliability, originality of design, and overall quality.

While the focus is still on precompetitive research, BRITE is much more interested in having a direct impact on the market than are the other EEC programs. Projects must be innovative, have a clear industrial potential, and be likely to have a substantial impact on industrial competitiveness in the medium to long term. Emphasis is placed on creating partnerships that are likely to be effective in future marketing efforts, as well as in research. Partners are also required to exploit results within three years of a project's completion, or they may be required to repay the EEC's share of funding.

In addition to direct funding, the commission also encourages cooperation by promoting privately funded "concerted-action projects." EEC support may include provision of a secretariat and coordination facilities, and financial assistance for meetings, workshops, seminars.

BRITE I

The BRITE program was launched in 1985, with a total budget of 360 MECU for the first four years (1985–1988).

Following the first call for proposals (1985), 103 projects with 495 participants were funded, for a total of 130 MECU. These projects have now been running for two years and are beginning to yield results. A second call was made late in 1987 for the remaining funds, bringing the total number of projects to about 150.

On the average, BRITE projects cost 1–2.5 MECU and involve at least ten man-years of research. They last a maximum of four years.

Priority Themes
The current BRITE projects focus on nine main areas:

- Reliability, wear, and deterioration: designing for reliability, corrosion, wear resistance, surface engineering
- Laser technology: high-beam lasers with industrial applications, delivery systems and equipment, manufacturing applications
- Joining techniques: new welding processes, improving current techniques, nonaerospace adhesive bonding, micro-joining techniques
- New testing methods: nondestructive testing (NDE), online testing, computer-aided testing
- CAD/CAM and mathematical modeling: advanced design and manufacturing techniques, computer-assisted techniques, advanced structural analysis
- Polymers, composites, new materials, power technology (such as plastics that conduct electricity)
- Membrane science and technology
- Catalysis and particle technology
- New production technologies for products made from flexible materials

Although it is a small program, BRITE has been very successful in encouraging international cooperation both horizontally (within an industry) and between different industries. Response to the program has been high. Over 550 proposals were submitted for the first call, so competition for projects is intense. In addition, the first "BRITE Technological Days" in December enjoyed the participation of over twelve hundred European industrialists from all the member states.

BRITE-EURAM

With encouraging results from the first BRITE phase, plus the recognition of new areas that need strengthening, a second phase of BRITE is being discussed, which should be finalized later this year. The second program will expand upon the results of the first, extending research and supporting the development of demonstration products from BRITE projects in some areas. The program will also be combined with EURAM, a small (160 MECU) EEC program for cooperative R&D in advanced materials. Given the critical importance of the design and manufacture of new materials to technological application and development, the commission felt that industrial needs would be better served if the two projects were combined.

EEC funding for the combined program will be nearly doubled, bringing the total budget of BRITE-EURAM to 680 MECU for 1989–92.

Ninety percent of this budget will be devoted to cost-shared applied research projects in the range of 1–3 MECU, and involving the participation of at least two industrial partners. Support will also be given to a limited number of demonstration projects.

Seven percent of the budget will be allocated for fundamental research, particularly in new materials. Projects will be in the range of 0.4 to 1 MECU and 10 man-years of activity. These projects will not require an industrial partner, but an industrial endorsement will be necessary.

The combined program will focus on:

• advanced materials technologies
• design methodology and assurance for products and processes
• manufacturing process technologies
• application of manufacturing technologies

In addition, BRITE-EURAM will attempt to encourage the participation of SMEs, by granting feasibility awards to help smaller organizations research and prepare project proposals. In select cases, the EEC will finance 75 percent of exploratory research for up to six months.

17. EUREKA is a program sponsored by nineteen European governments to promote international cooperation in advanced technologic research. Funding and support is provided independently by the governments of each member nation. Projects must include partners from more than one member nation and be able to demonstrate a significant expected benefit from cooperation. Unlike the EEC programs, EUREKA has a "ground up" structure. Projects are conceived and designed directly by industry according to their needs and prospects, and are then presented to the member nations for consideration. Projects may thus concern practically any area of advanced technological research, and they range from precompetitive work to the development of near-production demonstration projects. EUREKA was designed to complement EEC programs by filling in the ever-growing gap between research in advanced technology and product development. In general, EUREKA projects tends to be closer to production than those in EEC programs. The projects currently supported under the program total nearly 3.8 BECU.

EUREKA was founded in 1985 by President Mitterrand of France to enable

Europe to compete with the commercial spinoffs expected from the U.S. "Star Wars" program (Strategic Defense Initiative). It is an initiative for international cooperative R&D in advanced technology, with the aim of raising the productivity and competitiveness of Europe's industries and national economies.

Whereas the EEC programs are directed toward upstream precompetitive research, EUREKA promotes projects aimed directly at the development of products, processes, or services with worldwide market potential. Thus, while still "precompetitive" and within the rules of international competition, EUREKA projects tend to be much more directly market-driven than EEC projects.

EUREKA is a loose, decentralized organization of nineteen European countries, plus the EEC Commission. The organization itself does not provide any financial support for projects, but helps facilitate communication and cooperation between potential partners, and to spread relevant information to the EUREKA community.

Projects are organized by the participants, who are independently responsible for negotiating the terms of the agreement (on such issues as financing, management, and sharing of results), as well as determining its technical content.

There is no guiding framework plan as in the EEC programs, but projects generally fall under eight categories:

- information technology
- robotics and manufacturing
- lasers
- new materials
- biotechnology
- communications & audiovisual
- environmental protection
- transport technologies

Aside from industrial projects, member governments and the commission also join in projects for the development of modern infrastructures (i.e., telecommunications and transportation), and in areas such as environmental control that require international cooperation.

Financing of EUREKA projects is the responsibility of the participants. Although some member nations provide strong financial support for EUREKA projects (Italy has committed 816 billion lire to EUREKA projects), others only provide structural assistance. The EUREKA secretariat has ties with several banks and assists with finding private funding. EUREKA is also currently working with the EEC to organize a system to guarantee a portion of R&D loans, to encourage banks and other financial institutions to provide research loans.

The first EUREKA Conference of Ministers took place in Hannover in November 1985, where the first ten EUREKA projects were announced. Projects have since been announced periodically at five subsequent conferences.

To date, there are 213 EUREKA projects, involving over 1,000 organizations, and an estimated 3.8 billion ECU over the projected lifetime of the projects. This makes EUREKA the largest of all the European R&D programs in monetary terms.

The projects average five partners and three countries participating in each project. Nearly two thirds of all projects count the participation of one or more SME.

The size of EUREKA projects varies drastically, from under 1 million to 200 million ECU. Although there are six projects with an estimated budget of over 100 million ECU, half of all projects are under 10 million. The recent trend has also been toward smaller, more tightly defined projects.

Project Areas and Examples
I. INFORMATION TECHNOLOGY (25 PERCENT OF BUDGET)

Information technology is the largest research area, accounting for a quarter of the entire program budget. Projects range from fairly fundamental research in microelectronics to specific product development. A few examples:

- industrial development of amorphous silicon-based components for photo-electronic applications (2 countries, 7 years, 57 MECU)
- Cherise: project to develop, test and improve computer-image synthesis systems (2 countries, 4 years, 7.5 MECU)
- development of software system and hardware for use in farm crops management (2 countries, 3 years, 0.6 MECU)

II. ROBOTICS AND MANUFACTURING (17 PERCENT OF BUDGET)

- GEO: application of robotics to the construction industry. Goal of designing a robot for dangerous and laborious tasks on tall buildings and structures (2 countries, 7 years, 22 MECU)
- development of robot for detecting, collecting, and handling citrus fruit (2 countries, 5 years, 9 MECU)

Automated manufacturing is probably the fastest growing area in EUREKA, and there has been a recent surge in manufacturing-related projects. Many of these have been pursued under the "umbrella" project FAMOS, a twelve-nation initiative in flexible automated assembly. Through a number of different projects, FAMOS is involved in all aspects of automated-assembly systems development. Research includes work on computer-aided design and engineering, advanced and highly flexible automatic-assembly equipment (robots, programmable handling), new techniques in materials flow and control, and CIM aids for rational assembly operation. The various projects include:

- the design and integration of sensor-aided assembly systems with industrial robots (2 countries, 4 years, 10 MECU)
- flexible automated factory for the production of washing machines including automation of frames, motors, and electrical installation, and automatic quality control (3 countries, 5 years, 8.3 MECU)
- CIM pilot plants: improvement of information and materials flow, advanced hardware/software modules, advanced systems to improve product quality control (2 countries, 1 year, 1.3 MECU)
- refrigerator-compressor flexible-assembly system, design and development of a prototype (3 countries, 4 years, 23 MECU)

There are currently sixteen FAMOS projects in progress, many of which just began in the last year. In total, the projects involve fifty-two research years, and 150 MECU. Each project is expected to conclude with the development of a pilot plant incorporating the technologies developed. In addition to contributing to technical design, therefore, the program should also result in the construction of a series of state-of-the-art factories across Europe.

The FAMOS project enjoys strong support from many participating governments. The French government has allocated 40 million francs to FAMOS projects, while Italy has promised 50 percent government funding (totaling 100 million lire). FAMOS receives the largest portion of the Italian funds earmarked for EUREKA.

III. LASERS (6 PERCENT)

EUROLASER is another major "umbrella" project, which combines ten different countries in a program to develop the next generation of industrial lasers for material processing. The goal is being pursued through six different subprojects:

- CO2—laser system with a power range of 10 to 100 kw
- solid-state lasers with range 1 to 5 kw
- excimer lasers with output up to 10b kw
- CO^2 lasers of medium power (5 kw)
- free electron laser (fel)
- other systems with industrial & medical applications

The projects have forty participants overall, who specialize in various aspects of laser technology. They involve a total of thirty-one project-years and 226 MECU. Research in EUROLASER is coordinated with similar projects under the BRITE program.

IV. NEW MATERIALS (5 PERCENT)

In the project CARMAT 2000, organizations from France, Germany, Spain, the UK, and the Netherlands have combined in a five-year effort to develop new materials and new materials processes for car manufacture. Budget: 60 MECU. Other projects include:

- ceramics for diesel engines (4 years, 7.7 MECU)
- new polymer fibers for medical applications (5 years, 4 MECU)

V. BIOTECHNOLOGY (9 PERCENT)

- research and development of a malaria vaccine (2 countries, 3 years, 12.85 MECU)
- development of high-oil sunflower seeds suitable for growing in arid Mediterranean zones (2 countries, 7 years, 3.6 MECU)

VI. COMMUNICATIONS AND AUDIO-VISUAL (13 PERCENT)

Undoubtedly, one of the best-known and most successful EUREKA projects is HDTV, an initiative led by the giants of Europe's electronics industry, Philips and Thomson, to develop an advanced high-definition TV system. The project will produce major breakthroughs in television picture size and quality, as well as develop standards for incorporating the technology into the existing television environment. The ultimate goal is to create a next-generation product that can claim a leading share of the world market.

In addition to the main partners, twenty-seven other organizations are collaborating in the project, which is coordinated with several others in the ESPRIT and RACE programs. The project has a budget of 200 MECU for the first four-year phase (until 1990, when the partners will submit a full proposal for the development of an HDTV system). Significant gains have already been made in this phase, including the development of an intermediate HDTV system prototype, soon to be demonstrated at the Brighton radio and television show.

VII. ENVIRONMENT (11 PERCENT)

EUROTRAC is a major program in environmental protection that involves the cooperation of six European governments as well as private organizations. The purpose of the project is to analyze the composition and transportation of air pollution particles over Europe, in order to develop new methods for pollution control. EUROTRAC is an eight-year project, at an estimated 100 MECU.

VIII. TRANSPORT TECHNOLOGY (10 PERCENT)

EUROPOLIS is a project for developing an intelligent control system for urban traffic and advanced information control and monitor (4 countries, 7 years, 128 MECU).

Chapter 9

1. The details of Alexander Graham Bell's "photophone" invention are discussed in "Alexander Graham Bell and the Photophone: The Centennial of the Invention of Light-wave Communication, 1880–1980," by Forrest M. Mims, III, in *Optics News*, Vol. 6, No. 1, (1980). Mims quotes from Bell's notebooks on February 26, 1880.

2. Dr. K. C. Kao and Mr. G. A. Hockham of Standard Telecommunications Laboratories Ltd. wrote a paper that was originally submitted to the IEE on November 23, 1965, and revised on February 15, 1966. It suggested the use of dielectric fiber waveguides for light communications. The paper was presented in the IEE proceedings, Vol. 113, No. 7 (July 1966).

3. See, for example, Detlef Gloge of Bell Telephone Labs in a paper submitted on May 26, 1970 (after the Corning invention but before it was announced), entitled "Optical Waveguide Transmission." The paper was published in IEE proceedings (October 1970), Vol. 58, No. 10. Gloge argued that optical waveguides of the sort Corning invented would not be invented for a long time.

4. Very few countries have traditionally set up private phone companies, though there have been some moves toward privatization recently. At the time Lucy made his visits, the phone systems in Great Britain, France, Germany, Italy, Sweden, Holland, Belgium, and Japan were all fully state-owned.

5. As far back as my first visit to Japan in 1974, published documents from MITI had selected telecommunications as a major target area for the future. As described to me by a number of MITI officials in July 1974, telecommunications was seen as interrelated with microelectronics and computers and as essential to the development of the "information society" of the future. Two major efforts were conducted to promote the goal of bringing Japan to leader-

ship in "information industries." MITI took the lead in funding computer and microelectronics research and stimulating these industries in a variety of ways, while NTT, which reported to the Minister of Post and Telecommunications, took the lead on the telecommunications side.

Though MITI was not directly responsible for telecommunications, it did develop formal policy blueprints for how the industry should grow, and it advocated a policy of price subsidies, internal R&D development of all products from electric switching equipment to waveguides, and rapid modernization of the internal telecommunications infrastructures.

6. RCA was the first company to do work in the early 1950's on the scanners that eventually led to the development of the VCR. Ampex, an American company, introduced the first videotape recorder for broadcast use in 1956. During the 1960's, Japanese companies became aggressive in developing the videotape recorder, which eventually became the videocassette recorder, while U.S. companies kept research at a background level. After many fits and starts, Sony and JVC, a Matsushita subsidiary, brought VCRs to market in the mid-1970s. Today 80 percent of all VCRs in the world are Japanese-made, with most of the rest being made by Korean producers (Thomson and Philips of Europe have small-scale production). The analogy Duke was using referred to an American invention being commercialized by the Japanese.

7. Deregulation of the telecommunications industry was a fortuitous event for Corning. Since AT&T was committed to making its own fiber, Corning could not make significant headway in the United States as long as AT&T controlled almost all of the nation's phone lines. With deregulation, Corning had a natural market with independent phone companies, who were competing against AT&T and thus were happy to have an alternate source. The increased competition brought about by deregulation also helped the move toward waveguides in general. The lower costs that waveguides could provide became essential to success in the new competitive battles that emerged in the industry.

8. Actually, MITI and NTT were locked in a series of territorial disputes in the early 1980's, which reached the highest levels of government. These battles are discussed in the monograph *MITI, MPT and the Telecom Wars: How Japan Makes Policy for High Technology* (Brie Working Paper #21) by Chalmers Johnson (Berkeley, CA: Berkeley Roundtable on the International Economy, University of California, Berkeley, September 1986). In all likelihood, MITI, the MPT, and NTT all wanted to slow Corning down, but it is unclear whether it was a coordinated effort.

Index

ABOUT THE AUTHORS

IRA C. MAGAZINER has been an international business strategy consultant for fifteen years. He has done over two hundred studies in ten countries for companies such as General Electric, Corning Glass, Black & Decker, Volvo, Thomson Brandt, and Mitsubishi Chemicals. He has also put together economic growth strategies for a half-dozen governments. He has co-authored a number of books, including *Minding America's Business* and *Japanese Industrial Policy*. He graduated as valedictorian from Brown University in 1969 and attended Oxford University as a Rhodes Scholar. He lives in Bristol, Rhode Island, with his wife, Suzanne, and children, Seth, Jonathan, and Sarah.

MARK PATINKIN has spent the last ten years as a columnist for the *Providence Journal-Bulletin*. His column is syndicated nationally by the Scripps-Howard News Service, which reaches over three hundred newspapers. In 1985, he published *An African Journey*, a chronicle of a month spent in famine country. In 1987, a newspaper series he wrote on religious violence in Northern Ireland, India, and Beirut was one of two finalists for the Pulitzer Prize in international reporting. He graduated from Middlebury College in 1974. He lives in Providence, Rhode Island, with his wife, Heidi, and daughter, Ariel.